The **Silla**

Annals of the

Samguk Sagi

The Silla Annals of the Samguk Sagi

Published by The Academy of Korean Studies Press
Published in April 2012

Address The Academy of Korean Studies Press
              323 Haogae-ro, Bundang-gu, Seongnam-si, Gyeonggi-do, 463-791, Korea
Tel   82-31-708-5360
Fax 82-31-701-1343
website book.aks.ac.kr
Email akspress@aks.ac.kr

This book was translated and published with support by
The Acaderny of Korean Studies.

ISBN 978-89-7105-860-2 93910
Printed in Korea

The **Silla Annals** of the **Samguk Sagi**

Kim Pusik

translated by

Edward J. Shultz and
Hugh H.W. Kang
with Daniel C. Kane

THE ACADEMY OF KOREAN STUDIES PRESS

Preface

To agree to complete an annotated translation of an age-old history, as is the *Samguk sagi (History of the Three Kingdoms)*, with a set deadline, is a daunting task. The Academy of Korean Studies has been generous in allowing postponement on postponement—but there comes a time when one must reluctantly relinquish the manuscript. As a result, what you have here is an excellent translation into English of *The Silla Annals* of the *Samguk sagi;* but one that also may still lack the polished results that many of us expect.

While several individuals have been involved in this translation, the bulk of the work has been completed by Edward J. Shultz and Hugh H.W. Kang. Still, our thanks go to Daniel C. Kane, who provided a draft translation of one of the books in the annals and the introduction to this volume; Chizuko Allen, who helped with Japanese terminology; Richard D. McBride II, who helped ponder translations of Silla titles; Robert E. Buswell Jr., who was able to explicate Buddhist terminology; and Jonathan W. Best who has been helpful in answering many questions. Yi Sŭnghyŏn, a visiting PhD student from Sunggyungwan University, for a brief time provided some assistance. John C. Jamieson's dissertation, cited in the footnotes, helped guide us through several difficult sections of the annals. We have also benefited from the careful eye of our editor Henry Bennett, who has saved us from many embarrassing errors and from Kenneth R.

Robinson who graciously read the galleys with his sharp eyes. Any flaws that remain with this work rest with Edward J. Shultz and Hugh H.W. Kang.

We have also turned, in admiration, to the translation that Jonathan W. Best completed on *The Paekche Annals* of the *Samguk Sagi* as a guide. Readers will immediately notice differences between Best's translation and our translation—particularly in the annotations. To make *The Silla Annals* as accessible as possible to uninitiated students of early Korea, we have tried to limit footnotes to the bare essentials. Footnotes are used to identify geographic entries, to further explicate unclear terms and/or passages, and to introduce the reader to pertinent secondary sources. Within the notes the translators have, especially when further explanation has been required, relied heavily on the earlier Academy of Korean Studies Korean translation. Where possible, we have referred the more advanced reader to the detailed notes provided by the Academy of Korean Studies in their translation. Many notes are, in fact, translations of that Korean work. The serious student may wish to refer directly to the Korean version—however the annotated translation provided here should more than meet the needs of most students, general readers, and scholars who cannot read Korean.

When noting the actual text we have primarily cited the *Hanguk kojŏn ch'ongsŏ* edition published by Kyŏngin Munhwasa in 1973. However we have also extensively consulted the Academy of Korean Studies translation of the *Samguk Sagi* as a check to our own English translation and have regularly referred to the version of the original *Samguk sagi* published by the Academy of Korean Studies.

As Silla developed it introduced the regional administrative divisions of *pu, chu, kun,* and *hyŏn,* with the *pu* being the largest administrative unit and the *hyŏn* the smallest. Rather than translate these designations we have generally left them in Korean. The exception is *"pu,"* which we have rendered as "district." Similarly, when the term *"chin"* is used to designate a military unit, we have translated this as "garrison."

Personal names, geographic names, and terms in Korean have been Romanized according to the McCune-Reischauer system, the Pinyin system is used for Chinese, and the Hepburn system is used for Japanese. On first occurrence Korean and Chinese offices and titles are glossed with an English translation. Subsequently these terms are written with their English translation. In the case of Korean offices and titles, renderings into English, where possible, have followed the usages in *A New History of Korea* (Lee, 1984). In translating passages from the Chinese classics we have used, when available, the translations into English rendered by the early sinologist James Legge. For Chinese titles we have relied on Charles O. Hucker's *A Dictionary of Official Titles in Imperial China*

(Hucker, 1985).

A glossary of titles and offices, as well as a table of weights and measures, is provided at the end of the text. Included in the glossary are Korean and Chinese office titles with their English translations. Terms included in the table of weights and measures were selected on the basis of their frequency of use. An index is provided to help readers locate names, terms, titles, and/or topics within the text.

All dates are rendered according to the lunar calendar. At the start of each reign year, the date is rendered into the western calendar year. This is approximate, as the lunar and solar calendars do not exactly coincide, but there is no more than a one-year discrepancy.

Names of places and/or suffixes (e.g., monasteries, mountains, and rivers) are translated whenever possible; however redundancies such as Pulguk-sa Monastery have been avoided. Generally those mountains identified by a single character, such as Yangsan, have been rendered in the form "Mount Yangsan." Occasionally, however, in such cases as "T'ohamsan" for example, "Mount T'oham," which is an established usage, has been the preferred presentation.

Brackets […] are used when English has been added by the translators for clarification purposes. Korean terms translated by the current translators into English are also shown in brackets.

Braces {...} are used to indicate notes added by the original compilers of the *Samguk sagi.* We hope the readers benefit from this translation.

Edward J. Shultz
Honolulu

Contents

Introduction

This is the first English translation of *The Silla Pongi* (*Annals*) of the *Samguk sagi* (*History of the Three Kingdoms*). Compiled by the renowned Koryŏ-period scholar-official Kim Pusik (1075–1151) and his team of historians, they presented it, in 1145, to Koryŏ's King Injong.

For all of Korea's history as a unified nation, it has been the state of Silla—rather than its rivals for peninsular dominance, Koguryŏ and Paekche—that has been considered the source of the modern Korean nation and the exemplar of ancient Korea's achievements in politics, religion, and the arts. So it is somewhat surprising that *The Silla Annals* of the *Samguk sagi* are the last of that history's annals to see translation into English.[1]

One might argue this is, in part, the result of Silla's undisputed pride of place in the history of Korea. Silla has not engendered the controversy—and nothing sparks interest more than controversy—of Koguryŏ and, to a lesser extent, Paekche. The riches in what remains of Silla's material culture, as evidenced by the city of Kyŏngju and its environs, has perhaps also served to lessen the

---

1 *The Paekche Annals* appeared in 2006 (Jonathan W. Best, *A History of the Early Korean Kingdom of Paekche: Together with an Annotated Translation of the Paekche Annals of the Samguk Sagi*. Cambridge, MA: Harvard University Asia Center, 2006) followed by *The Koguryo Annals* in 2011 (Kim Pusik, *The Koguryŏ Annals of the Samguk Sagi*. Seongnam: The Academy of Korean Studies Press, 2011). A Russian translation of the *Samguk sagi* appeared also, in spurts, between 1959 and 2003. In the Russian case, *The Silla Annals* appeared first and, in fact, helped spur modern Russian studies of ancient Korea. See Kim Pu-sik, M.N. Pak, and L.R. Kontsevich, *Samkuk Sagi,* Moscow: Izd-vo vostochnoi litry, 1959.

urgency for an English translation of *The Silla Annals*. Still, however rich Silla may be, when compared to Koguryŏ and Paekche, in alternative textual material,[2] the *Samguk sagi* remains the undisputed primary source for the study of its history and the presentation of an English translation of *The Silla Annals* marks an important milestone.

Compiled several centuries after the last of the events it describes, the *Samguk sagi* is an oasis in the parched landscape of textual sources for the "Three Kingdoms" period of Korean history. And muddied as those waters may sometimes be, like the water in Wŏnhyo's "gourd," they do replenish.[3]

It has long been noted that Kim Pusik—a scion of the Kyŏngju Kim clan and a direct descendant of high-ranking Silla officials—largely displayed in his history a significant partiality towards Silla. *The Silla Annals* comprise approximately forty percent of the total annals (twelve of the twenty-eight total *kwŏn* [books]). Likewise, the history's biographies section (not available in English translation) deals largely with noted figures of Silla. Scholars and critics have also challenged Kim's chronology for the founding of the three kingdoms, wherein Silla is given precedence (though none of this history's founding dates for the

---

2   Important alternative sources for Silla history include the *Samguk yusa*, (*Memorabilia of the Three Kingdoms*, mid-thirteenth century), *Haedong kosŭng chŏn* (*Lives of Eminent Korean Monks*, 1215), surviving stele engravings such as the so-called *Sasan pi'myŏng* (*Four Mountain Steles*) attributed to the late-Silla scholar Ch'oe Chiwŏn, that same scholar's *Kyewŏn P'ilgyŏng chip* (*Plowing the Cassia Grove with a Writing Brush*, ca. 885), as well as contemporary or near contemporary Chinese and Japanese histories.

3   The staggered progress of the English translations reflects somewhat Kim Pusik and his team's multi-focused—and in the minds of strict neo-Confucianists, unorthodox—approach to the history of the kingdoms. In compiling separate annals for each of the three kingdoms, the *Samguk sagi* presents what amounts to a "*Rashomon*" approach to the early history of the peninsula: often relating the same story from different perspectives.

The **Silla Annals** of the **Samguk Sagi**

three kingdoms are tenable), as well as the historian's commentary, which is imbued with a strong sense of Silla legitimacy vis-à-vis its two rivals.[4]

Over the centuries the *Samguk sagi* has received criticism from every conceivable quarter. Traditional Confucianists and neo-Confucianists, for instance, censured it for its use of Silla terms and the employment of the term *pongi* ("annals," traditionally reserved for legitimate Chinese dynasties). Others condemn it, as well, for its depiction of marvels—such as stories related to the foundation of Silla and miraculous events surrounding the life of the Silla General Kim Yusin. To be fair, Kim Pusik himself recognizes in his historical commentaries that such stories are "too fantastic to be believed."

For an alternate perspective, others (most famously, Kim's near contemporary, Yi Kyubo) have criticized the *Samguk sagi* for its limited recording of marvels—namely the foundation myth of Koguryŏ.

In more contemporary times this account has been criticized for its wholesale exclusion of the history of Parhae as well as for its neglect of Koguryŏ. A more persistent complaint concerns its compilers' failure to use all the available sources (see n. 2). Perhaps the most caustic criticisms came from the Korean nationalist Sin Chaeho (1880–1936), who labeled Kim a sycophantic Sinophile in word and deed and in part responsible for what Sin Chaeho saw as the gradual emasculation of the Korean nation.

Certainly the *Samguk sagi,* as with any history, tells us as much

---

4   Kim Pusik was criticized by neo-Confucian scholars for giving equal place to all three kingdoms (in the sense that all three were given "annals" and thus regarded equally as legitimate states). One of the most significant of such critics was the late-Koryŏ–early-Chosŏn scholar Kwŏn Kŭn (1352–1409).

about the age in which it was written as it does about the age or ages it describes.[5] Regarding the question of Silla favoritism, however, considering that Silla's political life extended several centuries beyond the demise of Koguryŏ and Paekche and reached its apogee in the mid-eighth century, we should appreciate Kim Pusik's effort at fairness in naming his record the *History of the Three Kingdoms.*

As noted, *The Silla Annals* comprise the first twelve *kwŏn* of the twenty-eight-*kwŏn* annals section and cover the entire period from that state's putative founding in 57 BCE to 935 when Silla's final king Kyŏngsun surrendered to Wang Kŏn (T'aejo) of Koryŏ. In this retelling the *Samguk sagi* provides invaluable—and in many cases the only extant—insights into many facets of Silla history and culture and the Silla-Koryŏ transition period. Such insights address native belief systems, the unique nature of Silla Buddhism (though the *Samguk yusa* may be more valuable in this area), land tenure, social norms, gender relations, government structure, international relations, and, in particular, the chronic struggle between the landed lineage-group aristocracy and central power and the gradual decline of the Silla state this struggle engendered.

The Silla Annals comprise our basic understanding of Silla's "bone-rank" (*kolp'um*) system, one of Silla's distinguishing features. This system was characterized by Yi Kibaek, perhaps the most noted scholar of the period, as "a system that conferred or withheld a variety of special privileges, ranging from political preferment to aspects of everyday life, in accordance with the degree of respect due a person's bone-rank—that is, hereditary

---

5   For a fuller discussion of the form the *Samguk sagi* takes and the ideological imperatives and historiographical traditions that informed it, see the introduction to the English translation of *The Koguryŏ Annals* or the relevant portions of part 1 of Best's translation cited in n. 1 above.

bloodline."[6] The bone-rank system of Silla is a reflection of the rigidity of that state's structure and its persistent ties to its clan origins.[7]

The common thread connecting all of Silla's history is the struggle between the "blood" aristocracy and the monarchy or, more exactly, between aristocratic privilege and centralized power. *The Silla Annals* allow us to trace the trajectory of this dynamic as it moved, changed, and, for periods, found balance. However this divisiveness in Silla's political and social fabric provided opportunities for rival powers, external to Silla's traditional power centers, to emerge.

The final decline of Silla was characterized by the emergence of potent regional warlords, some from outside the aristocratic classes (i.e., the upper bone-ranks of the *kolp'um* system) that had traditionally monopolized political power in Silla. The causes of Silla's decline and fall continue to be the focus of intense scholarly inquiry and constitute their own historical subfield— "Late-Silla-Early-Koryŏ (Namal-Yŏch'o)" studies. The *Samguk sagi* remains the *sine qua non* for such research.

Silla's final century may be largely defined by the roles of its various social strata. In general terms these were the monarchy; the upper *"chingol"* ("true bone") ranks of Silla society—a class

6   Lee Ki-baik, *A New History of Korea* (trans. Edward W. Wagner with Edward J. Shultz; Cambridge, MA: Harvard University Press, 1984), 49. Lee (Yi Kibaek) was the pioneering scholar in the study of the head-rank six, as with much else regarding Silla. His groundbreaking study, "Silla yuktup'um yŏngu" (1970) was the first thorough treatment of Silla's head-rank six, and, by association, that kingdom's bone-rank system, and is still widely cited to this day. See Yi Kibaek, "Silla yuktup'um yŏngu" in *Sŏnggok nonch'ong* 2 (1971) and in *Silla chŏngch'i sahoesa yŏngu,* Seoul: Ilchokak, 1974.

7   Ideally the Monographs (*chi*) and Biographies (*yŏljŏn*) of the *Samguk sagi* should be read along with *The Silla Annals,* although these other materials have not yet been fully translated into English.

which controlled the highest offices of government and whose members alone were eligible to assume the kingship. Below them were the lower head ranks—most notably the *yuktup'um* (head-rank six), that is those below the *chingol* class but above the commoners and who were strictly limited in the office they might attain and the so-called *sŏngju* ("castle lords"), powerful figures in the Silla hinterland whose strength was gotten not through hereditary privilege but through the accumulation of land and resources and, ultimately, private armies. And finally there were the great mass of commoners, whose story is only to be inferred from the records of more court-centered histories or such recordings as Buddhist hagiographies.

As *The Silla Annals* approach the demise of Silla, thus closer to the lives of its compilers, the narrative becomes more nuanced, detailed, and dramatic. In its entry for the year 880 *The Silla Annals* relates how King Hŏngang climbed the ramparts of Kyŏngju and admired the view of his capital district, its neatly arranged streets and houses cheek-by-jowl with their tiled roofs testament to the city's wealth. Even at this eleventh hour in Silla's fortunes, to the Silla king it seemed the very picture of a domain boasting the twin riches of peace and prosperity.

This impression is confirmed by King Hŏngang's chief minister, Mingong, who tells the young monarch, "Since Your Majesty has ascended the throne, the forces of *yin* and *yang* are balanced, and the wind and rain have been timely. The years have been prosperous and the people have enough to eat. The borders have been peaceful and still, and the people on the streets have been happy. This is because of Your Majesty's virtue."

By including such a passage Kim Pusik was almost certainly aiming at irony, for that year offered a much starker reality. In the last decades of the ninth century Silla was a country in the final stages of a long and terminal illness. The man who would finally topple the teetering edifice was a three-year-old growing up in the region of modern Kaesŏng.

Kim Pusik later focuses his historical lens on another dramatic scene: the abdication of Silla's last king to the nascent power of Koryŏ. Terse though it is, the account in *The Silla Annals* conjures the scene with stirring effect. In the eleventh month of 935 a disconsolate King Kyŏngsun sent word to Wang Kŏn (T'aejo) of Koryŏ that events had forced upon the King the necessity of submitting to the authority of T'aejo. Kyŏngsun set off in the last Silla royal retinue to proffer both his personal submission and the *de facto* end of the thousand-year-old state of Silla.

This extraordinary procession, the *Samguk sagi* tells us, stretched for over 30 *li*[8] and was akin to a tribute mission, wafting fragrances (i.e., the smell of perfumed women) through the crisp winter air and with horses laden with Silla gold. Along the royal route curious crowds pressed, eager to be eyewitnesses to this pivotal moment. The pathos is not lost on Kim Pusik and the result is spellbinding history.

The *Samguk sagi,* and its annals in particular, may well be under-appreciated for how it reanimates an ancient past and emphasizes the human element, that common denominator of all history everywhere.

More than being simply a "Confucian-rationalist" history, the *Samguk sagi* conveys a sense of the tragedy of life. Kim Pusik had an eye for the dramatic, an appreciation of life's transience (he was, after all, Buddhist), and an abiding sympathy for the human condition. While we cannot be certain of the absolute accuracy of Kim Pusik's description of many events (he rarely references his

---

8   *Li:* approximately .75 kilometer (.5 mile).

sources), where other histories offer just "dust and bones" and lack human drama, *The Silla Annals* provides a sense of the human significance of ancient Korea. The *Samguk sagi* is the oldest surviving account of Korea's ancient past and one of the most extensive. Though there may be much to criticize, in the end there is a central truth: the enduring relevance of this extraordinary history.

The Silla
Annals of the
Samguk Sagi

Kŏsŏgan Hyŏkkŏse;
Ch'ach'aung Namhae; and
Isagŭm Yuri, T'arhae, P'asa,
Chima, and Ilsŏng

Book

1

Kŏsŏgan Hyŏkkŏse

Sijo [Founder Ancestor] had the family name Pak and the personal name Hyŏkkŏse.[1] He ascended the throne on *pyŏngjin* day [the twenty-fifth] of the fourth month {another source says it was on the fifteenth day of the first month}[2] in the first year [57 BCE] of the reign or Emperor Xiaoxuan of the Former Han[3] and took the

---

1   *Samguk yusa* (*The Memorabilia of the Three Kingdoms,* hereafter *SY*) Seoul: Minjok munhwa ch'ujinhoe, 1973, 1:12a–b, states that the name Hyŏkkŏse, also transliterated into "Pulgŏnae," meant in Silla "an enlightened ruler." Yi Pyŏngdo, in "Silla ŭi kiwŏn munje," *Hanguk kodaesa yŏngu* (hereafter *Hanguk kodae*) Seoul, 1976, 597, interpreted "Pulgŏnae" to mean the same as Hyŏkkŏse. He translated *hyŏk* to mean "bright or enlightened," and *kŏse* to mean "great" as *"kŏsŏ"* in Kŏsŏgan (Great Khan) which was Hyŏkkŏse's official title. See *Samguk sagi* (hereafter *SS*), Kyŏngin edition, Seoul, 1970, 1:1a. This allusion to the brightness of the sun is believed to reflect a probable infusion of the cult of nature worship into the Silla foundation legend. In the same reference above *SY,* citing another source, also indicates the legendary Chinese Holy Mother Sŏndo (Immortal Peach) as being Hyŏkkŏse's mother. For an elaborated narrative of the legend see *SY* 5:6a–7a.

2   All dates and months shown in this translation are based upon the lunar calendar, as in the original text.

3   As to the reliability of this foundation date there is considerable debate. Among those challenging this date and, in fact, doubting the veracity of the entire *SS* record before the middle of the fourth century are Imanishi Ryū, *Shiragishi kenkyū,* Tokyo, 1933, 8–10; Suematsu Yasukazu, "Kyū sangoku shiki to Sangoku shiki," *Seikyu shiso* 2 (1966): 8–9; and Yi Kibaek and Yi Kidong, *Hanguksa kangchwa* 1 (1982): 141. On the other hand some scholars, relying especially on new archaeological evidence, accept the start of Silla at this early date. See Kim Wŏlyong, "Samguk sidae ŭi kaesi e kwanhan ilgoch'al," *Tonga yŏngu* 7 (1967); "Saro yukch'on kwa Kyŏngju kobun," *Yŏksa hakpo* 70 (1976): 4–13, and Yi Chonguk, *Silla kukka hyŏngsŏngsa yŏngu* (hereafter *Silla hyŏngsŏng*) Seoul: Ilchogak, 1982, 16. See also Jonathan Best, *A History of the Early Korean Kingdom of Paekche* (hereafter *Paekche*), Cambridge, MA: Harvard University Asia Center,

title of *Kŏsŏgan*. At that time he was thirteen years old and the country was called Sŏnabŏl.[4]

Before this, people migrating from Chosŏn[5] spread out and lived in the mountains and valleys forming six villages[6] called: Yangsan Village of Alch'ŏn Stream, Kohŏ Village of Tolsan Mountain, Chinji Village {some say Kanjin} of Ch'wisan Mountain, Taesu Village of Musan Mountain, Kari Village of Kŭmsan Mountain, and Koya Village of Myŏnghwal Mountain. These became the six districts of Chinhan.[7] The village chief of Kohŏ, Lord Sobŏl,[8] looking at the foot of Yangsan Mountain saw a horse kneeling and neighing between trees near the Najŏng

---

2006, 8–9, for a discussion on this.

4   In *SY* "Sŏnabŏl" appears as "Sŏrabŏl." See *SY* 1:13a. Although variously translated, it is believed to mean "capital," as written by Iryŏn, the author of *SY*. For other interpretations see Academy of Korean Studies translation (Seoul: Choun munhwasa, 1996; hereafter *AKS*) 3:12, n. 6. It was not until the reign of King Chijŭng (500–514) that the country was formally called Silla.

5   Chosŏn, today known in history books as Ancient Chosŏn (Ko Chosŏn), was situated in northern Korea and southern Manchuria. This passage indicates that people were migrating from Chosŏn to Silla as Yan and Han China expanded into that area. Archaeological evidence also indicates northern influence in Silla's early beginnings. *Silla hyŏngsŏng* 16 and Yi Hyŏnhye, *Samhan sahoe hyŏngsŏng kwajŏng yŏngu,* Seoul: Ilchogak, 1984.

6   The boundaries of the six villages are open to speculation. *Hanguk kodae* 599–603 and Yi Kidong in *Silla kolp'umje sahoe wa hwarangdo* (hereafter *Kolp'um*), Seoul: Ilchogak, 1984, assert the six villages encompass the Kyŏngju basin. Kim Ch'ŏlchun in "Silla sangdae sahoe ŭi Dual Organization," *Yŏksa hakpo* 1–2 (1952; hereafter "Dual Organization"), states they cover the Kyŏngju region. *Silla hyŏngsŏng* 22–3 maintains that the six villages spread beyond the Kyŏngju basin but not over the entire Kyŏngsang region. *Silla hyŏngsŏng* also states the six villages evolved from a clan to a chiefdom society based on ranks. *Hanguk kodae,* on the other hand, identifies them as a clan society based on kinship and territory.

7   Chinhan was one of the Three Han and was located in the southeastern section of the Korean peninsula. Because the leader of the area was called King Chin by Han China, people in the Nangnang region called the area Chinhan, *Hanguk kodae* 238. *Silla hyŏngsŏng* 256–9 also suggests that the area under Chinhan control might have extended into the Han River Valley from south of the Yesŏng River to west of Ch'unch'ŏn, even though the area is generally believed to have been east of the Naktong River, which runs through the southeastern part of the peninsula.

8   Sobŏl-gong was also called Sobŏl-tori in *SY* 1:11b.

well, but when he approached, he found no horse, only a large egg.[9] Upon it splitting apart, out of the egg came a child, whom he [Lord Sobŏl] took home and raised.

After reaching over ten years of age the child was seen to be unusually precocious. The people of the six districts, believing his birth to be supernatural and mysterious, held him in high esteem. They then had him enthroned as their ruler. Because the Chin[han] people pronounced gourd [*ho*] as *pak,* and the large egg at first looked like a gourd, they made Pak his surname.[10] *Kŏsŏgan* means "King" in the Chin[han] language {some say this is a general term of respect for people of rank}.[11]

Year four [54 BCE], summer. On the first day of the fourth month, *sinch'uk* day, there was a solar eclipse.[12]

Year five [53 BCE], spring, first month. A dragon[13] was seen at

---

9   This tale is related in a somewhat different form in *SY*—see *SY* 1:11b–13a. Also of interest is that the births of Hyŏkkŏse and Aryŏng, his Queen, seem to be associated with well water—indicating a common ancient myth that regarded well water as the fountain of life. Besides Hyŏkkŏse, see also the birth of Queen Aryŏng in *SY* 1:1b–2a. *SY* notes that the horse was white, denoting an auspicious symbol of a heavenly messenger. *Dual Organization* 73 notes this as evidence of Northeast Asian immigrant influence in early Silla. The egg myth is also common in early Korean mythology as seen in the legends of King Tongmyŏng, King T'arhae, and King Suro. The egg could possibly symbolize the sun or the origin of life.

10 According to Yi Sungŭn, "Silla sidae sŏngssi ch'widŭk kwa kŭ ŭimi," *Hanguksaron* 6 (1980): 11–21, the use of the surname Pak in Silla does not appear until after the mid-sixth century.

11 The title *Kŏsŏgan* was used only for Hyŏkkŏse. Also called *Kŏsŭrhan* in *SY* 1:12b, its meaning is not clear but it might have been used by the Chinhan people as a term of respect for the ruler as indicated in *SY* or by Koguryŏ people to convey the idea of tribal chief, as asserted by *Hanguk kodae* 661.

12 See Park Sungnae, "Portentography in Korea," *Journal of Social Sciences and Humanities* 46 (1977): 51–71. Solar eclipses were carefully watched and used as harbingers. Of the sixty-six eclipses listed in *SS* many are also found in Chinese sources and correspond with Western records.

13 In East Asia dragons, as deities of water, were worshipped as positive signs. In *SS* dragons are noted twenty-one times, usually around wells or ponds when the location of their appearances were identified. See Kim Chŏngsuk, "Silla munhwa e nat'anan tongmul ŭi sangjing," *Silla munhwa* 7 (1990): 73–6. This myth is also

Aryŏng well and out of its rib cage on the right side a girl was born. An old woman[14] saw this and, believing it strange, took the girl, raised her, and borrowed the well's name to call her. When the girl grew up she looked virtuous and beautiful. The Founder Ancestor [Pak] hearing this, received her as his consort. Being wise in her conduct, she was able to help him domestically. Contemporaries called them the two sages.

Year eight [50 BCE]. The Wae [Wa][15] came with troops intending to invade our [coastal] region but, hearing of the Founder Ancestor's divine virtue, they withdrew.

Year nine [49 BCE], spring, third month. There was a comet in Wangnyang.[16]

Year fourteen [44 BCE], summer, fourth month. There was a comet in Orion's Belt.

Year seventeen [41 BCE]. The King, accompanied by his consort Aryŏng, inspected the six districts, promoting agriculture and sericulture to maximize the use of the land.

Year nineteen [39 BCE], spring, first month. The country of

---

recorded in *SY* 1:13a where it occurs not in the same year, but the year of Hyŏkkŏse's birth and the baby is said to have been born from the left side, as opposed to the right side, of the dragon's rib cage. It also records that the child had a beak on her mouth that fell off when she was bathed and that she was found not by an old woman but by the primogenitor and the people of the six villages.

14 Ch'oe Kwangsik, "Samguk sagi sojae nogu ŭi sŏnggyŏk," *Sach'ong* 25 (1981): 9, noting the frequent appearance of "old women" in *SS*, suggests this might be a term to denote a shaman. See also *AKS* 3:21–2, n. 27.

15 This is a term generally used for the inhabitants of the Japanese islands, as it is today. Hatada Takashi in "Sangoku shiki Shiragi hongi ni mieru Wa," *Nihon bunka to Chōsen,* 1975, has concluded, by pointing out that they invaded mostly Silla's east coast during the lean spring season, that obtaining food and other life-supporting products was the main objective of these raids in early Silla. *Paekche* 65-6 provides an excellent discussion of the term "Wae" and the political evolution of what today is referred to as Japan. "Wa" will be used for the early period up until the sixth century.

16 This is the twenty-eighth house in the eastern region of the sky—corresponding to Cassiopeia. The appearance of a comet was considered an evil omen.

The Silla Annals of the Samguk Sagi

Pyŏnhan[17] surrendered.

Year twenty-one [37 BCE]. The capital was constructed and was called Kŭmsŏng.[18] This year Koguryŏ's Founder Ancestor Tongmyŏng was enthroned.[19]

Year twenty-four [34 BCE], summer. On the last day of the sixth month, *imsin* day, there was a solar eclipse.

Year twenty-six [32 BCE], spring, first month. Palace halls were constructed in Kŭmsŏng.

Year thirty [28 BCE], summer. On the last day of the fourth month, *kihae* day, there was a solar eclipse. When Lelang people[20] leading troops came to invade, they saw that the frontier people did not lock their doors at night and left stacks of grain out in the open fields. They said to each other, "As the people of this region do not rob from each other, it must be said that this country practices the Way. If our troops move stealthily to raid them, as would thieves, how can we not feel ashamed?" Accordingly they withdrew [their troops].

---

17 This entry seems incorrect for such an early date unless it refers to one of Pyŏnhan's politically federated units. See *AKS* 3: 23, n. 34. Pyŏnhan, also called Pyŏnjin, may have been the area in the lower reaches of the Naktong River. Some of this area subsequently evolved into Kaya. In terms of customs and traditions, but not sacrificial rites, Pyŏnhan seem to have been similar to Chinhan.

18 See also *SS* 34. Yi Chonguk in *Silla sangdae wangwi kyesŭng yŏngu* (hereafter *Silla sangdae*), Kyŏngsan, 1980, 57, believes this area is just northwest of Namsan (South Mountain) in Kyŏngju. Kim Chŏnghak in "Anapchi chapki sang," *Pangmulgwan sinmun* 130 (1982) believes *"kŭmsŏng"* meant "royal city," or "capital." *"Sŏng"* has been translated as "fortress" throughout this translation.

19 Koguryŏ's progenitor is also known as Chumong (trad. 37–14 BCE). See *SS* 13:1a– 4a.

20 Nangnang (Chinese: Lelang) was one of the four Han Chinese commanderies and had its center where modern P'yŏngyang is today. Lelang dominated the area around P'yŏngyang from 108 BCE until it collapsed in 313. Yi Chonguk in "Saroguk ŭi sŏngjang kwa chinhan," *Hanguksa yŏngu* 25 (1979): 10, interprets this as evidence of Chinese Han people coming to the Silla area for trade. Ch'ŏn Kwanu in *Ko Chosŏnsa: Samhansa yŏngu* (hereafter *Samhansa*) Seoul, 1989, 180–1, sees this as a clash between Silla and the expanding Lelang.

Year thirty-two [26 BCE], autumn. On the last day of the eighth month, *ŭlmyo* day, there was a solar eclipse.

Year thirty-eight [20 BCE], spring, second month. [The King] sent Lord Ho on an official call to Mahan.[21] The Mahan King politely said to Lord Ho, "Chinhan and Pyŏnhan have been subordinated to our country but recently have not brought tributes dues. Is this the proper way of serving the esteemed power?"[22] He replied, "Ever since the two sages arose in our country, human affairs have been well conducted and the seasons have been orderly [hence] the warehouses are filled with stacked grains and the people are respectful and polite. Accordingly, among those displaced from Chinhan and came to Pyŏnhan, Lelang, and Wa, there are none who are not in awe in their hearts. My King yet, in his humility and modesty, sends me to cultivate friendly relations. This is going beyond what is required of propriety, yet Your Great Majesty in fearful anger threatened us with troops. What is the intention of Your Majesty?" The King of Mahan in indignation wanted to kill him [Lord Ho] but his close attendants remonstrated against this, so the King allowed him [Lord Ho] to return home.

Before this, many people from China, suffering from disorders in Qin, fled eastward, settling mostly east of Mahan where they lived among the people of Chinhan. As they gradually became prosperous Mahan people grew to dislike them, [starting to] blame them. Lord Ho's clan as well as his family name are unknown but,

---

21 Lord Ho, though mentioned as a man from Wa in this passage, is credited with first seeing Kim Alchi's mysterious appearance. See *SY* 1:16b–17a, Kim Alchi. Mahan is the area occupied by modern Kyŏnggi, Ch'ungch'ŏng, and Chŏlla provinces. It is said to have comprised fifty-four *soguk* (small political entities). For more on Mahan see *AKS* 3:50, n. 50.

22 "Serving the esteemed power" (*sadae*) has also been rendered as "serving the great."

originally, he was from Wa. Because he had earlier girded his waist with a gourd and crossed the sea coming here, he was called Lord Ho [Gourd].

Year thirty-nine [19 BCE]. The Mahan King died.[23] Someone suggested to the King, "Since the Western Han [Mahan] King earlier had insulted one of our envoys, now that they are in mourning we should send an expedition. If we attack that country now, wouldn't it be easy to pacify it?" The King replied, "Taking advantage of another's calamity is not right." He did not follow the suggestion but instead sent an official to offer condolences.

Year forty [18 BCE]. The Paekche founder Onjo ascended the throne.[24]

Year forty-three [15 BCE], spring. On the last day of the second month, *ŭlyu* day, there was a solar eclipse.

Year fifty-three [5 BCE]. An official from the Eastern Okchŏ[25] came and offered twenty well-bred horses saying, "My ruler heard that in South Han [Chinhan or Saro] a sage had appeared and therefore he sent me with these gifts."

Year fifty-four [4 BCE], spring. On the twenty-fourth day of the second month, *kiyu* [*ŭlyu*] day, a comet appeared in *Hago*.[26]

Year fifty-six [2 BCE], spring. On the first day of the first

---

23 It is unclear to whom this refers, but probably it is the same Mahan King mentioned above who had been called the King of Chin, as cited in the Chinese histories. See *Hou Hanshu* 85.

24 See also *The Paekche Annals, SS* 23:1a–2b. Paekche was probably one of the fifty-four entities of Mahan that established itself in the Han River Valley in central Korea. Onjo was said to have been the second son of Koguryŏ's founding King Tongmyŏng. See *AKS* 3:25–6, n. 43–4.

25 Eastern Okchŏ occupied the modern Hamhŭng area in northeastern Korea. It fell successively under the control of Wiman Chosŏn, the Han Commanderies, and then Koguryŏ. For more on the Eastern Okchŏ see *AKS* 3:26, n. 49.

26 *Hago* is the constellation of the Herd-Boy, also called Aquila. The *"kiyu"* entry appears to be in error. See *AKS* 3:27, n. 51. The correct date of the *SS* entry in this passage is the twenty-fourth day of the third month.

month, *sinch'uk* day, there was a solar eclipse.

Year fifty-nine [2], autumn. On the last day of the ninth month, *musin* day, there was a solar eclipse.

Year sixty [3], autumn, ninth month. Two dragons appeared in a well in Kŭmsŏng. A heavy thunderstorm hit and thunder shook the south gate of the city.

Year sixty-one [4], spring, third month. *Kŏsŏgan* Hyŏkkŏse died and was buried in Sanŭng [Snake Tomb] north of Tamam Monastery.[27]

Ch'ach'aung Namhae

Ch'ach'aung Namhae[28] ascended the throne [in 4]. {*Ch'ach'aung* is also called *Chach'ung*. Kim Taemun[29] said that in the (Silla) dialect this means "shaman" (*mu*). Because people believed that shamans served spirits and carried out sacrificial offerings they therefore, in awe, respected them. Eventually they called the

---

27 For a more detailed account see *SY* 1:13b. *SY* states that when the people of the capital tried to bury the King and Queen (who had also died), a large snake appeared preventing this. Accordingly the royal remains were divided into five parts and interred in pairs in five areas called the Five Tombs or Snake Tomb. But, as will be seen below, Hyŏkkŏse's descendants were also buried here and later it will be called the Five Tombs.

28 Yi Pyŏngdo, in his translation of the *Samguk sagi* (hereafter *SS 1977*), Seoul: Ulyu munhwasa, 1977, 5, suggests *"ch'ach'aung"* might be related to the the modern Korean term *"chung,"* for "monk," which originally might have meant "shaman," indicating this was an age when spiritual and temporal power were vested in one person. *SY,* royal tables, however, lists his royal title as *"kŏsŏgan."*

29 Kim Taemun was an eighth-century Silla noble and official who was also the author of a number of works on Silla, none of which are extant today. A brief biography of Kim may be found in *SS* 46:9b.

respected chief *Chach'ung.*} Namhae was Hyŏkkŏse's oldest legitimate son. Being tall and large he was [also] composed and kindly in nature, as he was wise and resourceful. His mother was Lady Aryŏng and his consort was Lady Unje {another source says his consort was Lady Aru}. He succeeded his father to the throne and this is the first year [of his reign].

| Commentary |[30] The rule that made the year following the year of the King's enthronement the first year of the reign is explained in detail in the *Chunqiu* (*Spring and Autumn Annals*).[31] This is a rule set by former kings that no one should alter. "Yixun" ["Yi's Instructions"][32] states, "As [King] Chengtang[33] had already died, it became Taijia's first year."[34] "Zhengyi" ["Correct Meaning" in the *Shujing* (*Classic of Documents*)][35] also states, "As [King] Chengtang had already died, that year then should be Taijia's first year." However the *Mencius* states, "Upon [King] [Cheng]tang's death, Taiding [as the heir] was yet to ascend the throne, [hence it

---

30 When East Asian historians compiled histories they often inserted their individual interpretations in to the general text in the form of these comments. *SS* has thirty-one such entries in its fifty *kwŏn* (books). See Edward J. Shultz, "Kim Pusik kwa Samguk sagi," *Hanguksa yŏngu* 73:6 (1991), and Chŏng Kubok, "Koryŏ sidae sahaksa yŏngu," unpublished PhD dissertation, Sŏgang University, 1985, 9–10.

31 *Chunqiu* is one of China's five classics and is a chronicle of the state of Lu supposedly compiled by Confucius.

32 "Yi's instructions" refers to the "Instructions of Yi Yin," which are found in the *Shujing* (*Classic of Documents;* hereafter *Shujing*) in which the admonitions are given to the son of King Tang of Shang by Yi Yin who was a minister of the Shang Emperor.

33 King Chengtang was the founder of the Shang dynasty which overthrew the Xia in China around the eighteenth-century BCE.

34 According to *Shiji* (*Records of the Historians;* hereafter *Shiji*) 3, Taijia was the fourth Shang King. See note 37 below. In the commentary that follows, Taijia appears as a younger brother to Waibing and Zhongren. In *Shiji,* however, Taijia is an elder brother to them. See *AKS* 3:30, n. 72.

35 The "Zhengyi" here is the *Shujing* "Zhengyi" ("The Correct Meaning") which was compiled by the Tang scholar officials Kong Yingda, Yan Shigu, et al.

was] two years for Waibing and four years for Zhongren."[36] I suspect the error [found] in the "Zhengyi" may have been due to the possible omission of a few words in "Yi's Instruction" in the *Shujing* (*Classic of Documents*).

Some people say, "In ancient times when a ruler ascended the throne, the first year of the new reign began after the elapse of a month, but in other cases after the elapse of a year it was then called the first year." If the first year started after the elapse of one month, it should be correct that Taijia's first year was [immediately] after [King] Chengtang had died. The *Mencius'* statement, "Taiding was yet to be enthroned," means Taiding did not take the throne but died. The [subsequent] statement, "two years for Waibing and four years for Zhongren" refers to Taiding's sons, [who were] Taijia's two brothers—one probably lived [reigned] for two years, the other for four years and then died [respectively]. [Hence, this is] how Taijia had succeeded [King] [Cheng]tang. The incredulous statement in the *Shiji* (*Records of the Historians*),[37] "Waibing and Zhongren are two rulers," is incorrect. According to the former, it is incorrect to make the previous King's last year the first year of the new reign.[38] If we follow the

---

36 *Shiji* 3. see *Ershi wushi*, Hong Kong: Hong Kong wenxue yenjiushe, 1959, 1:12, in its chronicle of Yin states that, although Taiding was King Tang's Crown Prince, he died before ascending the throne and so his younger brother Waiping ascended the throne and reigned for three years, and he then was followed by his brother Zhongren who ruled for four years. Some critics dispute this order of enthronements. *Shiji* also states that Taijia was the oldest grandson of King Chengtang. See *AKS* 3:30, n. 69–71.

37 The compilation of *Shiji* was completed by the great historian of the Former Han dynasty Sima Qian before his death in 85 BCE. It is a record of 1,300 years of China's past from the mythical Yellow Emperor to the Han Emperor Wudi in 130. For an English translation see Burton Watson, *Records of the Grand Historian*, New York: Columbia University Press, 1990.

38 The "former," as stated in the *Chunqiu*, refers to the way of determining the last year of the previous ruler as the first year of the new reign.

The Silla Annals of the Samguk Sagi

latter, it can be said that [they] had attained the decorum of the Shang people.[39]

Year one [4], autumn, seventh month. Lelang troops arrived and encircled Kŭmsŏng in several layers. The King addressed his attending officials saying, "The two sage rulers have departed from the country [died] and I, supported by the people, presumptuously occupy the throne and am fearful as if crossing a river. Now a neighboring country has attacked. This must be because of my lack of virtue. What should I do?" His attending officials replied, "These bandits, taking advantage of our period of mourning, have recklessly come to invade. As Heaven certainly will not assist them, they are not worth fearing." The enemy suddenly retreated.

Year three [6], spring, first month. [The court] erected a shrine to the Dynastic Founder.[40]

Winter, first day of the tenth month, *pyŏngjin* day. There was a solar eclipse.

Year five [8], spring, first month. The King, hearing of T'arhae's worthiness, married his oldest daughter to him.

Year seven [10], autumn, seventh month. T'arhae was made the rank of *taebo*[41] and placed in charge of governmental affairs and of defending the country.

Year eight [11], spring and summer. There was a drought.

Year eleven [14]. The Wa sent more than a hundred ships to plunder the homes of the people on the sea coast. The King

---

39 On the other hand, "the latter" refers to *Shujing* which asserts that the first year of the new reign is after the elapse of a year following the previous King's death. According to tradition the Shang Kingdom dominated the north-China plains approximately 1722–1122 BCE.

40 See *SS* 32 for an additional reference.

41 This rank is noted only in the earliest reigns and is later superseded by *ibŏlch'an* and *ich'an*. See *AKS* 3:32, n. 83.

dispatched the strong soldiers of the six districts to stop the Wa soldiers. Lelang, hearing that the country was abandoned, attacked Kŭmsŏng, causing [Silla] great urgency. At night there were shooting stars that fell into the enemy's camp. Many withdrew in fear and camped above Alch'ŏn River where they first built up twenty stone piles and then fled. A thousand soldiers from the six districts pursued them but, seeing the stone piles [stretching] from east of Mount T'oham[42] to Alch'ŏn Stream, they believed there were many enemies and so stopped.

Year thirteen [16], autumn, *muja* [last] day of the seventh month. There was a solar eclipse.

Year fifteen [18].[43] There was a drought in the capital.

Autumn, seventh month. There was [an infestation of] locusts. As the people were starving, [the court] opened the granaries to aid them.

Year sixteen [19], spring, second month. A man from Pungmyŏng,[44] while cultivating his fields, found King Ye's[45] seal which he presented [to the King].

Year nineteen [22]. There was a great pestilence and many people died.

Winter, eleventh month. Water did not freeze.

Year twenty [23], autumn. Venus entered *T'aemi*.[46]

Year twenty-one [24], autumn, ninth month. There was [an

---

42 Mount T'oham, southeast of Kyŏngju, is one of the five peaks of the Kyŏngju area and was an important point from which sea invaders could be detected.

43 *SY* 1:14b also notes that in this year seven Koguryŏ vassal states submitted to Silla.

44 *SS 1977* 7 believes this site is actually near modern Wŏnsan. *AKS* 3:33, n. 89, suggests the area was part of Eastern Ye land controlled by the Han Chinese commanderies.

45 The King of Yemaek, which is a kingdom believed to have been in northeastern Korea along the seacoast, probably received the seal from Han China.

46 *SS 1977* 7, citing Chinese records, indicates that this is a bad omen hinting at the possible death of an important figure.

infestation of] locusts. The King died and was buried in the garden of Sanŭngwŏn [Snake Tomb].

Isagŭm Yuri

Isagŭm Yuri ascended the throne [in 24]. He was [King] Namhae's Crown Prince and his mother was Lady Unje and his Queen was the daughter of *Kalmunwang* Ilchi.[47] {Some say the Queen was of the Pak lineage or the daughter of King Hŏru.} Earlier when [King] Namhae died, Yuri was to be enthroned. Because *Taebo* T'arhae was innately a man of virtue, he declined the throne. T'arhae said, "The throne is precious and not something an ordinary person like me can have. I have heard that noble and wise people have many teeth so let [us] test by having Yuri eat some rice cake to see [if he has many teeth]." As Yuri had many teeth, his attending officials all supported him to ascend to the throne, calling him *"Isagŭm."* This is what has been transmitted down from the past. Kim Taemun thus said, *"Isagŭm* is local dialect meaning "teeth."[48] Earlier as [King] Namhae was about to

---

47 The term *Kalmunwang* is used as an honorific title for men who are uncles or fathers-in-law to the King. See Yi Kibaek, "Silla sidae ŭi Kalmunwang" (hereafter "Kalmunwang"), *Silla chŏngch'i sahoesa yŏngu,* Seoul, 1974, 2–33. Ilchi's history is unclear but Yi Kibaek, on 10, suggests that he might be the father of King Yuri's Queen.

48 *SS 1977* 9 discusses possible meanings for this honorific. It was a term used for kings from Yuri to the eighteenth Silla King, Silsŏng. Having many teeth was a sign of being the oldest. Kim Ch'ŏlchun, in *Kodae sahoe* 143, suggests the change symbolized the foundation of a tribal league in Silla. It has been translated as "successor Prince" in Lee, Ki-baik, *A New History of Korea,* Cambridge, MA: Harvard University Press, 1984, p. 29.

die, he spoke to his son Yuri and son-in-law T'arhae saying, "After I die, from your two lineages of Pak and Sŏk, the oldest should succeed to the throne." Later the Kim lineage also rose and as the oldest person among the three lineages inherited [the throne], they called him *"Isagŭm."*

Year two [25], spring, second month. The King personally held sacrifices at the Dynastic Founder's Shrine and proclaimed a general amnesty.

Year five [28], winter, eleventh month. The King, inspecting the country and seeing an old woman starving, cold, and about to die, said, "I, an insignificant person, sit on the throne but cannot support the people, causing the old and young to reach this extreme [state]. This is my crime." He took off his clothes and covered her, giving her food to eat, and then commanded the concerned offices to search out [the country] and feed those widows, widowers, orphans, childless, old, and sick who could not support themselves. Thereupon many people from the neighboring states heard this and came in great numbers. This year the people's daily life was happy and peaceful. [The King] started to compose *Tosol-ga,* which marked the start of music and songs.

Year nine [32], spring. [The King] changed the names of the six districts and granted surnames.[49] Yangsanbu became Yangbu with the surname of Yi, Kohŏbu became Saryangbu with the surname

---

49 This development has stimulated considerable debate. Ch'oe Chaesŏk in *Hanguk kodae sa yŏngu* (hereafter *Hanguk kodaesa*), Seoul: Ilchisa, 1987, 373–4, asserts this began in Hyŏkkŏse's reign. Yi Chonguk accepts this entry at face value in "Silla sanggogi ŭi yuk ch'on kwa yuk pu," *Chintan hakpo* 49 (1980): 31. Yi Pyŏngdo states it happened in King Chabi's twelfth year (469) in *Hanguk kodae* 602. Kim Ch'ŏlchun, in *Dual Organization,* asserts it occurred in King Soji's reign, as does No T'aedon, "Samguk sidae pu e kwanhan yŏngu," *Hanguksaron* 2 (1975): 19. Finally, Yi Sungŭn in "Silla sidae sŏngssi ch'widŭk kwa kŭ ŭimi," *Hanguksaron* 6 (1980): 16–23, asserts that the use of royal surnames dates from the sixth century and that the linking of surnames with the six districts occurs during the process of unification in the seventh century.

Ch'oe, Taesubu became Chŏmnyangbu {or Moryang} with the surname Son, Kanjinbu became Ponp'ibu with the surname Chŏng, Karibu became Han'gibu with the surname Pae, and Myŏnghwalbu became Sŭppibu with the surname Sŏl. Also established were offices of seventeen ranks:[50] 1. *ibŏlch'an,* 2. *ich'ŏkch'an,* 3. *chapch'an,* 4. *p'ajinch'an,* 5. *taeach'an,* 6. *ach'an,* 7. *ilgich'an,* 8. *sach'an,* 9. *kŭppŏlch'an,* 10. *taenama,* 11. *nama,* 12. *taesa,* 13. *sosa,* 14. *kilsa,* 15. *taeo,* 16. *soo,* and 17. *chowi.*

The King already established the six districts, dividing them into two teams and having two Princesses each lead the women within one, forming them into friendly teams.

From the sixteenth day of the seventh month in autumn, everyday they met early in the yard of the larger district, weaving hemp. When it reached around ten at night they stopped.

Coming to the fifteenth day of the eighth month, they investigated to see who had more and who had less. The team that had more was given food and wine to thank the winners. Thereupon music, dance, and all types of games were presented and called *"kabae."* At that time a girl from the losing team got up and while dancing lamented, *"Hŭiso, hŭiso."* As these sounds were so sad and beautiful, later people took them and composed a song calling it *Hŭiso-gok.*

Year eleven [34]. In the capital the earth split open and a spring gushed out.

Summer, sixth month. There was a great flood.

Year thirteen [36], autumn, eighth month. Lelang invaded the northern frontier and attacked, destroying Mount T'asan Fortress.

Year fourteen [37]. The Koguryŏ King Muhyul[51] raided Lelang

---

50 See also *SS* 38.
51 This is Koguryŏ's third King, Great King Musin.

to destroy it. Five thousand people from that country came to surrender to Silla and were divided and settled in the six districts.

Year seventeen [40], autumn, ninth month. People from Hwaryŏ and Pullae[52] plotted together to lead horsemen to invade the northern borders. The leader of Maekkuk[53] with troops attacked from west of Kokha [winding river] and defeated them. The King was pleased and established good ties with Maek.

Year nineteen [42], autumn, eighth month. Generals from Maek, while hunting, captured birds and animals and presented them.

Year thirty-one [54], spring, second month. A comet appeared in the *Chagung* {*chami* (*ziwei*)} constellation.[54]

Year thirty-three [56], summer, fourth month. A dragon was seen in a well in Kŭmsŏng. Soon after a heavy rain came from the northwest.

Fifth month. A great wind uprooted trees.

Year thirty-four [57], autumn, ninth month. The King was seriously ill, and calling his officials said, "T'arhae in social standing is a royal relative of mine, his position is ministerial, and he is noted for his meritorious contributions. The talent of my two sons[55] is not as great as his. After I die, enable him to succeed to the throne. Do not disregard my instructions."

Winter, tenth month. The King died and was buried in the garden of Sanŭngwŏn.

52　These two districts, originally part of Imdun, were in eastern Lelang, see *SS 1977* 9. See also Yi Pyŏngdo, *Hanguk kodae,* 195–202.

53　This is a state allegedly located in the Chunch'ŏn region in central Korea. Chinese sources have placed it in the Liao/Manchurian region with Yeguk. *Nihon shoki* sees it as another name for Koguryŏ. See also Kim T'aekkyun, "Ch'unch'ŏn Maekkuk sŏl e kwanhan yŏngu," *Paeksan Hakpo* 30–1:131–8.

54　This is located north of the Big Dipper.

55　According to the *Silla Annals,* this refers to King Ilsŏng and King P'asa. However there is some evidence that indicates that King Ilsŏng was the son of *Kalmunwang* Pak Ado and King P'asa was the son of Naro. See *Silla Sangdae* 62–6.

　　　　The **Silla Annals** of the **Samguk Sagi**

Isagŭm T'arhae

Isagŭm T'arhae {one source says T'ohae} was enthroned [in 57]. His age was sixty-two and his surname was Sŏk. His Queen was Lady Ahyo. T'arhae originally was born in Tap'ana.[56] This country is 1,000 *li* northeast of Wa. Earlier this country's ruler married the daughter of the Queen's country [Yŏguk], making her his wife. After being pregnant for seven years, she gave birth to a great egg. The King said, "It is not a good omen for a person to give birth to an egg" and so he threw it out. His wife could not bear this and wrapped the egg with silk, together with treasures, put it in a chest, letting it float on the sea to drift away. It first reached the coast of Kŭmgwan [modern Kimhae region]. The people of Kŭmgwan, thinking it was strange, did not take it so it came to Chinhan's Ajin-p'o Harbor [in the Kyŏngju area]. This was in the thirty-ninth year [19 BCE] of the Dynastic Founder Hyŏkkŏse's reign.

At that time there was an old lady[57] at the coast who, with a rope, pulled it up and tied it to the shore. On opening the chest and looking at it, there was a small child. The woman took the child and raised it. When it grew it was 9 *ch'ŏk*[58] tall and its

---

56 See also *SY* 1:15a where it also says he came from Yongsŏngguk and mentions other states like Chŏngmyŏngguk. The Japanese scholar Mishina Shōei, in *Sangoku yūshi kōchō,* Tokyo, 1975, 490, states *Tap'ana* sounds like the Japanese word *Tajima* or *Tamana.* Others argue this points to a conquering or immigrating group under T'arhae coming from islands off the east or south coasts. See Kim Tujin, "Silla Sŏk T'arhae sinhwa ŭi sŏngnip kiban," (hereafter "Sŏk T'arhae"), *Hangukhak nonch'ong* 8 (1980): 11.

57 *SY* identifies this woman as an old fisherwoman named Ajin Ŭisŏn. She came from Chongyoguk, but its location is unclear. Kim Tujin in *Sŏk T'arhae* suggests she was a descendant of an earth-god lineage of a matrilineal society. See *SY* 1:15a.

58 Prior to Tang (seventh century), 1 *ch'ŏk* was approximately 24 centimeters (approximately 9.5 inches); from Tang forward, 1 *ch'ŏk* was approximately 30.5

bearing was outstanding and bright and in intelligence it surpassed other people. Some said, "This child does not know its surname. When the chest first reached here, there was a magpie that cried out and followed it. The abbreviated character for magpie is the character *"sŏk"* and so that was taken for his surname and, as he was *hae* [released] from the chest and came out, he was fittingly called T'arhae.[59] T'arhae first made his living as a fisherman and supported his mother. Not once was there any indication that he was lazy. His mother said, "You are an extraordinary person. Your features are very different from mine. Fittingly if you study you will achieve merit and fame." Thereupon he studied hard including the knowledge of geography. He viewed the residence of Lord Ho beneath Mount Yangsan[60] and, believing it was a propitious site, he plotted to take it and live there. The area later became Wŏlsŏng [Moon Fortress].[61] Reaching King Namhae's fifth year, hearing of his worthiness, [the King] had his daughter marry T'arhae. In the seventh year he was appointed *taebo* and entrusted with governmental affairs. When Yuri was on his death bed he said, "the previous King in his will said, 'after I die, regardless of whether it is my sons or son-in-law, whoever is older and wiser, he should inherit the throne. That is how I earlier became King and now we should transfer the throne that way.'"

Year two [58], spring, first month. [The King] made Lord Ho a *taebo*.

---

centimeters (12 inches).

59 Again *SY* 1:16a provides a more elaborate explanation, indicating that *sŏk* ("old") comes from T'arhae regaining his old house.

60 Lord Ho is first mentioned in Hyŏkkŏse's thirty-eighth year.

61 This is still visible in Kyŏngju today and is the site of ongoing archaeological research.

Second month. [The King] held sacrifices at the Dynastic Founder's Shrine.

Year three [59], spring, third month. When the King climbed Mount T'oham there was a dark cloud hovering over his head, and it lingered until after a while the cloud dissipated.

Summer, fifth month. Good ties were established with Wa and envoys were exchanged.

Sixth month. There was a comet in the *Ch'ŏnsŏn* constellation.

Year five [61], autumn, eighth month. The Mahan General Maengso surrendered Pogam Fortress.

Year seven [63], winter, tenth month. The Paekche King expanded his territory to Nangja Valley Fortress[62] and sent envoys asking to meet, but the King refused.

Year eight [64], autumn, eighth month. Paekche sent troops attacking Wasan Fortress.[63]

Winter, tenth month. They also attacked Kuyang Fortress.[64] The King sent 2,000 horsemen to chase—attacking and following them.

Twelfth month. There was an earthquake and no snow.

Year nine [65], spring, third month. The King heard at night the sound of a rooster crying in Sirim Forest west of Kŭmsŏng.[65] Waiting until dawn he sent Lord Ho to go and see it. There was a small gold-colored, chest hanging from the branch of a tree with a white rooster crying under it. Lord Ho returned to report it. The King sent a man to get the chest and open it. There was a small boy inside who was beautiful and looked extraordinary. The King,

---

62 See also *SS* 37; near modern Chŏngju. In King Sinmu's fifth year (685) it became Sŏwŏn, a minor capital.

63 This is Ch'ungbuk, Poŭn.

64 This is Ch'ungbuk, Koesan.

65 See also *SY* 1:16–7a for a somewhat similar account.

pleased, told his attendants saying, "How can this not be a son sent to me from Heaven to continue the succession." He took the boy and raised him. When he grew, he was bright and resourceful and was named Alchi. Because he came from a gold [*kŭm* or *kim*] chest, he was called Kim. They changed the name of Sirim to Kyerim and accordingly this became the name of the country.

Year ten [66]. Paekche attacked and took Wasan Fortress and had two hundred men live there and guard it. Then [Silla a little later] took it again.[66]

Year eleven [67], spring, first month. Because the Pak lineage was the noble family, they divided the country into districts of *chu* and *kun* [districts] for governing, calling the leaders *chuju* [chief] and *kunju* [chief].[67]

Second month. Sunjŏng became *ibŏlch'an*[68] and was put in charge of government affairs.

Year fourteen [70]. Paekche invaded.[69]

Year seventeen [73]. Wa invaded Mokch'ul Island. The King sent *Kakkan*[70] Uo to defend it, but to no success. Uo died there.

Year eighteen [74], autumn, eighth month. Paekche invaded the border region. [The King] sent troops to resist.[71]

Year nineteen [75]. There was a great drought with people starving. The [Court] opened the granaries to provide relief.

Winter, tenth month. Paekche attacked Wasan Fortress in the

---

66 See also *SS* 23:9a.

67 This system is not formalized until King Chijŭng's reign (500–514). *Chuju* and *kunju* were titles given to people who were dispatched to administer the *chu* and *kun*. See *AKS* 3:45–6, n. 162, and Sin Hyŏngsik, *Hanguk kodaesa ŭi Silla yŏngu* (Seoul: Ilchokak, 1984).

68 This was the first of Silla's seventeen ranks.

69 See also *SS* 23:9a.

70 This is another name for Silla's highest rank, *ibŏlch'an*.

71 See also *SS* 23:9b.

western region and occupied it.[72]

Year twenty [76], autumn, ninth month. [The King] sent troops to attack Paekche and retook Wasan Fortress.[73] The more than two hundred people living there who had come from Paekche were all killed.

Year twenty-one [77], autumn, eighth month. *Ach'an*[74] Kilmun fought with Kaya troops at Hwangsan-jin [ford][75] and captured more than a thousand of them. Kilmun became *p'ajinch'an*[76] and was rewarded for his merit.

Year twenty-three [79], spring, second month. A comet was seen in the east and then in the north [of the sky] for twenty days and then it disappeared.

Year twenty-four [80], summer, fourth month. There was a strong wind in the capital and a gate on the eastern side of Kŭmsŏng crumbled by itself.

Autumn, eighth month. The King died[77] and was buried north of the capital at Yangjŏng Hill.

Isagŭm P'asa

Isagŭm P'asa [in 80] was enthroned. He was King Yuri's second son. {Some say he was the son of Yuri's younger brother Naro

---

72 See also *SS* 23:9b.
73 See also *SS* 23:9b.
74 The sixth of Silla's seventeen ranks.
75 This is the Naktong River area between Kimhae and Yangsan.
76 The fourth of Silla's seventeen ranks.
77 *SY* 1:16a–b claims T'arhae died in his twenty-third year on the throne.

(Naero)}.[78] His Queen was Lady Sasŏng of the Kim lineage, the daughter of *Kalmunwang* Hŏru. Earlier, when T'arhae died, his officials wanted to enthrone Yuri's Crown Prince Ilsŏng as King. Some said that although Ilsŏng was the legitimate heir, his prestige and intelligence could not match that of P'asa. Accordingly, they enthroned [P'asa]. P'asa was frugal in expenses and thrifty in his needs. He loved the people and the people praised him.

Year two [81], spring, second month. The King held sacrifices at the Dynastic Founder's Shrine.

Third month. The King inspected the *chu* and *kun* districts and opened the granaries to aid the people. He reviewed [the cases] of those imprisoned and released those who had not committed crimes of the second degree.[79]

Year three [82], spring, first month. [The King] decreed, "Now the government granaries are exhausted and our military weapons are outdated and useless. If there is a disaster of a flood or drought, or enemy on the frontier, how could we protect ourselves? We ought to instruct the offices concerned to promote agriculture and sericulture and train troops to prepare for the unexpected.

Year five [84], spring, second month. Myŏngsŏn became *ich'an* and Yullyang became *p'ajinch'an*.

Summer, fifth month. The *kunju* [district chief] of Kot'a[80] presented a blue-colored cow. In Namsin-hyŏn[81] the barley grew

---

78 *Silla Sangdae*, citing *SY*, argues P'asa might be King Yuri's son.

79 A second-degree crime, requiring the death penalty either by hanging or beheading, was given to those guilty of treason or plotting treason. See *SS 1977* 15.

80 The area around Kyŏngbuk, Andong, see *SS 1977* 15. For late usesage see p. 59, note 16.

81 Silla had a number of regional designations such as *hyŏn* seen here and the *kun* which appear throughout *SS*. See note 84 below. The term *"kun"* is somewhat

The **Silla Annals** of the **Samguk Sagi**

abundantly with many shoots. As it was a bumper year, those who traveled did not carry provisions.

Year six [85], spring, first month. Paekche invaded the border area.[82]

Second month. Kilwŏn became *ach'an.*

Summer, fourth month. A strange star entered the *Chami* constellation.[83]

Year eight [87], autumn, seventh month. [The King] decreed, "I am without virtue. To the west is the enemy Paekche and to the south we touch Kaya. My virtue is not able to pacify them, my authority is insufficient to put them in awe. We ought to repair the fortresses and ramparts to be ready for an invasion." This month they constructed the two fortresses, Kaso and Madu.[84]

Year eleven [90], autumn, seventh month. [The King] dispatched ten officials to investigate if the *chu* chiefs and the *kun* chiefs were diligent in public affairs.[85] Those officials who had left the fields excessively decimated were demoted or dismissed.

Year fourteen [93], spring, first month. Yullyang became *ich'an* and Kyegi became *p'ajinch'an.*

Second month. The King traveled to Kosoburi-gun[86] and

---

problematic since, as seen below, it is translated as "prefecture" while on other occasions it appears as a military district—and at this early date neither usage seems applicable.

82   See also *SS* 23:9b.

83   See *SS 1977* 15. This is a star that is not normally seen and is considered an evil omen. See also note 54 above.

84   Kaso is Kyŏngnam, Kŏch'ang, Madu is in the Kyŏngbuk, Kyŏngsan-Wŏlsŏng region.

85   Silla developed a tiered local administrative structure with *chu, kun, hyŏn,* and *pu.* Roughly translated, *"chu"* is "province," *"kun"* is "prefecture," *"hyŏn"* is "county," and *"pu"* is "district." This work will maintain the original Korean terms.

86   *SS 1977* 15 suggests this might be in Chŏnbuk, Kobu, but questions the validity of this entry. *AKS* does not state the location of this site.

personally inquired [into the conditions of] the elderly and gave them grain.

Winter, tenth month. There was an earthquake in the capital.

Year fifteen [94], autumn, seventh month. Kaya bandits encircled Madu Fortress. The King dispatched *Ach'an* Kilwŏn who led a thousand horsemen to attack and drive them away.

Autumn, eighth month. [The King] reviewed troops in Alch'ŏn.

Year seventeen [96], autumn, seventh month. A storm blew from the south and uprooted large trees south of Kŭmsŏng.

Ninth month. Men from Kaya raided the southern region. [The King] sent the Kasŏng Fortress Chief Changse to resist, but he was killed by the enemy. The King, enraged, led 5,000 brave soldiers out to attack and defeated them, taking many prisoners of war.

Year eighteen [97], spring, first month. Troops were mobilized hoping to attack Kaya. That country's ruler sent emissaries requesting a pardon and the [mobilization] was suspended.

Year nineteen [98], summer, fourth month. The capital experienced a drought.

Year twenty-one [100], autumn, seventh month. It rained hail killing flying birds.

Winter, tenth month. There was an earthquake in the capital that knocked down the houses of people, causing death.

Year twenty-two [101], spring, second month. A fortress called Wŏlsŏng was constructed.

Autumn, seventh month. The King moved to reside in Wŏlsŏng.

Year twenty-three [102], autumn, eighth month. The kingdom of Ŭmjŭppŏl and the kingdom of Silchikkok[87] fought over

---

87 See *SS* 34:9a. The kingdom of Ŭmjŭppŏl is perhaps in modern Kyŏngju and the kingdom of Silchikkok is probably in modern Samch'ok, Kangwŏn province; see *SS* 35:12a.

territory and asked the King to adjudicate. The King, finding this to be difficult, said because King Suro of the kingdom of Kŭmgwan[88] is old and great in knowledge, he would summon him for consultation. [King] Suro offered an opinion that the contested land belonged to the kingdom of Ŭmjŭppŏl. Thereupon the King ordered the six districts to hold a banquet for King Suro. Five districts made their *ach'an* the chief [for the feast] and only Hangi district had a low-ranking person to manage it. [King] Suro was angry and ordered his slave T'amhari to kill the Hangi district chief Poje and return. The slave fled and entrusted himself to the house of the head chief of Ŭmjŭppŏl, T'ach'u. The King sent an official to search for the slave but T'ach'u would not send him. The King in anger attacked with troops the kingdom of Umjŭppŏl and the chief and the people surrendered themselves. The kings of the two kingdoms of Silchik and Aptok came to surrender.[89]

Winter, tenth month. Peach and plum trees blossomed.

Year twenty-five [104], spring, first month. Many shooting stars fell like rain but did not reach the ground.

Autumn, seventh month. The kingdom of Silchik rebelled. [The King] mobilized troops to suppress and pacify it and remove those remaining to the southern region.

Year twenty-six [105], spring, first month. Paekche sent an official asking for peace.

Second month. Three *ch'ŏk* of snow fell in the capital.

Year twenty-seven [106], spring, first month. [The King] made

---

88 *SY* 1:7a introduces King Suro as Kaya's first King. Yi Pyŏngdo believes he was the first King of the Kaya federation. *"Suro"* may mean "first to hatch from an egg," or "divine or high king," or the name possibly was derived from a Manchurian word meaning "divine." See *AKS* 3:49–50, n. 187.

89 Both *SY,* chronological tables, and *SS,* geographical section, indicate Aptok's surrender occurred in King Chima's reign (112–34). Aptok is in modern Kyŏngbuk, Kyŏngsan.

a trip to the kingdom of Aptok and offered relief to the poor and starving. In the third month he returned from Aptok.

Autumn, eighth month. [The King] ordered the Madu Fortress leader to attack Kaya.

Year twenty-nine [108], summer, fifth month. There was a great flood and people starved. [The King] dispatched officials to the ten circuits and opened the granaries to offer relief. He sent troops to attack the kingdoms of Piji,[90] Tabŏl, and Ch'op'al[91] to annex them.

Year thirty [109], autumn, seventh month. Locusts harmed crops. The King went around offering sacrifices to the mountains and streams to pray for relief. The locusts disappeared and [it turned into] a bumper year.

Year thirty-two [111], summer, fourth month. A city gate crumbled by itself.

From the fifth month to autumn, the seventh month, there was no rain.

Year thirty-three [112], winter, tenth month. The King died and was buried in Sanŭngwŏn.

Isagŭm Chima

Isagŭm Chima {some say Chimi} was King P'asa's legitimate son. His mother was Lady Sasŏng and his Queen was Lady Aerye of the

---

90 *Samhansa* 293 says this was in Kyŏngbuk, Yongil. *AKS* 3:50, n. 192, states the kingdom of Piji was Kyŏngnam, Ch'angnyŏng.

91 See *SS* 34. The kingdom of Tabŏl was Taegu and the kingdom of Ch'op'al was Kyŏngnam, Hapch'ŏn.

Kim lineage and daughter of *Kalmunwang* Maje. Earlier when King P'asa hunted in the Yuch'an Marsh, the Crown Prince followed him there. After the hunt when he passed Hangi district, *Ich'an* Hŏru entertained him. As he became intoxicated, Hŏru's wife together with her small daughter came out to dance. *Ich'an* Maje's wife also pulled out her daughter. When the Crown Prince saw her, he was pleased but Hŏru was not happy [with this]. The King spoke to Hŏru saying, "This area is called Taep'o. Here you have set up a lavish feast and tasty wine and through this banquet have brought much pleasure. You should be given the rank of *chuda*[92] which is above *ich'an*." Thereupon [the King] had Maje's daughter marry the Crown Prince, becoming his wife. *Chuda* was later called *kakkan*.

Year two [113], spring, second month. The King personally held sacrifices at the Dynastic Founder's Shrine. He appointed Ch'angyŏng to be an *ich'an* to participate in governmental affairs. Okkwŏn became *p'ajinch'an*, Singwŏn became *ilgilch'an,* and Sunsŏn became *kŭpch'an*.

Third month. Paekche sent envoys for a courtesy visit.

Year three [114], spring, third month. It rained hail damaging the barley shoots.

Summer, fourth month. There was a flood. [The King] reviewed [the cases of] those imprisoned and, except for those carrying the death penalty, freed the rest, completely pardoning them.

Year four [115], spring, second month. Kaya plundered the southern border area.

Autumn, seventh month. [The King] personally led an expedition against Kaya. As he led the infantry and cavalry across

---

92 Also read as *suburhan,* another name for *ibŏlch'an,* the highest rank in Silla. It later became the same as *kakkan.* See *SS 1977* 17. For another meaning of *chuda* see Yi Ut'ae, "Silla ch'on kwa ch'onju," *Hanguksaron* 7 (1981).

the Hwangsan River,[93] Kaya troops waited in ambush in a grove for them. The King did not realize this until just beforehand. As the ambush developed he was encircled several times. The King commanded the troops and attacked strenuously breaking through the encirclement and retreating.

Year five [116], autumn, eighth month. [The King] sent generals to invade Kaya and he led 10,000 elite troops to follow them. Kaya closed its fortress and firmly defended. Meeting a prolonged rain, [the Silla troops] withdrew.

Year nine [120], spring, second month. A large star fell to the ground west of Wŏlsŏng with a noise like thunder.

Third month. There was a great epidemic in the capital.

Year ten [121], spring, first month. Ikchong became *ich'an*, Hŭllyŏn became *p'ajinch'an,* and Imgwŏn became *ach'an.*

Second month. [Silla] constructed a mountain fortress at Taejŭngsan.[94]

Summer, fourth month. The Wa invaded the eastern coast.

Year eleven [122], summer, fourth month. A strong wind blew from the east uprooting trees and blowing tiles until night when it stopped. The people in the capital, because of rumors that the Wa had come in great numbers, rushed to hide in the mountains and valleys. The King commanded *Ich'an* Ikchong and others to order them to stop.

Autumn, seventh month. Flying locusts damaged the crops. The year saw famine and many robbers.

Year twelve [123], spring, third month. Silla made peace with Wa.

---

93 Hwangsan River is a branch of the Naktong River near Yangsan. See also Kim T'aesik, *Kaya yŏnmaengsa,* Seoul: Ilchokak, 1993.

94 See *SS* 34. This is probably the area around Tongnae in Pusan.

Summer, fourth month. A frost fell.

Fifth month. Houses east of Kŭmsŏng collapsed making a pond in which lotus flowers bloomed.

Year thirteen [124], autumn, last day of the ninth month, *kyŏngsin* day. There was a solar eclipse.

Year fourteen [125], spring, first month. The Malgal[95] entered in great numbers along the northern borders, killing and robbing people and clerks.

Autumn, seventh month. The [Malgal] again attacked the defense barricade at Taeryŏng and crossed the Iha River.[96] The King wrote to Paekche asking for help. Paekche sent five generals to assist. The invaders, on hearing this, retreated.

Year sixteen [127], autumn, first day of the seventh month, *kapsul* day. There was a solar eclipse.

Year seventeen [128], autumn, eighth month. There was a long comet spread across the sky.[97]

Winter, tenth month. There was an earthquake in the eastern part of the country.

Eleventh month. There was thunder.

Year eighteen [129], autumn. *Ich'an* Ch'angyŏng died and *P'ajinch'an* Okkwŏn became *ich'an* and participated in governmental affairs.

Year twenty [131], summer, fifth month. There was a heavy rain, washing away people's houses.

Year twenty-one [132], spring, second month. There was a fire

---

95 *SS 1977* 19 notes this refers to the Eastern Ye people who lived in the northern part of the Korean peninsula.

96 Taeryŏng might be modern Taegwallyŏng west of Kangwŏn, Kangnŭng. There are a number of suggestions as to the location of the Iha River: at Tŏgwŏn, Kangnŭng, or in the headwaters of the South Han River. See *AKS* 3:52, n. 207.

97 Usually the appearance of such a comet would indicate the possibility of a war occurring.

at the south gate of the palace.

Year twenty-three [134], spring and summer. There was a drought.

Autumn, eighth month. The King died but without sons.

Isagŭm Ilsŏng

Isagŭm Ilsŏng was enthroned [in 134]. He was King Yuri's oldest son {some say he was *Kalmunwang* Ilchi's son}. His Queen was of the Pak lineage, the daughter of King Chisorye.[98]

Year one [134], ninth month. There was a general amnesty.

Year two [135], spring, first month. The King personally held sacrifices at the Dynastic Founder's Shrine.

Year three [136], spring, second month. Ungsŏn became *ich'an* and was concurrently made administrator of all military affairs of the country. Kŭnjong became *ilgilch'an*.

Year four [137], spring, second month. The Malgal entered a frontier outpost and burned five barricades at Changnyŏng.[99]

Year five [138], spring, second month. [The King] established a Chŏngsadang[100] in Kŭmsŏng.

Autumn, seventh month. [The King] held a general inspection west of Alch'ŏn.

---

98 *Silla sangdae* 64–7, states he was also a *kalmunwang. SY,* tables section 6, says his father was King Norye, that is, the older brother of Yuri, King Chima.

99 The exact location of this site in unclear but *SS 1977* 19 suggests modern Kangwŏn province.

100 This is a new office where important state matters were discussed. See Yi Chonguk, *Silla hyŏngsŏng,* 206–11.

Winter, tenth month. [The King] toured the north and personally offered sacrifices at Mount T'aebaek.[101]

Year six [139], autumn, seventh month. A frost fell killing leguminous plants.

Eighth month. The Malgal raided Changnyŏng and took people as prisoners.

Winter, tenth month. They came again but the snow was severe so they retreated.

Year seven [140], spring, second month. [The King] set up barriers at Changnyŏng to defend against the Malgal.

Year eight [141], autumn, the last day of the ninth month, *sinhae* day. There was a solar eclipse.

Year nine [142], autumn, seventh month. [The King] summoned his officials to discuss officially sending an expedition against the Malgal. *Ich'an* Ungsŏn presented his case against it and so [the discussion] stopped.

Year ten [143], spring, second month. The royal palace was repaired.

Summer, sixth month, *ŭlch'uk* day. Mars infringed on Saturn.[102]

Winter, eleventh month. There was thunder.

Year eleven [144], spring, second month. [The King] decreed, "Agriculture is the foundation of governing and eating is what people believe to be Heaven's command. Have the various *chu* and *kun* repair and strengthen the dikes and reclaim and enlarge their fields." He also commanded, "Forbid the people from using

---

101 According to *AKS* 3:54, n. 219, this mountain is located on the border between modern Kyŏngbuk and Kangwŏn provinces. But this particular entry is somewhat questionable since it is doubtful that Silla's territory had expanded that far by this date.

102 When Mars appears it is interpreted to mean a war will occur. Saturn's appearance warns of impending disaster. *AKS* 3:54, n. 221–2.

gold, silver, pearls, and jade."

Year twelve [145]. In the spring and summer there was a drought but in the southern region it was most severe with people starving. [The court] transported its grain to relieve them.

Year thirteen [146], winter, tenth month. As the kingdom of Aptok rebelled, [the King] dispatched troops to pacify it and settle its remaining people to the southern region.

Year fourteen [147], autumn, seventh month. [The King] commanded his officials to recommend the wise and brave who could become military commanders.

Year fifteen [148]. [The King] conferred on Pak Ado the title of *kalmunwang*.[103] {In Silla those who were posthumously conferred with the title of King were called *kalmunwang*. Its meaning is not clear.}

Year sixteen [149], spring, first month. Tŭkhum became *sach'an*, Sŏnch'ung became *naema*.

Autumn, eighth month. There was a comet in *Ch'ŏnsi* constellation.[104]

Winter, eleventh month. There was lightning and in the capital there was a great epidemic.

---

103 There is some debate as to who Pak Ado was. According to *SS* 45, he was the grandfather of Pak Chesang or the great grandfather of King Mich'u (262–284). See Imanishi Ryū, "Shiragi kātsubun-ō-kō," *Shiragishi kenkyū,* 250; and Yi Kibaek, "Kalmungwang," 10–1. For the first mention of *kalmunwang* see above *Isagŭm* Yuri, n. 47. There were twenty-one men who held this title in Silla and they were all members of the kings' or queens' families. When the Kings were from the Pak clan, the fathers of the Queens were *kalmunwang*. When the Sŏks were kings, the fathers and materal grandfathers of the King became *kalmunwang*. After King Nulchi, as the throne passed from father to son, the brothers of the kings who never wore the crown were called *kalmunwang*. As kings became more authoritarian in the middle period, the practice of enfeofing men as *kalmunwang* completely stopped. But toward the end of Silla, as various lineages vied for the throne, when the leaders of a different lineage became king, the king's father was enfeofed *kalmunwang.*

104 This is located in the northeastern section of the heavens.

Year seventeen [150]. From summer, the fourth month, there was no rain until autumn, the seventh month, and then it rained.

Year eighteen [151], spring, second month. *Ich'an* Ungsŏn died Taesŏn became *ich'an* and was concurrently made administrator of all military affairs of the country.

Third month. It rained hail.

Year twenty [153], winter, tenth month. There was a fire at a palace gate. A comet was seen in the eastern sky and then again in the northern sky.

Year twenty-one [154], spring, second month. The King died.

The Silla
Annals of the
Samguk Sagi

Isagŭm Adalla, Pŏrhyu, Nahae,
Chobun, Ch'ŏmhae, Mich'u,
Yurye, Kirim, and Hŭrhae

Book

2

Isagŭm Adalla

Isagŭm Adalla was enthroned [in 154].[1] He was Ilsŏng's oldest son. His height was 7 *ch'ok* [2.1 meters] and he had a bulbous nose. His appearance was strange. His mother was of the Pak lineage, the daughter of King Chisorye. His Queen was Lady Naerye of the Pak lineage, the daughter of King Chima.

Year one [154], spring, third month. Kyewŏn became *ich'an* and was placed in charge of the country's military and governmental affairs.

Year two [155], spring, first month. [The King] personally held sacrifices at the Dynastic Founder's Shrine. There was a general amnesty. Hungsŏn became *ilgilch'an*.

Year three [156], summer, fourth month. Frost fell. A road was opened over Kyerip Pass.[2]

Year four [157], spring, second month. [The court] established two *hyŏn*, Kammul and Masan.[3]

Third month, the King inspected Changnyŏng Garrison and, in appreciation to the troops defending [the garrison], he gave each military garb.

Year five [158], spring, third month. [The court] opened

1 He was the last King of Silla's "early period" and the last of a succession of kings from the Pak lineage.
2 This is Kyŏngbuk, Mungyŏng
3 These locations are unclear but, possibly, in Kyŏngbuk or Ch'ungbuk. See *AKS* 3:56–7, n. 5–6.

Chungnyŏng [Pass].[4] The Wa came on a courtesy visit.

Year seven [160], summer, fourth month. There was heavy rain and Alch'ŏn overflowed washing away people's houses. The northern gate of Kŭmsŏng crumbled by itself.

Year eight [161], autumn, seventh month. Locusts destroyed grain. Many fish jumped out of the ocean and died.

Year nine [162]. The King inspected Sado Fortress[5] and expressed appreciation to the troops.

Year eleven [164], spring, second month. A dragon appeared in the capital.

Year twelve [165], winter, tenth month. *Ach'an* Kilsŏn[6] planned to rebel, but when it was discovered, fearing execution, he escaped to Paekche. The King sent letters seeking [his return] but Paekche did not allow this. The King in anger sent troops to chastise them. Paekche closed its fortress in defense and would not come out [to fight]. When our provisions were exhausted, we returned.

Year thirteen [166], spring, the first day of the first month, *sinhae* day. There was a solar eclipse.[7]

Year fourteen [167], autumn, seventh month. Paekche attacked and destroyed two fortresses in the western part of the country, captured 1,000 people, and left.[8]

Eighth month. [The King] ordered *Ilgilch'an* Hŭngsŏn to lead

---

4   This is between Kyŏngbuk and Ch'ungbuk.
5   Location is unclear, see *AKS* 3:57, n. 9. It was on an invasion route used by the Wa and the Wa took this fort in 292.
6   Kilsŏn also appears in *The Paekche Annals, SS* 23:11a–b, where his escape is noted as taking place in 155, not 165 as stated here. It is not clear which date is correct. The historian's comment, which follows this entry in *The Paekche Annals*, considers the action of the Paekche king to be in error.
7   See also *Hou Hanshu* 7, Huandi, ninth year.
8   See *SS* 23:12a.

twenty thousand soldiers to chastise them. The King also led eight thousand horsemen. They approached from the Han River. Paekche, greatly afraid, returned the men and women they had captured and begged for peace.

Year fifteen [168], summer, fourth month. *Ich'an* Kyewŏn died and Hŭngsŏn became *ich'an*.

Year seventeen [170], spring, second month. [The court] again repaired the Dynastic Founder's Shrine.

Autumn, seventh month. There was an earthquake in the capital, and frost and hail harmed grain.

Winter, tenth month. Paekche invaded the border area.[9]

Year eighteen [171], spring. As food was dear, people starved.

Year nineteen [172], spring, first month. Kudo[10] became *p'ajinch'an* and Kusuhye became *ilgilch'an*.

Second month. There was an incident at the Dynastic Founder's Shrine.[11] In the capital there was a great epidemic.

Year twenty [173], summer, fifth month. The Wa Queen Himiko[12] sent an envoy on a courtesy visit.

Year twenty-one, [174] spring, first month. Dust fell like rain.[13]

Second month. There was a drought and the wells and springs dried up.

Year thirty-one [184], spring, third month. The King died.

---

9 A similar entry is found in *SS* 23:12a.

10 He is a sixth-generation descendant of Kim Alchi and the father of King Mich'u and was named a *kalmunwang* in Mich'u's second year.

11 *Samhansa* 198 links this entry to a change in the royal lineage from Pak to Sŏk.

12 See also *Sanguoji* and *SS 1977* 23. Best, in "The Samguk sagi's Anomalous Reference to the Japanese Queen Himiko," *Proceedings of the the 10th ISKS International Conference on Korean Studies* 73-7, challenges this dating, suggesting that this event most likely occurred in 712.

13 This most likely refers to rain mixed with yellow dust that occasionally blows over Korea from the loess soil of north China.

Isagŭm Pŏrhyu

Isagŭm Pŏrhyu {or Parhwi} was enthroned [in 184]. His surname was Sŏk and he was the son of T'arhae's son *Kakkan* Kuch'u.[14] His mother was Lady Chijin Naerye of the Kim lineage. When Adalla died he had no sons and so the people of the country enthroned him [Pŏrhyu]. The King, divining wind and clouds, knew in advance whether there would be a flood or drought, whether the year's [harvest] would be one of plenty or scarcity, and he could tell if a person were honest or wicked. People called him a sage.

Year two [185], spring, first month. [The King] personally held sacrifices at the Dynastic Founder's Shrine and there was a general amnesty.

Second month. [The King] appointed *P'ajinch'an* Kudo and *Ilgilch'an* Kusuhye to be left [senior] and right [junior] *kunju* [military commanders] to chastise the kingdom of Somunguk.[15] The title of *kunju* starts from here.[16]

Year three [186], spring, first month. The King made a tour of inspection to the *chu* and *kun* observing the customs of the people.

Summer, last day of the fifth month, *imjin* day. There was a solar eclipse.[17]

Autumn, seventh month. Namsin-hyŏn presented an auspicious

---

14   *Samhansa* 30 suggests King Pŏrhyu was actually no blood relation to T'arhae but came from northern Korea to Silla and assumed T'arhae's lineage. See *AKS* 3:60, n. 22.

15   This is Kyŏngbuk, Ŭisŏng.

16   *SS 1977* 25 notes this also occurred in King Chijung's sixth year (505) and probably not in 185. The position in 505 was more of an administrative office while the 185 position mentioned first here oversaw military matters for short durations as needed.

17   See also *Hou Hanshu* 8, Lingdi, Chungbing 3. Yi Pyŏngdo, Yi Chaeho, and a P'yŏngyang translation of *SS* all assert this event occurred on *imsin* day.

ear of rice.[18]

Year four [187], spring, third month. [The King] commanded the *chu* and *kun* not to start public works projects because they will take away from the time for farming.

Winter, tenth month. In the northern region there was a great snow 10 *ch'ŏk* deep.[19]

Year five [188], spring, second month. Paekche came and attacked Mosan Fortress.[20] [The King] ordered *P'ajinch'an* Kudo to dispatch troops to resist them.

Year six [189], autumn, seventh month. Kudo fought with Paekche at Kuyang[21] and won over them. He killed or captured over 500 people.

Year seven [190], autumn, eighth month. Paekche raided the western border of Wŏnsanhyang and advanced and encircled Pugok Fortress.[22] Kudo led 500 elite horsemen to attack them. The Paekche troops pretended to flee. Kudo pursued them to Wasan, only to be defeated by Paekche. Because of Kudo's mistake, the King demoted him to a *sŏngju* [fortress commander] at Pugok and Sŏl Chi became left military commander.

Year eight [191], autumn, ninth month. A comet called "Banner of Chiyu" was seen in *Kaksŏng* and *Hangsŏng* constellations.[23]

---

18 This is regarded as an auspicious omen, *SS 1977* 25.

19 Ten *ch'ŏk* equal approximately 1 *chang*.

20 *SS 1977* 25 suggests this is an error. There are several possible sites for Mosan Fortress including Chŏnbuk, Namwŏn; Ch'ungbuk, Chinch'ŏn; or Kyŏngbuk, Ŭisŏng. This attack is also noted in *SS* 23:12b.

21 This battle is also listed in *SS* 23:12b. Its exact location in Ch'ungbuk is unclear. See *AKS* 3:61, n. 27.

22 Wŏnsanhyang is Kyŏngbuk or Ch'ungbuk, Chinch'ŏn, Yech'on. Pugok is either at modern Kyŏngbuk, Kunwi, or Ch'ungbuk, Koesan. See also *SS* 23:12b; *AKS* 3:61, n. 30.

23 This is one of the twenty-eight houses of heaven found in the eastern section of the sky. Its appearance is considered a warning of a future rebellion. Chiyu was a rebellious lord in ancient China. See also *Hou Hanshu* 9 and *Xiandi* 2–9.

Year nine [192], spring, first month. Kungnyang became *ach'an*. Sulmyŏng became *ilgilch'an*.

Fourth month. The capital had 3 *ch'ŏk* of snow.

Summer, fifth month. There was a heavy rain causing more than ten landslides in the mountains.

Year ten [193], spring, first day of the first month, *kabin* day. There was a solar eclipse.[24]

Third month. A woman in Hangi district gave birth to quintuplets of four boys and one girl.

Sixth month. The Wa people had a great epidemic and more than 1,000 people came seeking food.

Year eleven [194], summer, last day of the sixth month, *ŭlsa* day. There was a solar eclipse.[25]

Year thirteen [196], spring, second month. [The court] again repaired palace halls.

Third month. There was a drought.

Summer, fourth month. [Lightning/earthquake] shook both a big tree south of the palace and the eastern gate of Kŭmsŏng. The King died.

Isagŭm Naehae

Isagŭm Naehae was enthroned [in 196].[26] He was the grandson of King Pŏrhyu. His mother was Lady Naerye[27] and his Queen was of

---

24 See also *Hou Hanshu* 9, Xiandi 4:193.
25 See also *Hou Hanshu* 9, Xiandi 4:194.
26 *AKS* renders his name as Nahae.
27 This is the same name of King Adalla's Queen. Whether they are the same people

the Sŏk lineage and younger sister to King Chobun. His [King Naehae's] appearance was majestic and he was exceedingly talented. The former King's Crown Prince Kolchŏng and his second son Imae died earlier and the grandson by the first son was still young, thus they enthroned Imae's son and this was *Isagŭm* Naehae. This year, from the first to the fourth month, there was no rain but, on the day the King was enthroned, there was heavy rain, and the people happily welcomed it.

Year two [197], spring, first month. [The King] paid respects at the Dynastic Founder's Shrine.

Year three [198], summer, fourth month. A low-lying willow tree in front of the Dynastic Founder's Shrine rose up on its own.

Fifth month. As in the western part of the country there was heavy rain, [the court] exempted the *chu* and *hyŏn* that were flooded from grain and local products taxes for one year.

Autumn, seventh month. [The King] sent officials to make a call of consolation.

Year four [199], autumn, seventh month. Paekche invaded the border.[28]

Year five [200], autumn, seventh month. Venus was seen during the day. A frost fell killing the grass.

Ninth month, the first day, *kyŏngo* day. There was a solar eclipse.[29] The King held a grand review [of troops] at Alch'ŏn.

Year six [201], spring, second month. The kingdom of Kaya requested peace.

Third month, first day, *chŏngmyo* day. There was a solar eclipse. There was a great drought. [The court] reviewed all those

---

and she married Imae after Adalla died and gave birth to Naehae is unclear.

28   See also *SS* 23:12b for an identical entry.

29   See *Hou Hanshu,* Xuandi 210, Konan 6.

imprisoned and forgave those who had committed minor crimes.

Year eight [203], winter, tenth month. The Malgal violated the border. Peach and plum trees blossomed. People [suffered from] a great epidemic.

Year ten [205], spring, second month. Chinch'ung became *ilbŏlch'an* and participated in the country's governance.

Autumn, seventh month. Frost and hail destroyed grain. Venus infringed on the moon.

Eighth month. A fox cried in Kŭmsŏng and at the garden at the Dynastic Founder's Shrine.

Year twelve [207], spring, first month. Prince Iŭm {some say Naeŭm}[30] was appointed *ibŏlch'an* and concurrently was made administrator of all military affairs in the country.

Year thirteen [208], spring, second month. The King toured the western *kun* and *ŭp* [towns] for ten days and then returned.

Summer, fourth month. As the Wa invaded the border, the King dispatched *Ibŏlch'an* Iŭm to lead troops to resist them.

Year fourteen [209], autumn, seventh month. The eight countries above the ports [P'osang][31] plotted to invade Kara. A Kara prince came and asked for assistance. The King ordered the Crown Prince Uro[32] and *Ibŏlch'an* Iŭm to lead the soldiers of the

---

30 He is identified as King Naehae's Crown Prince in *SY* 5:24b and as a royal grandson in *SS* 48, biography of Mulgye. *AKS* renders his name as Naŭm.

31 Its location is unclear. It could well be Kaya. Yi Pyŏngdo believes it is one of the Kaya states in the Naktong River area. See *SS 1977* 27. Refer also to the above note 30 for *SY* entry. Some have translated "above the ports" as P'osang—however we have translated it as "above the ports" in accordance with the speculation offered by the Chosŏn scholar Chŏng Yagyong in his *Pyŏnjin pyŏlgo*. See also Kwŏn Chuhyŏn, "Ana Kaya sŏngip kwa palchŏn," *Kyemyŏng sahak* 4 (1993); Kim T'aesik, "Haman Anŭmguk ŭi sŏngjang kwa pyŏnjŏn," *Hanguk sahak yŏngu* 86 (1994); and Yi Kidong, *Hanguk kodae ŭi kukka wa sahoe* (hereafter *Kodae kukka*), Seoul: Ilchokak, 1985, 184–5.

32 Here he is identified as the Crown Prince. Uro was King Naehae's second son and when his older brother Iŭm died in Naehae's twenty-fifth year, Uro became Crown

six districts and go and help them. They attacked killing generals of the eight states and took away six thousand people imprisoned there and returned them.

Year fifteen [210], spring and summer. There was a drought. [The King] sent an official to review [the cases of] those imprisoned in the *kun* and *ŭp* and pardoned all except those who had committed the two crimes requiring a death sentence.[33]

Year sixteen [211], spring, first month. Hwŏngyŏn became *ich'an* and Yunjong became *ilgilch'an.*

Year seventeen [212], spring, third month. Kaya[34] sent a prince to be a hostage.

Summer, fifth month. There was a heavy rain washing away and submerging people's houses.

Year nineteen [214], spring, third month. A strong wind broke trees.

Autumn, seventh month. Paekche came and attacked Yogŏ Fortress in the western region[35] and killed the head of the fortress, Sŏl Pu. The King ordered *Ibŏlch'an* Iŭm to lead 6,000 elite troops to attack Paekche. They destroyed Sahyŏn Fortress.

Winter, twelfth month. There was thunder.

Year twenty-three [218], autumn, seventh month. The weapons in the arsenal came out "on their own." When Paekche people came and surrounded Changsan Fortress,[36] the King

---

Prince. See *Kodae kukka;* see also *SS* 45 for biography of Sŏk Uro.

33　The death penalty was given to those who rebelled or planned treason and it called for death by decapitation or strangulation. See Book 1, n. 78.

34　This state of Kaya cannot be precisely placed but it might be Kŭmgwan, Kaya, or Ana Kaya, that sought help when P'osang threatened to invade.

35　Both *The Paekche Annals, SS* 23:13a, and *Samguksa chŏryo* 3 place this same entry ten years earlier, in 204. But it is not clear which date is correct. The fortress is in Kyŏngbuk, Sangju, or Ch'ungbuk, Poŭn.

36　This is in the modern Kyŏngbuk, Kyŏngsan area. A similar entry is found in *SS* 24:1b.

personally led his troops out to attack and drive them away.

Year twenty-five [220], spring, third month. *Ibŏlch'an* Iŭm died. Ch'unghwŏn was made *ibŏlch'an* and concurrently was made administrator of all military affairs of the country.

Autumn, seventh month. The King held a grand military review west of Yangsan.[37]

Year twenty-seven [222], summer, fourth month. Hail harmed beans and barley. A person in Namsin-hyŏn died and after several months was resurrected.

Winter, tenth month. Paekche troops entered Udu-ju.[38] *Ibŏlch'an* Ch'unghwŏn led troops to resist them. Reaching Unggok he was defeated by the enemy. Alone he rode out and returned but was demoted to *chinju* [garrison chief]. Yŏnjin was made *ibŏlch'an* and concurrently was made administrator of all military affairs of the country.

Year twenty-nine [224], autumn, seventh month. *Ibŏlch'an* Yŏnjin fought against Paekche below Pongsan[39] and destroyed [Paekche], killing or capturing more than 1,000 people.

Eighth month. Silla constructed Pongsan Fortress.

Year thirty-one [226], spring. There was no rain until autumn, the seventh month, and then it rained. As people were starving, [the court] opened the granaries to relieve them.

Winter, tenth month. [The court] reviewed [the records of] all those imprisoned and pardoned those with minor crimes.

Year thirty-two [227], spring, second month. The King made a hunting tour of the *kun* and *ŭp* of the southwest and returned in

---

37 This is the area near South Mountain in Kyŏngju.

38 This is in modern Kangwŏn, Ch'unch'ŏn. As Silla territory only extended to this area much later, this entry is difficult to believe. See *SS 1977* 29. This area might be Kyŏngbuk, Yech'ŏn. See *SS* 24:1b–2a.

39 This location is unclear, but a similar entry is found in *SS* 24:2a.

the third month. *P'ajinch'an* Kanghwŏn became *ich'an*.

Year thirty-four [229], summer, fourth month. A snake cried in a southern warehouse for three days.

Autumn, ninth month. There was an earthquake.

Winter, tenth month. There was a heavy snow 5 *ch'ŏk* deep.

Year thirty-five [230], spring, third month. The King died.

Isagŭm Chobun

Isagŭm Chobun was enthroned {one source says the character was *kwi* (not *bun*)} [in 230]. His surname was Sŏk and he was the grandson of *Isagŭm* Pŏrhyu. His father was *Kalmunwang* Kolchŏng {some say Holchaeng}. His mother was Lady Okmo of the Kim lineage, the daughter of *Kalmunwang* Kudo. His wife was Lady Aihye, the daughter of King Naehae. When the former King was about to die, he willed that his son-in-law Chobun should succeed to the throne. The King was tall and in appearance was outstanding. In attending to affairs he made clear decisions. The people of the country respected him with awe.

Year one [230]. Yŏnch'ung was made *ich'an* and concurrently was put in charge of the country's military affairs.

Autumn, seventh month. [The King] paid respects at the Dynastic Founder's Shrine.

Year two [231], autumn, seventh month. *Ich'an* Uro became *taejanggun* [grand general] and destroyed the kingdom of Kammun and turned the territory into a *kun*.[40]

---

40 This is in the area of modern Kyŏngbuk, Kimch'on. See also *SS* 45.

Year three [232], summer, fourth month. The Wa unexpectedly appeared and surrounded Kŭmsŏng. When the King personally went out to fight, the enemy scattered and fled. The King sent lightly armed horsemen to pursue and attack them, killing or seizing over a thousand.

Year four [233], summer, fourth month. A strong wind blew tiles off house roofs.

Fifth month. The Wa troops invaded the eastern [coast].

Autumn, seventh month. *Ich'an* Uro fought the Wa at Sado[41] and, taking advantage of the wind, he set a fire and burned their ships. The enemy plunged into the water and were all killed.

Year six [235], spring, first month. The King made a tour of the east to comfort and aid [the people].

Year seven [236], spring, second month. The King of Kolbŏl,[42] Aŭmbu, led his people to come and surrender. [The King] granted them housing and land to [help] settle them in comfort and made their land into a *kun*.

Year eight [237], autumn, eighth month. Locusts destroyed grain.

Year eleven [240]. Paekche invaded the western region.[43]

Year thirteen [242], autumn. This was a year of plenty. Kot'a-gun presented auspicious rice.[44]

Year fifteen [244], spring, first month. *Ich'an* Uro became *sŏburhan*[45] and concurrently was made administrator of military affairs.

Year sixteen [245], winter, tenth month. Koguryŏ invaded the

---

41 This is Kyŏngbuk, Ŭidŏk.
42 This is Kyŏngbuk, Yŏngch'ŏn.
43 See also *SS* 24:3a.
44 This Kyŏngbuk, Andong.
45 This is another name for *ibŏlch'an,* see *SS* 1977 29.

northern region. Uro led troops out to attack them but did not succeed. Withdrawing to a defense barricade at Madu, that night got bitterly cold. Uro comforted his troops and built fires to keep them warm which moved their hearts with gratitude.[46]

Year seventeen [246], winter, tenth month. In the southeast there was a white vapor like a bolt of silk.

Eleventh month. There was an earthquake in the capital.

Year eighteen [247], summer, fifth month. The King died.

Isagŭm Ch'ŏmhae

Isagŭm Ch'ŏmhae was enthroned [in 247].[47] He was the younger brother, by the same mother, of King Chobun.

Year one [247], autumn, seventh month. [The King] held services at the Dynastic Founder's Shrine. The King named his father Kolchŏng to be *Kalmunwang* Sesin.

| Commentary | After Han Sundi's[48] enthronement, a responsible office memorialized, "The one who succeeds a person [on the throne] becomes that person's son. But one cannot offer sacrifices by lowering one's parents. This is the principle of honoring one's ancestors. Therefore the father who gives birth to an Emperor is called *Jin* [Parent] and his posthumous title is called *Dao* [The Grieved One] and that of his mother is called *Daohu* [The Grieved Queen] and the same follows for all the various

---

46 See also *SS* 17:2b and *SS* 45, Sŏk Uro's biography.

47 According to *SY*, chronological tables, he is known as Ihae, although the name Ch'ŏmhae is also noted for him.

48 The seventh Emperor of the Former Han dynasty, he reigned 74–47 BCE.

feudal lords [in accordance with their positions].[49] This is an eternal rule as it is in accordance with the dictates of the classics. Therefore, Later Han Emperor Guangmu and Song [Emperor] Yingzong all followed this and acted accordingly.[50] However there was no Silla king who did not respectfully call his father King even though he succeeded to the throne without being the son of the previous king. Not only this, but there was a similar practice in that they also enfeofed their fathers-in-law. This is such a deviation from the rule that it cannot be followed in practice.

Year two [248], spring, first month. *Ich'an* Changhwŏn became *sŏburhan* and participated in governmental affairs.

Second month. The King sent an envoy to Koguryŏ to conclude peace.[51]

Year three [249], summer, fourth month. The Wa killed *Sŏburhan* Uro.[52]

Autumn, seventh month. [The court] built the Namdang [Southern Hall] south of the palace. {Some call the Namdang the Todang (capital hall)}.[53] Yangbu became *ich'an*.

Year five [251], spring, first month. The King began to hold court in the (Southern Hall). A Hangi district person called Pudo was poor but did not try to curry favor. As he was skilled in

---

49 See *Hanshu* 63.

50 Emperor Gwangmu reigned from 25 to 57 and Emperor Yingzong from 1063 to 1067. Although both were members of the then-imperial family, they were not the sons of the preceding emperors. They were not allowed to offer sacrifices to their parents at the Imperial Ancestor's Shrine.

51 See *SS* 17:4b.

52 According to the biography section, *SS* 45, Uro died in King Ch'ŏmhae's seventh year (253).

53 The Namdang seems to have been a place to meet to discuss government affairs. Later, as affairs became more complicated, it was superseded by a number of offices. See "Kodae namdang ko," *Hanguk kodae*.

calligraphy and accounting, he became well known at that time. The King summoned him, making him *ach'an,* and entrusted him with the administration of the government warehouse.

Year seven [253], summer, fourth month. A dragon appeared in a pond east of the palace. South of Kŭmsŏng a low-lying plum tree grew upright on its own.

From the fifth to the seventh month there was no rain. [The King] offered prayers and sacrifices at the Dynastic Founder's Shrine and famous mountains and then there was rain—but this year had famine and many robbers.

Year nine [255], autumn, ninth month. Paekche invaded. *Ibŏlch'an* Ikchong fought a difficult battle against the enemy west of Koegok and was killed by the invaders.[54]

Winter, tenth month. Paekche attacked Pongsan Fortress but did not bring it down.[55]

Year ten [256], spring, third month. In the see east of the capital appeared three big fish 3 *chang* in length and 1 *chang* and 2 *chih* in height.[56]

Winter, tenth month, the last day of the month. There was a solar eclipse.

Year thirteen [259], autumn, seventh month. There was a drought and locusts. As this was a year of dearth, there were many robbers.

Year fourteen [260], summer. There was heavy rain and mountain slides in more than forty places.

Autumn, seventh month. A comet appeared in the eastern sky, lasting for twenty-five days and then disappearing.

---

54 See also *SS* 24:3b. Koegok is in Ch'ungbuk, Koesan.

55 See also *SS* 24:3b.

56 This probably refers to the sighting of whales. *Chih* is the equivalent of *chŏk.*

Year fifteen [261], spring, second month. [The court] constructed Talböl Fortress[57] and made *Naema* Kŭkchong a *sŏngju* [fortress commander].

Third month. Paekche sent an envoy requesting peace, but the request was not permitted.[58]

Winter, twelfth month, twenty-eighth day. The King was suddenly stricken and died.

Isagŭm Mich'u

Isagŭm Mich'u {one source says Mijo} was enthroned [in 262].[59] His surname was Kim. His mother was of the Pak lineage and the daughter of *Kalmunwang* Ich'il. His wife was Lady Kwangmyŏng of the Sŏk lineage and daughter of King Chobun. His ancestor Alchi appeared at Kyerim. King T'arhae took him and raised him in the palace and later made him *taebo*.[60] Alchi gave birth to Sehan. Sehan gave birth to Ado. Ado gave birth to Suryu. Suryu gave birth to Ukpo. Ukpo gave birth to Kudo and Kudo is Mich'u's father. As Ch'ŏmhae had no sons, the people of the country enthroned Mich'u. He is the first of the Kim lineage to rule the country.

---

57 This is in Taegu.

58 See also *SS* 24:5a.

59 According to the *SY*, chronological tables, he is also known as Miso or Mijo and is a seventh-generation descendant of Kim Alchi. It is believed the name Mich'u means original (*wŏn*) or root (*pun*) and, accordingly, primogenitor. See *AKS* 3:69, n. 89.

60 This is the only entry in the early sources that note that Alchi was appointed as *taebo*.

Year one [262], spring, third month. A dragon appeared in a pond east of the palace.

Autumn, seventh month. Kŭmsŏng's West Gate burned and the fire spread, burning more than a hundred people's houses.[61]

Year two [263], spring, second month. *Ich'an* Yangbu was made *sŏburhan* and concurrently was administrator of all military affairs in the country.

Second month. [The King] personally held sacrifices at the National Founder's Shrine.[62] There was a great amnesty, and [the King] enfeofed his father Kudo [posthumously] as *Kalmunwang.*

Year three [264], spring, second month. The King made a tour of inspection of the east and went to view the ocean.

Third month. [The King] went to Hwangsan and inquired into the [conditions of] the elderly and poor who could not support themselves and gave aid to relieve them.

Year five [266], autumn, eighth month. Paekche came to attack Pongsan Fortress. The fortress commander Chiksŏn led two hundred brave soldiers out to counterattack them. The enemy fled in defeat.[63] The King, hearing this, made Chiksŏn *ilgilch'an* and generously rewarded the soldiers.

Year seven [268]. Spring and summer saw no rain. [The King] met with his officials in the Southern Hall and personally inquired into the successes and failures of government and law. He also sent five officials on a tour of inspection to inquire into the peasants' burdens.

---

61 *SS 1977* 32 says one hundred houses burned. Yi Chaeho, *Samguk sagi* (hereafter *SS 1989*), Seoul, 1989, 56, and *AKS* SS 2:50 and Maema Kōsaku, "Shiragi ō no seji to kimei ni tsuite," *Tōyō gakuhō* 15:2 (1925) put the number at three hundred.

62 This is slightly different terminology, but it means the Founder's Shrine. See Ch'oe Kwangsik, "Kodae Hanguk ŭi kukka wa chesa," *Hangilsa,* Seoul, 1994, 165–74.

63 See also *SS* 24:5a.

Year eleven [272], spring, second month. [The King] decreed that all that injures farming should be completely removed.

Autumn, seventh month. Frost and hail fell damaging the grain.

Winter, eleventh month. Paekche invaded the border area.[64]

Year fifteen [276], spring, second month. The officials requested changes in the construction of palace halls. The King, fearing overburdening the people, did not allow it.

Year seventeen [278], summer, fourth month. A strong wind uprooted trees.

Winter, tenth month. Paekche troops came and encircled Koegok Fortress.[65] The King ordered *P'ajinch'an* Chŏngwŏn to lead troops to resist them.

Year nineteen [280], summer, fourth month. There was a drought and the court reviewed the records of those imprisoned.

Year twenty [281], spring, first month. Honggwŏn became *ich'an,* Yangjil became *ilgilch'an,* and Kwanggyŏm became *sach'an.*

Second month. [The King] paid respects at the Dynastic Founder's Shrine.

Autumn, ninth month. [The King] held a grand military review west of Yangsan.

Year twenty-two [283], autumn, ninth month. Paekche invaded the border area.[66]

Winter, tenth month. [When Paekche] encircled Koegok Fortress, [the King] commanded *Ilgilch'an* Yangjil to lead troops to resist them.

---

64   See also *SS* 24:5a.
65   See also *SS* 24:5b.
66   See also *SS* 24:5b.

Year twenty-three [284], spring, second month, The King made a tour of inspection and relief to the various fortresses in the western part of the kingdom.

Winter, tenth month. The King died and was buried at Taenŭng {also known as Chukchangnŭng}.[67]

Isagŭm Yurye

Isagŭm Yurye {according to the *Kogi (Ancient Record)*[68] two kings, the third and fourteenth, had the same name of Yuri or Yurye. It is unclear which is correct.} was enthroned [in 284]. He was King Chobun's oldest son. His mother was of the Pak lineage, the daughter of *Kalmunwang* Naeum.[69] Once at night she was out walking and the radiance of a star went into her mouth and she became pregnant. On the night [Yurye] was born, a strange fragrance filled the room.

Year two [285], spring, first month. [The King] paid respects at the Dynastic Founder's Shrine. Second month. *Ich'an* Honggwŏn became *sŏburhan* and charged with important government matters.

Year three [286], spring, first month. Paekche sent an envoy

---

67 See also *SY* 1:18a which states that the tomb was east of Hŭngyŏn Monastery.

68 *Kogi* may be a collection of ancient native works, in contrast to the foreign sources often relied on by the compilers. See Yi Kangnae, "Samguk sagi wa kogi," *Yongbong nonch'ong* 17–8 (1989). Chŏng Kubok argues that it is a single work. See Chŏng Kubok, "Samguk sagi ŭi wŏnjŏn ch'aryŏ," in *Samguk sagi ŭi wŏnjŏn kŏmt'o,* Songnam: Hanguk chŏngsin munhwa yŏnguwŏn, 1995.

69 *SS* 2 (year 230, above) states that King Chobun's wife was Lady Aihye, daughter of King Naehae. Because of the discrepancy here some suggest King Yurye was Chobun's grandson. See *Silla sangdae* 77.

requesting peace.[70]

Third month. There was a drought.

Year four [287], summer, fourth month. The Wa raided Illye district[71] and set it on fire. They captured 1,000 people and left with them.

Year six [289], summer, fifth month. The King, upon hearing that Wa troops approached, repaired his ships and readied his armor and his troops.

Year seven [290], summer, fifth month. As there was heavy rain, a Wŏlsŏng wall collapsed.

Year eight [291], spring, first month. Malgu was appointed *ibŏlch'an*.[72] As Malgu was loyal, incorruptible, and intelligent, the King always visited him, consulting on important governmental matters.

Year nine [292], summer, sixth month. Wa troops attacked and defeated Sado Fortress. The King commanded *Ilgilch'an* Taegok to lead troops to rescue without fail [the fortress].

Autumn, seventh month. There was a drought and a locust [infestation].

Year ten [293], spring, second month. [The court] rebuilt Sado Fortress and resettled more than eighty families of influential households from Sabŏl-ju.[73]

Year eleven [294], summer. Wa troops came and attacked Changbong Fortress, but did not succeed [in capturing it].

Autumn, seventh month. Tasa-gun presented auspicious rice.

---

70 See also *SS* 24:5b.

71 This district's location is unclear. *AKS* 3:72, n. 110, suggests it might be in Kyŏngbuk, Koryŏng.

72 Malgu, as son of Kudo, was King Mich'u's brother. He was King Naemul's father. See *AKS* 3:72, n. 111.

73 This is in Kyŏngbuk, Sangju

Year twelve [295], spring. The King addressing his officials said, "As the Wa repeatedly harass our fortresses and towns, the people are not able to live in peace. I would like to plan with Paekche to cross the sea all at once and attack their kingdom. What do you think of this?" *Sŏburhan* Honggwŏn replied, "Since we are not accustomed to naval warfare and if we dare to venture into an expedition far away, I fear the danger of the unexpected. Moreover, since Paekche has been deceitful on many occasions and always desired to swallow up our country, I also fear there will be difficulties with making plans with them." The King said, "You are right."

Year fourteen [297], spring, first month. Chiryang became *ich'an*. Changhŭn became *ilgilch'an* and Sunsŏn became *sach'an*. The kingdom of Isŏgo[74] came and attacked Kŭmsŏng. Our troops were deployed in a great number to defend but we were not able to drive them back. Suddenly strange troops arrived in a number that could not be estimated. All the people wore ear ornaments of bamboo leaves and joined our troops fighting against the enemy and defeating them. Afterwards people did not know where they returned to. Because some people saw tens of thousands of bamboo leaves piled at Chukchang tomb, the people said *ŭmbyŏng* [troops from the underworld] of the former King [Mich'u] helped them fight.[75]

Year fifteen [298], spring, second month. In the capital there was a heavy fog too thick to distinguish people. It lasted for five days and then cleared.

Winter, twelfth month. The King died.

---

74 This is in the Kyŏngbuk, Ch'ŏngdo region. See *AKS* 3:73, n. 115. See also *SY* 1:18a and 1:14b, under King Yuri, where it states that Yuri destroyed Isŏguk.

75 See *AKS* 3:73, n. 116, which explains these are believed to be forces from the underworld.

Isagŭm Kirim

Isagŭm Kirim {one source says Kirip} was enthroned [in 298]. He was the grandson of *Isagŭm* Chobun.[76] His father was *Ich'an* Kŏlsuk.[77] {Another source says Kŏlsuk was the grandson of Chobun.} As his personality was tolerant and generous, people all praised him.

Year two [299], spring, first month. Changhŭn became *ich'an* and concurrently was appointed to be the administrator of all military affairs of the country.

Second month, [the King] held sacrifices at the Dynastic Founder's Shrine.

Year three [300], spring, first month. [The court] exchanged envoys with the Wa.

Second month, the King made a tour of inspection to Piryŏrhol[78] and personally inquired into the elderly and poor and gave out grain in various amounts.

Third month. The King reached Udu-ju[79] and offered sacrifices while viewing [in the distance] Mount T'aebaek. Lelang and Taifang surrendered [to Silla].[80]

---

76 According to *SY,* royal tables, King Kiin was the second son of King Chobun's younger brother. Some contend that this could be read as the second son of King Chobun.

77 As *SY,* chronological tables, states King Kiin's mother was Lady Aihye. It is difficult to see King Kiin as King Chobun's son. See *Silla sangdae* 78. The character *"ich'an"* is unclear, Yi Cheho, in his translation, suggests it should be read as *"kakch'an."* See *SS 1989* 58. He also calls Kiin, Kirin.

78 Because this area, Hamnam Anbyŏn, did not become part of Silla until the sixth century, Yi Pyŏngdo questions this entry. *AKS* 3:74, n. 120, also doubts the veracity of this entry.

79 This is Kangwŏn, Ch'unch'on.

80 It is generally accepted that Lelang (Nangnang) fell to Koguryŏ in 313. Accordingly, it is difficult to accept this statement. *SS 1977* 35 concurs that the date of 300 is incorrect.

Year five [302]. Spring and summer, there was a drought.

Year seven [304], autumn, eighth month. There was an earthquake and a spring shot out.

Ninth month. In the capital there was an earthquake destroying people's houses and causing death.

Year ten [307]. The name of the kingdom was again called Silla.[81]

Year thirteen [310], summer, fifth month. Since the King was ill and remained in bed [without recovering, the court] proclaimed an amnesty freeing those in prison throughout the country.

Sixth month. The King died.

Isagŭm Hŭrhae

Isagŭm Hŭrhae was enthroned [in 310].[82] He was the grandson of King Naehae. His father was *Kakkan* Uro and his mother was Lady Myŏngwŏn, the daughter of King Chobun. Uro served the King with distinction and received many promotions, reaching *sŏburhan*.[83] Uro, seeing that Hŭrhae had an extraordinary appearance, was highly intelligent and his management of affairs was unlike others, addressed the various ministers and said, "This child is certainly the one who will make our family prosper." Thereupon when Kirim died without sons, the ranking officials

---

81 This is also said to have occurred in King Chijung's fourth year (503). *AKS* 3:74, n. 122, suggests this might mean the restoration of the name Silla or Saro from the term Kyerim which had been used since Kim Alchi's birth in the first century.

82 *SY*, chronological tables, calls him Kŏrhae.

83 *SS 1977* 35 translates this to read "Many times Uro was *sŏburhan*."

discussed saying, "Hŭrhae, although still young, has the virtue of one who is mature," so they supported his enthronement.

Year two [311], spring, first month. Kŭmni became *ach'an* and concurrently was appointed to be the administrator of all military affairs in the country.[84]

Second month. [The King] personally held sacrifices at the Dynastic Founder's Shrine.

Year three [312], spring, third month. As the King of Wa sent an envoy proposing the marriage of his son, [the court] sent the daughter of *Ach'an* Kŭmni.

Year four [313], autumn, seventh month. There was a drought and a locust [infestation]. As people were starving, [the court] sent an official to aid them with relief.

Year five [314], spring, first month. *Ach'an* Kŭmni was named *ich'an*.

Second month. Palace repairs were undertaken again but, because there was no rain, they were stopped.

Year eight [317], spring and summer. As there was a drought, the King personally reviewed those in prison and pardoned many.

Year nine [318], spring, second month. The King decreed, "Recently because of the ill effects of drought, the past years' [harvests] have not been as expected. Now, as the land looks fertile and rich and farming is about to begin, we should cease all that burdens the people."

Year twenty-one [330]. [The court] started to build Pyŏkkol-chi [pond]. Its shoreline was 1,800 *ch'ŏk* long.[85]

---

84 Best suggests the term *"pyŏngmasa"* could be rendered as "military and civil affairs."

85 *SS 1977* 36 notes this should be in *The Paekche Annals, SS. SY*, tables, states that this event occurred in King Hŭrhae's thirtieth year. The pond is located at Chŏnbuk, Kimje.

The **Silla Annals** of the **Samguk Sagi**

Year twenty-eight [337], spring, second month. [The court] sent an envoy on a courtesy visit to Paekche.[86]

Third month. It rained hail.

Summer, fourth month. Frost fell.

Year thirty-five [344], spring, second month. Wa sent an envoy requesting the King's daughter in marriage. [The King] declined because the daughter was already married.

Summer, fourth month. A strong wind uprooted a great tree south of the palace.

Year thirty-six [345], spring, first month. Kangse became *ibŏlch'an*.

Second month. The king or Wa sent an official letter severing ties.

Year thirty-seven [346]. Wa troops unexpectedly arrived at P'ungdo Island and plundered the households in the region and then advanced, encircling Kŭmsŏng, and hastily attacked. The King wanted to send out troops and confront them but *Ibŏlch'an* Kangse said that although the marauders had come from far away, their fighting spirit cannot be confronted now. It is best we delay by waiting until their troops are fatigued. The King approved this and closed the gates and did not go out. When the enemies' provisions were exhausted, and they were about to retreat, the King commanded Kangse to lead the elite troops to pursue, attacking and expelling them.

Year thirty-nine [348]. Water in a palace well suddenly overflowed.

Year forty-one [350], spring, third month. A crane nested in a corner of Wŏlsŏng.

Summer, fourth month. A heavy rain fell for ten days, the

---

86   See also *SS* 24:7b.

water was 3 to 4 *ch'ŏk* deep on the plains, submerging governmental and private houses, and in thirteen places there were mountain slides.

Year forty-seven [356], summer, fourth month. The King died.

The Silla
Annals of the
Samguk Sagi

Isagŭm Naemul and Silsŏng;
and *Maripkan* Nulchi, Chabi,
and Soji

Book

3

Isagǔm Naemul

Isagǔm Naemul {one source says Namil} was enthroned [in 356]. His surname was Kim and he was the grandson of *Kalmunwang* Kudo. His father was *Kakkan* Malgu and his mother was Lady Hyurye of the Kim lineage. His wife was of the Kim lineage and the daughter of King Mich'u. Since Hǔrhae died without sons, Naemul succeeded him {Malgu and *Isagǔm* Mich'u are brothers.}[1]

| Commentary | In selecting a wife one does not chose someone with the same surname in order to value differences.[2] Therefore when the Duke of Lu married a woman [with the same name] in Wu and Prince Jin had four concubines with the same name, the *Sibai* [Director or Punishments] of Chen and Zichan of Zheng severely criticized this.[3] But in Silla one not only selects

---

1   His name also appears as Namul. According to *SY,* chronological tables, kings from this time on are called *maripkan.* It is also at this time that the Kim lineage begins to monopolize the throne. For a complete discussion see *AKS* 3, n. 1–3. See Takeda Yukio, "Shiragi koppinsei no saikentō," *Tōyō bunko kenkyū* 67 (1975), as well as articles by Hamada Kōsaku (1990) and Suematsu Yasukazu (1954). *Isagǔm* Naemul is identified in *SY* as the son of the son of *Kalmunwang* Kudo or the younger brother of King Mich'u. See *Silla sangdae* 81–2 and Yi Kidong, "Silla Naemul wangson ǔi hyǒllok ǔisik," *Kolp'um* 64. It also seems unlikely that his wife was the daughter of King Mich'u since Mich'u preceded Naemul by more than one hundred years. Also of interest is that the above text identifies Mich'u as king but the footnote calls him *isagǔm.*

2   *Liji (Book of Rites)* states "One must not marry a wife of the same surname with himself." See Legge, James, translator, *Li Chi: Book of Rites,* New Hyde Park, NY: University Books, 1967, 1:78.

3   The Duke of Lu, whose surname was Chi, married a woman from Wu with the same surname, as did Prince Jin. The *Sibai* is an office that oversaw punishments.

wives from the same surname, but also from among nieces and maternal and paternal cousins, anyone can be a wife. Although foreign countries each have different customs, if one applies [these practices] to Chinese standards of propriety, then it is definitely counter to what is right. Only worse than this is the Xiongnu custom of incest between mother and child.[4]

Year two [357], spring. [The King] dispatched officials to inquire into the conditions of widowers, widows, orphans, and the childless and gave each three *sŏm*[5] of rice. And to those who especially exhibited filial and brotherly love, he gave them one grade elevation in their position.

Year three [358], spring, second month. [The King] personally held sacrifices at the Dynastic Founder's Shrine. A purple cloud enveloped above the shrine and divine sparrows gathered in the yard of the shrine.[6]

Year seven [362], summer, fourth month. The branches of trees in the garden of the Dynastic Founder's Shrine grew together.[7]

Year nine [364], summer, fourth month. Wa troops arrived in a great number. When the King heard this he was afraid he would not be able to check them. He made several thousand grass puppets, clothed them, armed them, lined them up beneath Mount T'oham, and hid 1,000 brave soldiers in a field east of Puhyŏn. The Wa, believing in the [strength] of their own numbers, directly

---

Zichan is the courtesy name for an official named Kongsun Qiao.

4 The Xiongnu were a northern nomadic group. See also *Shiji* 109 where it states that if the father dies, the son marries the father's second wife and if the older brother dies, the younger brother marries the older brother's wife.

5 Three *sŏm* is equivalent to 5.2 bushels.

6 A purple cloud occurred when there was an exceedingly virtuous monarch. The gathering of these birds was also a lucky omen.

7 This is also interpreted as an auspicious sign noting the prevalence of the King's virtue.

advanced and those hidden suddenly started to attack. The Wa fled in great defeat while [Silla] chased, killing nearly all.

Year eleven [366], spring, third month. Emissaries from Paekche came on a courtesy visit.[8]

Summer, fourth month. There was a great flood and landslides in thirteen places.

Year thirteen [368], spring. Paekche sent an emissary and presented two fine horses.[9]

Year seventeen [372], spring and summer. There was a drought and, as the year was barren, people starved and many became drifters. [The King] sent officials to open the granaries to offer relief.

Year eighteen [373]. Paekche's Mount Toksan Fortress chief came to surrender leading three hundred people.[10] The King accepted and settled them in the six districts. The Paekche king sent a letter saying, "Our two countries enjoy peace and friendship and have promised to be brothers. Now Your Majesty has accepted deserters. This truly transgresses the idea of friendly relations and is not what I expected from Your Majesty. Please return them." [The Silla king] replied, "People's minds are not unchanging and therefore they come and go as they please. Truly this is what they do. Your Majesty blames me instead of worrying about the people's peace of mind. How can you criticize me so harshly?" When the Paekche king heard this, he did not speak about it again.

---

8 See also *SS* 24:8a

9 See also *SS* 24:8a

10 See also *SS* 24:9a. This site is in Kyŏnggi, Ansŏng. Mount Toksan Fortress was built initially to guard against attacks from Lelang. King Kwanggaet'o of Koguryŏ moved people from P'yŏngyang to there. Best, *A History of the Early Kingdom of Paekche*, appendix 8, 444–8, provides a detailed discussion of Mount Toksan Fortress and its location.

Summer, fifth month. It rained fish in the capital.[11]

Year twenty-one [376], autumn, seventh month. Pusa-gun presented a deer with one antler.[12] It was a year of great plenty.

Year twenty-four [379], summer, fourth month. In Yangsan a small sparrow gave birth to a big bird.

Year twenty-six [381], spring and summer. There was a drought and as the year was barren, people starved. [The King] dispatched Widu to Fu Qin [former Qin] to present tribute products. Fu Jian [the Qin King] asked Widu,[13] "You have said that the conditions in Haedong [Korea] are not the same as in the past, what do you mean?" He replied, "Just as in China, changes in the age and [dynastic] names [occur]. How can we remain the same as in the past?"

Year thirty-three [388], summer, fourth month. There was an earthquake in the capital.

Sixth month. There was another earthquake.

Winter. [Water] did not freeze.

Year thirty-four [389], spring, first month. There was a great epidemic in the capital.

Second month. Dirt fell like rain.

Autumn, seventh month. As there was a locust [infestation], the grain did not ripen.

Year thirty-seven [392], spring, first month. Koguryŏ sent an envoy. Because he believed Koguryŏ to be powerful, the King sent

---

11 Although unclear, this could have been caused by a water spout.

12 This location is not clear although it may be Kyŏngnam, Hapch'ŏn. In China a deer with one antler is considered auspicious.

13 This case refers to the former Qin. Fu Jian was the third Emperor of the former Qin. He reigned 357–384. Silla had earlier, in 377, also sent an envoy to the former Qin. See *Zizhi tongjian* 104. That Silla sent several envoys to the Former Qin at this time indicated Silla was expanding its interest and entering on to the international stage.

Ich'an Taesŏji's son Silsŏng to be a hostage.[14]

Year thirty-eight [393], summer, fifth month. The Wa came, encircled Kŭmsŏng, and did not cease [their encirclement] for five days. The soldiers all requested to go out and fight. The King said, "Now the enemy have left their ships and come far inland. As they are prepared to die, we cannot confront them now." He closed the fortress gates and when the enemy retreated without any gain, the King first sent two hundred brave horsemen to cut off their route of retreat and then sent 1,000 foot soldiers to pursue them to Mount Toksan.[15] Attacking them from both sides, he greatly defeated them and captured or killed many.

Year forty [395], autumn, eighth month. The Malgal invaded the northern frontier. [The court] sent troops and greatly defeated them in the Silchik Plain.

Year forty-two [397], autumn, seventh month. In Hasŭlla in the northern region, as there was a drought and a locust infestation, resulting in a lean year, people starved. They bent the laws to pardon prisoners and again exempted the people from grain and local products taxes for one year.[16]

Year forty-four [399], autumn, seventh month. Flying locusts covered the fields.

Year forty-five [400], autumn, eighth month. A comet passed in the eastern sky.

Winter, tenth month. The King's horse in the royal stable kneeled on its knees and cried in sorrow, shedding tears.

Year forty-six [401], spring and summer. There was a drought.

---

14 See also *SS* 18:1b

15 This is in Kyŏngbuk, P'ohang.

16 Hasŭlla is the area around Kangwŏn, Kangnŭng, which had already fallen under Silla control.

Silsŏng, who had been a hostage in Koguryŏ, returned.

Year forty-seven [402], spring, second month. The King died.[17]

Isagŭm Silsŏng

Isagŭm Silsŏng was enthroned [in 402]. He is a descendant of Alchi and son of *Ich'an* Taesŏji. His mother was Lady Iri {*i* is also written as *ki*}, the daughter of *Agan* Sŏktŭngbo, and his wife was the daughter of King Mich'u.[18] Silsŏng was 7½ *ch'ŏk* tall. He was extremely bright and had deep insight. When Naemul died, his sons were young so the people of the kingdom enthroned Silsŏng to succeed him.[19]

Year one [402], third month. [The state] established amicable ties with the Wa and sent King Naemul's son Misahŭn[20] to be a hostage.

Year two [403], spring, first month. Misap'um became *sŏburhan* and put in charge of the country's military affairs.

Autumn, seventh month. Paekche invaded the border area.[21]

---

17 Although there is no mention in *SS* where he was buried, according to *SY,* chronological tables, he was buried southwest of Chŏmsŏngdae.

18 *SY,* chronological tables, refers to Silsŏng as a *maripkan* and lists his wife as Lady Yesŏng. *Agan* is rank six. As for his wife being the daughter of King Mich'u, this is unlikely, she rather should be considered a descendant of Mich'u.

19 Several scholars suggest the real reason Silsŏng became King is because of influence from Koguryŏ where he had been a hostage and action taken by the Sŏk lineage. See *Silla hyŏngsŏng* and Yi Kibaek and Yi Kidong, *Hanguksa kangchwa* 1 (1982).

20 According to *SY* 1:19a, King Naemul sent his third son, Mihae, to Wa and Mihae was not allowed to return home until he was forty. *Nihon shoki,* ninth year of Chuuai Tenno, calls him Misigoji, the son of King P'asa.

21 See also *SS* 25:4a.

Year three [404], spring, second month. [The King] paid respects at the Dynastic Founder's Shrine.

Year four [405], summer, fourth month. Wa troops came to attack Myŏnghwal Fortress[22] but withdrew without victory. The King led the cavalry and took a strategic point south of Mount Toksan and again fought, defeating them and killing or capturing more than three hundred.

Year five [406], autumn, seventh month. In the western part of the kingdom locusts damaged the grain.

Winter, tenth month. In the capital there was an earthquake.

Eleventh month. [Water] did not freeze.

Year six [407], spring, third month. The Wa invaded the eastern [coast].

Summer, sixth month. [The Wa] also invaded the southern area capturing and taking away a hundred people.

Year seven [408], spring, second month. The King heard that the Wa had established a camp on Tsushima. Housing military weapons and provisions, they planned to attack us. He wanted, before they had a chance [to attack us], to select our elite troops and attack and destroy their amassed troops. *Sŏburhan* Misap'um said, "I have heard that weapons are murderous and war is dangerous. Moreover when we cross the vast sea to attack others and if we lose the chance [to win], it will be too late to regret. It is not as good as relying on our rugged terrain to establish strategic fortifications, and resist them if they come and not let them treacherously invade us. When it is to our advantage, we can go out and capture them. This is the so called 'enticing others but not being enticed by others as the best strategy'." The King agreed to it.

---

22 This is located in eastern Kyŏngju.

Year eleven [412]. [The court] sent King Naemul's son Pokho as a hostage to Koguryŏ.[23]

Year twelve [413], autumn, eighth month. A cloud arose over Mount Nangsan[24] and it looked like a pavilion-tower. It gave out a fragrance and lasted for a long time without stopping. The King said, "This must be where a spirit had descended and wandered and should be an auspicious site." After this the people were forbidden from cutting trees.

A large bridge at P'yŏngyang-ju was newly constructed.[25]

Year fourteen [415], autumn, seventh month. [The King] held a large military review in Hyŏlsŏng Plain. The King also went to the south gate of Kŭmsŏng to watch archery.

Eighth month. [We] fought with the Wa at P'ungdo Island and defeated them.

Year fifteen [416], spring, third month. A large fish was caught on the eastern seashore and it had large horns. It was so large that it filled a cart.

Summer, fifth month. There was a landslide on Mount T'oham and a spring gushed 30 *ch'ŏk* high.

Year sixteen [417], summer, fifth month. The King died.

---

23 Here again *SY* 1:19a calls Pokho as Pokhae and says he is King Nulchi's younger brother. Pokho was kept in Koguryŏ for many years.

24 Located in Kyŏngju, Sach'ŏnwang Monastery is south of this mountain.

25 This is believed to be in the Chongno area of Seoul. But this is questionable since Silla did not occupy this area until the middle of the sixth century. See also references in *SS* 34 and 38. It also appears in *SY* 1:22a.

The **Silla Annals** of the **Samguk Sagi**

Maripkan Nulchi

Maripkan Nulchi was enthroned [417]. {Kim Taemun said, "The word *'marip'* is dialect meaning a post [*kwŏl*]. Post is pronounced as *'hamjo'* and was set up in accordance with one's rank. The King's post became the main post and those of officials followed beneath and so accordingly this word came to denote head of the government."}[26] He is the son of King Naemul. His mother was Lady Poban {one source says Naerye Kilp'o}, the daughter of King Mich'u. His wife was the daughter of King Silsŏng. In King Naemul's thirty-seventh year [on the throne], he sent Silsŏng as a hostage to Koguryŏ. When Silsŏng returned he became King. Resenting that he had been Naemul's hostage to a foreign country, he wanted to kill [Naemul's son] as revenge. He sent a man to invite a person whom he knew when in Koguryŏ and secretly told him if he saw Nulchi then to kill him. Accordingly [Silsŏng] ordered Nulchi to leave and [the Koguryŏ man] meeting him on the road saw Nulchi's appearance to be unusually elegant and beautiful with the air of a Prince. At last he confessed to him, "Your King commanded me to harm you, but now, seeing you, I cannot bear to kill you so treacherously." He then returned. Nulchi resented this and instead killed the King, enthroning himself.[27]

---

26 *SS 1977* 43 sees marip meaning "Your Majesty." Kim Taemun is reported to have written a number of histories. See SS 46 for his biography. See also Yi Kibaek, "Kim Taemun kwa kŭ ŭi sahak," *Yŏksa hakpo* 77 (1978).

27 *SY* 1:22a provides a slightly different account, noting that King Silsŏng asked that Koguryŏ troops come to Silla to help him kill Nulchi. Instead the Koguryŏ forces killed Silsŏng and enthroned Nulchi. See Yi Kibaek, "Silla Nulchi wanggye ŭi hyŏlyŏn ŭisik," in *Silla kolp'um chedo sahoe wa hwarangje*, Seoul: Ilchokak, 1984, and Suematsu Yasukazu "Shiragi Shonhosho," in *Shiragishi no shomondai*. *SY,* royal chronological tables, offers Naeji as another name for Nulchi. Yi Kidong believes it is at this time that father-son inheritance of the throne commenced. See "Silla Naemulwanggye ŭi holyŏn ŭisik," in *Kolp'um* 74.

Year two [418], spring, first month. [The King] paid respects at the Dynastic Founder's Shrine. The King's younger brother Pokho[28] returned from Koguryŏ with *Nama* Chesang.[29]

Autumn. The King's younger brother Misahŭn fled from Wa and returned.[30]

Year three [419], summer, fourth month. In Ugok a spring gushed forth.

Year four [420], spring and summer. There was a great drought.

Autumn, seventh month. A frost fell killing the grain and people starved. People were selling their children and grandchildren. [The King] reviewed [the cases of] those imprisoned, pardoning their crimes.

Year seven [423], summer, fourth month. [The King] entertained the elderly in the Southern Hall and personally gave food and granted rice and silk in varying amounts.

Year eight [424], spring, second month. [The King] sent an official to Koguryŏ to establish friendly ties.[31]

Year thirteen [429]. [The court] reconstructed Sije Dike. Its length was 2,170 *po*.[32]

Year fifteen [431], summer, fourth month. Wa troops invaded the eastern region and encircled Myŏnghwal Fortress but, with no victory, they returned.

---

28 According to *SY* 1:19a, Pokho is also called Pokhae. See note 23 above.

29 See *SS* 45 in the biographies section under Pak Chesang for additional information. *SY* differs slightly as it gives his surname as Kim and has him returning in Nulchi's ninth year. See *AKS* 3:85, n. 50.

30 See also *Nihon shoki* 9, Jingu, fifth year, third month.

31 See also *SS* 18:8a.

32 One *po* equaled one pace. See *AKS* 3:86, n. 53. Prior to Tang (seventh century), 1 *po* was about 6 *ch'ŏk* with 1 *ch'ŏk* approximately 24 centimeters (approximately 9.5 inches), so 1 *po* was approximately 1.44 meters (approximately 4.7 feet). From Tang forward, 1 *po* equalled 5 *ch'ŏk* with 1 *ch'ŏk* approximately 30.5 centimeters (12 inches), so 1 *po* was approximately 1.53 meters (5 feet).

Autumn, seventh month. A frost and hail fell destroying the grain.

Year sixteen [432], spring. As grain was very dear, people ate bark [fiber] from pine trees.

Year seventeen [433], summer, fifth month. Misahŭn died and was posthumously given the post of *sŏburhan*.

Autumn, seventh month. Paekche sent an envoy requesting peace. [The King] accepted.[33]

Year eighteen [434], spring, second month. The Paekche king sent two fine horses.

Autumn, ninth month. [The Paekche king] also sent a white hawk.

Winter, tenth month. [The King] used yellow gold and bright pearls as gifts to reciprocate Paekche's [good will].[34]

Year nineteen [435], spring, first month. A strong wind uprooted trees.

Second month. The court repaired the royal tombs of [many] generations.

Summer, fourth month. The King held services at the Dynastic Founder's Shrine.

Year twenty [436], summer, fourth month. It rained hail. [The King] reviewed [the cases of] those imprisoned.

Year twenty-two [438], summer, fourth month. In the mountains of Udu-gun,[35] water rushed out, washing away more than fifty houses. In the capital there was a strong wind with rain and hail. [The court] instructed people on how to use ox carts.[36]

---

33 See also *SS* 25:6a.

34 See also *SS* 25:6a–b. Paekche and Silla were joining together at this time to check Koguryŏ's growing power.

35 This is in Kangwŏn, Ch'unch'ŏn.

36 There are alternate ways in which this line has been translated. See *AKS* 3:86, n.

Year twenty-four [440]. The Wa raided the southern region, plundering and taking away people.[37]

Summer, sixth month. [The Wa] again invaded the eastern region.

Year twenty-five [441], spring, second month. Samul-hyŏn[38] presented a white pheasant with a long tail feather. The King prized it and granted the *hyŏn* clerk grain.

Year twenty-eight [444], summer, fourth month. Wa troops encircled Kŭmsŏng for ten days and, when their supplies were exhausted, they withdrew. The King wanted to send out troops to pursue them. His attending officers said, "According to opinions of military strategists, 'Do not press a foe too far—do not be too exacting'[39] so Your Majesty set aside this plan." The King did not listen and led several thousand horsemen pursuing them to east of Mount Toksan where they fought together and lost to the enemy. More than half of [Silla's] troops were killed. The King, turning pale in fear and alarm, cast aside his horse and went up a mountain. The enemy encircled several times. Suddenly, a dark fog fell and people could not see what was very close. The enemy said this was divine intervention and, collecting their troops, they withdrew and returned.

Year thirty-four [450], autumn, seventh month. A Koguryŏ border general was hunting on the plains of Silchik.[40] The Hasŭlla Fortress chief Samjik led troops out and in a surprise attack killed him. When the Koguryŏ king heard this he was angry and had a

---

58.

37   The characters used here, *"saenggu,"* can mean people, livestock, or slaves. See *AKS* 3:86, n. 59.

38   This is in Kyŏngnam, Sach'ŏn.

39   This is a quotation from Sunzi, *Treatise on War* (more commonly referenced as: Sun Tzu, *The Art of War*).

40   This is in Kangwŏn, Samch'ŏk.

[Koguryŏ] official come to inform saying, "I was very pleased to establish good ties with Your Majesty. But now you have dispatched troops and killed my border general. What kind of behavior is this?" He then raised troops and invaded our western region.[41] The King, with humble words, apologized and [the Koguryŏ troops] withdrew.

Year thirty-six [452], autumn, seventh month. Taesan-gun presented an auspicious rice stalk.

Year thirty-seven [453], spring and summer. There was a drought.

Autumn, seventh month. A pack of wolves entered Sirim.

Year thirty-eight [454], autumn, seventh month. Frost and hail damaged the grain.

Eighth month. Koguryŏ invaded [our] northern frontier.[42]

Year thirty-nine [455], winter, tenth month. Koguryŏ invaded Paekche.[43] The King sent troops to help them.

Year forty-one [457], spring, second month. A great wind uprooted trees.

Summer, fourth month. Frost fell injuring the barley.

Year forty-two [458], spring, second month. There was an earthquake and the south gate of Kŭmsŏng crumbled on its own.

Autumn, eighth month. The King died.

---

41 See also *SS* 18:10a.

42 See also *SS* 18:10a. This entry has the invasion starting in the seventh month.

43 This entry does not appear in either *The Paekche Annals, SS,* or *The Koguryŏ Annals, SS.*

Maripkan Chabi

Maripkan Chabi was enthroned [458]. He was the oldest son of King Nulchi and his mother was the daughter of King Silsŏng of the Kim lineage.

Year two [459], spring, second month. [The King] paid respects at the Dynastic Founder's Shrine.

Summer, fourth month. The Wa, with more than one hundred warships, raided the eastern region and advanced, encircling Wŏlsŏng. With arrows and rocks [falling] like rain from all over, the King defended the fortress. As the enemy was about to withdraw, [the King] sent out troops to attack and defeated them, chasing them north to the entrance to the sea.[44] More than half the enemy drowned.

Year four [461], spring, second month. The King took the daughter of *Sŏburhan* Misahŭn to be his Queen.[45]

Summer, fourth month. A dragon was seen in a Kŭmsŏng Well.

Year five [462], summer, fifth month. The Wa raided destroying Hwalgae Fortress and captured a thousand people and left.

Year six [463], spring, second month. The Wa invaded Samnyang Fortress,[46] but left without success. The King ordered Pŏlchi and Tŏkchi to lead troops and wait hiding along the road. In a surprise attack, they delivered a great defeat. Because the Wa had frequently invaded the territory, the King built two fortresses in the [coastal] region.

Autumn, seventh month. [The King] held a great military review.

---

44 This is the area around Kyŏngbuk, P'ohang. *AKS* 2:66 has a different rendering.
45 *SY,* chronological tables, claims his wife is the daughter of Pokho.
46 This is in Kyŏngnam, Yangsan.

Year eight [465], summer, fourth month. There was a flood and mountain slides in seventeen places.

Fifth month. In Sabŏl-gun[47] there was a locust [infestation].

Year ten [467], spring. [The King] ordered the concerned offices to repair battle ships.

Autumn, seventh month. The sky was red and a large star moved from the north to the southeast.

Year eleven [468], spring. Koguryŏ and the Malgal raided Silchik Fortress in the northern region.[48]

Autumn, ninth month. [The court] conscripted Hasŭlla people of fifteen years and above to build a fortress at Iha {another name for Iha is Ich'ŏn}.

Year twelve [469], spring, first month. [The King] established *pangni* [ward] names in the capital.[49]

Summer, fourth month. There was a flood in the western part of the country flooding that destroyed peoples' houses.

Autumn, seventh month. The King made a tour of inspection and relief through the *chu* and *kun* suffering from flooding.

Year thirteen [470]. [The state] constructed Samnyŏn [Three-Year] Mountain Fortress.[50] {It is called "Three-Year Mountain Fortress" because it took three years to construct.}

Year fourteen [471], spring, second month. Moro Fortress was constructed.[51]

Third month. In the capital land split open two *chang* in length and width. Muddy water gushed up.

---

47 This is in Kyŏngbuk, Sangju.

48 See *SS* 18:11a.

49 There were two divisions: *pang* and *li/ni*. Some scholars claim that *pang* was the larger unit, see Yi Pyŏngdo, *Hanguksa: kodaep'yŏn,* Seoul: 1959, 631. Others believe *li* was the larger unit, see *Silla hyŏngsŏng* 236.

50 This is in Ch'ungbuk, Poun.

51 Possibly in Kyŏngbuk, Kunwi, or P'ohang.

Winter, tenth month. There was a great epidemic.

Year sixteen [473], spring, first month. *Ach'an* Pŏlchi and *Kŭpch'an* Tŏkchi became senior and junior generals.

Autumn, seventh month. [The court] repaired Myŏnghwal Fortress.

Year seventeen [474]. [The court] constructed fortresses in Ilmo, Sasi, Kwangsŏk, Kurye, Taptal, Chwara, and other places.[52]

Autumn, seventh month. Koguryŏ King Kŏryŏn [Changsu] personally led troops attacking Paekche. Paekche's King Kyŏng[53] sent his son Munju to request aid. The King sent troops to assist them but, before they reached there, Paekche had already been defeated and Kyŏng suffered mortal wounds.[54]

Year eighteen [475], spring, first month. The King moved his residence to Myŏnghwal Fortress.

Year nineteen [476], summer, sixth month. The Wa [people] invaded the eastern frontier. The King commanded General Tŏkchi to attack and he defeated them, killing and capturing more than two hundred.

Year twenty [477], summer, fifth month. The Wa mobilized troops to invade using five routes but, in the end, they did not succeed and returned.

Year twenty-one [478], spring, second month. In the night there was a red glow resembling silk reaching from the earth to the sky.

---

52 Ilmo Fortress is in Ch'ungbuk, Ch'ŏngwŏn. Sasi Fortress is in Ch'ungnam, Ch'ongsŏng, although it is doubtful that Silla extended that far. Kwangsŏk Fortress is in Ch'ungbuk, Yŏngdong. Taptal Fortress is in Kyŏngbuk, Changju. Kurye Fortress is in Ch'ungbuk, Okch'ŏn, or Kyŏngbuk, Ch'ŏngdo. And Chwara Fortress is perhaps in Ch'ungbuk, Yŏngdong.

53 He is called Kyŏnsa in *The Paekche Annals, SS,* and is also known by his posthumous title of Kaero.

54 *The Koguryŏ Annals, SS* 18:12a, places this event one year later as does *The Paekche Annals, SS* 25:11a–12b.

The **Silla Annals** of the **Samguk Sagi**

Winter, tenth month. There was an earthquake in the capital.[55]

Year twenty-two [479], spring, second month, third day. The King died.

Maripkan Soji

Maripkan Soji {another sources says Pich'ŏ} was enthroned [479]. He was the oldest son of King Chabi. His mother was from the Kim lineage, the daughter of *Sŏburhan* Misahŭn. His wife was Lady Sŏnhye, the daughter of *Ibŏlch'an* Naesuk.[56] When Soji was young he was filial in conduct and kept himself respectful of others. People truly admired him.

Year one [479]. [The King] proclaimed a general amnesty and advanced the officials one step in rank.

Year two [480], spring, second month. [The King] held sacrifices at the Dynastic Founder's Shrine.

Summer, fifth month. In the capital there was a drought.

Winter, tenth month. Due to famine people were starving [so the court] opened the granaries and aided them.

Eleventh month. The Malgal invaded the northern frontier.

Year three [481], spring, second month. The King visited Piryŏl Fortress[57] to comfort the troops and gave out padded military uniforms.

---

55 These two entries for this year when considered together may well indicate volcanic activity.

56 *SY*, chronological tables, states he was King Chabi's third son. It also states his wife was the daughter of *Kalmunwang* Kibo.

57 This is in Hamnam, Anbyŏn.

Third month. Koguryŏ and the Malgal invaded the northern frontier and took Homyŏng and seven other fortresses. Their troops advanced to Milchilbu.[58] Our army was joined by support troops from Paekche and Kaya and they divided along different routes and resisted. The enemy was defeated and withdrew. [We] pursued and destroyed them west of Iha, beheading more than 1,000.

Year four [482], spring, second month. A strong wind uprooted trees and there was a fire in Kŭmsŏng's south gate.

Summer, fourth month. There was a prolonged rain. The King ordered all the officials in the country to review all those imprisoned.

Fifth month. The Wa invaded the frontier.

Year five [483], summer, fourth month. There was a great flood.

Autumn, seventh month. There was a great flood.

Winter, tenth month. The King visited the Ilsŏn area[59] to look into the peasant's suffering from disaster and gave out rice according to status.

Eleventh month. There was thunder and a great pestilence in the capital.

Year six [484], spring, first month. Oham became *ibŏlch'an*.

Third month, Saturn intruded on the moon and it rained hail.

Autumn, seventh month. Koguryŏ invaded the northern frontier. Our troops with Paekche jointly fought below Mount Mo

---

58 Inoue Hideo in his translation of the *Samguk sagi, Sankuo shiki,* Tokyo: Heibonsha, 1980, 83, surmises Homyŏng is either Kangwŏn, Kimhwa, or Chŏngnyŏng. There is some doubt as to whether Milchilbu is Kyŏngbuk, P'ohang. This incident is not found in *The Koguryŏ Annals, SS.*

59 This is in Kyŏngbuk, Kumi.

Fortress[60] and greatly destroyed them [Koguryŏ].

Year seven [485], spring, second month. [The court] constructed Kubŏl Fortress.[61]

Summer, fourth month. [The King] personally held sacrifices at the Dynastic Founder's Shrine and increased the number of households protecting the shrine to twenty.

Fifth month. Paekche came on a courtesy visit.[62]

Year eight [486], spring, first month. [The King] appointed *Ich'an* Silchuk to be a general and conscripted 3,000 corvee laborers from Ilsŏn to repair the two fortresses, Samnyŏn and Kulsan.[63]

Second month. Naesuk became *ibŏlch'an* and participated in the country's governance.

Summer, fourth month. The Wa invaded the frontier.

Autumn, eighth month. There was a large military review south of Mount Nangsan.

Year nine [487]. The court establised Singung Shrine in Naŭl.[64] Naŭl is the original place where the founder [*sijo*] was born.

Third month. [The court] established postal stations in the four directions and ordered the local offices to repair public roads.

Autumn, seventh month. They repaired Wŏlsŏng.

Winter, tenth month. There was thunder.

Year ten [488], spring, first month. The King moved his residence to Wŏlsŏng.

---

60 This may well be east of Kangwŏn, Ch'unch'ŏn.

61 Kubŏl is in Kyŏngbuk, Ŭisŏng.

62 See also *SS* 26:3b.

63 This is Ch'ungbuk, Okch'ŏn.

64 Singung is a shrine dedicated to King Michu. Others contend the shrine was dedicated to Alchi and Hyŏkkose. See *Silla sangdae* 94. See also Yi Kidong (Kidong Lee), "The Indigenous Religions of Silla: Their Diversity and Durability," *Korean Studies* 28 (2004): 6–7. *SS* 32 places this event in King Chijung's reign.

Second month. [The King] visited Ilsŏn-gun and inquired into the [condition] of widowers, widows, orphans, and the old without children, giving out grain according to status.

Third month. The King, on returning from Ilsŏn, pardoned those imprisoned in the *chu* and *kun* through which he passed except for those having committed the two types of crimes carrying the death penalty.

Summer, sixth month. Tongyang presented a turtle with six eyes. Under its belly was a character.

Autumn, seventh month. [The court] constructed Tona Fortress.[65]

Year eleven [489], spring, first month. Peasants roaming the countryside were returned to farming.

Autumn, ninth month. Koguryŏ attacked the northern border area reaching Kwahyŏn.

Winter, tenth month. [Koguryŏ] overwhelmed Mount Hosan Fortress.[66]

Year twelve [490], spring, second month. [The court] rebuilt Pira Fortress.[67]

Third month. A dragon was seen in the Ch'ura Well.[68] When the market in the capital first opened, goods from all areas were exchanged.

Year fourteen [492], spring and summer. There was a drought. The King, blaming himself, reduced the number of dishes he ate at ordinary times.

Year fifteen [493], spring, third month. Paekche's King Modae

---

65 This is in Kyŏngbuk, Sangju.
66 Kwahyŏn is in Kangwŏn, Hŭiyang-myŏn. See also *SS* 18:13a for the sacking of Mount Hosan Fortress.
67 Pira is in Kyŏngju.
68 The well is about seven *li* south of Kyŏngju.

[Tongsong] sent an envoy requesting [a bride] for marriage. The King selected *Ibŏlch'an* Piji's daughter and sent her.[69]

Autumn, seventh month. [The court] established two garrisons at Imhae and Changnyŏng to guard against the Wa marauders.[70]

Year sixteen [494], summer, fourth month. There was a great flood.

Autumn, seventh month. General Silchuk and others fought against Koguryŏ on the plains of Salsu but could not win. They retreated to protect Kyŏna Fortress where Koguryŏ troops surrounded them. Paekche's King Modae sent three thousand troops which helped end the encirclement.[71]

Year seventeen [495], spring, first month. The King personally held sacrifices at Singung Shrine.

Autumn, eighth month. Koguryŏ encircled Paekche's Ch'iyang Fortress. Paekche requested assistance. The King ordered General Tŏkchi to lead troops to help them and Koguryŏ troops scattered.[72] The Paekche king sent an official to bring thanks.

Year eighteen [496], spring, second month. Kaya sent a white pheasant with a tail feather 5 *ch'ŏk* long.

Third month. [The court] repaired the palace for a second time.

Summer, fifth month. There was heavy rain and Alch'ŏn Stream overflowed, submerging and washing away more than two hundred houses.

Autumn, seventh month. Koguryŏ attacked Mount Usan Fortress. General Silchuk attacked above Iha and destroyed them.[73]

---

69 *SS* 26:4a presents a similar entry but lists Piji as an *ach'an*.

70 *SS 1977* 49 places both sites east of Kyŏngju.

71 Kyŏna Fortress is probably in Ch'ungbuk, Koesan. For this battle see also *SS* 19:1b and *SS* 26:4b.

72 See *SS* 19:2a and *SS* 26:4b; the location of Ch'iyang Fortress is unclear.

73 Mount Usan Fortress might be in Ch'ungnam, Ch'ŏngyang. See also *SS* 192a.

Eighth month. The King toured the southern region to observe farming.

Year nineteen [497], summer, fourth month. The Wa intruded on the coast.

Autumn, seventh month. There was a drought and a locust infestation. [The King] ordered all officials each to recommend one talented person who can govern.

Eighth month. Koguryŏ attacked and defeated Mount Usan Fortress.[74]

Year twenty-two [500], spring, third month. The Wa attacked and defeated Changbong Garrison.

Summer, fourth month. A violent wind blew, uprooting trees. A dragon was seen near a Kŭmsŏng well and in the capital there was a thick yellow fog covering all over.

Autumn, ninth month. The King went to Nari-gun.[75] A person there named P'aro had a daughter called Pyŏkhwa who was sixteen and truly the country's beauty. Her father dressed her in fine embroidered silks and put her in a sedan chair, wrapping it with colorful silk and presenting it to the King. The King believed it to be food to eat and opened it to look at it, only to find a young girl. Taken aback, he did not receive her. When he returned to the palace he could not stop thinking about her and went [to her house] repeatedly incognito and bestowed on her royal favors. On one of the trips he passed through Kot'a-gun and stayed at an old woman's house. He asked her, "What kind of ruler do the people nowadays consider the King of this country to be?" The old lady responded, "The people consider him to be a sage but I alone doubt it. This is because I have heard that he visits a girl in Nari to

---

74 See *SS* 19:2b.

75 This is Kyŏngbuk, Yŏngju.

bestow favors several times dressed in disguise in ordinary clothes. Should a dragon don the clothes of a fish, he will be captured by a fisherman.[76] Now the King, although occupying the highest position, lacks self restraint. If this is being a sage, who isn't a sage?" When the King heard this he was very embarrassed and secretly brought the girl and placed her in separate quarters, where she gave birth to a son.

Winter, eleventh month. The King died.

---

76 This is based on a statement in *Shuoyuan,* a Han dynasty collection of anecdotes.

The Silla
Annals of the
Samguk Sagi

Maripkan Chijŭng; and Kings
Pŏphŭng, Chinhŭng, Chinji,
and Chinp'yŏng

Book
4

Maripkan Chijŭng

Maripkan Chijŭng was enthroned [in 500]. His surname was Kim and he was called Chidaero {another source says Chidoro and a third source says Chich'ŏllo}.[1] He was the great-grandson of King Naemul and the son of *Kalmunwang* Sŭppo and a younger second cousin to King Soji. His mother was Lady Chosaeng of the Kim lineage, the daughter of King Nulchi. His consort was Lady Yŏnje of the Pak lineage, the daughter of *Ich'an* Tŭnghŭn.[2] The King's physique was unusually large and his courage surpassed others.[3] As the former King died without any sons, [Chijŭng] thus inherited the throne. His age was 64.

| Commentary | Of those Silla's kings, one had the title of *Kŏsŏgan,* one *Ch'ach'aung,* sixteen *Isagŭm,* and four *Maripkan.*[4]

---

1   See *SY* 1:22b. In April 1989 a Silla stele was discovered containing the title *Kalmunwang* Chido. This is believed to mean *Maripkan* Chijung. It this is correct, it would cause the revision of the interpretation that kings like Chido, as *kalmunwang,* could not succeed to the throne. See *Kalmunwang* 27. Also see Yuri *isagŭm* in *SS* 1.

2   *SY,* chronological tables, states that Chijŭng's father was *Kalmunwang* Kibo, a younger brother of King Nulchi. His mother was Lady Chosaeng. It also mentions in *SY* 1:22b, Chich'ŏllo, that Chijŭng married the daughter of a noble of Moryang-pu. It is unclear if this is Lady Yŏnje.

3   *SY* 1: 22b–23a describes the King as possessing a 1.5 *ch'ŏk* penis and accordingly there was much difficulty in finding a suitable queen. Kim Ch'ŏlchun in "Koryŏ chunggi ŭi munhwa ŭisik kwa sahak sŏnggyŏk," *Hanguksa yŏngu* 9 (1973): 20, uses this as evidence of a phallus worshipping cult among the Silla people.

4   *SY* names King Naemul as the first *maripkan* while *SS* claims this title appears two kings later with Nulchi. Accordingly, *SY* claims there were fourteen kings called *isagŭm* and six with the title *maripkan.*

When Ch'oe Ch'iwŏn, the well-known Confucian scholar of late Silla, produced the *Chewang yŏndaenok* (*Chronology of Kings*),[5] all kings were accorded the title *Wang* without mentioning *Kŏsŏgan* and other titles. Is this because he considered these titles to be unrefined and inadequate? The *Zuo*[*juan*] and the *Han*[*shu*], which are Chinese histories, preserved the *Chu* term *gu youtu* and the Xiongnu term *chengli gutu* [for emperor].[6] Now, in recording Silla affairs, it is also fitting to preserve intact local terms.

Year three [502], spring, second month. The King commanded that live burials be forbidden.[7] When the former King died five boys and girls each were buried alive. This is what caused [this] command. The King personally held sacrifices at the Singung Shrine.

Third month. [The King] ordered each *chuju* [magistrate] and *kunju* [military governor] to promote agriculture.[8] They began to use oxen in farming.[9]

---

5   Ch'oe Ch'iwŏn was born in 857. This history is no longer extant but its title indicates that it was a chronology of Silla kings. It is believed that *SY,* chronological tables, copied Ch'oe Ch'iwŏn's work. See Yi Kibaek, "Uri yŏksarŭl ŏddŏgye polkŏs inga?" *Samsŏng munhwa mungo,* 1976, 28–31.

6   See *Zuozhuan* 10, Xuangong, fourth year, and *Hanshu,* Xiongnu section. *Gu youtu* means "raised on tiger's milk" and *chengli gutu* means "son of heaven."

7   Live burials were customary in Shang China, and seem to be associated with bronze age life on the Korean peninsula as well. With the growth of labor-intensive agriculture and the introduction of Buddhism, this custom was no longer practiced. Recent excavations have left scholars divided as to whether live burials were practiced in early Silla. See *AKS* 3:96–7, n. 13.

8   The terms *"kunju"* and *"chuju"* are first used in the eleventh year of King T'arhae's reign, see *AKS* 3:45, n. 162. By the sixth century, with Silla's territorial conquests and expansion, the military functions of these positions expanded. See *Kodae kukka* 169. Sin Hyŏngsik, in *Hanguk kodaesa ŭi Silla yŏngu,* Seoul, 1984, 205, suggests the *chuju* took primary responsibility for military matters and the *kunju* took charge of administrative matters and the encouragement of agriculture. See note 13 below for additional information.

9   *SY* 1:14b first mentions the use of ploughshares in King Yuri's reign. Advances in agriculture help explain Silla's economic success. See also *AKS* 3:97–8, n. 14. Yi Kidong asserts that agricultural productivity more than doubled at this time. See

Year four [503], winter, tenth month. Various officials said to the King, "Ever since the Dynastic Founder created the country, the name of the country was not settled, with some calling it Sara, some Saro and some Silla. We believe the Sin ["sil"; as in "Silla"] conveys the idea of virtuous nation building daily renewed and "la" gives the idea of encompassing all land, so it is fitting to use this as the name [for the state]. Reviewing all those who have ruled from ancient times on, everyone was called *che* [emperor] or *wang* [king]. From the time our Dynastic Founder created our country to now, there have been twenty-two generations [of rulers] and we have only used native terms. We have yet to establish respectful titles. Now we officials in agreement respectfully present to Your Majesty, the title "King of Silla." The King agreed.[10]

Year five [504], summer, fourth month. [The King] standardized rules for mourning garb and implemented them.

Autumn, ninth month. [The court] levied a corvée labor impressment and built twelve fortresses, including those at Pari, Misil, Chindŏk, and Korhwa.[11]

Year six [505], spring, second month. The King personally determined the *chu, kun,* and *hyŏn* in the country and established Silchik-chu and made Isabu[12] as *kunju* [military governor]. The

---

Kolp'um 325. More recently Chŏn Tŏkchae, "Sa-yuk segi nongŏp saengsallyŏk ŭi paltal kwa sahoe pyŏndong," *Yŏksa wa hyŏnsil* 4 (1990): 26, asserts it increased seventeen-fold.

10 Korean, Chinese, and Japanese histories have all offered a wide variety of names besides Silla. See *AKS* 3:12, n. 6. Silla has been called, for example, Sara, Saro, Sŏrabul, and Sŏnabul, see *AKS* 3:98–9, n. 15–7. The term *maripkan* was not discarded at this time. However, the term King *(wang)* is clearly used on a stele placed by King Chinhŭng in the middle of the sixth century.

11 Pari is Kangwŏn, Samch'ŏk; Misil is Kyŏngbuk, Pohang; and Korhwa is Kyŏngbuk, Yŏngch'ŏn.

12 He is a fourth-generation descendant of King Naemul. See also *SS* 44.

term *kunju* starts from this time.[13]

Eleventh month. For the first time the King commanded the offices concerned to store ice and regulate shipping.

Year seven [506], spring and summer. There was a drought and, due to famine, people starved. [The court] opened the granaries to provide relief.

Year ten [509], spring, first month. [The court] established the Eastern market in the capital.

Third month. [The court] constructed traps to prevent harm from wild animals.

Autumn, seventh month. A frost fell killing bean plants.

Year eleven [510], summer, fifth month. There was an earthquake destroying people's houses and killing some people.

Winter, tenth month. There was thunder.

Year thirteen [512], summer, sixth month. Usan-guk submitted to [Silla] and offered every year local products as tribute. Usan-guk is an island in the sea directly east of Myŏngju[14] and it is also called Ullŭng-do. It is about 100 *li* in area, and because of its rugged terrain, it never submitted. After *Ich'an* Isabu became military governor of Hasŭlla, he said, "As the Usan people are simple and cruel, it would be difficult to get them to submit by using force, but they could be brought to submission by devising a scheme." He made many wooden dummy lions and divided and placed them on battleships. Reaching that country's coast, deceivingly he said, "If you do not surrender then I will release these wild beasts to trample you to death." The people of the

---

13 A similar entry appears in King Pŏrhyu's second year (185). *Kunju* here stands for a centrally appointed military administrator of a locality. It is the highest official responsible for military and administrative matters in the *chu*. See note 8 above and, above, Book 1, n. 80 and n. 84.

14 This is in Kangwŏn, Kangnŭng.

*The **Silla Annals** of the **Samguk Sagi***

country became fearful and surrendered.

Year fifteen [514], spring, first month. [The court] established a minor capital at Asich'on.[15]

Autumn, seventh month. [The court] moved households from the six districts of the capital and the southern regions to resettle them [there]. The King died. His posthumous reign title was Chijŭng. The Silla tradition of conferring posthumous reign titles started here.[16]

King Pŏphŭng

King Pŏphŭng was enthroned [in 514]. His personal name was Wŏnjong. {According to *Cefu yuangui*, his surname was Mo and his personal name was T'ae.}[17] He was the oldest son of King Chijŭng. His mother was Lady Yŏnje and his wife was Lady Podo of the Pak lineage.[18] The King was 7 *ch'ŏk* tall, magnanimous, and loved the people.

Year three [516], spring, first month. [The King] personally

---

15 There is some debate over the location of Asich'on. Ch'ŏn Kwanu places it at Kyŏngbuk, Ŭisŏng; Yi Pyŏngdo in Kyŏngju; and Im Pyŏngt'ae in Kyŏngnam; Haman. Silla established minor capitals in the process of its territorial expansion to absorb other centers of power, to appease local sentiment, and to assert more direct control over these areas. See Im Pyŏngt'ae, "Silla sogyŏnggo," *Yŏksa hakpo* 35–6 (1967): 95–6.

16 This interpretation is questionable given that the posthumous naming of kings starts in the seventh century with T'aejong King Muyŏl. *SY*, chronological tables, states this custom begins in King Pŏphŭng's reign.

17 *Cefu yuangui* is a Song China encyclopedic text that was started in 1005 and completed in 1013.

18 According to *SY*, royal tables, his mother was Lady Yongje and his wife was Lady Pado.

held sacrifices at the Singung Shrine. A dragon was seen in a Yangsan Well.

Year four [517], summer, fourth month. [The court] first established the Ministry of Military Affairs.[19]

Year five [518], spring, second month. [The court] built Mount Chu Fortress.

Year seven [520], spring, first month. [The court] promulgated a code of laws[20] and introduced the regulations for official garb for the officialdom with the grades of red and purple.

Year eight [521]. [The court] sent envoys to Liang to present local products as tribute.[21]

Year nine [522], spring, third month. The Kaya king sent an envoy requesting marriage. The King sent the sister of *Ich'an* Pijobu.[22]

Year eleven [524], autumn, ninth month. The King went out to inspect the newly opened land in the southern boundary. The Kaya King came and met him.[23]

Year twelve [525], spring, second month. *Taeach'an* Idŭng

---

19 According to *SS,* treatise section, this occurred in King Pŏphŭng's third year [516]. The treatise and *Annals* sections frequently differ by one year. *AKS* suggests the *Annals* date is more trustworthy because during compilation, *Annals* relied on the first recorded documents which were annalistic chronologies. The year differences may be explained by the fact that the treatise section used the year of enthronement as the first year of the reign. The Ministry of Military Affairs was established as a result of Silla's expansion. See Sin Hyŏngsik, "Silla pyŏngburyŏnggo," *Yŏksa hakpo* 61 (1974).

20 The code of laws was based on those used in Jin. A stele from 524 in Ulchin that notes the enforcement of punishments adds credence to the authenticity of this entry.

21 This is a Chinese kingdom (502–557).

22 To study Kaya's royal lineage see Kim T'aesik, "Tae Kaya ŭi segye wa tosŏlchi," *Chindan hakpo* 81, 1996.

23 This probably was the last King of Kaya, Kim Kuhyŏng (521–532). See also Kim T'aesik, *Kaya yŏnmaengsa,* Seoul: Ilchokak, 1993.

became Sabŏl-chu military governor.[24]

Year fifteen [528]. The practice of Buddhism started.[25] Earlier in King Nulchi's reign, the monk Mukhoja came from Koguryŏ to Ilsŏn-gun.[26] A *kun* person named Morye constructed in his house a cave dwelling to provide a safe haven. At that time Liang sent envoys presenting clothing and incense.[27] The high-ranking officials did not know of incense or its use. They sent a person taking the incense and asked [about it] everywhere. Mukhoja saw it and told its name saying, "If you burn this incense a fragrance will spread and convey your sincerity to the sacred. Of the so-called 'sacred' nothing can surpass the three treasures. The first treasure is the Buddha, the second is the Dharma, and the third is the Sangha. If you burn this and ask for a wish, then you certainly will have a spiritual response." At that time the King's daughter was critically ill. The King sent Mukhoja to burn incense and offer a vow. As the King's daughter's illness quickly passed, the King was very pleased and lavishly presented food and gifts. [Muk]hoja set out to Morye and presented him the goods he received and then said, "I am now leaving and want to bid farewell." It is not known where he went after that.

In King Pich'ŏ's reign [Soji, 479–500], there was a monk called Ado {some write it Wado} who, with three attendants, came to

---

24 This is in Kyŏngbuk, Sangju.

25 According to *SY* 3:5b, Ado, this occurred in Pŏphŭng's fourteenth year (527). Scholars generally accept this date as it reflects information in earlier records. See Yi Kibaek, *Silla sidae ŭi kukka pulgyo wa yugyo,* Seoul: Hanguk yŏnguwŏn, 1978, 7–8.

26 The name Mukhoja means "foreigner with dark skin." Ilsŏn-gun is in Kyŏngbuk, Kumi.

27 Liang actually was not founded until 502. *Haedong kosŭng chŏn* suggests the envoys were from Wu. See Peter H. Lee, trans., *Lives of Eminent Korean Monks: The Haedong Kosŭng Chŏn* (hereafter *HK*), Cambridge, MA: Harvard University Press, 1969, 52.

Morye's house.[28] His rituals and ceremonies were similar in appearance to Mukhoja. After several years without any illness, he died. His three attendants remained lecturing on Buddhist *sutras* and *vinaya* [disciplinary rules] and later there were occasional converts to Buddhism. Thereupon the King also wanted to promote Buddhism but the ranking officials did not believe in it and only complained, making it difficult for the King. His confidant, Ich'adon {another source says Ch'ŏdo},[29] memorialized to the King, "I request Your Majesty to execute me by cutting off my head, to settle this issue." The King said, "Since my original intent was to promote the right way, it is wrong to kill an innocent person." He replied, "If this succeeds in getting the way, even though I die there will be no regrets." The King thereupon summoned his officials and asked about this. Together they said, "Looking at the monks' followers, they cut off their hair like boys and wear strange clothes, and their discourse is truly odd and teachings uncommon. Now if we follow them, we fear truly there will be regrets. Although we may commit a serious crime, we fear we do not dare support Your Majesty's decree." Ich'adon alone said, "Now what the ranking officials say is wrong. There should be an unusual man and only then is there an unusual event. Now I have heard that Buddhism is a profound belief and fear I cannot but believe in it." The King said, "What the multitude says is unalterable and only you alone say differently. I, however, cannot follow both ways." Accordingly, when lower officials were about to hand him over to be

---

28 See also *SY* 3:2a. Some say Ado is Mukhoja, others say this is the Ado who came to Koguryŏ in 374.

29 *SY* 3:5b–9a, Ich'adon, states he was from the Pak clan and great-grandson of Kalmunwang Sŭppo.

executed,[30] Ich'adon, facing death, said, "I am about to be executed in the name of Buddhism. If Buddha is divine, my death certainly will produce an unusual event." After the beheading, blood gushed and its color was white like milk.[31] The people considered it strange and never again attacked Buddhism. {Although this is based on Kim Taemun's *Kyerim chapchŏn*,[32] it is notably different from Han [Tae] *Naema* Kim Yonghaeng's monument inscription about the monk Ado.[33]}

Year sixteen [529]. [The King] issued a decree prohibiting the killing of living things.[34]

Year eighteen [531], spring, third month. [The King] ordered the offices concerned to repair the dikes.

Summer, fourth month. *Ich'an* Ch'ŏlbu became *sangdaedŭng* [extraordinary rank one] and oversaw the administration of state affairs. The office of *sangdaedŭng* began at this time and is like the *chaesang* [councilor of state] of today.[35]

Year nineteen [532]. The ruler of Kŭmgwan, Kim Kuhae,[36] and his wife and three sons—the oldest Nojong, the second Mudŏk, and the last Muryŏk—came with their country's treasury and

---

30 *SY* 3:5b–9a gives a slightly different interpretation showing the King's devotion to Buddhism.

31 This event is frequently linked with shamanism. But milk can also symbolize truth in a Buddhist context.

32 *Kyerim chapchŏn* is attributed to Kim Taemun. See Yi Kibaek, "Kim Taemun kwa kŭŭi sahak," *Yŏksa hakpo* 77 (1978).

33 *SY* 3:6a also quotes this source in its presentation.

34 *SY,* chronological tables, state that the King prohibited killing on ten memorial days.

35 The emergence of this office is a clear example of Silla state building. The office was frequently held by the most powerful noble. See Yi Kibaek, "Sangdaedŭng ko," *Silla chŏngch'i sahoesa yŏngu,* Seoul, 1974. The term *"sangdaedŭng"* refers to a superior subject and evolved from the term *"taedŭng"* who was a member of the Hwabaek Council. The *"sangdaedŭng"* presided over the council.

36 See also *SS* 41, Kim Yusin's biography. Kim Yusin's lineage traces through Kuhae and his son Murŏk. See also *SY* 2:48b–9a.

surrendered. The King attended to them with propriety and gave him [the former King of Kaya] the position of *sangdŭng* and made his country a *sigŭp* [fief]. His son Muryŏk served until he reached the title of *kakkan*.

Year twenty-one [534]. Extraordinary Rank One Ch'ŏlbu died.

Year twenty-three [536]. [The court] started using year titles and this year was called "Kŏnwŏn" [Establishing Year Titles] first year.[37]

Year twenty-five [538], spring, first month. [The King] instructed to allow officials receiving appointments to the provinces to take their families.

Year twenty-seven [540], autumn, seventh month. The King died. His posthumous name was Pŏphŭng. He was buried on a peak north of Aegong Monastery.

King Chinhŭng

King Chinhŭng was enthroned [540]. His personal name was Sammaekchong {another source writes Simmaekpu} and at that time he was seven years old.[38] He is the son of King Pŏphŭng's brother, *Kalmunwang* Ipchong. His mother was of the Kim lineage, the daughter of King Pŏphŭng, and his consort was Lady Sado of

---

37 The use of reign years was commonly practiced in China and inaugurating it here reveals a sense of maturity in Silla's dealings with China. Nevertheless *SS* did not rely on reign years for dating purposes.

38 According to *SY* 1:33b he was fifteen.

The **Silla Annals** of the **Samguk Sagi**

the Pak lineage.[39] As the King was young, the Queen Mother[40] assisted in government affairs.

Year one [540], eighth month. [The King] proclaimed a general amnesty and bestowed on the military and civil officials increases in rank by one grade.

Winter, tenth month. There was an earthquake and peach and plum trees bloomed.

Year two [541], spring, third month. It snowed 1 *ch'ŏk*. Isabu was appointed to be *pyŏngburyŏng* [Minister of the Ministry of Military Affairs] and entrusted with all the military matters in the country. Paekche sent an envoy requesting peace. The request was granted.

Year five [544], spring, second month. Hŭngnyun Monastery was completed.[41]

Third month. [The King] permitted people to leave their families to become monks and nuns to promote Buddhism.

Year six [545], autumn, seventh month. *Ich'an* Isabu memorialized to the King, "The history of a country records good and evil rulers and subjects, showing praise and blame forever. If there is no compilation of history, what can later generations learn?" The King profoundly agreed with this and commanded *Ach'an* Kŏch'ilbu[42] and others to bring men of letters from all over and have them compile a history.[43]

Year nine [548], spring, second month. Koguryŏ and Ye

---

39 According to *SY* 8b, royal tables, his mother was Chiso puin.
40 Yi Pyŏngdo, in his translation, *SS*, 1977, p. 56 suggests this refers to King Pŏphŭng's wife but this seems incorrect and at odds with the account.
41 Located in Kyŏngju, only its remains are visible today. It was the first royal temple.
42 See *SS* 44 for his biography. Of the Kim lineage, he was a fifth-generation descendant of King Naemul. The name of this compilation is unclear, although it is understood to be a history.
43 See Yi Kibaek, "Kodae kukka ŭi yŏksa insik," *Hanguksaron* 6 (1979).

[Tongye] people attacked Pakeche's Mount Toksan Fortress.[44] When Paekche asked for help, the King dispatched General Churyŏng, who led three thousand elite soldiers to attack them. The dead and captured were very numerous.

Year ten [549], spring. Liang sent an envoy who came with Kaktŏk,[45] a monk who had studied [in Liang], and carried Buddhist relics [*sari*]. The King had all the officials welcome them on the road in front of Hŭngnyun Monastery.

Year eleven [550], spring, first month. Paekche defeated Koguryŏ's Tosal Fortress.[46]

Third month, Koguryŏ captured Paekche's Kŭmhyŏn Fortress.[47] The King, taking advantage of the two countries' soldiers being exhausted, ordered *Ich'an* Isabu to deploy troops to attack them. He took the two fortresses and rebuilt and expanded them, placing 1,000 armed soldiers to defend them.

Year twelve [551], spring, first month. The reign year changed to Kaeguk first year.[48]

Third month. When the King inspected the defenses at Nangsan Fortress[49] he heard that Urŭk and his disciple Imun were well versed in music and especially invited them. The King was staying at Harim Palace[50] and he asked them to present their music. The two men had each composed new songs and

---

44   See also *SS* 19:8a, King Yangwŏn, fourth year. Some suggest this site is in Ch'ungbuk, Ch'ungju.

45   See *HK* 70–1. He was the first Silla monk to return from overseas.

46   See also *SS* 26:10a, King Sŏng, twenty-eighth year. Tosal is in Ch'ungnam, Ch'ŏnan.

47   Some claim this is in Ch'ungbuk, Chinch'ŏn, or Ch'ungnam, Yŏngi.

48   *AKS* 3:114, n. 90, suggests this might indicate that King Chinhŭng personally started to rule at this time.

49   This is in Ch'ungnam, Ch'ŏngju,

50   This is in Ch'ungbuk, Ch'ungju. Ch'ungju is by the South Han River.

performed them. Earlier the Kaya[51] king Kasil made a twelve-string *kayagŭm* to represent the rhythms of the twelve months. He also ordered Urŭk to compose melodies. When [Kaya] experienced unrest, he surrendered to us bringing his musical instruments. His musical [instrument] is called the *kayagŭm*. The King ordered Kŏch'ilbu and others to invade Koguryŏ and, riding on victory, they took ten *kun*.

Year thirteen [552]. The King ordered three people, Kyego,[52] Pŏpchi,[53] and Mandŏk, to study music under Urŭk. Urŭk, considering their abilities, taught Kyego the *kayagŭm,* Pŏpchi singing, and Mandŏk dance. When their training was completed the King ordered them to perform, saying, "This is no different from the music I heard earlier at Nangsan Fortress." He generously rewarded them there.

Year fourteen [553], spring, second month. The King ordered the offices concerned to construct a new palace east of Wŏlsŏng Fortress. As a golden dragon was seen in the area, the King became dubious of his plan and changed it, making the area a temple and giving it the name Hwangnyong [Imperial Dragon] Monastery.[54]

Autumn, seventh month. [Silla] took Paekche's northeastern periphery, established Sin-ju,[55] and named *Ach'an* Muryŏk as military governor.[56]

---

51 Yi Pyŏngdo believes this refers to Tae Kaya, around modern Koryŏng in Kyŏngbuk.

52 See *SS* 32:8a.

53 See *SS* 32:8a where he is called Chuji.

54 It took more than fifteen years to construct this monastery and its nine-storied pagoda became especially famous and is noted in *SY* 3:17b. This monastery carried a close affiliation with the court. See Yi Kibaek, "Hwangnyongsa wa kŭch'anggŏn," (hereafter "Hwangnyongsa"), *Silla sasangsa yŏngu,* Seoul:Ilchokak, 1986.

55 This is in Kyŏnggi, Kwangju.

56 Muryŏk was the son of Kim Kuhae and the grandfather of Kim Yusin.

Winter, tenth month. [The King] married a Paekche princess, making her a minor queen.[57]

Year fifteen [554], autumn, seventh month. [Silla] repaired Myŏnghwal Fortress.[58] The Paekche king Myŏngnong [Sŏng] came with Karyang[59] and attacked Mount Kwansan Fortress.[60] The military governor *Kakkan* Udŏk, *Ich'an* T'amji, and others resisted but to no avail. Sin-ju military governor Kim Muryŏk came with his *chu* soldiers to resist. When they were engaged in combat, *pijang* [colonel] of Samnyŏnsan-gun [Poun] *Kogan* Todo made a sudden attack, killing the Paekche King.[61] Thereupon the various armies riding on this victory soundly defeated them, beheading four *chwap'yŏng* and 29,600 soldiers.[62] Not a single horse returned.

Year sixteen [555], spring, first month. [The court] established Wansan-ju in Pisabŏl.[63]

Winter, tenth month. The King made a tour of inspection to Mount Pukhan to set the boundaries of his newly expanded territory.

Eleventh month. On returning from Mount Pukhan, he instructed that the districts [*chu* and *kun*] that he passed through should be exempt from one year of taxes and to pardon all those in prison except for those charged with crimes of the second

---

57 See also *SS* 26:10a.
58 This is in Ch'ungbuk, Okch'ŏn.
59 See Yi Pyŏngdo who believes this refers to Kaya.
60 This is also in the Ch'ungbuk, Okch'ŏn, region.
61 *Kogan* is the third rank in the Silla regional system. It corresponds to the ninth rank of *kŭpch'an* in the central-capital rank system. Samnyŏnsan is in Ch'ungnam, Poun.
62 *Chwap'yŏng* was the highest rank in the Paekche sixteen-grade scale. Best, in *Paekche* 336, also notes this battle.
63 This is in Kyŏngnam, Ch'angnyŏng, and not to be confused with the Chŏnbuk, Chŏnju, region.

degree.

Year seventeen [556], autumn, seventh month. [The court] established Piyŏrhol-chu[64] and *Sach'an* Sŏngjong became military governor.

Year eighteen [557]. Kugwŏn became a minor capital. [The court] abolished Sabŏl-chu and established Kammu-ju.[65] *Sach'an* Kijong became military governor. [The court] abolished Sin-ju and established Pukhansan-ju.[66]

Year nineteen [559], spring, second month. The court resettled the children of aristocratic families and powerful families of the six districts to Kugwŏn. *Naema* Sindŭk constructed a multi-arrow-shooting cannon and presented it [to the King]. It was placed on top of the fortress.

Year twenty-three [562], autumn, seventh month. Paekche invaded, plundering households on the border. The King sent out troops to defend, capturing or killing more than one thousand people.[67]

Ninth month. Kaya[68] rebelled. The King ordered Isabu to subjugate them and Sadaham to assist him. Sadaham, leading five thousand horsemen,[69] rode ahead entering Chŏndan Gate and erecting a white flag there. In the fortress [the people], being fearful, did not know what to do. Isabu led his troops to face them and at that time [Kaya] surrendered completely. In weighing

---

64   This is in the Anbyŏn region of Hamnam.

65   Kugwŏn is in Ch'ungbuk, Ch'ungju; Sabŏl-ju is in Kyŏngbuk, Sangju; and Kammu-ju is in Kyŏngbuk, Kimch'ŏn.

66   Sin-ju is in Kyŏnggi, Kwangju, and Mount Pukhan-ju is in the area north of the Han River in modern Seoul.

67   See also *SS* 27:1b.

68   *SS 1977* 59 also states this refers to Tae Kaya and is in the Kyŏngbuk, Koryong, region.

69   See *SS* 44 for Sadaham's biography where much of this event is recounted. He is a descendant of King Naemul.

merit, Sadaham's was greatest. The King rewarded him with fine-quality land and two hundred prisoners of war but Sadaham declined this three times. When the King forced him, he received the people and freed them to be commoners and divided the fields among his soldiers. The people of the country admired him.

Year twenty-five [564]. [The King] sent an envoy to present tribute to Northern Qi.[70]

Year twenty-six [565], spring, second month. Wusheng the emperor of Northern Qi sent a decree naming the King Commissioner with Extraordinary Power, Commandant of the Eastern Tributaries [*Sichijie Dongyi Xiaowei*], Lord of Nangnang, King of Silla.[71]

Autumn, eighth month. [The king] commanded *Ach'an* Ch'unbu to go out and defend Kugwŏn.

Ninth month. [The court] abolished Wansan-ju and established Taeya-ju.[72] Chen[73] sent the envoy Liu Si and the monk Mingguan on a courtesy visit, sending them with more than seventeen hundred volumes of Buddhist scriptures and commentaries.

Year twenty-seven [566], spring, second month. [The court] completed the construction of two monasteries, Kiwŏn and Silche.[74] [The King] named Prince Tongnyun, making him Crown Prince. [The court] sent an envoy to Chen presenting local products as tribute. The construction of Hwangnyong Monastery was completed.[75]

Year twenty-eight [567], spring, third month. [The court] sent

---

70 This is a northern Chinese state in modern Honam near Anyang.

71 Emperor Wusheng reigned from 562 to 565.

72 This is in Kyŏngnam, Hapch'ŏn.

73 This is a state that succeeded Liang China of the Six Dynasties. It fell to Sui in 589.

74 "Kiwon" is the name of a royal garden used by Sakyamuni. The Silla monk Sungyŏng, on returning from Tang, lived here.

75 *SY* and *HK* 54 claim construction ended in Chinhŭng's thirtieth year (569). See also *Hwangnyongsa.*

an envoy to Chen to present local products as tribute.

Year twenty-nine [568]. [The court] changed the reign title to T'aech'ang.

Summer, sixth month. [The court] sent an envoy to Chen to present local products as tribute.

Winter, tenth month. [The court] abolished Pukhansan-ju and established Namch'ŏn-ju and also abolished Piyŏrhol-chu and established Tarhol-chu.[76]

Year thirty-one [570], summer, sixth month. [The court] sent an envoy to Chen to present local products [as tribute.]

Year thirty-two [571]. [The court] sent an envoy to Chen to present local products as tribute.

Year thirty-three [572], spring, first month. [The court] changed the reign year to Hongje.

Third month. Crown Prince Tongnyun died. [The court] sent an envoy to Northern Qi to present tribute.

Winter, tenth month, twentieth day. For soldiers who died in battle, [the court] established, in the outer compounds of monasteries, P'algwan assemblies[77] that lasted for seven days.

Year thirty-five [574], spring, third month. Hwangnyong Monastery cast a 16 *ch'ŏk* statue of 35,007 *kun* of bronze and 10,198 *pun* of gold plate.[78]

Year thirty-six [575], spring and summer. There was a drought. The 16 *ch'ŏk* statue at Hwangnyong Monastery wept [with tears] reaching its feet.

---

76 Namch'ŏn-ju is in Kyŏnggi, Inch'ŏn, and Tarhol-chu is in Kangwŏn, Kosŏng.

77 P'algwan, known as the Assembly of Eight Prohibitions, is a Buddhist ceremony held in the eleventh month. For a fuller discussion see Sem Vermeersch, *The Power of the Buddhas,* Cambridge, MA: Harvard University Asia Center, 2008.

78 One *kŭn* is approximately 600 grams and *pun* can mean either approximately 0.25 centimeters (0.1 inches) or 28.4 grams (1 ounce).

Year thirty-seven [576], spring. [The court] began to uphold Wŏnhwa [as a leader].[79] Earlier the King and officials were distressed that they lacked a process to recognize people's talents and so they wished to have many people mingle to observe their conduct, and afterwards recommend them for selection. Accordingly, they selected two beautiful girls, named Nammo and Chunjŏng, and gathered more than three hundred people as their followers. But the two girls competed over their beauty and were jealous of each other. Chunjŏng lured Nammo to her private residence and strongly urged her to drink wine. As she became drunk, she was dragged and thrown into a river, killing her. Chunjŏng [in turn] was executed. Their followers became disorganized and dispersed.

After that event they then selected a handsome boy and adorned him, calling him Hwarang, to uphold him [as a leader].[80] Followers gathered like clouds, sometimes to refine each other's sense of morality and honesty, sometimes to enjoy collectively music and song, and to train in and appreciate mountains and streams, going far and wide. Because of this they knew if a man were corrupt or honest, and selected those who were good and recommended them to the court. Thus Kim Taemun, in the *Hwarang segi*,[81] wrote, "Wise advisers and loyal subjects excelled

---

79 This is a description of the Hwarang order. A similar description appears in *SY* 3:22b–23a.

80 There has been extensive research on the Hwarang. See for example "Silla hwarangdo ŭi sahoehakchŏk koch'al" in *Kolp'um*. The term "Hwarang" can mean both the leader of the group and the group itself. One source states it began in 514, another source states 540.

81 This text was long believed to be lost but in 1989 a copy was reported to have been discovered. Several scholars, such as Yi Chonguk, attest to this text's authenticity while others cast serious doubt. See No T'aedon, "P'ilsabon hwarang segi ŭi saryojŏk kach'e," *Yŏksa hakpo* 147 (1995). See also Richard D. McBride, "Silla Buddhism and the *Hwarang segi* Manuscripts," *Korean Studies* 31 (2007).

out of this. Outstanding generals and brave soldiers were produced from this." Ch'oe Ch'iwŏn in his introduction on the "Nallang" stele[82] wrote, "Our country has a mysterious principle called 'Pungnyu.' The origin of this teaching can be found in detail in the history of the Hwarang and, in fact, includes the three teachings[83] which transform people when exposed to them. [The idea of] 'At home filial to your family, outside the home loyal to the state' is taught by the Minister of Punishments in Lu [Confucius]. 'Following the doctrine of inaction and the practice of teaching without words,' is the principle of the scribe of Zhou Taoism [Lao Tzu]. 'Not to do anything evil, to practice reverentially everything good.' This is the teaching of the Prince of India [Buddha]."[84] The *Xinluo Guoji* [*Silla kukki*], by Linghu Cheng of Tang,[85] states, "They selected the handsome boys of the nobility and adorned them, powdering their faces and calling them Hwarang. The people of the country all respected and supported them."

The Dharma Master Anhong went to Sui China in search of the Dharma and returned with two monks, including the foreign [Indian] monk Vimala, and presented the *Lankāvatāra* and *Śrīmālā sūtras*, along with *śarīra* [relics] of the Buddha.[86]

Autumn, eighth month. The King died. His posthumous title was Chinhŭng and he was buried at a peak north of Aegong Monastery. The King, enthroned at an early age, supported

---

82 This is from a stele that is no longer extant.

83 The three teachings are Buddhism, Confucianism, and Taoism.

84 Robert E. Buswell Jr. of UCLA referenced this particular quotation in a personal message noting the line is indeed a famous passage that is thought to summarize the teachings of all the Buddhas throughout the eons. It even has its own designation in the canon, *avavāda* or *ovādapātimokkha*.

85 This is a record written by a Tang envoy to Silla in 768.

86 Buswell provided the Sanskrit titles for these sutras.

Buddhism singlemindedly. Toward the end of his life he shaved his head and donned the robes of a monk, calling himself Pŏpun until his death. The Queen too, following him, became a nun and lived at Yŏnghŭng Monastery. When she died the people of the country buried her with appropriate rituals.

King Chinji

King Chinji was enthroned [in 576]. His personal name was Saryun {another source states Kŭmnyun}. He was King Chinhŭng's second son. His mother was Lady Sado and his consort was Lady Chido.[87] Because the Crown Prince died early, Chinji was enthroned.

Year one [576]. *Ich'an* Kŏch'ilbu became extraordinary rank one and was put in charge of the country's affairs.

Year two [577], spring, second month. The King personally held sacrifices at the Singung Shrine and proclaimed a great amnesty.

Winter, tenth month. Paekche invaded the *chu* and *kun* of the western region.[88] The King ordered *Ich'an* Sejong[89] to set out, leading troops, and attack, defeating them north of Ilsŏn. They beheaded 3,700 people and built Naerisŏ Fortress.

Year three [578], autumn, seventh month. [The court] sent an

---

87 According to *SY*, royal tables, his mother was the daughter of *Kakkan* Yŏngsa of the Pak lineage and his consort was the daughter of Lord Kio of the Pak lineage.

88 See also *SS* 27:1b–2a.

89 *AKS* 3:126, n.165, speculates that this may be another name for Noribu, who was killed in the tenth year of King Chinp'yŏng [588].

envoy to Chen to present local products as tribute. Silla accorded to Paekche Mount Arya Fortress.[90]

Year four [579], spring, second month. Paekche constructed Unghyŏn Fortress and Songsul Fortress to block the passage to Mount Sasan Fortress, Mijihyŏn Fortress, and Naerisŏ Fortress.

Autumn, seventh month, seventeenth day. The King died. His posthumous title was Chinji and he was buried north of Yŏnggyŏng Monastery.

King Chinp'yŏng

King Chinp'yŏng was enthroned [in 579]. His personal name was Paekchŏng[91] and he was the son of King Chinhŭng's Crown Prince Tongnyun. His mother was Lady Manho {another source states Mannae} of the Kim lineage who was the daughter of *Kalmunwang* Ipchong. His consort was Lady Maya of the Kim lineage who was the daughter of *Kalmunwang* Poksŭng.[92] From when the King was born, his appearance was unusual and his physique was exceedingly large.[93] He was resolute in his thinking,

---

90 This is in Chŏnbuk, Iksan. This incident is not mentioned in *The Paekche Annals, SS,* and scholars dispute the authenticity of the character *"yŏ"* (accorded). *SS 1977* 63 notes it should be read as "attack."

91 This name is derived from the father of Sakyamuni. The practice of giving Buddhist names to members of the Silla royal family starts from the reign of King Chinp'yŏng.

92 According *SY,* royal tables, 19, his mother was also called Lady Mallyŏng. His second wife was Lady Sŭngmu of the Son lineage. Maya is the name of Sakyamuni's mother.

93 *SY* 1: 35a states the King was 11 *ch'ŏk* tall. It also notes that once, when visiting Ch'ŏnju Monastery, three stone steps broke under his weight.

wise, and perceptive.

Year one [579], eighth month. *Ich'an* Noribu became extraordinary rank one.[94] The King enfeofed his younger brothers, Paekpan as *Kalmunwang* Chinjŏng and Kukpan as *Kalmunwang* Chinan.[95]

Year two [580], spring, second month. The King personally held sacrifices in the Singung Shrine. *Ich'an* Hujik became Minister of the Ministry of Military Affairs.[96]

Year three [581], spring, first month. [The court] established the Wihwabu, which is like the present Ministry of Personnel Affairs [Ibu].[97]

Year five [583], spring, first month. [The court] established the Sŏnbusŏ [Office of Shipping] with a director [*taegam*] and deputy director [*chegam*].[98]

Year six [584], spring, second month. The reign year was changed to Kŏnbok.

Third month. [The court] established the Chobu [Ministry of Taxation][99] under a minister who was put in charge of taxation, and the Sŭngbu [Ministry of Transportation] under a minister who was put in charge of overseeing transportation [horses and vehicles].

---

94 Some assert he is the same man as Sejong who led troops to defeat Paekche in the second year of King Chinji's reign, but others contend he is the same person as the oldest son of King Kuhae, Kŭmgwan Kaya's last king. See Kim T'aesik, 1996, 22–3.

95 His daughter will become in the future Queen Chindŏk. Paekpan is the name of Sakyamuni's uncle. The preface *chin* is found on the names of many kings and queens at this time, and carried the idea, according to Buddhist beliefs, of being invested. Kukpan, as noted above, is also a Buddhist name.

96 He is the great-grandson of King Chijŭng.

97 See also *SS* 38.

98 According to the *Koryŏsa*, "Chikkwan-ji," section 1, this office was subordinate to the Office of Military Affairs (Pyŏngbu) and became an independent office in King Munmu's eighteenth year [678]. See *SS 1977* 65.

99 See *SS* 38.

Year seven [585], spring, third month. As there was a drought, the King avoided his ceremonial halls and reduced the number of dishes in his daily meals.[100] He went to the Southern Hall and personally reviewed the records of those imprisoned.

Autumn, seventh month. The eminent monk Chimyŏng entered Chen seeking to learn the dharma.[101]

Year eight [586], spring, first month. [The court] established the Yebu [Ministry of Rites] under two ministers.[102]

Summer, fifth month. There was thunder and shooting stars fell like rain.

Year nine [587], autumn, seventh month. Taese and Kuch'il were two men who sailed out into the sea. Taese, King Naemul's seventh-generation descendant and the son of *Ich'an* Tongdae, was extraordinarily gifted. From his young age he had the idea of traveling overseas. Befriending a monk called Tamsu, he once said, "Spending an entire life in the confines of the mountains and valleys of Silla, how would it be different from a fish in a pond or a bird in a cage, never knowing the vastness of the blue oceans or the spaciousness and stillness of the mountains and forests? Some day in the future, riding on a raft across the sea, I wish to reach Wu-Yue[103] to seek teachers in the sacred mountains to search for the Way. If I can transform myself from an ordinary person and if Taoist immortality can be learned, then I would be

---

100 A similar practice was common in China where emperors were expected to be frugal in times of difficulty as a way to atone for possible wrongdoing. This practice mentioned here may show evidence of growing Chinese influence within the court.

101 When he returned to Silla in 602 the King appointed him to the *Taedŏk* rank. See *HK* 72–3 for details on his life.

102 In China this was a ministry to oversee education, rituals, and foreign affairs.

103 These are not actual countries but refer to the region south of the Yangzi River in China.

flying, riding the wind through the vast emptiness of Heaven. This would be a truly marvelous and extraordinary act worth watching in the world. Can you join me?" Tamsu was not willing to go so Taese left and, seeking a companion, he ran into a person named Kuch'il. He [Kuch'il] was high-minded with unusual integrity. Together they visited the temples of South Mountain. Suddenly there was wind and rain and falling leaves floating in the puddles of a garden. Taese talked with Kuch'il saying, "As I would like to roam with you to the western regions, for now let's each take a leaf, pretend it is a boat, and see which gets there first." After a while Taese's leaf was ahead and Taese laughed saying, "It looks like I am going, doesn't it?" Kuch'il, in anger, said, "I am also a man, why can't I go also?" Taese knew he was with him and confided his intentions to him. Kuch'il said, "That is my wish too" and, in the end having each other as friends, they sailed out from the Southern Sea but no one later knows where they went.

Year ten [588], winter, tenth month. Extraordinary Rank One Noribu died and *Ich'an* Suŭlbu became extraordinary rank one.

Year eleven [589], spring, third month. Wŏngwang, dharma master [*pŏpsa*], went to Chen seeking the dharma.[104]

Autumn, seventh month. In the western part of the country there was a flood, submerging 30,360 houses, and more than two hundred people died. The King dispatched officials to offer the survivors relief.

Year thirteen [591], spring, second month. [The court] established the Yŏnggaekpu [Ministry of Protocol] under two

---

104 Wŏngwang was one of Silla's most renowned monks. His biography can be found in *SY* 4:1a and *HK* 74–82.

The **Silla Annals** of the **Samguk Sagi**

ministers.[105]

Autumn, seventh month. [The court] built Namsan Fortress which was 2,854 po in circumference.

Year fifteen [593], autumn, seventh month. [The court] rebuilt Myŏnghwal Fortress. Its circumference was 3,000 po and [rebuilt also] Mount Sŏhyŏng Fortress whose circumference was 2,000 po.

Year sixteen [594]. The Sui Emperor [sent] an edict conferring on [the King] the title of Senior Commander [Shanggaifu], Lord of Nangnang, King of Silla.

Year eighteen [596], spring, third month. The eminent monk Tamyuk went to Sui seeking the dharma.[106] [The court] sent an envoy to Sui to present local products as tribute goods.

Winter, tenth month. There was a fire in Yŏnghŭng Monastery that spread and burned three hundred fifty houses. The King personally went to help.

Year nineteen [597]. Samnang Monastery was completed.[107]

Year twenty-two [600]. The eminent monk Wŏngwang returned [from Sui] accompanying the Silla tribute envoy *Nama* Chemun and *Taesa* Hoengch'ŏn.

Year twenty-four [602]. [The King] sent the envoy *Taenama* Sanggun to Sui to present local products as tribute.

Autumn, eighth month. Paekche attacked Amak Fortress.[108] The King had [the Silla] troops counterattack and soundly defeated them. Kwisan and Ch'uhang died here.[109]

Ninth month. The eminent monk Chimyŏng returned from Sui with tribute envoy Sanggun. As the King revered Lord Chimyŏng's

---

105 This is an office to greet foreign guests.
106 See also *HK* 73.
107 Its remains have been found in Kyŏngju.
108 This fortress is located in Chŏnbuk, Namwŏn. See also *SS* 27:3b–4a.
109 Kwisan's biography is in *SS* 45. He was from the Saryŏng district of Kyŏngju.

adherence to Buddhist vows, he made him *Taedŏk*.[110]

Year twenty-five [603], autumn, eighth month. Koguryŏ invaded Mount Pukhan Fortress. The King personally led ten thousand soldiers to stop them.[111]

Year twenty-six [604], autumn, seventh month. [The court] sent as tributary envoys *Taenama* Manse and Hyemun and others to Sui. [The court] abolished Namch'ŏn-ju [Ich'on] and reestablished Pukhansan-ju.

Year twenty-seven [605], spring, third month. The eminent monk Tamyuk returned from Sui accompanying the [Silla] tribute envoy Hyemun.

Autumn, eighth month. [The court] dispatched troops to invade Paekche.[112]

Year thirty [608]. The King, worrying that Koguryŏ had repeatedly invaded [Silla's] land, wanted to ask Sui troops to punish Koguryŏ and asked Wŏngwang to compose a letter requesting military aid. Wŏngwang said, "To seek ones own preservation while destroying others should not be the conduct of a Buddhist monk, but as I live in Your Majesty's land and consume Your Majesty's water and food [vegetables], how could I dare not to follow Your command?" and then wrote accordingly.

Second month. Koguryŏ invaded [Silla's] northern border, capturing eight thousand people.

Fourth month. Koguryŏ conquered Mount Umyŏng Fortress.[113]

Year thirty-one [609], spring, first month. The land below Moji Peak burned.[114] It was 4 *po* wide, 8 *po* long, and 5 *po* deep and

---

110 This is a title of prestige given to monks of high esteem.

111 See also *SS* 20:2b.

112 See also *SS* 27:4b.

113 See also *SS* 20:3a.

114 This site is located in Kyŏngju and is probably evidence of a natural gas emission.

lasted until the fifteenth of the tenth month.

Year thirty-three [611]. The King sent an envoy to Sui with a memorial requesting troops. Emperor Yangdi [of Sui] granted it. That which concerns the movement of troops is recorded in *The Koguryŏ Annals*.[115]

Winter, tenth month. Paekche troops encircled Kagam Fortress for a hundred days.[116] Hyŏn magistrate Ch'andŏk vigorously defended but, exhausting his strength, he died and the fortress fell.[117]

Year thirty-five [613], spring. There was a drought.

Summer, fourth month. A frost fell.

Autumn, seventh month. When the Sui envoy Wang Shiyi arrived at Hwangnyong Monastery, a *Paekkojwa* [a Buddhist Hundred-Seat Assembly] was held,[118] inviting Wŏngwang and other dharma masters to lecture on the *sutras*.

Year thirty-six [614], spring, second month. [The court] abolished Sabŏl-chu and established Ilsŏn-ju and made *Ilgilch'an* Ilbu a military governor. Yŏnghŭng Monastery's earthen Buddha fell apart on itself and, not long after, King Chinhŭng's Queen, the Buddhist nun [Piguni, Bhiksuni][119] died.

Year thirty-seven [615], spring, second month. The King held a *taebo* banquet lasting for three days.[120]

---

115 See *SS* 20:3b. This account also appears in *Suishi* 3 and *Tongji zizhuan* 131.

116 This fortress may be in the Koesan region of Ch'ungbuk or in Kyŏnggi, Ansan.

117 Ch'andŏk is also mentioned in the biography section, *SS* 47, under Haeron.

118 The Assembly is a Buddhist assembly based on the Inwang sutra [Sutra for Humane Kings] to which leading monks are invited. This is the first record of this event in Korean history.

119 According to *SY* and *HK* 62, King Pŏphŭng's Queen was called Piguni or Myobŏp and stayed and died at Yŏnghŭng Monastery. But since Yŏnghŭng Monastery had not been constructed at King Pŏphŭng's time, this woman was probably not King Chinhŭng's Queen.

120 The *Taebo* banquet was held when the country had a reason to celebrate. At this

Winter, tenth month. There was an earthquake.

Year thirty-eight [616], winter, tenth month. Paekche attacked Mount Mosan Fortress.[121]

Year forty [618]. The military governor of Mount Pukhan-ju, Pyŏnp'um, planned to retake Kajam Fortress and dispatched troops to fight with Paekche. Haeron followed the troops and fought the enemy with all his strength, but died. Haeron was Ch'andŏk's son.[122]

Year forty-three [621], autumn, seventh month. [The King] sent an envoy to the Tang court to present local products as tribute. [The Tang Emperor] Gaozu personally entreated him and sent *Tongzhi sanji hangshi* [Senior Recorder for Comprehensive Duty] Liu Wensu on a courtesy visit and presented an imperial letter, a screen, and three hundred *tuan* [bolts] of silk.[123]

Year forty-four [622], spring, first month. The King personally visited Hwangnyong Monastery.

Second month. *Ich'an* Yongsu was given the position of *chŏnjungsŏng* [palace administrator] in the Naesŏng [Palace Bureau].[124] Earlier in the King's seventh year an official was appointed to Taegung Palace, Yanggung Palace, and Saryanggung Palace each. Now a single palace administrator in the Naesŏng was in charge of all three palaces.

Year forty-five [623], spring, first month. [The court] established two *taegam* [director] positions in the Ministry of Military Affairs.

Winter, tenth month. [The court] sent an envoy to Great Tang

---

time the King distributed food and wine to all his subjects.
121 See *SS* 27:5a.
122 See Haeron's biography in *SS* 47.
123 This was the first Silla envoy to the Tang court.
124 Yongsu is the son of King Chinji and the father of King Muyŏl.

to present tribute. Paekche attacked Nŭngno-hyŏn.[125]

Year forty-six [624], spring, first month. [The court] established six director positions in the Siwibu [Office of Royal Guards], one director in the Sangsasŏ [Office of Awards], and one director in the Taedosŏ [Office of Clerical Affairs].[126] Third month. Tang's Gaozu sent an envoy investing the King with the titles *Zhuguo* [Pillar of State], Lord of Nangnang-gun, King of Silla.

Winter, tenth month. Paekche troops encircled our six fortresses at Sokham, Aengjam, Kijam, Pongjam, Kihyŏn, and Hyŏlch'aek.[127] Thereupon three fortresses were either destroyed or surrendered. *Kŭpch'an* Nulch'oe, combining the troops of the three fortresses, Pongjam, Aengjam, and Kihyŏn, firmly defended, but unable to prevail, he died there.[128]

Year forty-seven [625], winter, eleventh month. [The King] sent an envoy to Great Tang to present tribute and at the same time accused Koguryŏ of blocking the passage so that envoys could not get to the [Tang] court and [accused] them of several invasions.

Year forty-eight [626], autumn, seventh month. [The King] sent an official to Great Tang to present tribute. Tang Gaozu sent Zhu Zishe who came with a decree encouraging [Silla] to establish peaceful relations with Koguryŏ.

Eighth month. Paekche attacked Chujae Fortress. The head of the Tongso Fortress fought dying in battle.[129] Koho Fortress was

---

125 See *SS* 27:5b.

126 The Siwibu oversaw the defense of the palace and the king. The Sangsasŏng was an office in the Ch'angbu (Ministry of Storage). The Taedosŏ was an office in the Ministry of Rites that supervised monks and their practices.

127 Sokham is in Kyŏngnam, Hamyang, as is Aengham. Kijam is believed to be in the Chinju area of Kyŏngnam and Hyŏlch'aek is in Kyŏngnam, Sanch'ong-gun.

128 For Nulch'oe's biography see *SS* 47.

129 See also *SS* 27:6a. *The Paekche Annals, SS,* states that the King was in the fortress,

constructed.[130]

Year forty-nine [627], spring, third month. There were strong winds and it rained dirt for five days.

Summer, sixth month. [The court] sent an envoy to Great Tang to present tribute.

Autumn, seventh month. The Paekche general Sagŏl attacked two fortresses in the western periphery, capturing more than three hundred men and women.[131]

Eighth month. A frost fell destroying grain.

Winter, eleventh month. [The court] sent an envoy to Great Tang to present tribute.

Year fifty [628], spring, second month. Paekche encircled Kajam Fortress.[132] The King dispatched troops to attack and destroyed them.

Summer. There was a great drought. They moved the market and drew a dragon to pray for rain.[133]

Autumn and winter. People, in starvation, sold their children.

Year fifty [629], autumn, eighth month. The King sent *Taejanggun* [Grand Generals] Yongch'un and Sŏhyŏn and *Pujanggun* [Adjutant General] Yusin to attack Koguryŏ's Nangbi Fortress.[134] Koguryŏ troops came out of the fortress lined up in formation and their troops' strength looked truly vitalized. Our troops seeing them were terrorized, losing their heart to fight.

---

but this is believed to be in error.

130 Koho Fortress is believed to be south of Kyŏngju's South Mountain.

131 See also *SS* 27:6a.

132 See *SS* 27:6b.

133 Silla people believed moving the market south from an area that had a strong *ŭm* (female) element to one with *yang* (male) features would cause rain to occur. They also believed dragons could summon rain clouds.

134 Yongch'un is another name for Yongsu. Sŏhyŏn is the eleventh-generation descendant of King Suro of Kŭmgwan Kaya and the father of Kim Yusin. See *SS* 41–3 for the biography of Kim Yusin.

The Silla Annals of the Samguk Sagi

Yusin said, "I have heard, 'if you shake the collar, a fur garment will be straightened. To pull the guide ropes then the net is stretched out.' How can I take this to be my basic principle?" He then jumped on his horse, unsheathed his spear, advancing forward toward the enemy's camp. Going back and forth, each time he beheaded generals and captured their flags. The various armies, riding on victory, beat their drums and marched forth to attack, beheading more than five thousand. The fortress then surrendered.

Ninth month. [The court] sent an envoy to Great Tang to present tribute.

Year fifty-two [630]. In the garden in the main palace a crack opened in the ground.

Year fifty-three [631], spring, second month. A white dog climbed up a palace wall.

Summer, fifth month. *Ich'an* Ch'ilsuk and *Ach'an* Sŏkp'um planned to revolt. When the King became aware of it he captured Ch'ilsuk, beheading him in the eastern market, and banished nine generations of his relatives. *Ach'an* Sŏkp'um ran away but when he reached Paekche's borders, wanting to see his wife and children, he returned to Mount Ch'ongsan, hiding by day and walking by night. Seeing a woodcutter there, he took off his clothes, changing them for the woodcutter's clothes. Dressed [as a woodcutter] and carrying firewood, he secretly reached his house where he was captured and executed.

Autumn, seventh month. [The court] sent an envoy to Great Tang to present two beautiful girls. Wei Zheng believed it was not correct to receive them.[135] The Emperor cheerfully said, "If we

---

135 Wei Zheng was a civil official and scholar during the reign of Tang Daizong. See *Jiu Tangshu* 51 for his biography.

thought about returning to their home country those two parrots presented by Linyi [Annam] that cried about the bitter cold [in China], how much more would these two girls separated so far away from their relatives, think of returning?" Accompanying them with an envoy, he returned them. A white rainbow disappeared into a palace well. Saturn infringed on the moon.

Year fifty-four [632], spring, first month. The King died, his posthumous reign title was Chinp'yŏng and he was buried in Hanji. Tang Daizong, in an edict, posthumously conferred on him the title of *Zuoguang Ludaifu* [Left Master of Supreme Happiness] and a condolence gift of two hundred *tuan* [bolts] of silk. {*Kogi* [The Ancient Record] states that the King died in the first month of the sixth year, *imjin,* of *zhenguan* [*chŏnggwan*]. *Xin Tangshu* and *Zizhi tongjian* both say in *xingmao,* fifth year, of *zhenguan,* Silla's King Chinp'yŏng died. Why this error?}

Queens Sŏndŏk and Chindŏk
and King T'aejong Muyŏl

Book

5

Queen Sŏndŏk

Queen Sŏndŏk was enthroned [632]. Her personal name was Tŏngman and she was the oldest daughter of King Chinp'yŏng.[1] Her mother, Lady Maya, was of the Kim lineage. Tŏngman by nature was generous, humane, and intelligent. When the King died without a son, the people of the country enthroned Tŏkman and gave her the title *Sŏngjo hwanggo*.[2] In the time of the former King, he obtained from China a painting of peonies and some peony seeds which he showed to Tŏngman.[3] Tŏngman said, "although these flowers appear to be very beautiful, they must have no fragrance." The King laughed saying, "How do you know this?" She replied, "The flowers are painted without butterflies, so I know this. Generally if girls are extremely beautiful, boys will follow them. If flowers have fragrance, the bees and butterflies will follow. Accordingly, although these flowers are very beautiful,

---

1   Here the Queen's posthumous reign title is Sŏndŏk but, according to *Tangshu*, this was the Queen's name during her lifetime. The name Tŏngman may well be an example of the Buddhist-style royal name that frequently was used in middle and late Silla. See "Dual Organization" 92. The character *"tŏk"* (virtue) probably conveys the idea of Buddhist charity and the character *"man"* frequently was appended to the names of women. However *SY* 1:25b indicates that *man,* meaning "ten thousand," was an alternate character.

2   This title has been rendered "hallowed royal grandmother" and might well indicate the growing consciousness of a royal family called *sŏnggol*. See Yi Kibaek and Yi Kidong, *Hanguksa kangchwa* 1 (1982), 186.

3   According to *SY* 1:25b, the Tang emperor Taizong sent the picture and seeds. The flowers were red, white, and purple. The peony was considered Tang's state flower and a cherished symbol.

in designing the painting without bees or butterflies, they must be flowers without fragrance." In planting the flower seeds, it was ultimately as she had said. Her prescience was like this.

Year one [632], second month. *Taesin* [Great Minister] Ŭlche oversaw the administration of government affairs.

Summer, fifth month. There was a drought but, coming to the sixth month, it rained.[4]

Winter, tenth month. [The court] sent officials to inquire into the conditions of the widows, widowers, orphaned, and the old without children in the country who could not support themselves and aided them.

Twelfth month. [The court] sent an envoy to Great Tang to present tribute.

Year two [633], spring, first month. [The Queen] personally held sacrifices in the Singung Shrine, proclaimed a general amnesty, and exempted taxes for the various *chu* and *kun* for one year.

Second month. There was an earthquake in the capital.

Autumn, seventh month. [The court] sent an envoy to Great Tang to present tribute.

Eighth month. Paekche invaded the western region.[5]

Year three [634], spring, first month. The reign year was changed to Inp'yŏng and Punhwang Monastery was completed.

Third month. Hail fell as big as chestnuts.

Year four [635]. Tang sent an envoy to carry a *tujŏl* [confidential medallion of identification] investing the Queen as Pillar of State, Lady of Nangnang, Queen of Silla, to have her

---

4   According to *The Paekche Annals, SS* 27:7a, Paekche fought Silla at this time.
5   According to *AKS* 3:141, n. 9, this is the area around Kyŏngnam, Koryŏng. See also *SS* 27:7a.

succeed her father's investiture.[6] Yŏngmyo Monastery was completed.[7]

Winter, tenth month. [The court] sent Ich'an Sup'um and Yongsu {another source says Yongch'un} to tour and look into [the condition of] the chu and hyŏn.

Year five [636], spring, first month. [The Queen] appointed Ich'an Sup'um to be extraordinary rank one.

Third month. As the Queen was ill, medicine and prayers were given but to no avail.[8] At Hwangnyong Monastery [the court] held a Hundred-Seat Assembly, assembled monks to lecture on the Sutra for Humane Kings, and ordained one hundred monks.

Summer, fifth month. Frogs gathered in a great number west of the palace at Jade Gate Pond.[9] The Queen, hearing this, called her attendants, saying, "The bull frogs have anger in their eyes looking like that of soldiers. I once heard in the southwestern region there was a place called 'Jade Gate Valley.'[10] Have perhaps some neighboring country's troops secretly infiltrated there?" She commanded General Alch'ŏn and P'ilt'an to lead troops to go and search for them.[11] As expected, Paekche General Uso, wishing to lead a raid on Mount Toksan Fortress, led five hundred armed troops who came hiding there. Alch'ŏn made a surprise attack

---

6   According to the Silla section of *Tangshu,* the Queen was invested *kun wang* and not *kun kong. Kun wang* was the highest rank, 1a, while *kun kong* was the next lower rank, 1b. See also *AKS* 3:142, n. 12.

7   An important Buddhist monastery located in Kyŏngju, it was the site of royal services. See also *SY* 4:20b.

8   The exorcist Milbon helped cure the Queen. See *SY* 5:1a.

9   See also *SY* 1:25b–26a for a somewhat similar account.

10 *SS* 27:7b–8a notes a Paekche invasion into this area, which was probably in the Sŏngju-Hapch'ŏn region of western Kyŏngsang. "Jade Gate Valley" conveys the idea of the female vagina. See Kim T'aesik, "Paekche ŭi Kaya chiyŏk kwangyesa," *Paekche ŭi chungang kwa chibang,* Taejŏn: Ch'ungnam University, 1997, 75–82.

11 As the section "Pilt'an to lead troops to go and search for them" is missing from the original *SS,* this passage was completed based on the entry in *SY* 1:26a.

killing them all.[12] Dharma Master Chajang went to Tang seeking the dharma.[13]

Year six [637], spring, first month. *Ich'an* Sajin became *sŏburhan*.

Autumn, seventh month. Alch'ŏn became grand general.

Year seven [638], spring, third month. South of Ch'ilchung Fortress there was a boulder that moved 35 *po* on its own.[14]

Autumn, ninth month. Yellow flowers fell like rain.[15]

Tenth month. Koguryŏ attacked Ch'ilchung Fortress in the northern region. The people, alarmed and agitated, fled into the mountain valleys. The Queen ordered Grand General Alch'ŏn to assemble the people and reassure them.

Eleventh month. Alch'ŏn fought with Koguryŏ troops outside Ch'ilchung Fortress, overcoming them [Koguryŏ]. He killed or captured very many.

Year eight [639], spring, second month. Hasŭlla-ju was made the northern minor capital and *Sach'an* Chinju was ordered to defend it.

Autumn, seventh month. The water in the Eastern Sea was red and turned warmer, killing fish and turtles.

Year nine [640], summer, fifth month. The Queen sent sons to

---

12 In *SS* 27:8a the text reports that Uso resisted but was captured. The location of Mount Toksan Fortress was probably in the Kumi area of Kyŏngbuk, although there were several fortresses with this name. See *AKS* 3:144, n. 20.

13 Chajang was one of Silla's eminent monks. His biography appears in *SY* 4:13a–16a. This has been translated into English in Lee, Peter H., ed., *Sourcebook of Korean Civilization* (hereafter *"Sourcebook"*), New York: Columbia University Press, 1993, 1:83–7.

14 This fortress sat on strategic ground just south of the Imjin River that alternately was controlled by Silla and Koguryŏ. See *AKS* 3:146, n. 30.

15 The meaning of this entry is unclear unless it refers to falling leaves or heavy yellow dust.

Tang requesting they enter Guoxue [the National University].[16] At this time [Tang] Taizong widely gathered the world-renowned Confucian scholars, making them teach there. Frequently he visited Guozijian [the Imperial College] and had them lecture.[17] Among the students who were versed in more than one of the great classics,[18] many were made eligible for government posts. Since Taizong increased the size of the school to twelve hundred *kan* [bays] and the number of students to 3,260, those who wanted to study there gathered like clouds in the capital [Changan]. Koguryŏ, Paekche, Gaochang [Koch'ang], and Turfan [T'obŏn][19] also sent sons to study there.

Year eleven [642], spring, first month. [The court] sent an envoy to Great Tang to present local products.

Autumn, seventh month. Paekche's King Ŭija mobilized a great number of troops and attacked, taking some forty fortresses in the western part of the country.[20]

Eighth month. Paekche also plotted with Koguryŏ to take Tanghang Fortress[21] to cut the route back to Tang. The Queen sent an envoy to inform Taizong of this urgency. In this month the Pakeche General Yunch'ung, leading troops, attacked and destroyed Taeya Fortress.[22] *Todok* [Commander-in-Chief] *Ich'an* P'umsŏk, *Saji* Chukchuk,[23] and Yongsŏk and others died in battle.

---

16   An identical passage is found in *Zizhi tongjian* 195.

17   *AKS* 3:146, n. 29, suggests that the government school and the Imperial College may be the same thing.

18   The great classics include *Liji (Book of Rites), Analects,* and *Spring and Autumn Annals.*

19   Gaochang and Tur fan were two states in western China. Gaochang was in Xinjiang and Tufan was in Sichuan. See *AKS* 3:147, n. 32–3.

20   See also *SS* 28:1b.

21   This is in Kyŏnggi, Hwasŏng.

22   See also *SS* 28:1b. Taeya was in Kyŏngnam, Hapch'ŏn.

23   *Saji* is also called a *sosa*, a Silla rank. See Chukchuk's biography in *SS* 47:12b–13b.

Winter. The Queen was going to attack Paekche in retaliation for the battle at Taeya Fortress. She sent *Ich'an* Kim Ch'unch'u to Koguryŏ to request troops. Earlier when Taeya was defeated, Commander-in-Chief P'umsŏk's wife died there. She was Ch'unch'u's daughter. When Ch'unch'u heard this he leaned against a pillar and stood all day long without blinking his eyes and not even noticing if people and things passed in front of him. After some time passed, he uttered, "Alas, being a man as I am, how can I not avenge Paekche?" Immediately in an audience with the Queen he said, "I wish to support an envoy to Koguryŏ to request troops and avenge my hatred for Paekche." The Queen approved this.

Koguryŏ's King Kojang [P'ojang], having already heard of Ch'unch'u's fame, met him and afterward had his troops guard [Ch'unch'u] closely. Ch'unch'u said to the King, "Now Paekche has lost its senses and has become like a long snake or a big pig [that covets everything] and invaded our territory. My Queen wants to borrow the troops and horses of your great country to [help] wash away our shame. Thus she sent me your subject to convey her order to Your Majesty." The Koguryŏ king replied, "Chungnyŏng Pass was originally in our territory. If you return the land northwest of Chungnyŏng to us, we will send our troops."[24] Ch'unch'u replied, "I came to uphold my Queen's order to request troops. Your Majesty has no intention to aid your neighbor in this difficulty but only with threats demand the return of land. Even if I will die, I do not know about anything else [other than my Queen's order]." Angry with [Ch'unch'u's] disrespect, he imprisoned him in an annex. Ch'unch'u secretly had a man report

---

P'umsŏk, of the Kim lineage, was Kim Ch'unch'u's son-in-law.

24 See also Kim Yusin's biography, *SS* 40–2, for further elaboration.

this to his Queen. The Queen ordered Grand General Kim Yusin to lead a death squad of 10,000 to go there. Yusin led the troops across the Han River entering into Koguryŏ's southern border. When the Koguryŏ King learned of this, he released Ch'unch'u to return home. Yusin became military governor of Amnyang-ju.

Year twelve [643], spring, first month. [The court] sent an envoy to Great Tang to present local products.

Third month. The eminent monk Chajang, who went to Tang in search of the dharma, returned.

Autumn, ninth month. [The court] sent an envoy to the Great Tang Emperor who presented the following: "Koguryŏ and Paekche have on several occasions invaded our country, attacking several tens of our fortresses. The two countries in alliance wish to take from us. Now in this ninth month they are about to greatly mobilize, and under these circumstances [my] country will certainly not be able to survive. So my country has earnestly sent me to request [aid] from your country. I beg of you to send a few troops to assist us."[25] The Emperor told the envoy, "I truly pity your country being invaded by those two countries and I sent envoys a number of times to bring peace among your three states. However Paekche and Koguryŏ, as soon as the envoys returned, changed their mind and plotted to divide and swallow your territory. What ingenious strategy does your country want to use to avoid this peril of destruction?" The envoy said, "My Queen, having exhausted all our options, only wants to report this urgency to your country, hoping the best for our country's survival." The Emperor said, "If we sparingly dispatch our frontier troops, accompanied by the Khitan and Malgal, directly to Liaodong, your country by itself will be relieved from the

---

25 See *Cefu yuangui* 991, Zhenguan, seventeenth year, ninth month.

encirclement for about one year. After this, if the enemy becomes aware of no more troops being deployed, they will return and invade at will causing turmoil to all four countries and leaving your country too with no peace. This is the first option. I am also able to provide you with several thousand pieces of red clothes and red banners. As the two armies [of Paekche and Koguryŏ] arrive, we can set up and display them. When they see this, they will think they are our troops and will certainly all scatter in disarray. This is the second option. The country of Paekche, trusting the turbulence of the ocean, neglects military preparations. Men and women in complete disregard of social mores enjoy themselves holding endless banquets. I can deploy several tens of hundreds of ships loaded with armed soldiers, silently cross the sea, and directly attack that country. But because your country has a woman as a ruler, neighboring states belittle it. As you have lost the authority of the ruler, thus inviting the enemy to attack, no year will enjoy peace. I want to send one of my royal relatives to be with the ruler of your country but as this ruler cannot do the job alone, I will need to send troops to guard. I will wait for your country to become peaceful and then transfer it to you to govern. This is the third option. You should fittingly deliberate on these and [decide] which one in the future to follow." The envoy merely made an acknowledgement without replying. The Emperor lamented, thinking "these rustic simpletons can do no more than request troops and report emergencies."

Year thirteen [644], spring, first month. [The court] sent an envoy to Great Tang to present local products. [Tang] Taizong sent *Sinungcheng* [Aide to the Court of National Granaries] Xiangli Xuanzhuang to carry an imperial letter addressed to Koguryŏ stating, "Silla has entrusted its fate to my country. Its tribute is never wanting. You and Paekche had better immediately cease hostilities. If you attack again next year, I will be forced to dispatch troops to attack your country." [Yŏn] Kaesomun spoke to Xuanzhuang saying, "Koguryŏ and Silla have had a split for a long time. In the past when Sui made repeated invasions, Silla took advantage of this conflict to grab 500 *li* of Koguryŏ territory and occupied all of the fortresses and towns there. If they do not return these fortresses and land, I fear this war we will never be able to end." Xuanzhuang replied, "Do you need to dig up things from the past?" Somun in the end did not comply.

Autumn, ninth month. The Queen, appointing [Kim] Yusin to be grand general, ordered him to lead troops to attack Paekche. [Silla] greatly defeated them and took seven fortresses.

Year fourteen [645], spring, first month. [The court] sent an envoy to Great Tang to present local products. [Kim] Yusin, returning after subduing Paekche, did not even have time to see the Queen because a major Paekche force came again and attacked the [border] regions. The Queen ordered him to resist them and so, without reaching his home, he went out to attack and defeat them, beheading 2,000. Upon returning home he reported [his victory] to the Queen but again, before he even reached his home, there was an urgent notification that Paekche had again invaded the territory. The Queen, considering the urgency of the situation, said, "The country's survival depends upon you. Please, without shrinking from your task, go out and plan." Yusin, again without returning to his home, trained his troops day and night. Marching on the road westward, as he passed by the gate of his house, everyone in the house looked at him and shed tears, but Lord Yusin went on without looking back.[26]

---

26 The biography of Kim Yusin in *SS* 41 offers a slightly different narrative, stating that Kim Yusin, after going 50 *po* beyond his house, asked for water from his house. On drinking it he confided that the water from his house still had its old

Third month. The pagoda at Hwangnyong Monastery was built following Chajang's request.

Summer, fifth month. As [Tang] Taizong personally led an expedition against Koguryŏ, the Queen sent out thirty thousand troops to help. [Meanwhile] Paekche, taking advantage of the power vacuum, raided seven fortresses in the western part of the country.

Winter, eleventh month. *Ich'an* Pidam became extraordinary rank one.

Year sixteen [647], spring, first month. Pidam and Yŏmjong, believing a Queen is not fit to govern well, plotted a rebellion and raised troops, but could not succeed.[27] On the eighth day the Queen died.[28] Her posthumous reign title was Sŏndŏk and she was buried at Nangsan. {*Tangshu* states she died in the twenty-first year of *zhengguan* [647]. *Zizhi Tongjian* states it was the twenty-fifth year. According to this history [SS], *Tongjian* is wrong}.[29]

| Commentary | As I understand, in ancient times there was Lady Nüwa[30] who assisted Fuxi in administering the nine districts, but she was not the son of heaven. Coming to Empress Lu[31] and Wu Zhao,[32] they assisted young and inexperienced

---

flavor.

27 This revolt witnessed a clash between the power of the central aristocrats in the Hwabaek Council who sided with Pidam and the supporters of stronger royal authority who sided with the monarch. See *Kolp'um* 83-4.

28 *AKS* 3:156, n. 81, speculates that, because of Pidam's revolt, the Queen might actually have abdicated.

29 See *Tangshu* 220, Silla section, *zhengguan* 21, and *Zizhi tongjian* 198, *Taizong zhengguan* 22.

30 She is a legendary sister of Fuxi who was one of the three early legendary rulers of China. There is debate as to whether she is one of the three legendary emperors. She is depicted as having the body of a snake and the head of a human. Fuxi is credited with teaching the arts of hunting and fishing, domesticating animals, and instituting family life.

31 The wife of Han Emperor Gaozu

rulers, and made decisions as if they were emperors. The histories did not officially label them as rulers but only called them "High Empress Dowager" Lady Lu and "Heavenly Empress Dowager" Lady Wu. According to the laws of heaven, *yang* is firm and *yin* is gentle and according to the laws of man, man is honorable and woman is demeaning. How can one permit an old woman to leave the woman's quarters and determine the governmental affairs of the state? Silla, helping a woman to rise to occupy the royal throne, is a product of an age of unrest. It is fortunate that the state did not collapse. There is a phrase in *Shiji* (*Records of the Historians*), "The hen does not announce the morning"[33] and in *Yijing* (*The Book of Changes*) there is the phrase, "An emaciated sow still seeks to romp around."[34] How can this not be a warning?

Queen Chindŏk

Queen Chindŏk was enthroned [in 647]. Her personal name was Sŭngman and she was the daughter of *Kalmunwang* Kukpan {another source says Kukpun}[35] who was the younger brother by the same mother of King Chinp'yŏng. Her mother was Lady

---

32　Tang Empress Wu Zhao was a concubine of Taizong and wife of Gaozong.

33　The full quote is, "The hen does not announce the morning. The crowing of a hen in the morning indicates the subversion of the family." See *Shijing,* part 5, book 2, verse 5.

34　See *Yijing,* hexagram 44. See Richard Wilhelm translation *The Iching or Book of Change* Princeton: Princeton University Press, 1977, 172.

35　The character *chin* comes from Buddhist texts as well as the name Sŭngman. The use of Buddhist names by monarchs ends here. During her reign Silla starts to use extensively Chinese practices. As she was the last ruler of Hallowed Bone (Sŏngol) status, *SY* states her reign marks the end of Silla's "ancient period."

Wŏlmyŏng of the Pak lineage. Sŭngman's appearance was portly and beautiful. She was 7 *ch'ŏk* tall and her hands went past her knees.

Year one [647], first month, seventeenth day. Pidam was executed along with thirty people connected with him.

Second month. *Ich'an* Alch'ŏn became extraordinary rank one and *Taeach'an* Susŭng became the Udu-ju[36] military governor. Tang Taizong sent an envoy carrying a confidential medallion of identification conferring posthumously the former Queen as *Guanglu Daifu* [Grand Mistress for Splendid Happiness] and invested the Queen as Pillar of State, enfeofing her *Chun* [Queen] of Nangnang-gun.[37]

Autumn, seventh month. [The court] sent an envoy to Tang to express gratitude and changed the reign year to T'aehwa [Great Peace].[38]

Eighth month. A comet came out of the southern sky and many stars moved north.[39]

Winter, eleventh month. Paekche troops encircled three fortresses—Mount Musan, Kammul, and Tongjam.[40] The Queen sent [Kim] Yusin, who led ten thousand foot soldiers and horsemen, to resist them. They fought an uphill battle and were nearly exhausted when Yusin's subordinate Pinyŏngja and Pinyŏngja's son Kŏjin charged the enemy camp and fought to

---

36 This is in Kangwŏn Ch'unch'ŏn.
37 As seen earlier, Nangnang [Lelang]-gun was a Chinese administrative unit in northern Korea that disappeared in the early fourth century.
38 This covered the years 647 to 650. This is the last Silla reign title as Silla subsequently adopted Chinese reign titles. *SY* and the Kim Yusin biography in *SS* both state this starts one year later in 648.
39 Although *AKS* is silent, the Yi Pyŏngdo edition notes that the next sixteen characters are unclear.
40 These fortresses are located in Chŏnbuk, Muju; Kyŏngbuk, Kŭmnyŭng; and Kyŏngbuk, Kumi; respectively. See also *SS* 28:2a–b.

death,[41] [thereupon] boosting the morale of all [the soldiers] who attacked, beheading more than 3,000.

Eleventh month. The Queen personally held sacrifices at the Singung Shrine.[42]

Year two [648], spring, first month. [The court] sent an envoy to Great Tang to present tribute.

Third month. Paekche's General Ŭijik invaded the western frontier and defeated Yogŏ and more than ten fortresses. The Queen, disturbed by this, commanded Aptok-chu Commander-in Chief [Kim] Yusin to plan [to counter] this. Yusin thereupon urging and instructing his troops, was preparing to dispatch his troops when Ŭijik counter-attacked him. Yusin divided his army along three routes and attacked from different sides. When the Paekche troops fled in defeat, Yusin pursued them north killing nearly all.[43] The Queen was pleased and rewarded the soldiers by rank.

Winter. [The court] sent the tribute envoy Han Chirhŏ to the Tang court. [Tang] Taizong ordered a censor to ask, "As Silla treats China [as a tributary sovereign], how can they use a different reign year?" [Han] Chirhŏ said, "From a long time ago the Heavenly Court [China] never provided us with a calendar, thereupon since our former King Pŏphŭng, we have used our own reign years. If Your Majesty's court commanded us, how would our small country dare do otherwise?" Taizong acknowledged this. [The court] sent *Ich'an* Kim Ch'unch'u and his son Munwang[44] to the Tang court. Taizong sent *Guangluqing* [Chief

---

41 See biography in *SS* 47:11b–12a.

42 According to *Nihon shoki* 25, "Hyodokki," Kim Ch'unch'u visited Japan as an envoy at this time. Korean texts make no mention of such a visit.

43 These events are briefly recorded in *SS* 28:2b. See also Kim Yusin's biography.

44 This is Kim Ch'unch'u's third son who is also known by the name Munjŏng. See

Minister for Splendid Happiness] Liu Xing to the suburbs to welcome. Reaching the palace and seeing Ch'unch'u's appearance was truly exceptional, he generously received him. Ch'unch'u requested to visit *Guoxie* [the National University] to observe the ceremony honoring Confucius and hear the lectures. Taizong permitted this and then presented his personally composed *Wentang* [*Ont'ang*] inscription,[45] the *Jinci* [*Jinsa*] inscription[46] which he wrote, and the newly completed *Jinshu (History of Jin)*.

On the day he was summoned to a banquet, [Taizong] presented very generously gold and silk and asked, "Do you have anything on your mind?" Ch'unch'u bowing down said, "My country is situated in a far corner of the sea but has served Your Majesty's court successively for many years. Paekche being strong and cunning has several times invaded and moreover last year penetrated deep [into our country], attacking and taking ten or twenty fortresses and blocking our passage to your court. If Your Majesty cannot lend your imperial troops to exterminate this evil, then the people of my country will become completely imprisoned, and we can never again hope to cross the sea to present tribute." Taizong in profound agreement permitted the dispatch of troops. Ch'unch'u also requested to change [Silla's] ceremonial gowns to follow China's system. Thereupon the court sent out rare clothing and presented it to Ch'unch'u and his attendants and decreed that Ch'unch'u hold the rank of *Tejin* and Munwang the rank of *Zuowuwei jiangjun* [General of the Left

---

Jiu Tangshu 199.

45 See *AKS* 3:159, n. 97. This is a piece the Emperor wrote when he went hunting and returned to an area his father had visited.

46 Taizong wrote this at a shrine in Shanxi where Emperor Gaozu had held services. See *AKS* 3:159, n. 99.

Militant Guard].[47] When he [Ch'unch'u] was to return home, the [Emperor] summoned officials of the third rank and above and held a banquet for them. His treatment and courtesy [toward them] was very complete. Ch'unch'u humbly spoke, "I have seven sons[48] and wish that Your Majesty would have them as *suwei* [imperial resident guards] at your side."[49] [Taizong] then commanded his son Munwang [different character] and Taegam [] [][][50] to stay [as guards]. When Ch'unch'u was returning, he met on the sea a Koguryŏ patrol. Ch'unch'u's attendant, On Kunhae, donning a high ceremonial cap and the clothes of a high official, sat on top of the ship. The patrol, seeing him, thought he was Ch'unch'u and captured and killed him. Ch'unch'u rode a small ship, reaching Silla. When the Queen heard this she sighed in pain and posthumously named [On] Kunhae to be *taeach'an* and generously rewarded his grandchildren.

Year three [649], spring, first month. [The court] started to wear Chinese-style robes and caps.[51]

Autumn, eighth month. Paekche general Ŭnsang led many troops coming to attack to take Sŏkt'o and seven fortresses.[52] The Queen commanded Grand General [Kim] Yusin and generals Chinch'un, Chukchi, Ch'ŏnjon, and others to go out and resist

---

47 *"Tejin"* was a two-b rank in the civil bureaucracy and *"Zuowuwei jiangjun"* was a three-a rank in the military hierarchy. This same information is also found on the tomb inscription for Kim Inmun.

48 *SY* 1:30a states he had nine sons in all.

49 By serving as imperial resident guards, he in effect was sending his sons there to serve as "hostages" to show his support for Tang. See Sin Hyŏngsik "Silla ŭi tae Tang kyosŏpsange nat'anan sukwi e taehan ilgoch'al." *Yŏksa kyoyuk* 9 (October 1966).

50 [][][] denotes missing characters.

51 See also garb section below. The use of Chinese garb by the officialdom began in 520, Pŏphŭng's seventh year.

52 See also *SS* 28:2b.

them. Back and forth they fought for ten days without resolution. They went and camped under Tosal Fortress. Yusin spoke to all saying, "Paekche people will certainly come today to spy on us. Pretend you do not know anything and do not ask any questions." He then had people move among the soldiers saying, "Guard your positions firmly and do not move. We are waiting for tomorrow when relief troops will arrive and then we can engage in a decisive battle." When the spies heard this, they returned and reported it to Ŭnsang. [Ŭn]sang and others, thinking there would be an increase in troops, could not but have doubt and fear. Thereupon Yusin and others advanced to attack and soundly defeated them, killing and capturing a hundred officers and beheading 8,980 soldiers. They captured 10,000 battle horses and the number of captured items like weapons could not be counted.

Year four [650], summer, fourth month. [The Queen] decreed that *chingol* [true bone] officials in government positions[53] should carry a staff of office.

Sixth month. [The court] sent an envoy to Great T'ang to report the destruction of the Paekche forces. The Queen weaved on silk and composed a five-rhyme verse "T'aep'yŏngsong [Song of Great Peace]" and sent Ch'unch'u's son Pŏmmin[54] to present it to the Tang Emperor. The verse is as follows:

As Great Tang commences a new imperial rule, the Emperor's lofty ambition shines forth,
As war ended, peace prevailed throughout the world[55]
Cultivating the virtue of the former kings.

---

53 This is the second highest rank in the *kolp'um* system. See *AKS* 3:162, n. 113.

54 Pŏmmin is the future King Munmu who will complete Silla's unification after he comes to the throne in 661.

55 See *AKS* 3:163, n. 117. Many of these expressions here and below come from classical Chinese sources such as *Shangshu*.

As he reveres Heaven, the four seasons are orderly.

In managing all things, everything sparkles.

His endless benevolence is in company with the sun and the moon.

Cherishing the propitiousness of the time, [the world] moves toward peace.

How glittering are the flags! How vibrant are the marching bands!

Those outlying barbarians who disobey his orders will be punished by Heaven, falling down on the blades of swords.

With good customs spreading all over

From near and far, happy auguries have competingly appeared.

The four seasons are orderly and splendid like a jade flame[56]

The Seven Luminaries revolve throughout the universe[57]

Only sacred mountains produce able ministers,[58]

While the Emperor employs loyal and honest [subjects].

Just as the Five Emperors and Three Sovereigns accomplished complete virtue[59]

So may our Tang Dynasty forever be splendid.

Gaozong, in commending him, appointed Pŏmmin to be *Daifuqing* [Chamberlain for the Palace Revenues] and he returned. This year the court started to use the Chinese reign-year Yinghui.

| Commentary | The three dynasties [of Xia, Shang, and

---

56 Despite their differences, the four seasons are in harmony, splendid like a jade flame.

57 These are the sun and moon and five bright planets.

58 The appearance of talented and benevolent subjects generation after generation is because of the spirits of the sacred mountains.

59 The Five Emperors include the legendary Huangdi, Yao, and Shun, and the Three Sovereigns were Fuxi, Shennung, and Huangdi. See Charles O. Hucker, *China's Imperial Past,* Stanford: Stanford University Press, 1975, 22–3.

Zhou] changed the first day of the [lunar] new year and later generations gave reign titles because all considered this standardization [unification] a great event that would renew everything the people saw and heard [experienced]. If [a country] were not taking advantage of the time and rising side by side to compete for control of the world, or if a cunning man were not taking advantage of feuds to covet the imperial throne, then a small country in the periphery, being an imperial subject, truly cannot honestly use illegitimate reign titles. That Silla single-mindedly supports China and sends envoys overseas in ships loaded with tribute gifts, going one after another in succession, using its own year titles from the reign of [King] Pŏphŭng is indeed incomprehensible. Still many years would pass continuing this mistake which they had inherited. There was much hesitation even after Tang Taizong's reproach. Silla then accepted and started to use Tang reign titles. Although there is little that could have been done, they were able to change this mistake that they continued.

Year five [651], spring, first day of the first month. The Queen went to Chowŏn Hall to receive New Year's greetings from the officialdom. The ritual of New Year's greetings begins here.[60]

Second month. The court changed the name of *P'umju* to *Chipsabu* [Chancellery Office] and appointed *P'ajinch'an* Chukchi to be *Chungsi* [Chief Minister] of the Chancellery Office and made him in charge of important security matters[61] [][][] [The court]

---

60 This tradition first appeared in Chinese courts as early as the second century BCE at the start of the Former Han dynasty.

61 *Chipsabu* was the highest administrative office headed by the *Chungsi*. The *Chungsi* was in charge of important governmental affairs and assisted the king. He was an important official in strengthening royal authority. See Yi Kibaek, "Silla chipsabu ŭi sŏngnip," *Silla chŏngch'i sahoe sa yŏngu*. The *P'umju* initially served as a personal council to the king, concerning itself with finances. But in 584, when tax matters were transferred to the Office of Taxation, the *P'umju* continued to handle expenses. See *SS* 38 and Yi Kibaek, "P'umjugo," in *Silla chŏngch'i sahoe sa*

sent *P'ajinch'an* Kim Inmun to Tang to present tribute and then to stay as an imperial guard.[62]

Year six [652], spring, first month. *P'ajinch'an* Ch'ŏnhyo became *chwari pangburyŏng* [Senior Minister of the Ministry of Law].[63] [The court] sent an envoy to Great Tang to present tribute.

Third month, in the capital there was a heavy snow. The south gate of the palace collapsed for no apparent reason.

Year seven [653], winter, tenth month. [The court] sent an envoy to Tang to present *kŭmch'ong* cloth.

Year eight [654], spring, third month. The Queen died. Her posthumous title was Chindŏk. She was buried in Saryang-bu [district]. When Tang Gaozong heard this he held mourning at Yingguang Gate and had *Taichangcheng* [Aide for Ceremonies] Zhang Wensu as commissioner to offer condolences and confer on her posthumously the title *Gaifu yidong sansi* [Commander Unequalled in Honor][64] together with three hundred bolts of silk. People of Silla referred to the twenty-eight rulers from Silla's founder [Pak] Hyŏkkŏse to Chindŏk as *Sŏnggol* [Hallowed-Bone]. From [King] Muyŏl to the last King they are called *Chingol* [True-Bone].[65] Linghu Cheng of Tang, in *Xinluoji* (*Records of Silla*), states, "The royal lineage of this country is called the first bone and the other aristocrats are the second bone."[66]

---

yŏngu.

62 The second son of Ch'unch'u, he accompanied Tang troops in the subjugation of Paekche and then fought with Silla soldiers against Koguryŏ. He died in 694 in the Tang capital of Changan. See his biography in *SS* 44:5a–8a.

63 This was an office in the central government that oversaw the penal code.

64 This was rank 1b in the Tang civil system. She was the first of many Silla monarchs to receive this enfeofment. Koguryŏ monarchs received a similar rank from Sui.

65 The change from *sŏnggol* to *chingol* and its significance has been noted by many. See, for exanaple Yi Kidong, *Kolp'um;* Yi Chonguk; and *Hanguk kodae.*

66 *Xin Tangshu* 220, relying heavily on *Xinluoji,* has a more detailed account.

King T'aejong Muyŏl

King T'aejong Muyŏl was enthroned [654]. His personal name was Ch'unch'u and he was the son of *Ich'an* Yongch'un {another source says Yongsu}, the son of King Chinji. {The *Tangshu*, in error, says he was the younger brother of Queen Chindŏk.} His mother was Lady Ch'ŏnmyŏng, the daughter of King Chinp'yŏng. His consort was Lady Munmyŏng, the daughter of *Kakch'an* Sŏhyŏn.[67]

Being in appearance exceptional and great,[68] the King from an early age had the ambition to rule the world. [Advancing] successively under [Queen] Chindŏk, his rank reached the position of *ich'an*. The Tang Emperor conferred on him [giving him] the title of *chijin*. When [Queen] Chindŏk died, the officialdom requested that *Ich'an* Alch'ŏn be the regent. Alch'ŏn firmly declined, saying, "I am old and without any virtue of note. Now [in terms of] high moral repute and prudence, there is no one as good as Lord Ch'unch'u. He in fact is an exceedingly well-fit person to rule the country." Thereupon when they supported him to be king, [Kim] Ch'unch'u declined three times but then ascended to the throne.[69]

Year one [654], summer, fourth month. [The King] posthumously invested his father as Great King Munhŭng and his mother as Queen Dowager Munjŏng. There was a general amnesty.

Fifth month. [The King] commanded Yangsu to be Minister of

---

67 She was the second sister of Kim Yusin.
68 According to *SY* 1:30a–b, he ate three bushels of rice and nine pheasants a day. *Nihon shoki,* Taika, third year, describes him as having a handsome face and being a good conversationalist.
69 See *SS* 42 for additional discussion of Kim Yusin's role in this action.

the Ministry of Law to examine and discuss the law code and revise the more than sixty statutes of administrative law in the Ministry of Law. Tang sent a commissioner with special powers carrying a warrant to invest the King as Commander Unequalled in Honor, King of Silla. The King sent an envoy to Tang to express his thanks.

Year two [655], spring, first month. *Ich'an* Kŭmgang became extraordinary rank one. *P'ajinch'an* Munch'ung became Chancellor. Koguryŏ, with Paekche and the Malgal, joined troops to invade our northern border region and captured thirty-three fortresses. The King sent an envoy to Tang to seek assistance.

Third month. Tang sent *Yingzhou dudu* [Commander in Chief] Cheng Mingzhen and *Zuoyouwei zhonglangjiang* [Left and Right Guard Commandant] Su Dingfang to deploy troops to attack Koguryŏ. [The King] installed his oldest son Pŏmmin to be Crown Prince and his second son Munwang to be *ich'an*. Noch'a became *haech'an*, Int'ae became *kakch'an*, and Chigyŏng and Kaewŏn each became *ich'an*.[70]

Winter, tenth month, Usu-ju presented a white deer, Kulbul-gun presented a white hog that had one head, two bodies, and eight feet.[71] The King's daughter Chijo married *Taekakch'an* [Kim] Yusin.[72] The court built a drum tower inside Wŏlsŏng.

Year three [656]. Kim Inmun, returning from Tang, was named military governor and oversaw the construction of Mount Changsan Fortress.[73]

---

70 These are all sons of the King.

71 Usu-ju is in Kangwŏn, Ch'unch'ŏn and Kulbul-gun is in Kyŏngbuk, Andong.

72 The character for *"Chijo"* is different when she appears in *SS* 43. Because Kim Yusin was sixty-one at this time, it is likely that this entry has been misplaced here.

73 According to *SS* 44:5a–8a, this event occurred two to three years earlier. He was rewarded with a *sigŭp* of three hundred households. Mount Chang is in Kyŏngbuk,

Autumn, seventh month. [The King] sent his son Munwang, General of the Umuwi [Right Militant Guards], to Tang to attend the court.

Year four [657], autumn, seventh month. Ilsŏn-gun had a flood and over three hundred people drowned. Land on the eastern side of Mount T'oham burned lasting for three years and then going out.[74] The gate of Hŭngnyun Monastery collapsed by itself. A rock north of [][][] fell, smashing into small bits like rice. It tasted like stale granary rice.

Year five [658], spring, first month. Chief Minister Munch'ung again became *ich'an*. Munwang became chief minister.

Third month. Because the land at Hasŭlla [Kangnŭng] was adjacent to Malgal [land], the people could not [enjoy] peace. Because of this [the King] lowered it from a [minor] capital to a *chu* and established a commander-in-chief to guard it and also made Silchik to be *Pukchin* [north garrison].[75]

Year six [659], summer, fourth month. As Paekche frequently intruded on our borders,[76] the King was going to attack them and sent an envoy to Tang to seek troops.

Autumn, eighth month. *Ach'an* Chinju became Minister of Military Affairs.

Ninth month. Hasŭlla presented a white bird. In the middle of the Kigun River in Kongju a large fish, 100 *ch'ŏk* in length, appeared dead. Those who ate it died.

Winter, tenth month. While the King was holding court, his face showed concern because his request for troops from [Tang] received no reply. Suddenly there were men who came before the

Kyŏngsan.

74 This probably refers to volcanic activity.

75 Silchik is Kangwŏn Samch'ŏk.

76 See *SS* 28:5a.

King who looked like the deceased officials Changch'un and P'arang.[77] They said, "Although we are [only] dead skeletons, we still carry a desire to help our country. Yesterday we went to Great Tang and came to know that the Emperor has commanded Grand General Su Dingfang and others to lead troops next year in the fifth month to come to attack Paekche. We have made this report to you because Your Majesty has been anxiously waiting for this reply." Having spoken they disappeared. The King was very surprised and felt it was strange. He richly rewarded the descendants of these two families and ordered the offices concerned to construct Changŭi Monastery in Hansan-ju to pray for their repose.[78]

Year seven [660], spring, first month. Extraordinary Rank One Kŭmgang died. *Ich'an* Kim Yusin became extraordinary rank one.

Third month. [Tang] Gaozong commanded *Zouyouwei dajiangzhun* [Left and Right Guard Grand General] Su Dingfang to be *Shenqiudao dazongguan* [Adjutant Grand Commandant], Kim Inmun to be assistant adjutant grand commander, and *Zuoxiaowei jiangzhun* [General of the Left Courageous Guard] Liu Boying and others to lead a land and sea force of 130,000 soldiers and sailors [][][] to subdue Paekche.[79] He also commanded the King to be Adjutant Grand Commander of Uido {Chinese: Yuyi} and to lead troops to reinforce [][][].[80]

---

77 These were deceased officials who had died fighting Paekche. *SY* 1:37a provides a slightly different account of this incident.

78 This monastery no longer exists, although at one time it was situated in the area north of modern Hyojadong in central Seoul.

79 Characters are missing in the text. However AKS editors, as well as Yi Pyongdo, have offered the reconstruction as it appears here. *SS,* in other sections, provides this same count as does *SY.* However the Chinese *Jiu Tangshu* and *Zizhi tongjian* say Tang dispatched only 100,000 men.

80 Missing characters here, and unless otherwise noted, have been restored based on the *AKS* translation. John C. Jamieson, "The Samguk sagi and the Unification

Summer, fifth month, twenty-sixth day. The King with Yusin, Chinju, Ch'ŏnjon, and others led the troops out of the capital.

Sixth month, eighteenth day. They reached Namch'ŏnjŏng.[81] Dingfang departed from Laizhou,[82] with his many ships spread over 1,000 *li,* and they sailed east following the current.

Twenty-first day. The King sent his Crown Prince Pŏmmin to lead one hundred warships and he met Dingfang at Tŏngmul Island.[83] Dingfang said to Pŏmmin, "I would like to reach the south of Paekche on the tenth day of the seventh month and meet up with your King's troops to crush [the Paekche king] Ŭija's capital. Pŏmmin replied, "My Great King is now waiting for your great force and when he hears that you have arrived, he will certainly gulp down his breakfast in bed and rush to come." Dingfang in his delight had Pŏmmin return and enlist Silla forces. When Pŏmmin, on arrival, reported on the vastness of Dingfang's forces, the King was beside himself with delight. [The King] also commanded the Crown Prince, Grand General Yusin, Generals P'umil and Hŭmch'un {another source writes "sun" for "ch'un"} to lead 50,000 crack forces in concert with them. The King went to Kŭmdol Fortress.[84]

Autumn, seventh month, ninth day. Yusin and others advanced their army to the plains of Mount Hwangsan.[85] Paekche's General Kyebaek led his troops and, first occupying a rugged position,

---

Wars," unpublished PhD dissertation, University of California, Berkeley, 1969, 232, n. 7, suggests *Yuyi dao* (circuit, not island) was a mythical name for Korea.

81 This is in Kyŏnggi, Ich'ŏn, one of the ten *chŏng* of Silla's regional military commands.

82 This is on the northern coast of Shandong, Yixian; see *AKS* 3:179, n. 195.

83 This island is in Hwanghae, Ongjin. *SY* lists it as Tŏngmul Island but with a different character for *"mul."* It is also referred to as Tŏkchŏk Island.

84 This is in Kyŏngbuk, Sangju.

85 Ch'ungnam, Nonsan, near Kaet'ae Monastery.

they set up three camps and waited. Yusin and others divided their army into three routes, and four times they fought without a decision, exhausting their troops. General Hŭmsun said to his son Pangul, "For a subject nothing is greater than loyalty and for a son nothing is greater than filial piety. In facing a crisis, to offer one's life, both loyalty and filial piety will be fulfilled." Pangul responded, "Humbly, I understand your command." Thereupon he entered the battle fighting valiantly to his death. Left General P'umil summoned his son Kwanjang {another source says Kwanch'ang}[86] and, standing him in front of his horse, pointed to the officers who were waiting and said, "Although my son is about sixteen years old, his determination is courageous. In today's battle he can be a great model for the three armies." Kwanjang [][][] responding promptly on an armored horse and grabbing a single spear in his hand, he dashed into the enemy's camp. But he was captured [][][] by the enemy and brought back alive [][][] to Kyebaek. Kyebaek on removing [the boy's] helmet, and endeared by his youth and courage, could not bare to harm him and sighed, saying, "We are unable to match Silla. If their youth are like this, how much more are their mature men?" He then allowed him to return alive. Kwanjang reported to his father, "When I dashed into the enemy camp, it was not because I feared death that I was unable to kill their general and snatch their standards." As soon as he finished speaking, he scooped water with his bare hands from a well, drank it, and then headed back to the enemy camp, fighting with urgency. Kyebaek captured and beheaded him, and sent the head back tied to his horse's saddle. P'umil, taking the head, with blood flowing onto his sleeve, said, "My son's face looks as if he were alive; it is fortunate indeed that

---

86 See *SS* 47.

he was able to die for the King." When the three armies saw this they were filled with indignation and with the resolve to fight to death. They beat their drums and cried out going into battle. The Paekche forces were soundly defeated, killing Kyebaek and capturing *Chwap'yŏng* Ch'ungsang, Sangyŏng, and twenty others.

On the same day Dingfang and Assistant Adjutant Grand Commander Kim Inmun and others reached Kibŏlp'o[87] where they encountered the Paekche forces, struck their advancing forces, and soundly defeated them. When Yusin and others reached the Tang camp, Dingfang was going to behead Silla *Tokkun* [Commander] Kim Munyŏng {another source writes another character for *yŏng*} at the entrance to the camp because Yusin and others came after the agreed time. Yusin addressed his troops saying, "The great general [Su Dingfang] did not witness the battle at Mount Hwangsan and yet is treating our late arrival as a crime. Being guiltless I cannot accept this indignity. We must first fight a decisive battle with Tang and then crush Paekche." He grabbed his battle axe and stood at the entrance to the camp, with his hair raised up in anger, and the jeweled sword at his waist leaping instinctively from its scabbard.[88] Dingfang's Right General Dong Baoliang, stepping on his foot, said, "The Silla army is going to revolt." There upon Dingfang freed Munyŏng from his crime.

The Paekche Prince *Chwap'yŏng* Kakka sent a message to the Tang general pleading they withdraw their troops. On the twelfth day the Tang and Silla forces [][][] encircled Ŭija's capital and advanced to the plains of Soburi. Because of some [apprehensions] [][][] Dingfang was unable to move forward, but Yusin persuaded

---

87 This is at the confluence of the Paek and Ungjin rivers in Ch'ungnam.

88 This is almost verbatim from Jamieson 80a.

him and then the two armies courageously charged ahead side by side along four routes. The Paekche prince again sent his *sangchwap'yŏng*[89] to present abundant sacrificial foods and delicacies which Dingfang refused. The King's son by a concubine personally, with the six *chwap'yŏng*, went before him to beg for pardon but they too were spurned. On the thirteenth day, King Ŭija led his aides and secretly at night fled to Ungjin Fortress for protection. Ŭija's son Yung and *Taejwap'yŏng* Ch'ŏnbok and others came out to surrender. Pŏmmin had Yung kneel in front of his horse and, spitting in his face, cursed, "Your father wantonly killed my younger sister and buried her in the middle of a prison. This for the past twenty years has vexed my heart and caused me anxiety. Now today your life rests in my hands." Yung lay flat out on the ground without a word.

On the eighteenth day Ŭija led the Crown Prince and the soldiers of the Ungjin *pangnyŏng*[90] defense corps out of Ungjin Fortress to surrender. The King heard of the surrender and on the twenty-ninth day came he came from Kŭmdol Fortress to Soburi and sent *Chegam* [Deputy Director] Ch'ŏnbok to Great Tang to announce the victory.

Eighth month, second day. They held a great banquet to honor the officers and soldiers. The King, with Dingfang and the various generals, sat high at the front of the hall. Ŭija and his son Yung sat low at the back of the hall and they occasionally had Ŭija serve wine. Among the Paekche *chwap'yŏng*, and all the officials, there was none who did not choke with tears and weep. On this day they captured and beheaded Moch'ŏk. Moch'ŏk was originally

---

89 This is the leader of the *chwap'yŏng* council of six *chwap'yŏng*.

90 The *pangnyŏng* was in charge of Ungjin Fortress, one of the five regions of Paekche.

from Silla but, on defeat, had fled to Paekche and with Kŏmil of Taeya Fortress plotted to surrender this fortress and therefore was decapitated. Kŏmil also was taken and his crimes were listed: 1, In Taeya Fortress you plotted with Moch'ŏk to lead Paekche troops and burn down the granary, resulting in starvation and causing the defeat of the fortress. This is your first crime. 2, You forced the murder of P'umsŏk and his wife. This is your second crime. 3, You came with Paekche to attack Silla. This is your third crime. They dismembered his four limbs and tossed the corpse into a river.

Remaining Paekche bandits held fortresses at Namjam and Chŏnghyŏn [][][].[91] *Chwapy'ŏng* Chŏngmu assembled a group and encamped at Tusiwŏnak[92] and plundered the Tang and Silla people. On the twenty-sixth day [we] attacked the great wooden barricade at Imjon[93] but, as the [Paekche] forces were too many and the terrain too rugged, [we] were not able to win but only attacked and destroyed a small barricade.

Ninth month, third day. *Langjiang* [Vice Commandant] Liu Renyuan with 10,000 troops garrisoned at Sabi Fortress. Prince Int'ae, *Sach'an* Ilwŏn, and *Kŭpch'an* Kilna, along with 7,000 soldiers, assisted them. Dingfang had the Paekche King, the royal clan, as well as ninety-three court officials, and 12,000 people from Sabi, board vessels to Tang.[94] Kim Inmun, *Sach'an* Yudon, and *Taenama* Chungji and others accompanied them.

On the twenty-third, remnant Paekche enemies entered Sabi planning to capture those who had surrendered. *Liushou* [Garrison Commander Liu] Renyuan had Tang and Silla troops go after and

---

91 This is in Taejŏn.
92 This is presumed to be in Chŏnbuk, Muju.
93 This is in Ch'ungnam, Yesan.
94 One could surmise that Su is taking these people to Tang to use them as possible hostages.

attack them. The enemy retreated, ascending Sabi's southern pass, and fortified four or five barricades, camping there and waiting for opportunities to plunder the fortress town. [Other] Paekche people in more than twenty fortresses rebelled and joined them. The Tang Emperor dispatched Left Guard Commandant Wang Wendu to be Ungjin *todok* [governor].

On the twenty-eighth, on reaching Mount Samnyŏn Fortress, he delivered the imperial decree. Wendu stood facing east and [our] Great King faced west. After delivering the decree, as Wendu was about to bestow imperial gifts on the King, he suddenly became ill and died on the spot. Subordinates instead completed the ceremony.

Tenth month, ninth day. The King led the Crown Prince and various forces to attack Irye Fortress.[95] On the eighteenth day, they took the fortress and placed government officials there to hold it. More than twenty other Paekche fortresses in fear also surrendered. On the thirtieth day they attacked the troops at the military barricades at the Sabi southern pass, beheading 1,500 people.

Eleventh month, first day. Koguryŏ invaded and attacked Ch'iljung Fortress and *Kunju* [Commander] P'ilbu died fighting.[96] On the fifth day the King crossed Kyet'an rapids to attack the mountain fortress at Wanghŭng Monastery and on the seventh day he was victorious and beheaded seven hundred people. On the twenty-second the King returned from Paekche to deliberate the merit of his soldiers and promoted Sŏnbok, a soldier in the Kyegŭm Banner, to be *kŭpch'an* and *Kunsa* [Army Supervisor]

---

95 This is in Ch'ungnam, Nonsan.
96 *AKS* 3:188, n. 240, suggests P'ilbu was a *kunju* (commander) while in *SS* 47 he is called a *hyŏllyŏng* (magistrate).

Tujil to be *kogan*.[97] The four who died in battle, Yusaji, Mijihwal, Pohongi, and Sŏlyu, were granted varying positions [in accordance with their merit]. Paekche men were also given appointments based on their ability. *Chwap'yŏng* Ch'ungsang and Sangyŏng and *Talsol* Chagan were granted the rank of *ilgilch'an* and the position of *ch'onggwan* [adjutant grand commander]. *Ŭnsol* Musu was given the rank of *taenama* and the position of *taegam* [director]. And *Ŭnsol* Insu received the rank of *taenama* and the position of *chegam* [deputy director].

Year eight [661], spring, second month. Remaining Paekche enemies came and attacked Sabi Fortress. The King ordered *Ich'an* P'umil to be general of the *Taedang* [Grand Banner][98] and *Chapch'an* Munwang, *Taeach'an* Yangdo, *Ich'an* Ch'ungsang, and others to be his deputies. *Chapch'an* Munch'ung was made general of Sangju[99] and *Ach'an* Chinwang his deputy. *Ach'an* Ŭibok was made general of Haju. Muhol and Ukch'ŏn became directors of Namch'ŏn.[100] Munp'um became general of the *Sŏdang* [Oath Banner] and Ŭigwang became general of the *Nangdang* [Junior Banner] and went to assist.[101]

Third month, fifth day. Arriving at the mid-point, P'umil divided the army under his command and went forward, first reaching south of Turyangyun Fortress {Yun can also be written

---

97 See *AKS* 3:189, n. 244. *Kunsa* is a low ranking military position in the Kyegŭm Banner. See Kimura Makoto, "Shiragi gun kansei no kakuritsu katei to sonshisei," *Chōsenshi kenkyūkai ronbunshū* 13 (1976): 17–20.

98 This is the highest office in Silla's six-*chŏng* (garrison) structure. Each *chŏng* was commanded by men of "True Bone" status who lived in the capital.

99 Sangju was one of the six *chŏng* (garrisons) of Silla and today is in the Sangju region (different *"sang"* character) of Kyŏngbuk.

100 Haju also is one of the six *chŏng* and was first at Kyŏngnam, Ch'angnyŏng, and then at Kyŏngbuk, Kyŏngsan. Namch'ŏn is in Kyŏnggi, Ich'ŏn.

101 *Nokkŭm sŏdang* is the highest military position among the nine Silla *sŏdang*. *Nangdang* is also part of the nine *sŏdang* system.

as I}[102] where he searched for a place to set up camp. The Paekche [enemy], seeing our ranks were yet to be fully organized, attacked unexpectedly, forcing our army to flee in disarray and scatter northward. On the twelfth day the great army came and camped outside Kosabi Fortress[103] and advanced to attack Turyangyun Fortress. But, after one month and six days, they were not able to win.

Summer, fourth month, nineteenth day. The troops were withdrawn. The Great Banner and the Oath Banner went first and the Haju army followed to Pingolyang where they met the Paekche army and fought but withdrew in defeat. Although those killed were comparatively few, there were great losses in weapons and carts loaded with military supplies. The [forces of] Sangju and the Junior Banner encountered the enemy at Mount Kaksan[104] and attacked forth overcoming them and they entered the Paekche fort, beheading two thousand. When the King heard of [his] army's defeat, he was very shocked and had Generals Kŭmsun, Chinhŭm, Ch'ŏnjon, and Chukchi dispatched to help and reinforce their troops. However when they reached Kasihye port,[105] they heard the army had withdrawn to Kasoch'ŏn[106] and so they returned. Because of the generals' defeats in battle, the King deliberated penalties by rank.

Fifth month, ninth day {another source says eleventh}. Koguryŏ General Noeŭmsin and Malgal General Saenghae joined forces and came attacking Sulch'ŏn Fortress[107] but to no avail and

---

102 This is in Ch'ungnam Ch'ŏngyang.
103 This is in Chŏnbuk, Chŏngŭp.
104 This is in Chŏnbuk, Chŏngŭp.
105 This is in Kyŏngbuk, Koryŏng.
106 This is in Kyŏngnam, Kŏch'ang.
107 This is in Kyŏnggi, Yŏju.

so [they] shifted the attack to Mount Pukhan Fortress, lining up mobile weapons that hurled rocks that smashed the battlements and buildings of the fortress. *Taesa* [Fortress Commander] Tongt'ach'ŏn got men to lay out iron caltrops outside the fortress so that people and horses were unable to advance. He dismantled the storage houses at Anyang Monastery to transport the lumber to build towers in places where the fortress had been damaged. He made rope nets on which he hung cow leather, horse hide, and cotton cloth and put an arrow-shooting canon inside to defend. At that time in the fortress there were only 2,800 men and women. Fortress Commander Tongt'ach'ŏn was able to exhort the young and old to fight the powerful enemy for more than twenty days. But with provisions exhausted and strength sapped, he earnestly prayed to heaven and suddenly there was a great star [meteor] that fell into the enemy camp and it rained and thunder shook. The enemy, perplexed and frightened, lifted the siege and departed. The King commended and rewarded Tongt'ach'ŏn and elevated him to the post of *taenama*. Aptok-chu was moved to Taeya[108] and *Ach'an* Chongjŏng was appointed governor.

Sixth month. The water in the well at Taegwan Monastery turned to blood. On the land in Kŭmma-gun blood flowed over 5 *po* wide. The King died. His posthumous title was Muyŏl and he was buried north of Yŏnggyŏng Monastery and presented with the title of *t'aejong*. When [Tang] Gaozong learned of his death, he conducted a mourning ritual at Luocheng Gate.

---

108 The area west of the Naktong River had fallen to Paekche in 642 and at this time returned to Silla.

The **Silla Annals** of the **Samguk Sagi**

The Silla
Annals of the
Samguk Sagi

King Munmu – Part One

Book

6

King Munmu — Part One

King Munmu ascended the throne [in 661]. His personal name was Pŏmmin and he was the oldest son of King T'aejong [King Muyŏl]. His mother was Lady Kim, Queen-Consort Munmyŏng, the youngest daughter of Sop'an[1] [Kim] Sŏhyŏn and [Kim] Yusin's younger sister. Her older sister dreamed that she climbed and sat on top of Mount Sŏhyŏng[2] where she urinated and it flowed to all corners of the country. Waking from her dream she told her younger sister. The younger sister playfully said, "I would like to buy your dream." And so she gave her a brocade skirt as the price of the dream. Several days later, Yusin was playing kick-ball[3] with Lord Ch'unch'u and stepped on a sash on Ch'unch'u's garment pulling it off. Yusin said, "Fortunately, my house is nearby, please come over and we will mend the sash." And so they went together to his house. As wine was served he [Yusin] casually called his sister Pohŭi to bring a needle and thread to sew. For some reason[4] the older sister did not appear, but his younger sister came forward to sew it on.[5] Lightly made up and neatly dressed, her

---

1   This was the third level in Silla's seventeen-rank order.
2   Located in the western part of Kyŏngju, it is also know as Mount Sŏndo.
3   This is a traditional Korean game where players kick a ball to each other.
4   *SY* 1:29b claims she did not wish to appear, claiming it was improper.
5   See *SY* 1:29b-30a provides a slightly different account of this encounter noting that Kim Yusin on discovering his sister was pregnant wanted to burn her to death but he was stopped by Queen Sŏndŏk who allowed Kim Ch'unch'u to rescue her. Shortly after they were married.

beauty dazzled those around her. Ch'unch'u on seeing her was delighted, requested marriage, and completed the ceremony. Shortly after she became pregnant and gave birth to a son who is called Pŏmmin, and his [Pŏmmin's] Queen was Queen Chaŭi, daughter of *P'ajinch'an* Sŏnp'um.[6]

Pŏmmin's stature and appearance were outstanding and he was bright and quite resourceful. At the start of the *Yonghui* [years][7] he went to Tang where [Tang] Gaozong conferred on him the title of *Daifuzheng* [Chamberlain for the Palace Revenue]. In [Silla] T'aejong's first year [654], as *p'ajinch'an*, [Pŏmmin] was appointed Minister of the Ministry of Military Affairs and shortly after became Crown Prince. In Xianqing, fifth year [660], when T'aejong together with the Tang General Su Dingfang defeated Paekche, Pŏmmin was with them and achieved great merit. Reaching this he was enthroned.

Year one [661], sixth month. Imperial Resident Guards[8] Inmun, Yudon, and others, who had been staying in Tang, returned and informed the King, "The [Tang] Emperor has already sent Su Dingfang commanding thirty-five naval and land-route forces[9] to attack Koguryŏ. He commanded Your Majesty to deploy troops to support him. Although Your Majesty at present is in mourning, it

---

6   See *AKS* 3:196, n. 11, which indicates Chaŭi's name could be written as Chanul, and 3:197, n. 12, for further information on Sŏnp'um.

7   This is the period from 650 to 655 during Tang Gaozong's reign.

8   According to Jamieson 239, "*suwei,* literally "Night Guard," and originally a "corps of officers charged with the responsibility of keeping watch at the imperial inner chambers" were Silla aristocratic youth who, as night guards, played both political and diplomatic roles and, during the unification wars, assisted Tang troops on the Korean peninsula. See Sin Hyŏngsik, "Silla ŭi tae Tang kyosŏpsange nat'anan sukwi e taehan ilgoch'al," *Yŏksa kyoyuk* 9 (October 1966), and Book 5, n. 49.

9   *To* ("route") could also be read as "circuit," although there were only ten at this time. "Route" seems a more appropriate translation.

would be difficult to disobey this command of the Emperor."[10]

Autumn, seventh month, seventeenth day. Kim Yusin was appointed grand general; Inmun, Chinju, and Hŭmdol were appointed generals of the Grand Banner;[11] Ch'ŏnjon, Chukchi, and Ch'ŏnp'um were appointed Adjutant Grand Commanders of the *Kwi* [Noble] Banner;[12] P'umil, Ch'ungsang, and Ŭibok were appointed Adjutant Grand Commanders of Sangju; Chinhŭm, Chungsin, and Chagan were appointed Adjutant Grand Commanders of Haju;[13] Kungwan, Suse, and Kosun were appointed Adjutant Grand Commanders of Namch'ŏn-ju; and Sulsil, Talgwan, and Munyŏng were appointed Adjutant Grand Commanders of Suyak-chu. Munhun and Chinsun were appointed Adjutant Grand Commanders of Hasŏ-ju, Chinbok was appointed Adjutant Grand Commander of the Oath Banner, Ŭigwang was appointed Adjutant Grand Commander of the Junior Banner, and Wiji was appointed director of the Kyegŭm Banner.[14]

Eighth month. The Great King, leading various generals, arrived at Siigok Garrison[15] where they stayed. []️[]️[][16] A messenger

---

10 According to Jamieson 249, "The order was not heeded, according to Munmu's response to Xue Rengui in 671." Silla was hesitant to attack Koguryŏ before Paekche had been completely pacified and also remained suspicious of Tang's designs.

11 *Taedang* (Grand Banner) was one of the six *chŏng* of the Silla military units that were in Kyŏngju.

12 Along with the Grand Banner, *Kwidang* (Noble Banner) was the largest unit in the six *chŏng*. See Yi Sŏngsi, "Shiragi 6 tang no saikentō," *Chōsen gakuhō* 92 (1979). See also note 27 below.

13 Haju was in Kyŏngnam, Ch'angnyŏng, but subsequently moved to the Hapch'ŏn area.

14 This is the name of the highest position in the *Kyegŭm* Banner which was established in the first year of King Munmu.

15 This may be Namch'ŏnjŏng, which is located in Kyŏnggi, Ich'ŏn, or Kyŏngbuk, Kumi.

16 It is surmised, based on the entry in *Samguksa chŏryo,* that the two missing characters are *"si yu,"* meaning "at that time." See *AKS* 3:200, n. 30.

came reporting, "Remnants of the Paekche forces relying on Mount Ongsan Fortress[17] have blocked the road preventing our advance."[18] So the Great King first sent a messenger to persuade them [to stop] but they did not listen.

Ninth month, nineteenth day. The Great King then advanced to Unghyŏn Garrison and assembled the various adjutant grand commanders and directors and went in person to make a pledge. On the twenty-fifth day he advanced his army to surround Mount Ongsan Fortress and on the twenty-seventh he first burned the great wooden barricade and then beheaded several thousand men, finally defeating them. In evaluating merit, the *kakkan* and *ich'an* who were adjutant grand commanders were granted a sword and those adjutant grand commanders who were *chapch'an*, *p'ajinch'an,* or *taeach'an* were granted a halberd, and those below were raised one rank. They constructed Unghyŏn Fortress. Adjutant grand commander of Sangju P'umil, Ilmosan-gun *Taesu* [Governor][19] Taedang and Governor of Sasisan-gun[20] Ch'ŏlch'ŏn and others led troops to attack Usul Fortress[21] and beheaded a thousand people. Paekche people *Talsol* Chobok and *Ŭnsol*[22] P'aga planned with many others to surrender and [the King] conferred on Chobok the rank of *kŭpch'an*, making him governor of Kot'aya-gun and to P'aga the rank of *kŭpch'an* together with land, housing, and clothing.

Winter, tenth month, twenty-ninth day. When the Great King

---

17 This fortress is believed to be Mount Kyejok Fortress which is located in modern Taejŏn.
18 Again there are several characters missing in this passage.
19 Ilmosan-gun is in Ch'ungbok, Ch'ŏnggwŏn. *Taesu* (governor) was the office in charge of a *kun.*
20 This is in Ch'ungnam, Hongsŏng.
21 This at Taedŏk-gu in Taejŏn.
22 *Talsol* and *Ŭnsol* are Paekche official ranks, see Best, 42–4.

learned of the arrival of a Tang imperial messenger, he returned to the capital. The Tang emissary offered condolences and held at imperial command services for the former king, giving five hundred bolts of various colors of silk. [Kim] Yusin and others rested their troops waiting for further orders. When Hanzi Route[23] Adjutant Grand Commander Liu Demin arrived he relayed an imperial decree to transport military provisions to P'yŏngyang.

Year two [662], spring, first month. The Tang emissary remained at his official quarters. At that time he conferred on the King the title of Commander Unequalled in Honor, Supreme Pillar of State, King of Nangnang-gun, King of Silla. *Ich'an* Munhun became *chungsi* [chief minister].[24] The King commanded Yusin, along with Inmun, Yangdo, and others, nine generals in total, to go to P'yŏngyang with more than two thousand wagons loaded with four thousand *sŏk* of rice and more than twenty-two thousand *sŏk* of unhusked rice.[25] On the eighteenth day they lodged at P'ungsuch'on. As the conditions were icy, the roads became dangerous and the carts were unable to proceed so they loaded the provisions on cows and horses. On the twenty-third day they crossed Ch'ilchung River, reaching Sanyang.[26] Director of the Noble Banner[27] Sŏngch'ŏn and *Kunsa* [Army Supervisor]

---

23 Jamieson 240, n. 39, states that Hanzi is the area of modern Hwanghae and was once part of the Lelang Han commandery.

24 See year 651, above, and accompanying note 65. Jamieson 242, n. 40, indicates that the name lasted until 747 when it was changed to *sijung*.

25 According to Jamieson 242, n. 41, the "use of the word '*cho*,' 'tribute or rental grains,' is unusual in the *SGSG* [SS], appearing to be a special Korean usage denoting a grain between husked rice and millet." Yi Pyŏngdo translates it as *pyŏ* or "unhusked rice."

26 This river is located in Kyŏnggi, P'aju, and Sanyang is north of the Imjin River in Hwanghae.

27 *Chegam,* or deputy director, seen earlier in 660, was a military position established in 562. There were five deputy directors in the Noble Banner.

Sulch'ŏn encountered the enemy soldiers at Ihyŏn and attacked, killing them.

Second month, first day. Yusin and others reached Changsae,[28] a distance of 36,000 *po* from P'yŏngyang and sent ahead *Pogigam*[29] Yŏlgi and others, totaling fifteen, to the Tang camp. On this day, as the wind and snow were freezing cold, many men and horses froze to death. On the sixth day they reached Yango[30] and Yusin sent *Ach'an* Yangdo and Director Insŏn to the Tang camp to give them provisions and to present to [Su] Dongfang 5,700 [*pún*; 570 *taels*] of silver,[31] 30 bolts of fine cloth, 30 *ryang* [*taels*] of hair, and 19 *taels* of ox bile.[32] After Dongfang received the provisions he stopped fighting and returned home. When Yusin and others heard that the Tang troops had departed, he also turned around, crossing the Kwach'on [stream].[33] The Koguryŏ forces pursued him and he turned around his army to fight and beheaded more than 10,000 people, capturing *Sohyŏng*[34] Adahye and others and over 10,000 weapons. In evaluating their merit, the [court] gave goods, land, and slaves from Ponp'i Palace,[35] dividing them

---

28 This is in Hwanghae, Suan.

29 *Pogigam* is a military office in the six garrisons of the Silla nine banners and in charge of the infantry and cavalry.

30 This is thought to be modern p'yŏngyang.

31 The original text reads 5,700 p'un [Chinese fen].

32 According to Jamieson 242, n. 42–3, "one hundred parts *(p'un)* equals one *tael* *(yang)* or slightly more than an ounce." Ox bile is used in medicine. See Edward H. Schafer, *The Golden Peaches of Samarkand,* 191–2. Hair could be used to wrap feet and heads for warmth.

33 This is located in P'aju, Kyŏnggi.

34 This is a relatively low Koguryŏ rank. For rank listings see Lee Ki-baik, translated by Edward W. Wagner with Edward J. Shultz, A *New History of Korea,* 52.

35 This is believed to be the main palace of the Sŏk lineage. According to Jamieson 243, n. 45, "The Ponp'i Palace is said to have been situated at the birthplace of the Sŏk clan." It is one of several in the Kyŏngju environs. *SS,* treatise section on bureaucracy, states it was built in 681. Jamieson notes, "It is a mystery as to why the property should be divided at this time."

equally between Yusin and Inmun. There was a fire at Yŏngmyo Monastery.[36] The ruler of T'amna, *Chwap'yŏng* Todongŭngnyul {another source says *jin* [in place of *nyul*]} surrendered. Because T'amna, from the Mudŏk period[37] on, was under Paekche control, the leader had the title of *chwap'yŏng*. Thereupon on surrendering [T'amna] became a subordinate state [to Silla].

Third month. There was a general amnesty. Because the King had already pacified Paekche he commanded the agencies concerned to prepare a great banquet.

Autumn, seventh month. [The King] sent *Ich'an* Kim Inmun to Tang to present tribute.

Eighth month. Remnant Paekche forces gathered, camping at Naesaji Fortress,[38] to cause unrest. [The King] sent Hŭmsun and others, totaling nineteen generals, to attack and destroy them. As Adjutant Grand Commander of the Grand Banner Chinju and Adjutant Grand Commander of Namch'ŏn-ju Chinhŭm, feigning illness, relaxed, and did not attend to state affairs, they were executed and their entire families were eliminated. *Sach'an* Yŏdong flogged his mother and then fell rain and a thunderbolt, killing him, and on his body there were seen inscribed three characters *su ak dang* {of which the middle character is indiscernible in its meaning}. Namch'ŏn-ju presented a white magpie.

Year three [663], spring, first month. A large storehouse [Changch'ang] was constructed at Sin Fortress on South

---

36 Per Jamieson 243, n. 46, this monastery burned three times between 663 and 668.

37 As there is no Paekche king by this name, some feel this is a misprint for Widŏk, see *SS 1977* 92. Some suggest this is the period of Tang Wude (618–626). According to *SS* 26 T'amna first came under Paekche control in King Munju's second year (476). See also *AKS* 3:203, n. 53.

38 This is Taejŏn.

Mountain.[39] Pusan Fortress was also constructed.[40]

Second month. Hŭmsun and Ch'ŏnjon led troops attacking and seizing Paekche's Kŏyŏl Fortress, beheading over seven hundred people and also attacking and defeating Kŏmul Fortress and Sap'yŏng Fortress. They attacked Tŏkan Fortress[41] and beheaded 1,070 people.

Summer, fourth month. Great Tang designated our country Kyerim *Dadudufu* [Superior Area Command] and the King *Dadudu* [Area Commander in Chief].

Fifth month. Yŏngmyo Monastery gate was jolted. The former Paekche Commander Poksin[42] and the monk Toch'im welcomed the former Prince Puyŏ P'ung,[43] enthroning him [King]. They surrounded *Liangjiang* [Vice Commander] Liu Renyuan who remained at Ungjin Fortress. The Tang Emperor sent a decree to [Lui] Jengui that he assume the concurrent position of Prefect of Taebang prefecture and take charge of former *Dudu* [Commander-in-Chief] Wang Wentu's forces and, with our troops, head toward the Paekche camp. Every time they fought they defeated the enemy—as nothing could hinder them as they advanced. Poksin and others ended their siege of [Liu] Renyuan and retreated to

---

39 The large storehouse, according to *SY* 2, was 50 *po* [15 meters] long and 15 *po* [4.5 meters] wide. The remains of Sin Fortress are still visible on South Mountain in Kyŏngju. See Yi Chonguk, "Namsan sinsŏngp'irul taehae pon Silla ŭi chibang t'ongch'i cheje," *Yŏksa hakpo* 64 (1974): 1–69.

40 This is a few miles west of Kyŏngju and its remains also are still visible.

41 Kŏyŏl Fortress is in Kyŏngnam, Kŏch'ang; Kŏmul is in Chŏnbuk, Changsu; Sap'yŏng is near Kŏmul; and Tŏkan is in Chŏnbuk, Imsil. See Kim T'aesik, *Kaya yŏnmaengsa* 123. Tŏkan Fortress is in Ch'ungnam, Nonsan.

42 Poksin is the nephew of King Mu and had once been sent to Tang and also Japan. He led the failed Paekche restoration. See *SS* 28. See also *AKS* 3:205, n. 56. See also Best 399–400.

43 He is the son of King Ŭija. In 631 he went to Japan. In 663 Japan sent 5,000 men to help restore him to power but this force was defeated at the Battle of the Paek River. See *SS* 28 and Best.

protect Imjon Fortress.[44] Shortly after Poksin killed Toch'im and, combining with his forces and calling together all other rebel forces, their power greatly expanded. Rengui joined with Renguan, took off their armor to rest their troops, and then called for reinforcements. An imperial decree had *Youweiwei jiangzhun* [General of the Right Awesome Guard] Sun Renshi lead 400,000[45] soldiers to Tŏngmul Island and then on to Ungjin-pu [district] Fortress. The King commanded Kim Yusin and others, totaling twenty eight {another source states thirty} generals, to join forces and attack and seize Turŭngyun Fortress {another source writes *rŭng* as *yang*}, Churyu,[46] and other fortresses, defeating them all. Puyŏ Pung fled for his life.[47] Princes Ch'ungsŭng[48] and Ch'ungji and others led their people and surrendered but Chijusin alone held out at Imjon Fortress and did not surrender.

Winter, tenth month. From the twenty-first day on, [Silla] attacked him but to no avail and on the fourth day of the eleventh month they withdrew their troops. On reaching Sŏlli Garrison {it could be written as *"sŏl"* or *"hu"*}, they evaluated merit and made grants accordingly. There was a general amnesty. They made clothing and distributed it to the Tang troops that remained.

Year four [664], spring, first month. Kim Yusin, because of his age, requested to retire but it was not accepted. He was given a small table and staff.[49] *Ach'an* Kungwan became governor of

---

44 This is in Ch'ungnam, Yesan.
45 Acording to *Zizhi tongjian* 200, he led seven thousand men.
46 Turŭngyun Fortress is in Ch'ungnam, Ch'ŏngyang. Churyu Fortress could be any number of sites in Ch'ungnam or Chŏnbuk.
47 He fled to Koguryŏ and, when Tang defeated Koguryŏ, he was exiled to China.
48 Ch'ungsung had been in Japan and returned to Paekche with the restoration movement.
49 Per Jamieson 246, n. 52, Kim was seventy years old at this time. The award of the table (Jamieson states it was as an elbow rest) and staff were traditional gifts to honored subjects.

Hansan-ju. A decree was issued also permitting women to wear Chinese court garments.

Second month. It was ordered that the offices concerned settle twenty households each [to care for] the royal tumuli.[50] *Kakkan* Kim Inmun and *Ich'an* Ch'ŏnjon, together with Tang *Chishi* [Imperial Emissary] Liu Renyuan and Puyŏ Yung of Paekche made an alliance at Ungjin.[51]

Third month. Some Paekche remnant groups held Mount Sabi Fortress and rebelled. The governor of Ungjin dispatched troops that attacked and destroyed them.[52] There was an earthquake. Sŏngch'ŏn, Kuil, twenty-eight people in total, were sent to Ungjin district fortress to study Tang music.[53]

Autumn, seventh month. The King commanded Generals Inmun, P'umil, Kungwan, Munyŏng, and others to lead the troops of the two *chu*, Ilsŏn and Hansan, along with forces from [Ungjin] district fortress, to attack and they destroyed Koguryŏ's Tolsa Fortress.

Eighth month, fourteenth day. There was an earthquake destroying people's houses and it was especially severe in the southern region. [The King] forbade people from taking their wealth and land and donating it, as they pleased, to monasteries.

Year five [665], spring, second month. Chief Minister Munhun,

---

50 It was customary for royal tombs to be protected and maintained in this manner. See Cho Insŏng, "Kwanggaet'o wangnŭngbi t'onghae pon Koguryŏ ŭi sumyoje," *Hanguksa simin kangchwa* 3 (1988): 104–7.

51 Per Jamieson 246, n. 53, "The dogged insistence on the part of Tang generals for Silla to enter into an amnesty pledge with the Paekche elements to whom Tang had already given recognition and official status is not recorded in the Chinese histories, the original source for this account being the Munmu missive of 671." Silla resisted an oath in 663 but entered into one in 664 and 665.

52 For greater details on this battle see *SS* 43 Kim Yusin's biography and *AKS* 3:228, n. 83.

53 According to *AKS* 1:75, n. 27, *Samguksa chŏryo* puts this figure at thirty-eight.

because of age, retired and *Ich'an* Chinbok became chief minister. As *Ich'an* Munwang[54] died, his funeral was conducted with the rites of a Prince. Tang Emperor [Gaozong] dispatched an envoy to offer condolences and at the same time he presented one set of purple clothing, one belt, one hundred *p'il* [bolts] of variegated silk gauze, and two hundred bolts of raw silk. The King presented the Tang envoy with even more generous amounts of gold and silk.

Autumn, eighth month. The King made an alliance[55] with Imperial Emissary Liu Renyuan and the governor of Ungjin Puyŏ Yung at Ungjin's Mount Ch'wiri.[56] Earlier Paekche from Puyŏ Chang's [King Mu of Paekche, 600–640] reign had made an alliance with Koguryŏ and often invaded our territory. We sent envoys to Tang seeking help [so frequently] that they saw each other on the road. After Su Dingfang had pacified Paekche and had returned his troops [to Tang], the people remaining there again rebelled. The King, with Grand Defender Liu Renyuan, Liu Rengui, and others, for a number of years planned a strategy and gradually pacified them when Tang Gaozong commanded Puyŏ Yung to return [home to Paekche], quiet the remaining people, and conclude a peace with us. At this time a white horse was sacrificed and a covenant concluded by first praying to the deities of Heaven and Earth as well as to the deities of the streams and valleys. They then smeared their lips with blood. The covenant read as follows:[57]

"In the past, the former King of Paekche was at a loss as to

---

54 He is the son of King Muyŏl and one of Munmu's younger brothers.
55 Jamieson 248, n. 56, provides a detailed discussion of this agreement and the sources where it can be found.
56 This is in Ch'ungnam, Kongju. See also *AKS* 3:208, n. 85.
57 This is adapted from Jamieson 104–7.

right and wrong: he was unfriendly to good neighbors and not cordial to relatives;[58] he collaborated with Koguryŏ, contacting the Wa state, and together they became vicious, invading Silla and plundering its villages and fortresses, leaving hardly a year with peace. The Son of Heaven, who pities any creature deprived of its habitat and feels compassion for innocent people, frequently sent envoys to bring about friendly relations. Yet, relying on their rugged land and the great distance [from China], [Paekche] scorned imperial wishes.

The Emperor became enraged at this and conducted an expedition to rectify the situation and wherever his flags and banners went, a single battle saw complete resolution. Truly he could have turned palace and residence grounds into marshland and ponds as a warning to [Paekche's] descendants; he could have plugged up their source and plucked up their roots as admonitions for later generations. But 'embrace the yielding, punish the rebellious' was the admirable rule of former kings; 'revive the dying, connect the breaking'[59] was the constant pattern of sages of old, and action must be modeled on the ancients and will be transmitted through records of the past. It was thus that [the Emperor] established Puyŏ Yung of the former state of Paekche and Chamberlain of the Ministry of Husbandry and chief administrator[60] as governor of Ungjin to maintain [Paekche's] ancestral sacrifices and preserve his mulberry and catalpa trees.[61]

---

58 "Relatives" refers to a marriage contracted in 493, in compliance with a Paekche request, between Paekche's King Tongsŏng and the daughter of a Silla nobleman.

59 As noted by Jamieson, "Embrace the yielding," is seen in *Zhongyong (Doctrine of the Mean)*, Legge, 409, and the second "revive the dying," appears in *Zhongyong*, Legge, 411, New York: Paragon, 1966.

60 For a brief period during the Tang, from 662 to 670, the normally encountered term for this ministry, *"sinong,"* was changed to *"sijia."*

61 These are planted by one's ancestors, hence, one's birthplace.

He will rely on Silla to be a good neighbor forever. Each will free themselves from emotions of the past and conclude new treaties of amity. Each will become tribute states, obeying the [imperial] command forever.

Further, General of the Right Awesome Guard, Duke of Lucheng District Liu Renyuan was sent as envoy to personally exhort and persuade so as to make known and bring to fruition the Imperial will. They [Silla and Paekche] will make a pact involving marriage and repeat its pledge. They will slaughter a sacrificial animal and smear their lips with its blood. There will be mutual sincerity for all times. They will give each other relief in calamity and aid in disaster, with the bonds of indebtedness of brothers. They will reverently receive the silken sounds [Imperial commands] and not dare fail in observing them.[62] After the agreement they will both maintain constant fidelity.[63] Should one waiver in his virtue[64] and breach the covenant, raising arms and mobilizing people to encroach upon the other's border, the all-knowing gods will be watching and rain down hundreds of calamities upon him. He will never raise his sons and grandsons so that no one will maintain his dynastic altars. With the performance of sacrifices to his ancestors obliterated, no trace of his lineage will remain.

Hence, they will make an iron covenant written in gold[65] and preserve it in the [royal] ancestral shrine so that descendants for myriad generations will dare not violate it.

---

62 Echoing the *Zuozhuan;* see Legge, 71.

63 *"Suihan"* alludes to a passage in *Analects* IX:27 where the resistance of the pine and cypress is marveled at. The trees are cited metaphorically in reference to firmness of principle under adversity. See *Analects* 144.

64 See *Shijing* 97; *Book of Songs* 104.

65 Han Gaozu used the term "iron contract" or "gold contract" to indicate an official document. See *AKS* 3:210, n. 90.

Hear this, oh gods. Accept this offering and give blessings.[66] Text composed by Liu Rengui."

After smearing blood on their lips, the sacrificed animals and other goods were placed in the ground at the north side of the [national] altar and the covenant was placed in our [Silla] tombs. Thereupon Liu Rengui led our emissaries as well as the four emissaries of Paekche, T'amna, and Japan [Wa], sailed westward across the sea, returning to participate in services at Mount Tai.[67] [The King] named Prince Chŏngmyŏng to be his Crown Prince and declared a general amnesty.

Winter. The people of Ilsŏn-ju and Kŏyŏl-chu, these two *chu*, were ordered to transport military supplies to Hasŏ-ju. In the past ten *sim* of silk was one bolt. This has been changed so that one bolt is 7 *po* in length and 2 *ch'ŏk* in width.[68]

Year six [666], spring, second month. There was an earthquake in the capital.

Summer, fourth month. There was a fire at Yŏngmyo Monastery. There was a general amnesty. Ch'ŏnjon's son Hallim and Yusin's son Samgwang at the rank of *nama* entered Tang as imperial resident guards. Having already pacified Paekche, the King wanted to destroy Koguryŏ and requested troops from Tang.

Winter, twelfth month. Tang named Li Chi to be *Liaodongdao xingzhun dadudu* [Adjutant Grand Commander-in-Chief of Liaodong] and *Silie shaochangbao* [Junior Executive Attendant of

---

66 Similar invocations are seen in more than one of the *Odes;* see, for example, Legge, 253, 620; and Waley, *Songs,* 195, 251.

67 *AKS* 3:210, n. 91, notes that this same information is found in several Chinese sources.

68 As noted earlier, 1 *po* (pace) at this time was approximately 1.53 meters. As 1 *sim* was approximately 2.03 meters (80 inches), and 1 *ch'ŏk* equaled 24 centimeters (9.5 inches), the length of a bolt of cloth is now reduced by nearly half. See Jamieson 252, n. 67. See also Yi Ut'ae, "Hanguk kodae ŭi ch'ŏkto," *T'aedong kojŏn yŏngu* 1 (1984): 13. See also *AKS* 3:210, n. 93–94.

the Ministry of Personnel] Hao Chujun of Anlu as his deputy in attacking Koguryŏ. Yŏn Chŏngt'o,[69] a high Koguryŏ noble, came to surrender with twelve fortresses, 763 households, and 3,543 people. Chŏngt'o and twenty-four of his subordinates were given clothing, food, and housing and were settled in eight of their fortresses that remained intact in the capital as well as several *chu* and districts. And they dispatched soldiers to garrison and guard them.

Year seven [667], autumn, seventh month. For three days a [court] banquet was held. The Tang Emperor decreed that Chigyŏng and Kaewŏn become generals and join in the Liaodong campaign.[70] The King at once made Chigyŏng a *p'ajinch'an* and Kaewŏn a *taeach'an*. The Emperor again decreed that *Taeach'an* Irwŏn become *Yunhui Jiangzhun* [Yunhui General of the Cloud-like Flags].[71] The King ordered [Irwŏn] to receive the imperial decree in the palace courtyard. He sent *Taenama* Chŭphangse to Tang with tribute goods. [Tang] Gaozong ordered Liu Renyuan and Kim Int'ae[72] to follow the route through Piyŏl and enlisted our soldiers to follow two routes, Tagok and Haegok, and to meet in P'yŏngyang.[73]

Autumn, eighth month. The King led thirty generals including

---

69   He is the younger brother of Yŏn Kaesomun.

70   Jamieson 253, n. 72, "Chigyŏng and Kaewŏn were King Munmu's fifth- and sixth-younger brothers, respectively. The "Liaodong Campaign" was the name used by Tang for the attack on Koguryŏ whose territories at that time stretched deep into the Manchurian area."

71   This is a Tang honorary-rank three.

72   Kim Int'ae was the son of King Muyŏl's concubine.

73   According to Jamieson 253, n. 73, "The routes presumably lead from the southwest (Paekche) in the first instance and the southeast (Silla) in the second toward the Koguryŏ capital." *AKS* 3:211, n. 101, suggests Taegok is located in Hwanghae, P'yŏngsan, and Haegok is also located in Hwanghae. According to *Kuksa taesajŏn*, Piyŏl is located in Hamgyŏng namdo.

Taegakkan Kim Yusin and departed the capital. In the ninth month they reached Hansŏng Garrison and waited for the Duke of Ying.[74]

Winter, tenth month, second day. The Duke of Ying reached 200 *li* north of P'yŏngyang Fortress. He selected and dispatched *Taenama* Kangsim, who was village head[75] of Yidonghye village, to lead a Khitan cavalry of eighty men past Ajinham Fortress[76] and, reaching Hansŏng, he transmitted an imperial letter urging troops on for an [early] engagement to which the Great King agreed.

Eleventh month, eleventh day. On reaching Changsae, it was learned that the Duke of Ying had returned and so the King's troops also returned.[77] At this time he granted Kangsim the rank of *kŭpch'an* and five hundred *sŏk* of millet.

Twelfth month. Chief Minister Munhun died. Tang Garrison General Liu Renyuan announced the decree of the Son of Heaven that [Silla] would aid in the conquest of Koguryŏ and gave to the King the standards of a grand general.

Year eight [668], spring. Ama[78] came and surrendered. Wŏngi and [Yŏn] Chŏngt'o were sent to Tang. Chŏngt'o remained there and did not return and only Wŏngi came back. There was an imperial decree stating that from now on women would be forbidden [as tribute].[79]

---

74 This is Li Shiji, or Li Ji. The Ying state is around present day Yingshan in Hubei. See Jamieson 253, n. 74.

75 See also *AKS* 3:212, n. 103.

76 This is in the Ch'ŏlwŏn area of Kangwŏn.

77 The original text has the word "encounter." However, according to the *Samguksa chŏryo* it is "returned." See *AKS* 1:78, n. 55.

78 According to Jamieson 255, n. 76, this is probably an island off the coast of Chŏnnam, presumably south of Yŏsu. See *AKS* 3:212, n. 105.

79 According to Jamieson 255, n. 77, "'Women were, except for a [sic] brief moralistic periods, welcome items of tribute by the Tang Chinese." Gaozong in this instance appears to be agreeing with his father's dictum. See Schafer, *Golden Peaches,* op

Third month. *Pajinch'an* Chigyŏng became chief minister. Piyŏrhol-ju[80] was established and *P'ajinch'an* Yongmun was named its area commander-in-chief.

Summer, fourth month. A comet held at *Ch'ŏnsŏn* [the Celestial Ship].[81]

Sixth month, twelfth day. *Liaodong anfufu dashi* [Deputy Pacification Chief of Liaodong], *Liaodong xingzhun* [Adjutant Deputy Grand Commander of Liaodong], concurrent Pacification Commander in Chief, Adjutant Commander in Chief, Right Councilor, Acting Left Mentor of the Heir Apparent, Supreme Pillar of the State, Dynasty Founding Baron of Luocheng Liu Rengui received an imperial decree and, with Imperial Resident Guard *Sach'an* Kim Samgwang, they reached Tanghang Garrison. The King had *Kakkan* Kim Inmun meet them with an elaborate [court] ceremony. Thereupon the *Youxiang* [Right Councilor Liu] having concluded an agreement [to mobilize troops] went toward Ch'ŏngang. On the twenty-first day *Taegakkan* Kim Yusin became Grand Banner Supreme Adjutant Grand Commander; *Kakkan* Kim Inmun, Hŭmsun, Ch'ŏnjon, Munch'ung, *Chapch'an* Chinbok, *P'ajinch'an* Chigyŏng, *Taeach'an* Yangdo, Kaewŏn, and Hŭmdol became Grand Banner Adjutant Grand Commanders; *Yich'an* Chinsun {another source writes it *"ch'un"*} and Chukchi became Kyŏngjŏng [Capital Banner] Adjutant Grand Commanders; *Ich'an* P'umil, *Chapch'an* Munhun, and *Taeach'an* Ch'ŏnp'um became *Kwidang* [Noble Banner] Adjutant Grand Commanders; *Ich'an* Int'ae became *Piyŏldo* Adjutant Grand Commander; *Chapch'an*

cit., 44–5.

80 This is located in the southern part of Hamgyŏng and shows that Silla was quickly taking over Koguryŏ territory, see Jamieson 255, n. 78.

81 Jamieson 256, n. 79, points out that the "Celestial Ship" is "the main star in a group of seven north of Musca Borealis constellation.

Kungwan, *Taeach'an* Toyu, and *Ach'an* Yongjang became Hansŏng-ju *haenggun* [Field] Adjutant Grand Commanders; *Chapch'an* Sungsin, *Taeach'an* Munyŏng, and *Ach'an* Pokse became Piyŏl-ju Field Adjutant Grand Commanders; *P'ajinch'an* Sŏngwang, *Ach'an* Changsun, and Sunjang became Hasŏ-ju Field Adjutant Grand Commanders, *P'ajinch'an* Ŭibok and *Ach'an* Ch'ŏngwang became Oath Banner Adjutant Grand Commanders, and *Ach'an* Ilwŏn and Hŭngwŏn became *Kyegŭm* Banner Adjutant Grand Commanders. On the twenty-second day [Ungjin] district fortress Liu Renyuan sent *Kwigan* Mihil to report the submission of two *kun* and twelve fortresses including Koguryŏ's Taegok Fortress, Han Fortress, and others. The King sent *Ilgilch'an* Chingong with congratulations. Inmun, Ch'ŏnjun, Toyu, and others led the military forces of Ilsŏn-ju and seven *kun* and of Hansŏng-ju to the Tang camp. On the twenty-seventh the King departed from the capital to the Tang troops. On the twenty-ninth commanders of the various routes departed. The King had Yusin, because of an illness, remain in the capital. Inmun and others met the Duke of Ying and advanced the army to the foot of Mount Yŏngnyu {Yŏngnyu is 20 *li* north of Sŏgyŏng [the Western Capital]}.

Autumn, seventh month, sixteenth day. The King proceeded next to Hansŏng-ju where he instructed the various commanders to go and meet the Tang troops. Munyŏng and others on the plains of Sach'ŏn [stream] met and fought the Koguryŏ troops soundly defeating them there.

Ninth month, twenty-first day. Together with Tang troops, they surrounded P'yŏngyang. The Koguryŏ King [Pojang] first sent Chŏn [Yŏn] Namsan[82] and others to meet with the Duke of Ying

---

82 He is Yŏn Kaesomun's third son. See also SS 49. Tang Gaozu had changed his

and request to surrender. Thereupon the Duke of Ying with King Pojang, Princes Pongnam and Tŏngnam, high officials, and more than 200,000 people returned to Tang. *Kakkan* Kim Inmun and *Taeach'an* Choju accompanied the Duke of Ying and returned and Int'ae, Ŭibok, Suse, Ch'ŏngwang, and Hŭngwŏn followed. Earlier when the Tang army pacified Koguryŏ, the King set out from Hansŏng for P'yŏngyang. On proceeding to Hilch'ayang, he learned that the Tang generals had already returned and so he turned back to Hansŏng.

Winter, tenth month, twenty-second day. The King granted Yusin the rank of *t'aedae kakkan*[83] and Inmun was granted the rank of *tae kakkan*. In addition the *ich'an* and generals all became *kakkan*. All those who were *sop'an* and below were raised one rank. As Grand Banner *Sogam* [Junior Director] Pondŭk was first in merit in the battle of Sach'ŏn, and Hansan-ju Junior Director Pak Kyŏnghan was first in merit in killing military governor Sult'al in P'yŏngyang, and Hŭgangnyŏng Sŏnguk was first in merit in fighting at the great gate in P'yŏngyang, each was awarded the rank of *ilgilch'an* and 1,000 *sŏk* of unhulled rice. As Oath Banner *Tangju* [Chief] Kim Tunsan was first in merit in fighting in the P'yŏngyang military camp, he was awarded the rank of *sach'an* and 700 *sŏk* of unhulled rice. As Puggŏ, the *Kunsa* [Army Commander] of Mount Namhan, was first in merit in the battle of P'yŏngyang's northern gate, he was awarded the rank of *sulgan*[84] and granted 1,000 *sŏk* of millet. As Kugi, the Army

---

name from Yŏn. For a fuller account of the battle of P'yŏngyang see *The Koguryŏ Annals, SS,* King Pojang 27.

83 This was a special rank within the Silla rank order meaning great supreme *kakkan*.

84 This is a regional rank given to people in the countryside at level two in the eleven-grade rank system. See Yi Ut'ae, "Silla Ch'on kwa Ch'onju," *Hanguksaron* 7 (1981): 114.

Commander of Puyang[85] was first in merit in fighting at the southern bridge in P'yŏngyang, he was granted the rank of *sulgan* and 700 *sŏk* of millet. As Sehwal, the *ka* [interim] Army Commander of Piyŏrhol was first in merit in fighting at the minor fortress of P'yŏngyang, he was granted the rank of *kogan* and 500 *sŏk* of millet. As Kim Sanggyŏng, Junior Director of Hansan-ju, lost his life in battle at Sach'ŏn and was first in merit, he was awarded the rank of *ilgilch'an* and granted 1,000 *sŏk* of unhusked rice. *Sach'an* Kuyul of Asul[86] fought in the battle of Sach'ŏn where he went beneath a bridge, waded across a stream, and went out to fight with the enemy, scoring a great victory. Because he did this without orders and on his own pursued this dangerous course, and although he was first in merit, [his deeds] were not recorded. Burning with anger, he wanted to hang himself, but a bystander saved him so he did not die. On the twenty-fifth day the King, on returning to his country, stopped at Yoktol station where Kugwŏn[87] *Sasin* [Attending Subject] *Taeach'an* Yongjang personally offered a banquet to entertain the King and those in attendance. As soon as the music began, Nŭngan, the fifteen-year-old son of *Nama* Kinju presented the dances of Kaya.[88] The King, seeing [the dancer] had classical neat features and was lovely, summoned him forward, patted him on the back, and urged him to drink from his golden wine cup and generously presented gifts of silk.

Eleventh month, fifth day. The King entered the capital with

---

85 Puyang is in Kangwŏn, P'yŏnggang.
86 This is in Ch'ungnam, Asin.
87 Kugwŏn is in Ch'ungbuk, Ch'ungju.
88 Kugwŏn was an area in which the Kaya ruling class had settled and so it became a center of Kaya culture. See Im Pyŏngt'ae, "Silla sogyŏnggo," *Yŏksa hakpo* 35-6 (1967): 86-9.

7,000 Koguryŏ prisoners. On the sixth day he led his military and civil officials, and paying respects at the shrine of his forebears, reported, "Respectfully following the intentions of my honored forebears, with the Great Tang, we mobilized righteous troops to challenge the crimes of Paekche and Koguryŏ. The arch villains, bowing down, pled guilty, making peaceful the destiny of the country. We hereby make this report, may the gods listen to it." On the eighteenth day goods were awarded to those who died in battle; those of junior director rank and above each received ten [] [][] bolts and their followers received twenty bolts.

Twelfth month. There was a fire at Yŏngmyo Monastery.

Year nine [669], spring, first month. Dharma master Sinhye became *Chŏnggwan* [Scribal Inspector] in the *Taesŏsŏng* [Central Secretariate].[89] The Tang monk Ban arrived and transmitted the Tang Emperor's order requesting loadstone.[90]

Second month, twenty-first day. The Great King met with his ranking officials and handed down this decree:[91]

"In the past, Silla was cut off by two states. The North attacked and the West invaded, frequently leaving [Silla] with no peace. The bleached bones of its warriors heaped high in the fields, heads and torsos were scattered far apart.

Our former King, pitying the people being cruelly harmed and disregarding his well-being, crossed the sea to enter Tang to seek troops.[92] Originally his wish was to pacify those two states and abolish war forever, to expurgate the deep enmity of generations

---

89 Jamieson 260, n. 87, states "the functions of this office are obscure." Talented monks were selected to fill it. Jamieson translates it as "senior scribe." See also *AKS* 3:216, n. 132.

90 Jamieson 260, n. 88, states "Lodestone, a frequent tribute from Korea, was apparently used for medicinal purposes." See Schafer, *Golden Peaches,* 181.

91 See Jamieson 118–9 for reference.

92 Jamieson notes here that this is a reference to King Muyŏl's trip to Tang in 648.

and make whole again the people's shattered lives. But whereas Paekche was pacified, Ko[gu]ryŏ had yet to be destroyed when I inherited the task of overcoming them. Finally I have completed the goal cherished by the former King. The two enemies have now been pacified. Peace and tranquility prevail all over. Those who demonstrated merit in battle have all been presented with rewards, and the souls of those who died in battle have been posthumously granted treasures for their repose.

However, among those in prison, those yet to receive the grace of royal sympathy as well as those suffering in cangues and shackles, have still to be granted the favor of starting anew. When I think of this I can neither eat nor sleep in comfort. Now there can be an amnesty throughout the country.

Before dawn of the twenty-first day of the second month in the second year of the Zongzhang period [669], all those imprisoned, other than for the 'five great crimes'[93] who received the death sentence, will be released, regardless of the severity of their crimes. Since the last amnesty those who committed crimes or were stripped of their ranks will be restored as before. As for thieves, although they will be set free, [they still must make recompensation] and there will be no deadline for the collection of recompensation for those who lack resources. As to those impoverished people who obtained grains from others, should they be from poor crop areas, they need return neither the original amount nor any interest. Those from good harvest areas need only return the principal amount when this year's crop is harvested. Interest need not be repaid. The [amnesty terms] are in effect for the next thirty days []][]. The offices concerned will

---

93 Jamieson 261, n. 93, translates the five great crimes as "The Five Defiances," noting this includes murder of one's lord, mother, father, grandfather, or grandmother.

dutifully carry them out."

Summer, fifth month. As the people of these three *kun,* Ch'ŏnjŏng-gun, Piyŏrhol-gun, and Kangnyŏn-gun, were starving, they opened the granaries to provide relief and sent *Kŭpch'an* Kijinsan and others to Tang to present two *sang* [boxes] of loadstone. They also sent *Kakkan* Hŭmsun and *P'ajinch'an* Yangdo to Tang to offer apologies.[94]

Winter. A Tang envoy arrived to transmit a decree and returned to Tang with a bow master, the artisan *Sach'an* Kujinch'ŏn. [In the decree the Emperor] ordered he make a wooden bow [but] it shot an arrow [only] 30 *po.*[95] The Emperor questioned him, "I have heard in your country you can make bows that shoot arrows for 1,000 *po,* so why is it that this bow shoots no more than 30 *po?*" [Kujinch'ŏn] answered, "It is because the material is not good. If I had wood from my country, I could make one to do that." On this the Emperor sent an envoy to fetch the [proper] wood and soon *Taenama* Poknan brought the wood. Again the Emperor ordered him to remake it and it shot 60 *po.* When asked the reason, he answered, "I do not know the reason, but perhaps because when the wood was transferred across the sea it was impacted by humidity." The Emperor suspected that he was [purposely] not making the bow and even though he threatened him with severe punishment, to the end he did not display his talent.

The King gave out 174 horse corrals:[96] twenty-two went to the

---

94 It is unclear as to why Silla was offering apologies although it might relate to the fact that Silla had occupied some Paekche territory or, as Jamieson 261, n. 96, suggests, "to plead Silla's case in relation to Li Ji's accusation of their failure to meet battle schedules."

95 Thirty *"po"* is about 45.9 meters. See Yi Ut'ae, "Hanguk kodae." According to *AKS* 3:217, n. 139, as noted earlier, the length of the *"po"* measurement changed in the Tang period.

96 Jamieson 262, n. 97, "The text here reads *ku* (nine), a likely error for *pŏm.*"

Sonae,[97] ten to government offices, six to *T'adae kakkan* Yusin, and five to *Tae kakkan* Inmun. Seven *kakkan* each received three, five *ich'an* each received two, six *p'ajinch'an* and eight *tae ach'an* each received one, and the remaining seventy-four were appropriately distributed.

Year ten [670], spring, first month. Tang Gaozong allowed Hŭmsun to return home but Yangdo was detained and remained in prison where he died. This was because the King had dared to occupy, without authority, Paekche land and people. The Emperor seethed with anger and again detained [Silla] envoys.

Third month. *Sach'an* Sŏl Oyu together with Koguryŏ *T'aedaehyŏng* Ko Yŏnmu, each led ten thousand elite soldiers across the Yalu River to Okkol. [][][] Malgal troops had gone ahead to Kaedonyang and waited there.

Summer, fourth month, fourth day. Fighting started with our troops winning a great victory and killing and capturing countless numbers. As Tang troops continuously arrived, our troops retreated and occupied Paeksŏng Fortress.[98]

Sixth month. A Koguryŏ man from Surim Fortress,[99] *Taehyŏng* Mojam,[100] gathered the remaining people from Kungmo Fortress to south of the P'aesu River.[101] They killed Tang government officials, the monk Pŏpan, and others and headed to Silla. On arriving at Saya Island[102] in the Western Sea, they saw the great minister from Koguryŏ, the son of Yŏn Chŏngt'o, Ansŭng. They

---

97 This is believed to be an office, the *Sŭngbu,* that made horse carts; see Yi Pyŏngdo 103. However it might have meant the court.
98 This is in Kyŏnggi, Ansŏng.
99 This is in Kyŏnggi, P'aju.
100 Jamieson 264–5, n. 104, suggests there are a number of inconsistencies in this account.
101 This is the Taedong River.
102 This is Tŏkchŏk Island in Ongjin, Kyŏnggi.

The Silla Annals of the Samguk Sagi

escorted him to Hansŏng Fortress and made him the ruler. They sent *Sohyŏng* Tasik to Silla who pleadingly announced,

"The accepted principle of the world is to restore fallen states and continue interrupted lineages, and we can only look to Silla with this hope. The previous kings of our country saw their demise because they lost the Way. Now we have received our nation's high noble Ansŭng and endorse him to be our lord. It is our wish to act as a fence and screen [protecting frontier] and forever serve with utmost loyalty."

The King settled them in Kŭmmajŏ in the western part of the country.[103] As a woman in Hangi district gave birth at one time to three boys and one girl, the [King] sent 200 *sŏk* of millet.

Autumn, seventh month. The King was suspicious that remaining Paekche people were going to rebel again and so he sent *Taeach'an* Yudon to the Ungjin governor to seek a harmonious relationship, but they did not comply. [Instead] they dispatched *Sama* Yegun[104] to spy on Silla. The King, knowing that they plotted against us, detained Yegun and would not return him and [instead] enlisted troops to attack Paekche. P'umil, Munch'ung, Chungsin, Ŭigwan,[105] Ch'ŏngwan, and others attacked and seized sixty-three fortresses and resettled those people to the interior [of Silla]. Ch'ŏnjon, Chukchi, and others captured seven fortresses and beheaded 2,000. Kungwan, Munyŏng, and others captured twelve fortresses and attacked barbarian soldiers, beheading seven thousand, and they captured

---

103 This is in Iksan, Chŏnbuk. Jamieson 265, n. 105, indicates this was a direct challenge to Tang. Ansŭng remained here until 683 when he was moved to the Silla capital.

104 *SS* suggests that there is a textual error here and his name should be read as Nigun. See Munmu's letter of 671, *AKS* 3:219, n. 151. Yegun had been detained in Silla for several years and also visited Japan.

105 His daughter married Ansŭng.

very many war horses and weapons. The King returned. Because Chungsin, Ŭigwan, Talgwan, Hŭngwŏn, and others camped at [][] [] monastery and retreated, this is a crime that deserves death. But they were forgiven and only lost their positions. Ch'anggilu, [][][] *il* were each given the rank of *kŭpch'an* and differing amounts of unhusked rice. The King sent *Sach'an* Sumisan to enfeof Ansŭng as the King of Koguryŏ. The enfeofment proclamation stated:

In the first year of Xianheng,[106] in the year *kyŏngo*, in autumn, the first day of the eighth month, on *sinch'uk* day, I, the King of Silla, command the enfeofment of the Koguryŏ heir Ansŭng. Your founding King, King Chungmo[107] accumulated virtue on the northern mountains and built merit in the southern seas, his commanding presence spread across Ch'ŏnggu,[108] and his humane instructions covered Hyŏnt'o.[109] His descendants followed in succession without interruption, and they expanded the land over 1,000 *li* for about eight hundred years. [But] coming to the two brothers Namgŏn[110] and Namsan, calamity arose in the family[111] as a schism among relatives occurred, destroying the family and the country and extinguishing the ancestral shrines and the dynastic altars. The people were agitated with no place to put their trust. You went to the fields and the mountains to escape danger and difficulties and put your trust personally in a neighboring state [Silla]. You are like Duke Wen of Zhen in your wandering and suffering and like the Marquis of Wei in restoring

---

106 These are the reign years 670–673 of Tang Gaozong.
107 This refers to the Dynastic Founder King Tongmyŏng.
108 This is another name for Korea. Jamieson 266, n. 109, states this is "a poetic name for the land to the northeast of China, a legendary paradise."
109 This is another name for Koguryŏ.
110 He is the second son of Yŏn Kaesomun.
111 Jamieson 267, n. 112, translates this as "reverential screen," a metaphor for rulers.

The Silla Annals of the Samguk Sagi

a destroyed state.[112] Now people cannot exist without a ruler as 'august heaven must have one to entrust with the Mandate.'[113] Since you alone are the true successor of the former kings, who else, if not you, can lead the ancestral sacrifices? With sincerity I send the envoy *Ilgilch'an* Kim Sumisan and others to open this command to name you King of Koguryŏ. You must fittingly gather and soothe your displaced people and restore the ancient connections, and forever as [friendly] neighboring countries [we must] conduct affairs as brothers. Honor this, honor this. Along with this I send 2,000 *sŏk* of non-glutinous rice, 1 armored horse, 5 bolts of thin silk, 10 bolts each of pongee and linen, and 15 *ch'ing* [135 kilograms][114] of cotton. You [the king] should accept this."

Twelfth month, Saturn passed into [through] the moon. In the capital there was an earthquake. Chief Minister Chigyŏng retired. The country of Wa changed its name to Japan. They say they took this name because they are near to where the sun rises.[115] Hansan-ju Adjutant Grand Commander Suse seized Paekche []. When this affair became known, they dispatched *Taeach'an* Chinju to punish them. {[]}[116]

---

112 Jamieson 267, n. 114, states these are two personalities of the Eastern Zhou. Duke Wen lived among foreign tribes when his father murdered his brother who was the heir apparent. Duke Wen later returned to restore the legitimate line. "The Marquis of Wei, Duke Xuan, was installed by subordinates to his older brother's position once an usurper was done away with."

113 Jamieson 267, n. 115, notes that this phrase is modeled on one in *Shijing*.

114 One *ch'ing* is approximately 9 kilograms (19.8 pounds). According to Jamieson 267, n. 116, 1 *ch'ing* equals 15 *kŭn*.

115 A similar passage is found in *Xin Tangshu*. See *AKS* 3:220, n. 162.

116 The text has a footnote of seventeen characters, five of which cannot be read—rendering the footnote unintelligible.

The Silla
Annals of the
Samguk Sagi

King Munmu – Part Two

Book

7

King Munmu — Part Two

Year eleven [671], spring, first month. *Ich'an* Yewŏn became chief minister. [Silla] dispatched troops to invade Paekche. In the battle south of Ungjin, *Tangju* [Banner Chief] Pugwa[1] was killed. Malgal troops came and encircled Sŏlgu Fortress[2] but could not bring it down. They were about to withdraw when we sent out troops to attack them, beheading more than 300 people. On learning that Tang troops wanted to come and aid Paekche, [Silla] dispatched *Taeach'an* Chingong, *Ach'an* [][][] to defend Ongp'o. A white fish jumped into [ten characters missing], 10 *pun.*

Summer, fourth month. [Lightning] shook the south gate of Hŭngnyun Monastery.

Sixth month. General Chukchi and others were dispatched to lead troops to trample the grain at Paekche's Karim Fortress[3] and then fought against Tang forces at Sŏksŏng Fortress,[4] beheading 5,300 people and capturing two Paekche generals and six Tang

---

1 *Tangju* (Banner Chief) is a military office that, in middle and late Silla, shifted to be a position in the regional system, equivalent to a county magistrate. See Yi Chonguk, "Namsan sinsŏngp'irŭl t'onghayŏ pon Silla ŭi chibang t'ongch'i ch'eje," *Yŏksa hakpo* 64 (1974) and Chu Podon, "Silla chunggo ŭi chibang t'ongch'i chojik e taehayŏ," *Hanguksa yŏngu* 23 (1979). For Pugwa see his brother Ch'wido's biography in *SS* 47.
2 This is in Hamnam, Anbyŏn.
3 This is in Ch'ungnam, Puyŏ.
4 This is also in Ch'ungnam, Puyŏ. See Yun Mubyŏng and Sŏng Chuyŏk, "Paekche sansŏng ŭi sindohyŏng, *Paekche yŏngu* 8 (1977).

Guoi [Courageous Garrison] vice commanders.

Autumn, seventh month, twenty-sixth day. Great Tang commander Xue Rengui had Dharma Master Imyun[5] to carry a letter stating:[6]

Field Area Commander-in-Chief Xue Rengui sends this letter to the King of Silla. Following the promise of the Heavenly Mandate, we came to this border [swiftly] covering 10,000 *li* like a dry wind and crossing 3,000 *li* of a great ocean. I have learned that [your] contriving mind has shifted somewhat and you misuse martial strength at border fortresses, that you discard "Youye's half-a-word [honesty]"[7] and abandon the "single promise of Housheng [trustworthiness]."[8] The elder brother is becoming a treacherous chief while the younger brother is the loyal servant.[9] The flower and its base[10] have been severed while the moon of longing over separation shines in vain. Truly, when [relations between] the two sides are discussed, one cannot but sigh in regret.

Your former King Muyŏl,[11] in planning and governing, toiled tirelessly among hundreds of fortresses [across the country]. He

---

5   See *AKS* 3:223, n. 9.

6   This letter and notes are adapted from the Jamieson 128 translation.

7   A metaphor for honesty originating in *Analects* 12:12. Youye is the name of Confucius' disciple Zilu, a man of such honesty that he elicited complete trust from others. Even a fragment of what he said was of such felicity as to allow decisions to be based on it.

8   A reference to Houying, an aged recluse of the Warring States period who provided Xinling Zhun with successful tactical plans for breaking a Qin siege. Unable to join in the battle because of his age, he vowed to kill himself as a sacrifice to the campaign and he carried out his vow.

9   This is undoubtedly a reference to Paekche as younger brother and Silla as older brother.

10 A metaphor for brotherly love.

11 See *AKS* 3:224, n. 13. The passage refers to him as Kaebu which was taken from a title given him when he ascended the throne.

was vexed by Paekche incursions to the west and alarmed by Ko[gu]ryŏ plundering to the north. Because there were battles frequently across the countryside, silkworm rearing maidens could not meet the mulberry season and plowmen missed their tilling times. [The former king's] age approached sixty, nearing his twilight years,[12] yet, unafraid of the dangers of navigating the sea, he traveled far across Marquis Yang's hazards [of waves] to devote his heart to the land of China and to touch his forehead at gate of the imperial palace.[13] He fully described [Silla's] isolation and weakness and discussed with clarity the encroachments and harassment. On hearing this heartfelt disclosure, one could not help but be overcome with sorrow. Taizong Wendi,[14] whose bearing commanded the world and whose spirit prevailed over the universe just like the nine changes of Bangu and the one palm of Chuling,[15] did not rest for a day from supporting the fallen and rescuing the weak. He received your late lord with pity and sympathetically accepted his requests. Within but one day he personally and repeatedly favored him with light carriages and fine steeds, handsome clothing, and the finest herbs. Having already accepted this grace, as they discussed military matters, their bond was as that of fish and water, as clear as set in stone.

---

12 The text literally reads "approached the age of the docile ear" which is from the *Analects* II:4, "...At sixty I heard (the bidding of Heaven) with a docile ear...." It goes on, as translated by Jamieson, "The elm's shadow encroached more each day." As to the actual age of Muyŏl, it was probably closer to 45 or 46. See *AKS*. 3:224, n. 14.

13 This is a reference to Muyŏl's troop request trip to Tang in 648. "Marquis Yang" is the "God of the Waves."

14 This was the first posthumous name for Taizong,

15 According to Jamieson, these two figures from Chinese folklore are cited to illustrate Taizong's deftness in the administration of an immense empire. Bangu altered original chaos in nine ways on one day to organize the universe and Chuling, a giant god, bifurcated a mountain with his hands and feet so that the rivers were able to flow into the land.

The late [Silla] lord stayed continuously in the [palace of] thousands of phoenix locks and myriad crane portals [bolts and keys] where he was feasted at wine banquets. They [Emperor and King] chatted and laughed by palace stairs shining like gold, then conferred on military matters. Setting the date [to attack] and giving boisterous aid, straightaway they made a decisive deployment and attacked by land and sea. At this time frontier plants had shed their blossoms then, and elm flowers had shed their seeds.[16]

In the Zhubi war[17] Wendi personally campaigned—in pity for others and in commiseration with their pains—which certainly is the depth of his righteous action. Yet soon after, the mountains and seas changed form and the sun and moon lost their rays [with the death of Taizong]. The Sage [Gaozong] resumed the good works[18] [of his father] and Your Majesty, too, carried on your family [legacy]. Relying on each other as vines growing on stones, you dispatched troops together for the expedition preparing for battle, thereby following the will of your father.

For more than several decades China was wearied but still opened frequently its treasuries and daily hastened to supply fodder. For the benefit of Silla [the land of blue islands], troops of China [the yellow earth] were raised, valuing [Silla's] usefulness

---

16 Much of the erudite diction which characterizes General Xue's style in this document is obscure and not seen in standard lexical or quotation collection sources. The gist of the description of the meeting between Taizong and Muyŏl seems to be, however, that they were planning an attack at some future but then unspecified date. "Phoenix locks" and "crane portals" seem to refer to the tight security of the palace. See also *AKS* 3:225, n. 22.

17 This is the 644–645 campaign against Koguryŏ in which Taizong participated. This occurred in the Liaodong area where Mount Zhubi is located. See also *AKS* 3:225, n. 23.

18 As per Jamieson, "A metaphor for the successor, carrying on well the traditions of his predecessor," from *Shijing;* see *Book of Songs* 265.

The **Silla Annals** of the **Samguk Sagi**

and shunning its uselessness. How could we not know when to stop but it was simply because we feared betraying the trust of our forefathers!

Now the strong marauders have been wiped clean, your bitter enemies have lost their state, and you, the King, have once again regained your armies and treasures. Your heart and strength should not waiver so that China and Silla will be of mutual assistance. Then we can melt down our weapons to transform your country [Silla] which has suffered from a lack of essentials. You will naturally attend to the well-being of your country and hand it down to your descendants. This is about what historians would make a laudatory comment.[19]

But now you Your Majesty has discarded a foundation of safety and scorned a policy which would maintain a constant [course]. Afar, you betray the will of Heaven and nearby, reject the words of your father. You treat Heaven's timely [opportunity] with rude contempt and commit deception in neighborly relations. In your country, a far out-of-the-way place, where troops have been drafted from every household and year after year has seen the rising of arms, where widows must pull grain wagons and the young till garrison land, you have neither the sustenance to maintain yourself nor defense should you attack. You may supplant your losses with what you can acquire and preserve, but you do not balance large and small [that is do not know your capacity] and confuse the adverse and the favorable. It

---

19 Jamieson offers a more literary translation, "You should be an unwavering 'heart and backbone' (loyal reliable subject) so that the inner (Tang) and the outer (Silla) may aid each other. Melt down your arrowheads and make the 'empty room' your principle." This is taken from a Zhuangzi metaphor, "When a room is open, light enters naturally, and when the frame or heart is free from extraneous concerns, pure truth can be understood." He goes on, "Then you may naturally 'leave plans to your descendants, secure comfort and support to your sons,'" which is a quote from *Shijing;* see *Book of Songs.*

is as if to proceed gripping the pellet bow while unaware of the danger of the dry well[20] or to move ahead to snatch the cicada and not know of the oriole's formidable presence.[21] It illustrates Your Majesty's inability to judge capacity!

From the outset, during the days of the former King [Muyŏl], he was a recipient of Heaven's care. However, you falsely displayed sincere decorum while harboring evil in your heart, you followed selfish desires while coveting the Emperor's supreme merit, and you shamelessly seek grace in front of the Emperor while planning to rebel in the back. You are not honoring your former lord's [legacy]. Surely one should observe an oath "until the Yellow River runs dry"[22] and [maintain] one's honor [as clear] as the frost.[23] To transgress the will of one's lord is disloyalty; to oppose one's father's will is unfilial. Can you [King] take comfort in bearing these two labels on your person?

You, Kings, both father and son, were suddenly one morning enthroned as Heaven's compassion extended afar to you and its awesome might supported you. When all the adjoining provinces and commanderies one after the other became disorderly, as a result, imperial decrees of investiture were received and thereby you submitted yourself as an imperial subject. You sat and studied the classics and prepared yourself with thoroughness in the Odes and Rites. You heard of propriety yet did not conform, saw goodness but belittled it. You listened to scheming words and are

---

20 This is an allusion to the parable of a girl so fond of eating chicken that she stalked a bird so intently that she paid no attention to where she was going and fell into an abandoned well and died.

21 This is another parable against covetousness.

22 Per Jamieson, this is literally, "Until the River is as a belt," which is from an enfeofment pledge quoted in *Shiji* referring to an "impossible occurrence."

23 This, too, undoubtedly quotes a classical covenant.

confused by the god of surveillance,[24] thus, showing indifference to the foundation of your noble lineage, you prolong the demands of the devil's rapprochements. You supported the former King's flourishing accomplishments while harboring devious thought. Internally you have eliminated officials under suspicion and externally have brought on the arrival of mighty troops. How can this be taken as wise?

Further, Ansŭng of Ko[gu]ryŏ is still young and immature, and within his remaining villages and surviving fortresses, the living have been reduced by half. Consequently he is unsure of himself and thus lacks the ability to take up the responsibility of governing the country.[25] I, [Xue] Rengui, hoisted the sails of our storied ships to catch the wind and, with banners in a line, circuited the northern shore. I felt pity for him in the past when he was like a "bird wounded by an arrow"[26] on his wing and could not bear to attack him. Yet he [now] depends on outside aid! What a foolish blunder is this!

The Emperor, whose grace is boundless and whose humaneness extends afar, whose love is warm like the suns rays, with brilliance like spring flowers, heard this news from afar and was saddened, but, disbelieving, ordered me to come to observe the situation. You, Your Majesty, not only were you unable to send men out to inquire after us, nor did you treat our troops with meat and wine. Rather, you conveniently concealed armor-clad troops on the hillsides and hid soldiers at river mouths to sneakingly crawl

---

24 Literally "Ears and eyes," which is probably criticism of Silla's reconnaissance activities, the term often being used as a metonym for spy.

25 Literally, as per Jamieson, "Unable to bear the weight of his collar and belt" which means his territories: the mountains and rivers of his land surround just as his collar and belt enwrap his body.

26 This passage means one once struck by misfortune or disaster trembles when encountering it again.

through the forest thickets and pant for breath on grass-tangled slopes. Stealthily the "self-gnawing" spear is raised;[27] nowhere is there a sign of joint support.

The great [Tang] army is yet to be deployed, [but] our scout force set out, and as they scanned the ocean and sailed the rivers, even the fish were startled and birds fled. In such a situation one can see what one should do, so please know how to stop your blundering and blind delusion. Upon undertaking great endeavors, one does not covet petty gains, and if one wants to hold to high integrity, one must rely on exceptional and rare qualities. For it is inevitable that the untrained phoenix will be watched by wolves.

The Han [Chinese] cavalry of General Gao [Kan] and Li Jinxing's border tribe troops [Khitan and Malgal troops],[28] the navy of Wu and Chu and the troublesome forces of You and Bing,[29] have assembled like clouds from the four directions. They line up in their ships and descend and rely on rugged spots to construct fortifications and reclaim wild areas to make them arable. This, Your Majesty, will be a fatal [illness] for you.

If Your Majesty makes those who toil to sing and want to straighten out what went wrong, then you must discuss the causes in detail and outline clearly [the circumstances] of both sides. I, Rengui, who early attended the Emperor[30] and was personally

---

27 This indicates self destructive action, acts which will later be regretted. This quotes the *Zuozhuan,* see Legge 5: 78–9.

28 General Gao led an expedition on to Silla territory in 671 and Li also was a Tang general of northern origins.

29 Wu and Chu are areas in south China; You and Bing are areas in north China. This is a reference to the recruitment of seamen from the south and vicious warriors from the northern areas.

30 Here, literally, "the Great Chariot," that ridden by the Emperor and often quoted as a metonym for the Emperor himself.

entrusted with responsibility, will then record [those facts] to inform [the throne] in a memorial. The problems will certainly be resolved. Why do you hesitate and entwine yourself? Ah! In the past you were a man of loyalty and honor; now you are a treacherous subject. What a regret that the propitious beginning would end adversely. What a tragedy that those who at first were of the same [mind] are in the end estranged.

The wind is strong, the air is sharp; leaves fall and time [passes] sadly. When I climb the mountains and gaze afar, pain strikes in my breast. Since Your Majesty is clever and quick witted, a man of refined and imposing presence, you should return to the principle of modesty and maintain a mind that follows the Way.[31] Thus, will sacrificial rites be timely[32] and royal succession [will continue][33] without change. To foresee blessings and receive [Heaven's] protection, let this be Your Majesty's policy. Even in the midst of a severe clashing of swords, envoys must come and go. I now have dispatched Your Majesty's monk Imyun to bring you this letter in which I present a few [of my thoughts].

The Great King in a letter replied:

In the year of Zhenguan [648], the Former King [Muyŏl] entered the Imperial Court, had an audience, and personally received the gracious decree of Taizong, Wenhuang-di which stated:

"Our present attacks on Ko[gu]ryŏ are for but one reason: We take pity on you Silla, hemmed in by two states, always invaded

---

31 Literally, "augments the modest" which is from the *Yijing, Book of Changes,* 119. The second allusion, a "right according" mind, has not been located.

32 Literally, the "feeding of blood," which refers to ancestral sacrifices, necessarily attended to symbolize the continuity of the state.

33 Literally, the "bundle of (white) rush," which is another reference to continuity of the state, here alluding to an ancient investiture ceremony where the Emperor gave the Prince a bundle of earth wrapped in white rush, symbolic of purity.

and humiliated with never a year of peace. Territory is not what I covet; riches and people are things I possess. When we subdue the two countries, both [the territory] south of P'yŏngyang and the land of Paekche will all be given to you Silla, for eternal tranquility."

The Emperor bestowed on him the stratagems and battle schedules.

The people of Silla all, on hearing of this imperial decree, every man built up his strength and every household waited to serve. [But] before the great campaign could be concluded, Wendi passed on with the present ruler ascending the throne, continuing the former favor. The kindness repeatedly shown has been even greater than in past days. Our brothers and children were conferred with high ranks and titles.[34] Since high antiquity there has not been such a degree of honor and favor. We will pulverize our bodies and smash our bones[35] in the desire to serve to the utmost, and smear our livers and brains with the dust of the plains[36] in the hope of repaying even one ten-thousandth [of what has been bestowed on us.].

Coming to the fifth year of Xianqing [660], His Imperial Eminence [Gaozong] was moved by the fact that our Former King's [Muyŏl's] goals had not yet been realized and wished to conclude this task inherited from former days. He sent his navy, gave orders to his generals, and dispatched a large number of sailors. [Our] Former King [Muyŏl] was old and weak and unable

---

34 Literally, "clutched the gold (seal) and suspended the purple (pouch)," which is a metaphor for official status and a reference to Silla royal scions who had been granted titles at the Tang court. The "gold" is the gold seal of office and the "purple" is the purple pouch which held the seal and which, in terms of standard court dress, was suspended from the waist belt.
35 This is a metaphor for utmost expenditures of effort in the service of others.
36 In others words, sacrifice our lives.

to accompany his armies, yet, always remembering the former grace, he forced himself to go to the border and appointed me to lead our troops to meet the great [Tang] army.[37] The two sides joined forces, together advancing by sea and land. Just as the [Tang] naval forces entered the mouth of the [Paek] river, the [Silla] armies had already defeated the major enemy troops.[38] The two forces reached the royal capital and together subdued the entire state [of Paekche].

After the pacification, our Former King then, with Superior Area Commander Su [Dingfang] had 10,000 Chinese troops remain, and, in addition, Silla dispatched [the King's] younger brother [Prince] Int'ae in command of 7,000 troops so as to guard Ungjin together.

After the great [Tang] army returned, the enemy subject Poksin rose up west of the [Paek] river, sought out and regrouped [Paekche] remnants, and laid siege pressuring the fortress at the Ungjin area command. He first destroyed the outer barricades, capturing all the military provisions, then attacked the district fortress and came close to bringing it down. He then built encampments at four spots adjacent to the district fortress to hold the siege, whereupon it became impossible to enter or leave. I led troops there and broke the siege, destroying all the surrounding enemy fortresses. First I relieved the forces from immediate danger, then I carried provisions, thus 10,000 troops of China escaped the tiger's jaw and the starving forces garrisoned there were spared "bartering children and eating them."[39]

---

37   That is, the Tang troops.

38   This is a reference to Silla's successful campaign against Paekche's eastern flank. The Paek River, now called the Kŭm River, flows by Kongju and Puyŏ before reaching the sea.

39   This is from *Zuozhuan*, see Legge 326 and 328.

Coming to the sixth year [661], Poksin's forces gradually increased and had invaded and taken the area east of the river. A thousand Chinese troops from Ungjin set out to strike the enemy but, instead, were beaten by them without a man returning. With this defeat, Ungjin's troop requests for troops continued day and night. Silla, suffering from widespread plague, was unable to mobilize military forces, yet it was difficult to refuse the pressing requests and so [untested] troops were sent out. They went to lay siege to Churyu Fortress but, the enemy, aware that they were few in number, struck right away and inflicted heavy losses on the military forces. [Our force] returned with no gain. Fortresses in the southern area all rebelled together then and sided with Poksin who, riding on victory, laid yet another siege of the district fortress. This severed the road to Ungjin, causing shortages in salt and bean paste.[40] We immediately recruited able-bodied young men to slip in through the road with salt to relieve their distress.

In the sixth month our Former King died. Although the funeral ceremonies had just been completed, but not yet out of the mourning period, we were unable to hasten to respond to requests for rescue [from Ungjin]. Yet there was an imperial edict, ordering us to mobilize troops to send to the north again.[41] Then, *Zongguan* [Area Commander in Chief] of Hamja Route[42] Liu Demin's group came with an imperial edict appointing Silla to supply and transport provisions to the forces at P'yŏngyang. A messenger came from Ungjin at that time and described in detail the district fortress's precarious isolation. Area Commander-in Chief Liu and

---

40 Jamieson suggests this also may be read "salt and bean paste," one necessary for food preservation and the other a protein supply.

41 Jamieson indicates that this section of the text appears to be corrupted. And, as will be seen below, there is a discrepancy with the timing of Liu's mission.

42 Hamja was one of the *hyŏn* originally in Lelang commandery.

I deliberated and I said that if provisions were transported first toward P'yŏngyang it was likely that the Ungjin route would be severed and, should the Ungjin route be severed, Chinese troops garrisoned there would fall into enemy hands. So Area Commander Liu went along with me then, first striking Ongsan Fortress. Ongsan was taken and, further, a fortress was built at Unghyŏn, and the road to Ungjin reopened.

In the twelfth month Ungjin's provisions were exhausted. It was feared that shipment to Ungjin first would be a violation of the [Imperial] edict, yet if a shipment were sent to P'yŏngyang, then I feared Ungjin would have no grains. So the old and weak were used for transporting to Ungjin and strong, elite, troops were to head for P'yŏngyang. Snowstorms on the road were encountered by those taking grains to Ungjin; men and horses were completely wiped out, not one in a hundred returning.

In the first month of Longshuo period's second year [662], Area Commander-in-Chief Liu set out to bring military provisions toward P'yŏngyang along with Silla's Commander of the Two River Routes Kim Yusin and others.[43] Dreary rains had fallen throughout the month at that time, with freezing blizzards and extreme cold, so that men and horses froze to death, making it impossible for all the provisions they carried to reach their destination. The great [Tang] army at P'yŏngyang also wanted to return and Silla's military force, because their supplies were exhausted, also headed back. The soldiers were starving and cold, their hands and feet frostbitten, and countless numbers of them fell dead on the road. As they advanced as far as the Horo River,[44]

---

43 Jamieson notes that this rank is possibly incorrectly transmitted as it appears nowhere else in SS.

44 This river has been referred to as Kwach'ŏn Stream. It appears to be the Imjin River flowing by Kyŏnggi, P'aju. See AKS 3:228, n. 50.

Ko[gu]ryŏ forces soon came in pursuit and lined up in formation [ready to fight] along the bank of the river. Silla's force, which had been starved and weary for days and days, feared that the enemy would maintain a long pursuit, so crossed the river before the enemy did, then [turned and] fought with them. Our advance force had clashed but briefly when the enemy scattered and then our troops assembled and returned.

Not a month had passed after their return when repeated demands for grain came from Ungjin district fortress. Tens of thousands of sacks[45] were sent in all, to Ungjin in the south and P'yŏngyang in the north. Supplying two places at once, tiny Silla's manpower was sapped to the extreme and oxen and horses wiped out. As farming was not done in a timely way, the annual grains did not ripen and every kernel stored in our granaries was transported away. Although there was not even sufficient food for the people of Silla, provisions for Ungjin's Chinese troops were more than ample. Moreover, it had been long since the garrisoned Chinese troops left their homes and their clothing was so tattered and worn that none had a complete piece of cloth covering his body. Silla [thereupon] urged its people to supply them with clothes according to the season.

Protector General Liu Renyuan, protecting far away an isolated fortress with the enemy on all sides, was constantly subject to attacks and siege by Paekche, but was always relieved and rescued by Silla. As for 10,000 Chinese troops, they were clothed and fed for four years [by] Silla. From Renyuan on down and from the troops on up, in their skin and bones [origins] they were born from the soil of China [the land of Han] but their flesh and blood

---

45 *Hu* (Chinese) is *kok* in Korean; it is the equivalent of approximately 44 liters (40 quarts-US dry; 10 gallons-US dry; 5 pecks-US; 1.25 bushels-US) and is translated here as "sack."

was all Silla. And although its indebtedness to the graces of the state [Tang] was unlimited, Silla's devoted loyalty, too, is deserving of acknowledgement.

In the Longshuo period's third year [663], when Area Commander-in-Chief Sun Renshi led troops here to rescue [Ungjin] district fortress, Silla military forces also set out to join the campaign and advanced to the area beneath Churyu Fortress. At this time ships and troops from Wa had come to aid Paekche and one thousand Japanese ships were anchored in the Paek River,[46] while elite cavalry from Paekche guarded them high up from the shore. Silla's spirited horsemen, being China's vanguard, first destroyed the [Paekche] encampment ranks on the shore, whereupon Churyu lost its courage and immediately surrendered. After the southern area was pacified, we turned our troops to attack to the north where Imjon Fortress alone vainly persisted without surrendering. The two forces [Silla and Tang] combined strength to strike the fortress together, but resistance was so firm that we could not take it. Silla was about to return then when *Shouzhu* [Grand Officer] Du[47] said, "The [Imperial] edict reads, 'After the pacification meet to make an alliance [with Paekche],' and so, even though Imjon Fortress alone has yet to surrender, you now should make an alliance." Silla believed "The [Imperial] edict directed 'meet to make an alliance after the pacification.' Since Imjon has not yet surrendered, we cannot say 'the pacification is already completed.' Furthermore, Paekche is deceptive and treacherous in a hundred ways and endlessly fickle. Now if we join in an alliance [with Paekche], we fear 'self-

---

46 The Paek River or Paengma River are names given to the lower reaches of the Kŭm River which flows into the sea at about the thirty-sixth parallel. See note 38 above.

47 A reference to Du Shuang, whose name appears in the Tang histories in discussions of the Paekche campaign, but who has no official biography.

gnawing' consequences later."[48] Thus Silla made a request to halt the forming of an alliance.

In the first year of Linde [664], a stern edict was again passed down rebuking us for not meeting to make an alliance, whereupon we immediately dispatched men to Ungnyŏng [Pass] to erect an altar and make an alliance. So the place where the alliance was made became the border between the two. Although a meeting to make an alliance was not at all desired, we could not dare disobey the edict.

Once again, an altar was built at Mount Ch'wiri, and, with Imperial Emissary Liu Renyuan, lips were smeared with blood and we made an oath together. It was sworn that our pledge [would endure as] the hills and streams. Boundary markers were erected to be our permanent borders. People would be able to dwell therein, each carrying on their livelihood.

In the second year of Qienfeng [667], hearing of the Superior Area Commander, the Duke of Ying's[49] expedition to Liao, I went toward Hansŏng-ju and dispatched troops to gather at the border. Since Silla's military forces were unable to go in [to attack Koguryŏ] alone, three times we sent out scouts and continuously dispatched ships to watch for the great [Tang] army. As the scouts all on returning said that the great [Tang] army had not yet reached P'yŏngyang, we struck at Ko[gu]ryŏ's Ch'ilchung Fortress to clear open roads and wait for the great [Tang] army's arrival. When the fortress [Ch'ilchung] was just on the verge of falling, Kang Sim, an emissary of the Duke of Ying came and said, "In compliance with the orders of the Superior Area Commander

---

48 See *AKS* 3:229, n. 53. This means hurting yourself but there is nothing you can do about it.

49 In 637 Li Ji was enfeofed the Duke of Ying or the Duke of the state of Ying. See also *AKS* 3:211, n. 97.

[Duke of Ying], Silla military forces must not attack the fortress, but must quickly head toward P'yŏngyang to supply troop provisions." The command was issued to hasten to meet [the Tang army], but when Silla's military forces had proceeded as far as Sugok Fortress,[50] they heard that the great [Tang] army had already returned and so pulled out.

In the third year of Qianfeng [668], Director Kim Poga was sent off by sea to obtain the Duke of Ying's directives and returned with the [Duke's] order that Silla military forces hasten toward P'yŏngyang to assemble. In the fifth month, Minister of the Right Liu [Rengui] came and [further] Silla military forces were sent out with him to hasten toward P'yŏngyang. I, too, went to Hansŏng-ju to inspect the military forces. It was at this time that troops of both China and the frontier peoples[51] were assembled together at the Sasu River and [Yŏn] Namgŏn sent out his troops in hopes of a single decisive victory. Silla's military force, alone as the vanguard, straightaway smashed [Namgŏn's] main ranks, crushing and demoralizing the [Koguryŏ] troops within P'yŏngyang Fortress. Thereupon the Duke of Ying again selected five hundred of Silla's spirited horsemen to first enter through the fortress gates and finally destroyed P'yŏngyang, reaping great success.

With this, Silla's soldiers said, "Since our expedition has started, nine years have already passed. We have exhausted all our strength but have at last pacified the two countries and today realize the long-held hope cherished for generations. It is fitting that our state be given grace for applying its full loyalty and the people rewarded for doing their utmost." The Duke of Ying then

---

50   This fortress is believed to be in Hwanghae, Sinye-gun. See *AKS* 3:229, n. 55.
51   This refers to the Malgal and Khitan serving the Tang.

revealed, "Silla's earlier failure to meet campaign schedules must also be taken into consideration." Upon hearing this, Silla soldiers became increasingly agitated. Further, our generals who had established merit were all described in the record and sent to the Court. No sooner had they arrived at the capital [Changan] than it was said, "There is no one of merit in Silla." When the generals returned, the people were even more frightened.

Further, the fortress at Piyŏl[52] originally belonged to Silla but was attacked and taken by Ko[gu]ryŏ some thirty years ago. Silla regained this fortress, resettled people there, and installed officials to safeguard it. This fortress was taken again [by Tang] and returned to Ko[gu]ryŏ. Moreover, from the time of Paekche's pacification on through the subjugation of Ko[gu]ryŏ, we applied full loyalty, exerted all our efforts and did not fail [your] country, yet suddenly, for some unknown transgression, we have been abandoned overnight. And in spite of such grievances, there has never been a thought of rebellion.

In the first year of the Zongzhang period [668], Paekche shifted boundaries and changed markers where the alliance was made, obtaining our land through encroachment. They lured our slaves and enticed our people, then hid them in their interior. And although we made repeated demands to obtain them [that is land and peoples], they were never returned. Again, news came which stated: "Your country [Tang] is repairing its ships, ostensibly for an attack on Wa, but in reality for a strike at Silla." The people, learning of this, were surprised and restless. Further, a Paekche woman was given in marriage to Pak Toyu, the commander-in-chief of Hansŏng. There was a joint plot to steal Silla's weapons and strike a surprise raid on one of the *chu*. Luckily, when Silla

52   This fortress is located in the Anbyŏn region of South Hamgyŏng.

learned of the matter, Toyu was immediately beheaded and their plot did not materialize.

In the sixth month of Xianheng's first year [670], Ko[gu]ryŏ plotted a rebellion and killed all Chinese officials. Silla wanted to send troops immediately, but first notified Ungjin saying, "Ko[gu] ryŏ has already rebelled and we must attack. Since we are both subjects of the Emperor, it is proper to campaign together against the evil enemy. There should be deliberations regarding the sending of troops and we request that you send your officials here so as to map strategy together." Paekche's *Sama* [Adjutant] Migun[53] came here and deliberated with us saying, "After we have deployed troops, I fear there will be mutual suspicion between us. We had better have officials of both sides exchange hostages." Thereupon Kim Yudon along with Paekche's Chief Recorder Sumi Changgwi of [Ungjin] district fortress and others were forthwith appointed to go to the district for discussion of the hostage exchange. Even though Paekche approved the exchange of hostages, she still had military forces amassed within the fortress and when we arrived at the area beneath the fortress, they immediately came in the night to attack.

In the seventh month [of 670], when [Silla] tributary envoy Kim Hŭmsun and others arrived and were about to demark the borders by examining the maps and verifying the facts, we [discovered] we were to separate and return all of Paekche's old land. The Yellow River was not yet as a belt nor was Mount Tai as a whetstone![54] Yet within three or four years, [the land] was once given and once taken away and Silla's people felt that their

---

53   This is the *sima* (Chinese: *sama*), "adjutant," of Ungjin Fortress, see *AKS* 3:230, n. 61.

54   This is a sarcastic reference back to the Xue letter.

original hope had been thwarted. They said, "Silla and Paekche have been mortal enemies for generations. Judging from Paekche's actions at present, if they are allowed to set themselves apart as a single country, one hundred years hence our descendants will have been swallowed up by them. Silla [being an inseparable ally] is [like] a part of your country [Tang] and cannot be separated into two countries. Our wish is to be one family and without affliction for long years ahead."

In the ninth month of last year, having recorded all those facts, we dispatched an envoy to present a memorial to the Court, but [rough seas] forced him back. Another emissary was then sent who was also unable to reach his destination. Thereafter, when due to frigid winds and fierce waves we had still not memorialized [the Court], Paekche fabricated the story in a memorial that Silla had rebelled.

Silla on the one hand lost the favor of the [Tang] high minister [Duke of Ying] and on the other hand later was slandered by Paekche. Wherever we turn we are blamed so as to be unable to explain our loyalty and sincerity. Calumny such as this daily meets the ears of the Emperor while not once is there word of our single-minded loyalty.

The messenger Imyun came, bringing your most gracious letter, and we learned that You, Grand Commander, braving rough seas, have come far from abroad. We should have properly sent emissaries to the outskirts to welcome you and treat you with meat and wine. But being some distance away in a different fortress, I was unable to observe proper ceremony to welcome you on time. Please do not take offence [to my failure].

We have unrolled and read Your Honor's letter which wholly assumes that Silla is already traitorous. Since this is not our true position, we are anxiously alarmed and fearful. If we enumerate ourselves how much we have contributed, we fear this will bring criticism. Yet by accepting censure with sealed lips, we fear we may fall into an unfortunate fate. Therefore we now briefly enumerate these false accusations to record that we have not been traitorous.

The country [Tang] has not yet sent even a single emissary to inquire into reasons and [instead] hastily dispatched tens of thousands of troops to overthrow our kingdom. Multi-decked warships cover the blue sea and are lined bow to stern in the mouth of the river to rescue Ungjin[55] and destroy our Silla. Alas! Before the two states had been pacified we hustled about as directed and sent [by Tang], while now that the beast has been done in, it is we who are invaded and are at the mercy of the chief [Tang].[56] It is Paekche, the seditious bandit, who is given Yongchi's prize[57] while Silla, who has given her life for Han, received Dinggong's death sentence.[58]

Yet even if the sun's rays did not shine around them, the impulse of the sun flower and bean leaf would still be to turn toward the sun. You, Grand Commander, are endowed with the hero's elegance and bear the superior ability of both a minister and general. Complete in all Seven Virtues and versed in the Nine

---

55 *AKS* 1:89, n. 21–2, citing the *Samguksa chŏryo,* used the character "to rescue" in place of "criticize."

56 This is taken from *Shiji* 92, meaning that Silla's contributions are being directed by Tang.

57 This alludes to an event that is reputed to have occurred as the Han dynasty's Liu Bang was consolidating his dynasty. Although Yongchi was hated by the Han ruler and his life had been spared only because of merit in battle, Liu Bang chose to enfeof him first and thereby signal to his other generals that if a fief were given to Yongchi first, none of them would go without. See Jamieson 279 n. 172.

58 Dinggong, a general under Xiangyou, was executed by Liu Bang after his defeat of Xiangyou. Liu claimed that his defeat of Xiangyou was made possible by men like Dinggong and the execution was to serve as a warning against disloyalty.

Schools,[59] you execute the imperial judgment with care and [do not] punish the innocent recklessly. And before the imperial troops are sent forth, you have first [a letter] inquiring into reasons. Through this letter to you, we dare set forth [the facts to prove] we are not rebellious. We beg you, Grand Commander, to seriously consider it yourself, then explain the situation [to the Emperor] in a memorial."

Submitted by Kim Pŏmmin, Area Commander-in-Chief of Kyerim Prefecture, Grand General of the Left [Militant] Guard, Commander Unequalled in Honor, Supreme Pillar of State, King of Silla.

Soburi-ju was established and *Ach'an* Chinwang was made *todok* [commander-in chief].[60]

Ninth month. Tang General Gao Kan and others lead 40,000 frontier troops to P'yŏngyang where, digging deep trenches and building high ramparts, they invaded Taebang.[61]

Winter, ten month, sixth day. [We] attacked more than seventy Tang cargo ships and captured *Liangjang* [Vice Commandant] Qianer Dahou[62] and more than one hundred soldiers. The number of people who drowned cannot be estimated. As *Kŭpch'an*

---

59 The "seven virtues" of military genius are "the repression of cruelty, the calling in of the weapons of war, the preservation of the great appointment, the firm establishment of one's merit, the giving repose to the people, the harmonizing all (the States), the enlargement of the general wealth." See *Zuozhuan*, Legge 351 and 320. The "nine schools" into which pre-Qin philosophers were categorized by Liu Xin in the Han-shu's *Treatise on Literature* were Confucianism, Taoism, Yin-yang theories, Legalism, Logic, Moism, Diplomatism, Eclecticism, and Agrarianism. See also Feng Yu-lan, *A Short History of Chinese Philosophy,* New York: Free Press, 1960, 31–2.

60 This is Puyŏ. Chinwang, in 661, as an *ach'an,* participated in the attack on Sabi Fortress.

61 This same narration appears in 672 below, indicating this entry may be in error.

62 According to Jamieson 281, n. 179, this officer was returned to Tang in the following year and appears to have been a foreigner, perhaps of Koguryŏ ancestry. The term *Dahou* means "grand marquis."

The **Silla Annals** of the **Samguk Sagi**

Tangch'ŏn was first in merit, he was given the rank of *sach'an*.

Year twelve [672], spring, first month. The King sent generals to attack Paekche's Kosŏng Fortress,[63] subduing it.

Second month. [Silla] attacked Paekche's Karim Fortress but to no avail.

Autumn, seventh month. Tang General Gao Kan led 10,000 troops and Li Jinxing led 30,000 troops coming at the same time to P'yŏngyang where they established eight garrisons and camped there.

Eighth month. They attacked Hansi Fortress and Maŭp Fortress,[64] subduing them. The troops advanced to 500 *po* from Paeksu Fortress[65] where they encamped. Our troops with Koguryŏ troops fought [Tang in resistance], beheading several thousand. When Gao Kan retreated, we pursued them to Sŏngmun[66] and fought them but our troops suffered a defeat with *Taeach'an* Hyoch'ŏn, *Sach'an* Ŭimun, Sanse, *Ach'an* Nŭngsin, Tusŏn, *Ilgilch'an* An Naham, Yangsin, and others dying. [We] constructed Chujang Fortress in Hansan-ju.[67] Its circumferences was 4,360 *po*.

Ninth month. A comet appeared seven times in the northern skies. The King, because Paekche had earlier gone and slandered Silla to the Tang and requested troops to attack us, and because [the King] believed this to be urgent, he did not [have time] to report this before he sent out troops to fight them. Because of this the Tang court considered this a crime against them and so [Silla]

---

63 This is believed to be Sabi Fortress. See *SS 1977* 119.
64 This is believed to be in the P'yŏngyang area along the banks of the Taedong River.
65 This may be in Kyŏnggi, P'aju, or Hwanghae, Chaeryŏng.
66 This is in Hwanghae, Tanhung, or Kyŏnggi, Hwasŏng.
67 This is the site of Namhan Mountain Fortress.

sent *Kŭpch'an* Wŏnch'ŏn and *Nama* Pyŏnsan along with those under custody—Naval Vice Commandant Qianer Dahou, Laizhou *Sima* [Adjutant] Wang Yi,[68] Ponyŏl-ju *Zhangshi* [Administrator] Wang Yi, Ungju Commander-in-Chief Deputy Adjutant Yegun, Chŭngsan Adjutant Pŏpch'ong, and 170 soldiers—to present a memorial begging for pardon. It stated:[69]

I, your subject's crime, deserving of the punishment of death, respectfully state that formerly when we were as if hanging by our heels,[70] we received aid and relief from afar and thus were able to escape slaughter. Though we pulverize our bodies and smash our bones, it would be insufficient to repay such great mercy. Even crushing our heads into ashes and dust we could not recompense such kindness.

But our bitter enemy, Paekche, has encroached upon our borders and implicated imperial troops in order to destroy us, your subjects, and thus erase their shame. Fearing destruction we [acted] to preserve ourselves, yet, unjustly labeled as perverse traitors, we are involved in a crime difficult to pardon. I, your subject, fear that were we punished before having stated the facts, we will live as disobedient subjects and in death be a ghost of one who betrayed grace. Hence, the facts of the case are respectfully recorded and the throne memorialized at the risk of death. Prostrate, I beg that they will be heard even briefly by Your Majesty and that the causes will receive Your enlightened judgment.

From generations past we, your subjects, have unfailingly presented tribute. Recently, because of Paekche, we have

---

68 Laizhou is on the Shandong peninsula.

69 This is adapted from Jamieson 153–5.

70 As per Jamieson, helpless suffering, a metaphor from Mencius; see Legge 184.

The **Silla Annals** of the **Samguk Sagi**

repeatedly failed to send tribute missions, so that now Your Majesty has had to issue pronouncements and order Your generals to punish our crime, for which even death would be insufficient punishment. All the bamboo on South Mountain[71] is not enough for writing our crimes; the woods of Baoxie [Valley][72] are not enough for making the shackles we your subjects [deserve]. Make reservoirs of our shrines and altars, chop and slice my body. If [Your Majesty] would hear the facts and confer a decision, I would happily accept slaughter. My coffin and funeral carriage are by my side, my muddied forehead is still not dry [muddied from kowtowing]; I await the Court [order] with bloody tears and, prostrate, listen for the punishment.

Prostrate, it is my thought that because Your Majesty the Emperor has the brilliance of the sun and moon, the rays of your tolerance will shine to every corner. Your virtue combining heaven and earth will nourish all living things [plants and animals]. Your virtue that fosters life will reach even lowly insects.[73] Your kind mind that loathes killing engulfs the birds and fish. If you were to pardon us because we obey, and grace us permitting our bodies to be intact, even if I died, it would not be different from being alive. Although it is not my wish, I dare to reveal what I hold in my heart. Unable to win over the thought of throwing myself on my sword, I humbly dispatch Wŏnch'ŏn and others to offer this report in acknowledgement of my crime. Prostrate, I await the Imperial edict. I bow before you. I bow before you. My crime is deserving of death. My crime is deserving

---

71 This refers to Zhongnan Mountain, west of Changan, one of China's holy mountains. The timber grown there was noted for its natural straightness. See also Legge, *The She King* 197–8.

72 A valley in the above-mentioned Zhongnan Mountains, noted for its select woods.

73 From *Daodejing;* see Legge, *The Text of Taoism* 1:94.

of death.

Along with this [memorial] they presented 33,500 *pun* of silver, 33,000 *pun* of copper, 400 needles, 120 *pun* of ox bile, 20 *pun* of gold, 6 *p'il* of forty-*sŭng* cloth,[74] and 60 *p'il* of thirty-*sŭng* cloth. This year as grain was dear, people were starving.

Year thirteen [673] spring, first month. A meteor fell between Hwangnyong Monastery and the Chaesŏng.[75] Kang Su[76] became *sach'an* and was given every year 200 *sŏk* of grain.

Second month. [The court] expanded Sŏhyŏng Mountain Fortress.

Summer, sixth month. A tiger entered the great palace grounds and was killed.

Autumn, seventh month, first day. [Kim] Yusin died. *Ach'an* Taet'o planned a rebellion to side with Tang but, as the event was discovered, he was executed and his wife and children were made people of low social standing.

Eighth month. *P'ajinch'an* Ch'ŏn Kwang became a chief minister. [The court] expanded Sayŏl Mount Fortress.

Ninth month. [They] constructed Kugwŏn Fortress {it was the old Wanjang Fortress}, Pukhyŏng Mount Fortress, Somun Mount Fortress, Isan Fortress, Chuyang Fortress in Suyak-chu {also called Chiram Fortress}, Chujam Fortress in Tarhan-gun, Manhŭngsa Mount Fortress in Kŏyŏl-chu, and Kolchaeng-hyŏn Fortress in Samnyang-ju.[77] The King sent *Taeach'an* Ch'ŏlch'ŏn and others to command a hundred battleships to guard the West Sea [Yellow

---

74 According to Jamieson 283, n. 191, 80-warp thread might equal one *sŭng*.

75 This refers to Panwŏlsŏng or the royal palace. See Jamieson 284, n. 194.

76 See also *SS* 46.

77 Pukhyŏng Mount Fortress is in Kyŏngju; Somun Mount Fortress is in Kyŏngbuk, Ŭisŏng; Isan Fortress is in Kyŏngbuk Koryŏng; Chuyang Fortress is in Kangwŏn, Ch'unch'ŏn; Tarhangun Fortress is in Kangwŏn province; and Kŏyŏl-ju Fortress is in Kyŏngnam, Kŏch'ang.

Sea]. Tang troops with Malgal and Khitan troops came invading the northern boundary. Fighting in nine engagements our soldiers defeated them, beheading more than 2,000. The number of Tang troops that drowned in the Hŏro and Wangbong rivers cannot be estimated.[78]

Winter. Tang troops attacked Koguryŏ's Ujam Fortress,[79] subduing it. The Khitan and Malgal forces attacked Taeyang Fortress and Tongja Fortress,[80] destroying them. [The court] established the Wasajŏng[81] for the first time with two positions in the *chu* and one in the *kun*. Earlier, when King T'aejong destroyed Paekche, he abolished frontier guards but, reaching this, it was reestablished.

Year fourteen [674], spring, first month. *Taenama* Tŏkpok, who had gone to Tang as an imperial resident guard to study calendrical matters, returned and brought a new corrected calendar.[82]

Because the King accepted Koguryŏ people who had rebelled and occupied Paekche's former territory and had the people secure it, Tang Gaozong in great anger sent a decree stripping the King of his office. The King's brother Grand General of Uhyowiwŏn, Duke of Imhae-gun, Kim Inmun at that time was in the [Tang] capital. [The Emperor] enthroned him the King of Silla, had him return to his country [Silla], and named *Zuoshuzi zhongshiwenxia* [Grandee of the Secretariate Chancellery] Liu Rengui Adjutant Grand Commander of Kyerim Circuit and Chief Minister of the

---

78 *AKS* 3:235, n. 93, suggests this is in the Koyang area in the Han River estuary.
79 This is in Hwanghae, Kimch'ŏn.
80 Taeyang Fortress is in Kangwŏn, Kŭmgang, in the Democratic People's Republic of Korea (North Korea) and Tongja Fortress is in Kyŏnggi, Kimp'o.
81 This is a rural office that handled inspections of accounts and the execution of justice. According to *SS* 40, 133 positions were created at this time in 673.
82 Tang, in 666, adopted the calendar used by the Sui Emperor and used it until 728.

Weiweiqing [Court Imperial Regalia] Li Pi as Grand General of the Uryŏng army. Li Jinxing became a deputy and dispatched troops to come and attack [Silla].

Second month. Inside the palace they dug a pond, constructed mountains, planted flowers and grass, and raised exotic birds and animals there.[83]

Autumn, seventh month. There was a wind storm that destroyed Hwangnyong Monastery's Buddha Hall.

Eighth month. There was a major review of troops beneath Sŏhyŏng Mountain.

Ninth month. Dharma Master Ŭian was named *taesŏsŏng*[84] and Ansŭng enfeofed King Podŏk. {In King Munmu's tenth year Ansŭng was enfeofed King of Koguryŏ and now he is enfeofed again. Whether the word Podŏk is the same meaning as submission or a place name is not known.} [The King] went to Yŏngmyo Monastery on the front road where he reviewed troops and watched *Ach'an* Sŏl Sujin's Six-Column Maneuver.[85]

Year fifteen [675], spring, first month. Seals cast in copper for all central and provincial offices were made and distributed.

Second month. Liu Rengui destroyed our troops at Chiljung Fortress. Rengui pulled his troops and returned. It was decreed that Li Jinxing would be Andong Garrison *fudashi* [in-charge of pacification] and govern that area. The King thereupon sent an envoy to [Tang] to present tribute and apologize for his crimes. The Emperor pardoned him and restored his royal title. Kim

---

83 This is most likely Annapchi Pond which was reconstructed in Kyŏngju in 1970. See Yi Kibaek, "Manghaejŏn kwa Imhaejŏn," *Silla sasangsa yŏngu,* Seoul: Ilchokak, 1986.

84 This was a clerical office first established in King Chinhŭng's reign, and by Queen Chindŏk's reign two people had held this appointment.

85 See Jamieson 160. See also *AKS* 3:235, n. 105.

Inmun who was en route returned and was enfeofed Duke of Imhae-gun. However, much of Paekche territory was taken [by Silla], occupying up to Koguryŏ's southern border, forming *chu* and *kun*. When Silla heard that Tang troops with Khitan and Malgal were coming to invade, it sent out the Nine Armies to prepare for them.

Autumn, ninth month. Because Kim Chinju, father of imperial resident guard, and student P'unghun had been executed in Silla,[86] Xue Rengui had P'unghun guide troops to come and attack Ch'ŏnsŏng Fortress.[87] Our general Munhun and others fought back defeating them, beheading 1,400 and seizing forty battleships. Rengui broke the siege, retreated, and captured 1,000 war horses. On the twenty-ninth day Li Jinxing led 200,000 troops and camped at Maech'o Fortress.[88] Our troops attacked and pushed them out, taking 30,380 battle horses and, in addition, a similar amount of weapons.[89] [The King] sent an envoy to Tang to present tribute of local products. Following the Anbuk River,[90] [Silla] established checkpoints and fortresses and also constructed Ch'ŏlgwan Fortress.[91] The Malgal entered Adal Fortress[92] to pillage it. Fortress Commander Sona[93] resisted in battle but was killed. Tang troops with Khitan and Malgal came and encircled

---

86 There is discrepancy as to when he was executed. This account occurred in the eighth month of 662. But another passage in *SS* has him alive in 670. A study by Kwŏn Tŏkyong suggests he died between 670 and 675. See *AKS* 3:236, n. 107.

87 This is also known as Paeksu Fortress and is located in Kyŏnggi, P'aju, or Hwanghae, Chaeryŏng.

88 This is in Kyŏnggi, Yangju.

89 Jamieson 286, n. 206, points out that in *Xin Tangshu* 220 one fifteen-character line gives the victory to Li Jinxing's army.

90 This river flows north in Hamnam.

91 This is in Hamnam, Munch'ŏn.

92 This is in Kangwŏn, Ich'ŏn.

93 See biography in *SS* 47.

Ch'ilchung Fortress but could not take it. *Sosu* Yu Tong died in battle. The Malgal also encircled Chŏngmok Fortress[94] and destroyed it. *Hyŏllyŏng* [Hyŏn magistrate] T'algi led the people to resist but, exhausting their strength, they all died. Tang troops again encircled Sŏkhyŏn Fortress and captured it. Hyŏn magistrate Sŏnbaek, Silmo, and others fought strenuously but died. Our troops fought with Tang forces eighteen times in battles of various sizes, winning in all of them, and beheaded 6,047 and took two hundred battle horses.

Year sixteen [676], spring, second month. The eminent monk Ŭisang received the royal decree and established Pusŏk Monastery.[95]

Autumn, seventh month. A comet appeared between *Pukha* and *Chŏksu*[96] and was 6 to 7 *po* long. Tang forces came and attacked Torim Fortress,[97] capturing it. Hyŏn magistrate Kŏsiji died in battle. [The court] built Yanggung Palace.

Winter, eleventh month. *Sach'an* Sidŭk led naval forces and fought against Xue Rengui at Soburi-ju's Kibŏlp'o but was greatly defeated. But, advancing again, and in twenty-two battles of varying sizes, he won, beheading more than 4,000. *Chaesang* [Councilor of State] Chinsun requested to retire but was not allowed. He was given a small table and cane.

Year seventeen [677], spring, third month. [The King] watched shooting practice at the south gate of Kangmu Hall. The *Chwa Sanokkwan*[98] was first established. Soburi-ju presented a white

---

94 This is in Kangwŏn, Hoeyang-gun.

95 Ŭisang (625–702) was the founder in Korea of Hwaŭm (the Flower-Garland School). He built this temple in Kyŏngbuk, Yŏngju.

96 These stars are in the vicinity of Gemini. See also *AKS* 3:239, n. 119–20, which states *Pukha* is three stars within *Gemini* and *Chŏksu* is to the west of *Pukha*.

97 This is in Kangwŏn, Tongch'ŏn.

98 This office (Left Salary Office) oversaw the administration of salaries and stipends.

falcon.

Year eighteen [678], spring, first month. [The court] appointed one person to be Minister of the Office of Shipping to oversee shipping matters and placed one person of *kyŏng* rank each in the Chwau Ibangbu [Ministry of Law].[99] [The court] established Pugwŏn[100] as a minor capital and named *Taeach'an* Ogi to oversee it.

Third month. *Taeach'an* Ch'unjang became chief minister.

Summer, fourth month. *Ach'an* Ch'ŏnhun became commander-in-chief of Mujin-ju.

Fifth month. Pugwŏn presented an odd bird with a pattern on its feathers and hair on its shins

Year nineteen [679], spring, first month. Chief minister Ch'unjang, because of illness, was relieved and *Sŏburhan* Ch'ŏnjon became chief minister.

Second month. [The court] sent an official to put T'amna in order. The palace was repaired again and it was quite grand and beautiful.

Summer, fourth month. The Fitful Glitter [Mars] held at Feather Grove.[101]

Sixth month, *T'aebaek* [Venus] intruded on the moon and a falling star invaded Orion.

Autumn, eighth month. Venus intruded on the moon. *Kakkan* Ch'ŏnjon died. [The court] built the Eastern Palace [as the Crown Prince's residence] and started to name the various gates around

---

It had one director, two principle clerks, and four scribes. In 680 Silla established the Right Salary Office. See *SS* 38 and *AKS* 3: 239, n. 123.

99 The Ibangbu oversaw legal matters similar to the Ministry of Punishments in later periods.

100 This Kangwŏn, Wŏnju.

101 According to Jamieson 166. "Fitful Glitter" is attributed to Needham 3:398. See also *AKS* 3:240, n. 127.

the palace. [The construction of] Sach'ŏnwang Monastery was completed. [The court] expanded South Mountain Fortress.

Year twenty [680], spring, second month. *Ich'an* Kim Kungwan became extraordinary rank one. [The King] presented to King Podŏk Ansŭng vessels made of gold and silver and 100 *tan* of multi-colored silk and also presented the King's younger sister {another source says this Kim is *Chapch'an* Ŭigwan's daughter}[102] to be his wife, and also sent the following missive:

"At the root of human relations, that of husband and wife should come first, and at the base of royal governance, producing heirs is the most important. Dear King, 'As your magpie's nest is empty and the cock's crow is on your mind'[103] [it seems you are thinking of finding a wife]. You cannot go for a long time without a wife to assist you, so that you will not lose the great undertaking of establishing your [royal] household. Now I have selected a good time and a good day and according to established conventions have [sent] my sister's daughter to be your spouse. You [King] can fittingly unify our feelings and principles and, upholding the sacrifices to our ancestors, produce an abundance of offspring and make it a flourishing bedrock forever. How can this not be splendid! How can this not be beautiful!"

Summer, fifth month. The Koguryŏ King [sent] *Taejanggun* [Grand General] Yŏnmu and others to submit a memorial:[104]

I, your subject, Ansŭng report that *Taeach'an* Kim Kwanjang on arrival respectfully announced your instructions and presented

---

102 In the missive that follows and in Ansŭng's response, the woman is referred to as the King's niece and so it should read as "sister's daughter."

103 The "magpie's nest" is from *Shiji* 20 which, as Jamieson 291, n. 225, states, "Sings of marriage between royal houses of different states." The "cock's crow" is also from *Shiji* 150–1 which, per Jamieson, is "interpreted as singing of the model mate."

104 This is adapted from Jamieson 167–9

your missive which made your niece the consort of my lowly domain. Accordingly she arrived here on the fifteenth day of the fourth month.

Delight and apprehension so mingle in my heart that I know not what to do. I recall that the imperial daughter [of the Emperor Yao] was sent down to Gui in marriage and the royal daughter [of Zhou] was sent in marriage to the Qi [kingdom] in principle to elevate sagely virtue and in total disregard of commoner [status].[105] Yet I, your subject, am nothing but mediocre, lacking in talent and conduct worthy of note. I luckily met good fortune, have basked under sagely influence and received at every turn extraordinary favor, none of which could ever be repaid. Nevertheless I am repeatedly the beneficiary of your favor and have been allowed to be your relative through marriage.

"At once, the 'luxuriant flowers' have manifest blessings and 'reserved and subdued'[106] will constitute the virtuous [wife]." With an auspicious moon and a good hour, we have returned to my unworthy quarters. What I received on one morning I could not have obtained in one hundred million years. This is something I never wished for, a delight beyond expectations. How could only one or two generations receive this grace alone? From my founding ancestor on, all take delight in this.

As I, your subject, have yet to receive the contents of your missive and dared not to go personally directly to your Court, yet, unable to contain my joy and delight, I humbly dispatch my great general *T'aedaehyŏng* Yŏnmu to present this memorial."

---

105 As per Jamieson, Gui is the surname of Shun to whom Yao gave his second daughter in marriage because of his virtue. Shun was a commoner at that time; see *Shiji* 26–7. The second allusion is again to *Shijing* and is an ode describing marriage of a royal daughter to a feudal prince; see *Shijing*.

106 These two expressions are from the same ode noted above, praising the qualities of the royal daughter.

Kŭmgwan's minor capital was established in Kaya-gun.

Year twenty-one [681], spring, first month, first day. For an entire day it was dark like night. *Sach'an* Musŏn led 3,000 elite troops and guarded Piyŏrhol.[107] [The court] established the *U* [Right] *sanokkwan* office.[108]

Summer, fifth month. There was an earthquake. A shooting star intruded into *Samdaesŏng* [Orion].

Sixth month. The Celestial Dog fell to the southwest.[109] The King wanted to construct a new wall around the capital and asked the monk Ŭisang about it. He replied, "Even if you live in a grass house on wild plains, if you follow the correct path, your karma will last long. If it were not truly so, even if you construct the wall making the people work hard, there will be no gain." The King then stopped the construction.[110]

Autumn, seventh month, first day. As the King died, his posthumous name was Munmu. His officials, according to his will, buried him in an estuary in the East Sea at a great rock.[111] According to popular legend the King was transformed into a dragon and accordingly they called it "Great King's Stone." His last testament stated:[112]

"Encountering a time of disorder and facing wars, I campaigned to the west and battled to the north. I secured the land, smote the traitorous, summoned the cooperative, and, in the end, brought

---

107 This is in the Anbyŏn region in Hamnam.

108 In 677 the court had established the Left Office and this office, too, presumably oversaw stipends and salaries. It had one director, two clerks, and four scribes.

109 Apparently a meteor, the term "Celestial Dog," or "Heavenly Dog Star," refers to such falling objects and dates back at least as far as *Shijing* in Chinese tradition, perhaps in reference to the wailing sound they made.

110 *SY* 2:3b presents a somewhat similar statement by Ŭisang, noting this was written by the monk.

111 This site can still be viewed off the coast near Kyŏngju.

112 This translation is adapted from Jamieson 170–3.

peace to all both near and far. Above, I consoled the concern bequeathed by my ancestors and below, avenged the long-borne hatred of two generations [my father and his sons]. Rewards were given generously to both perished and survivors, titles awarded fairly to those of our kingdom and abroad. Arms were melted into agricultural implements bringing benevolence and longevity to the masses, lessening taxes, [and] reducing corvee labor. Families were adequately supplied and people were satiated. As a result people found tranquility and no fears within the land. Granaries are stocked high like mountains and prisons have grown over with weeds. I can say that I have no shame before the gods and the people equally and did not trample on the wishes of the bureaucrats and the people.

Despite all the difficulties, I am afflicted with a serious disease. Still toiling myself with government and reforms, my illness grew worse. That life passes leaving only names to remain has been the same in the past as now. That suddenly one faces death [the vast night], why should it be regretted?

The Crown Prince has accumulated bright virtue since his youth and for long has occupied the 'thunder'[113] position. Officials from various ministers of state on down to functionaries must not neglect their duty toward the departed nor be heedless of proper service toward the living. Since the ceremonial master of the ancestral shrines and altars to the gods of soil and grain cannot be vacant [even for a moment], the Crown Prince should succeed to the royal throne immediately before my casket.

Moreover the mountains and valleys change and shift, while generations push on. From King Wu's North Hill tomb one cannot

---

113 "Thunder" is one of the eight trigrams and symbolizes the oldest son and east, the position of the Crown Prince's quarters. See Jamieson 294, n. 232.

see the brilliance of the incense burner made of gold in the shape of a duck. As to the ruler of Wei's wish for his western tumulus viewpoint, do we hear more than the name 'Copper Sparrow'?[114] Omnipotent heroes of bygone days end as mounds on which shepherds and woodcutters sing while foxes and rabbits are burrowing in the sides. They are needless wastes of funds and only remain as an object of criticism in writings. They wantonly sap men's strength yet cannot help the soul within.

When I quietly contemplate all this, I am filled with unceasing pain. Such things are not to be desired. Ten days immediately after my death [the placing of silk-cotton][115] in the Court outside of the Warehouse Gate, cremate me in the fashion of the Western Country [India]. As to the degree of mourning, there are established levels, but frugality is to be rigorously followed in the funeral procedures. As for the protection in the border fortresses and garrisons as well as the levying of taxes in the prefectures and commanderies, that which is not essential should be reviewed and abolished. And if there be inapplicable law codes or procedures,[116] correct them immediately.

Inform all far or near so that my intent will be known while those in charge will carry it out."

114 As per Jamieson 295, n. 236, this is an allusion to Caocao's last will enjoining his ministers and concubines to perform elaborate sacrificial rituals in the Copper Sparrow Tower which overlooked his gravesite. See also the Chinese text *Yedou gushi*.

115 This is in reference to the practice of placing cotton on the mouth and nose of the dying to watch for the last signs of breathing.

116 The original refers to four types of laws: criminal law, administrative law, amendments and additions to imperial decrees, and procedures in implementing the law.

The **Silla Annals** of the **Samguk Sagi**

The Silla
Annals of the
Samguk Sagi

Kings Sinmun, Hyoso, and Sŏngdŏk

Book

8

King Sinmun

King Sinmun (r. 681–692) ascended the throne. His personal name was Chŏngmyŏng {Myŏng's adult name was Ilch'o}.[1] He was the oldest son of Great King Munmu and his mother was Queen Chaŭi {another source writes it as "Chaŭi" with a different character}. His Queen was Lady Kim, the daughter of the *Sop'an* Hŭmdol, whom he married when he was Crown Prince. For a long time they were without children. [However] she was subsequently expelled from the palace when his [Sinmun's] father-in-law [Kim Hŭmdol] was implicated in a rebellion. He [Sinmun] was installed as Crown Prince in the fifth year of King Munmu [665]. Reaching this, he ascended the throne. Tang Gaozong sent an envoy investing him as King of Silla and, accordingly, he inherited the ranks and titles of his predecessor [Munmu].

Year one [681], eighth month. *Sŏburhan* Chinbok was named extraordinary rank one. On the eighth day *Sop'an* Kim Hŭmdol, *P'anjinch'an* Hŭngwŏn, *Taeach'an* Chingong, and others plotted rebellion and were put to death.[2] On the thirteenth day King

---

1   *SY* 3 records his name as Ilcho. It was customary when a man turned twenty that he took an adult name.

2   The rebellion of Kim Hŭmdol was one of the greatest of the political upheavals faced by Silla during its middle period and its suppression provided an opportunity for the Silla King to enhance royal authority. See Inoue Hideo, "Shiragi seiji taisei no hensen katei," *Kodaishi kōza* 4 (1962): 220; Kang Sŏngwŏn, "Silla sidae panyŏkŭi yŏksajŏk sŏnggyŏk," *Hanguksa yŏngu* 43 (1983): 34–5, 3; and Kim Sut'ae, "Silla Sinmunwangdae chŏnjaewanggwŏn ŭi hangnipgwa Kim

Podŏk[3] dispatched *Sohyŏng* Sudŏkkae to congratulate the successful suppression of the rebels. On the sixteenth day a directive was issued:

To reward the meritorious is a laudable custom of the ancient sages and to punish the criminal was the exemplary law of former kings. By my paltry body and through my insignificant virtue I have sought to preserve the lofty dynastic foundation. Neglecting even to eat, from early dawn until retirement late in the night, I have labored with high officials to ensure the tranquility of the kingdom. Who could have imagined that such a rebellion would arise in the capital during the mourning period! The rebel leaders, the officials Hŭmdol, Hŭngwŏn, Chingong, and others, did not rise to their offices from ability but rather through acts of favor. From start to finish they proceeded recklessly, squandering wealth, engaging in activities neither benevolent nor virtuous, and wielding power indiscriminately—treating officials with arrogance [and] deceiving high and low alike. Without compunction they made a daily show of their greed, giving free reign to their personal tyranny. They summoned to their sides cunning and nefarious [cohorts] and, conspiring with palace courtiers, spreading their ill-effect all over to give aid to bad elements, they set a date and time wishing to stage the rebellion.

First relying on the assistance of heaven and earth and receiving the benefits [assistance] from the souls of the dynastic shrines, the plotting of Hŭmdol and others was exposed because

---

Hŭmdol ran," *Hanguk munhwa* 9 (1992): 157–79.

3 Podŏk was the crowned name of Ansun (alternately, Ansŭng; dates unknown). He was a high-ranking official of late Koguryŏ. Some Chinese sources cite Ansŭng as the grandson of King Pojang, the last King of Koguryŏ, whereas *SS* describes him elsewhere as, alternately, a son of King Pojang and a grandson of Yŏn Kaesomun. The date and circumstances of Ansŭng's death are unknown. See *The Koguryŏ Annals, SS* 22, n. 190.

of their accumulated evil and overflowing crimes. This is what men and gods would reject as it would not be permissible to heaven and earth. There is nothing that would be greater in violating righteous principle and harming convention. Therefore I mustered soldiers to eliminate this gang of owls and tiger-like brutality[4] and some fled to hills and valleys and some returned in submission to the royal palace. Now I have searched out remnants who were less important and gotten rid of them all by execution. Thus in three or four days all the leaders of the criminals were purged. Although these executions were taken with little choice, these measures have startled the people. How could I forget even for a moment my concerns and shame. But now the fugitive outlaws have been completely purged and anxieties near and far extinguished. I have ordered the demobilization of the mustered soldiers and cavalry. Let the pronouncement of these developments be promulgated in the four directions.

On the twenty-eighth day *Ich'an* Kungwan was beheaded and a directive was issued:

The role of serving the King has loyalty as its fundamental principle. The basic principle of being an official is that one cannot have two minds. The Minister of the Ministry of Military Affairs *Ich'an* Kungwan, in accordance with set orders of rank, was eventually promoted to the highest office. Yet he did not show to the court unstained integrity in correcting royal mistakes and supplementing the King's shortcomings. Neither did he unfailingly support royal commands nor manifest faithful loyalty to the dynasty. Growing intimate with the traitor Hŭmdol and

---

4   In Chinese tradition owlets, *xiao* (Korean: *hyo*), were thought to devour their own mother and so were maligned as "unfilial." Similarly, the *jing* (Korean: *kyŏng*) was a tiger-like beast reputed to hunt and eat its own parent. Thus a brutal and unfilial person was sometimes referred to as *"xiaojing."*

others, he learned of their plans for rebellion yet did not let this be known. Not only did he show no concern for the nation's welfare but he failed even to meet the duties of his post. How could he repeatedly hold such critical positions as state minister yet allow the laws of the land to become so muddled? Fittingly, like others, he must be punished to serve as a warning to later generations. Kungwan and one of his legitimate sons shall be forced to commit suicide. Let this pronouncement of these matters be promulgated throughout so that all will know it.

Winter, tenth month. The office of *Siwigam* [Director of Royal Bodyguard] was abolished and six generals were appointed.[5]

Year two [682], spring, first month. The King personally made offerings at the Singung Shrine and granted a general amnesty.

Summer, fourth month. The Ministry of Personnel Affairs was set up with two ministers who were put in charge of recommending officials.[6]

Fifth month. *T'aebaek* [Venus] intruded on the moon.

Sixth month. The National Academy was established with one *kyŏng* [director].[7] Set up, as well, were a *Kongjangbugam* [Director

5 *Siwigam* was Director of the *Siwibu,* an office established in the fifth year (652) of Queen Chindŏk, apparently to manage the royal palace and provide a royal bodyguard. Yi Mungi, "Silla siwibu ŭi sŏngnip gwa sŏnggyŏk," *Yŏksa kyoyuk nonjip* 9 (1986): 34–5.

6 This office was established in the third year (582) of King Chinp'yŏng and charged with the selection, appointment, and dismissal of state officials. *SS,* monograph on ranks and offices, part 1, notes that in the second year of King Sinmun two *Kŭmhasin* (Officials of the Lotus Lapel) were first appointed and that a third was appointed in the fifth year (685) of that king's reign. That same monograph states that in the sixth year (806) of King Aejang the office of *kŭmhasin* was changed to simply that of "director." Based upon this, it would seem that *SS* mistakenly records here that Sinmun appointed two directors when it should read he appointed two *kŭmhasin.*

7 The *Kukhak* (National Academy) was established under the Ministry of Rites to train and educate members of Silla's expanding officialdom in the Confucian classics and rituals. Its name changed briefly to *Taehakgam* during the reign of King Kyŏngdŏk (r. 742–765) but reverted to *Kukhak* in the subsequent reign of

of the Ministry of Works] and a *Ch'aechŏngam* [Director of Adornments and Lacquer].[8]

Year three [683], spring, second month. Sunji was named chief minister. The youngest daughter of *Ilgilch'an* Kim Hŭmun[9] was designated to become a royal consort. Earlier *Ich'an* Munyŏng and *P'ajinch'an* Samgwang were sent to set the date [of the marriage], while *Taeach'an* Chisang was dispatched carrying wedding gifts to the bride's home,[10] namely fifteen carts of silk; one hundred thirty-five carts containing rice, liquor, oil, honey, soy, soy-bean curd, and dried meats; and one hundred fifty carts of tax [grain].

Summer, fourth month. One *ch'ŏk* of snow fell in the fields.

Fifth month, seventh day. *Ich'an* Munyŏng and Kaewŏn were sent to the home [of the bride] and invested her as royal consort. On that same day, between 5 a.m. and 7 a.m., *P'ajinch'an* Taesang and Sonmun and *Ach'an* Chwaya and Kilsuk and others were sent, together with their wives and thirty ladies each from the wards of Yangbu and Saryangbu,[11] to welcome the bride [to the palace]. On both sides of the carriage ridden by the consort were many attendant ladies and government officials. Arriving at the

King Hyegong (r. 765–780).

8 The Director of the Ministry of Works was chosen from among the *Taenama*, officials of the tenth office rank of Silla officialdom. *SS* 38 records that this ministry was also established by King Sinmun in this year. The Director of Adornments and Lacquer was selected from among the *Nama* and *Taenama* officials. See *SS* 38.

9 Kim Hŭmun, an eighth-generation descendant of Silla's King Naemul (r. 356–402), was a noted general and member of the Hwarang corps. See his biography in *SS* 47.

10 To present a formal marriage request the would-be groom would send gifts to the home of the would-be bride.

11 Yangbu and Saryangbu were two wards of the Silla capital of Kyŏngju and have their origins in the names of two clan groupings that, along with others, combined to form the early Silla state.

north gate of the palace, she got down [from the carriage] and entered the palace.

Winter, tenth month. Ansŭng, King Podŏk, was summoned and made *Sop'an*, granted the [royal] surname of Kim, and made to reside in the capital where he was granted a magnificent residence and a fertile piece of land. A comet entered the *Ogŏ* [Five-Cart] constellation.[12]

Year four [684], winter, tenth month. From dusk to dawn the sky was aflame with shooting stars.

Eleventh month. While stationed at Kŭmmajŏ,[13] the nephew of Ansŭng, General Taemun, plotted rebellion and, when it was discovered, he was executed. The remaining plotters, witnessing the execution of Taemun, killed several government officials, seized the town, and rebelled. The King ordered troops to put down the revolt and, in the ensuing fighting, Banner Chief P'ipsil was killed.[14] On seizing the town the people there were gathered up and resettled in the *chu* and *kun* to the south and the area was thereafter named Kŭmma-gun {Other sources had Taemun as Silbok}.[15]

Year five [685], spring. Wansan-ju was restored and Yongwŏn was appointed its adjutant grand commander. Ch'ŏng-ju was created out of Kŏyŏl-chu,[16] creating the system of nine *chu* for the

---

12 The constellation is named alternately as *Ch'ŏngŏ* (Chinese: *Tianju*), *Ak* (Chinese: *Yue*), *Ch'ŏnch'ang* (Chinese: *Tiancang*), *Kagong* (Chinese: *Kegong*), and *Kyŏngsŏng* (Chinese: *Qingxing*).

13 Modern Kŭmma-myŏn is the city of Iksan, North Cholla province. It had been established as part of the Kingdom of Podŏk granted to Ansŭng in 670 by Silla's King Munmu.

14 A native of the Saryang district of Kyŏngju. He was the son of Ch'wibok. Rather than *tangju* (banner chief), *SS* 47 gives P'ipsil's position as *Kwidang chegam* (Deputy Director of the Noble Banner).

15 See *SS* 47, Taemun is referred to as Silbok.

16 Ch'ŏngju was located in the area of modern Chinju city, South Kyŏngsang. Its

first time.[17] *Taeach'an* Pokse was then appointed Adjutant Grand Commander [of Ch'ŏng-ju.] The *sogyŏng* [minor capital] of Sŏwŏn[18] was established and *Ach'an* Wŏnt'ae[19] was appointed its *sasin* [mayor].[20] The minor capital of Namwŏn[21] was established and families from the *chu* and *kun* were divided and settled there to live. Pongsŏng Monastery was completed.[22]

Summer, fourth month. Mangdŏk Monastery was completed.[23]

Year six [686], spring, first month. *Ich'an* Taejang {*jang* alternately is written with another character} was appointed chief minister. The *Yejakpu* [Department of Buildings and Maintenance] was established with two directors.[24]

Second month. The four *hyŏn* of Sŏksan, Masan, Kosan, and Sap'yŏng were established.[25] Sabi-ju was made into a *kun* while

name was changed to Kangju during the reign of King Kyŏngdŏk (r. 742–765) but reverted to Ch'ŏngju during the reign of King Hyegong (r. 765–780).

17 Referring to the system of nine *chu* completed in the fifth year of King Sinmun, though reorganized slightly during the sixth and seventh years of that king's reign. These nine provinces were Ilsŏn, Samnyang, Hansan, Suyak, Hasŭlla, Sobu, Wansan, Ch'ŏng, and Palla. In part the reorganization of Silla territory into nine *chu* was a symbolic reference to the system of nine provinces that characterized China during the reign of King Yu, legendary founder of China's Xia dynasty.

18 This is modern Ch'ŏngju city in North Ch'ungch'ŏng province. During the reign of King Kyŏngdŏk its designation was changed to that of *kyŏng* (capital city).

19 He is the father of Sŏngjŏng (alternately, Ŏmjŏng), a secondary consort of the future King Sŏngdŏk. (r. 702–737).

20 During Silla, an official in charge of a secondary capital. The position was also known as *sadaedŭng*.

21 This is in modern Namwŏn in North Cholla province.

22 A monastery located in modern Tongsŏngdong in Kyŏngju. *SY* 5 relates that the temple was established by King Sinmun in the fifth year (685) of his reign upon the advice of the monk Hyet'ong. The temple is also known as Sinch'ung Pongsŏng Monastery.

23 A monastery located in modern Paebandong, Kyŏngju. See *SY* 2.

24 A department responsible for the building and maintenance of royal and government structures. It was also called *Yejakchŏn.*

25 Sŏksan was located in modern Puyŏ, South Ch'ungch'ŏng; Masan district was located in modern Sŏch'ŏn-gun, South Ch'ungch'ŏng; Kosan was located in modern Yesan-gun, South Ch'ungch'ŏng; and Sap'yŏng was located in modern

Ungch'ŏn-gun was made into a *chu*. Palla-ju was made into a *kun* while Mujin-gun was made into a *chu*.[26] [The Court] sent an envoy to Tang requesting copies of the *Book of Rites* and other literary works.[27] The Empress Wu[28] issued orders to the offices concerned to copy the *Jixiong yaoli*[29] and select the most worthy portions of the *Wenguan cilin*[30] and compile them into a work of fifty volumes that was then granted [to the Silla envoys].

Year seven [687], spring, second month. [The King's] first son was born. On that day the weather was dark and gloomy with severe thunder and lightning.

Third month. Ilsŏn-ju was abolished and Sabŏl-chu was established with *P'ajinch'an* Kwanjang named as its adjutant grand commander.

Summer, fourth month. The chief of the *Umsŏngsŏ* [Office of Music][31] was renamed from *changgwan* [chief] to *kyŏng* [director]. [The Court] sent high officials to the Royal Ancestral Shrine to

---

Tangjin-gun, South Ch'ungch'ŏng.

26 Palla-ju refers to the modern region around Naju city, South Cholla. It is unclear when it was first established as a *chu*.

27 This request by Silla is mentioned in both *Jiu Tangshu* 199 and *Xin Tangshu* 220. The request for such works is likely connected to the establishment of the *Kukhak* four years previous. Hamada Kōsaku, "Shiragi no kokugaku to kentō ryūgakusei," *Kumatsushū* 2 (1980): 60–1.

28 Wu Zetian (r. 690–705) had been one of the favored concubines of Emperor Taizong of Tang and went on to become the concubine of his son Emperor Gaozong, under whom she was eventually named Empress consort. Empress Wu ruled China, formally declaring herself Empress in 690 and establishing a new dynasty, the Zhou.

29 Literally "the necessary ceremonial and mourning rites," two of the standard *wuli* (five rites).

30 *Wenguan cilin* (*Forest of Officials' Poetry and Prose*) was an anthology compiled in early Tang by Xu Jingzong and others and filled an astounding 1,000 volumes. In Japan twenty-three of the original thousand volumes have survived.

31 A government office under the Ministry of Rites that was responsible for music. The date of its establishment is not known but the earliest reference to it dates from the fifth year (651) of Queen Chindŏk.

offer sacrifices stating:

I, as King, respectfully speak to the souls of Great King T'aejo,[32] Great King Chinji,[33] Great King Munhŭng,[34] Great King T'aejong,[35] and Great King Munmu. Though lacking both ability and virtue, I have been made heir to your most lofty and unfinished work, to which I care and dedicate myself day and night without rest or respite. Owing to the care of the ancestral tombs, and protected by the blessings of Heaven and Earth, peace and tranquility prevail in the four corners [of the kingdom]. Foreign guests from far lands come loaded with treasurers. We have come to this point through transparent justice without litigation. Lately, in my duties as King, I have lost the way and morals have deviated from the way of Heaven. The stars are strange in their motions, the sun has lost its brilliance and fallen into gloom so that my body shivers and I seem as one at the bottom of a deep pond or valley. Respectfully, I send officials so and so of such and such offices to set up unworthy offerings before the ancestral spirits who look very much alive.[36] Prostrating myself before you, I wish you would understand the insignificance of my sincerity and pitying my insignificant self, I beseech that you might make bountiful the four seasons, smoothly

---

32 Most scholars posit this to be the thirteenth King of Silla, the first Silla monarch of the Kim clan, Mich'u Isagŭm. Other theories have proposed the first Silla monarch to be Pak Hyŏkkŏse, the founder of the Kim clan Kim Alchi; or the seventeenth King of Silla, Naemul, under whom the Silla monarchy was firmly established under the Kim house.

33 King Chinji (r. 576–579).

34 Referring to Yongch'un (alternately, Yongsu), father of Kim Ch'unch'u (later King Muyŏl). During the first year (654) of the reign of King Muyŏl he was granted the ceremonial title of Great King Munhŭng.

35 King T'aejong Muyŏl (Kim Ch'unch'u; r. 654–661).

36 Meaning to make offerings reverently, as if the spirits themselves were present.

establish the five admonishments [for the ruler],[37] make bountiful the crops and eradicate illness, so that food being plentiful and morality and proper ceremony observed, the land will be in order and at peace, banditry disappear, and the way leading to our descendants full of good fortune. Respectfully I beseech you.

Fifth month. A royal directive was issued to grant *kwallyojŏn* [emolument land] to all civil and military officials according to rank.[38]

Autumn. Fortresses were constructed at the two *chu* of Sabŏl and Samnyang.

Year eight [688], spring, first month. Chief Minister Taejang died and so *Ich'an* Wŏnsa was named chief minister.

Second month. The position of director was assigned to the Office of Shipping.

Year nine [689], spring, first month. A royal directive was handed down to abolish the system of *nogŭp* [stipend villages] for both the central and provincial officials and instead a graded system of annual *cho* [grain rents] was established.[39]

---

37 See *AKS* 3:250, n. 41, as adapted from *Hanshu* 85. "The Five Admonishments" instructed the ruler to: 1) conduct yourself properly, 2) maintain proper relations with women, 3) treat your close attendants properly, 4) measure merit and rewards judiciously, and 5) improve your officials by treating them virtuously.

38 There have been various scholarly interpretations of this brief passage and they may be divided roughly into two categories. First, that it constituted merely a regularization and formalization of the *chikchŏn* (office-land) system already in effect as a salary system for officials. See Paek Namun, *Chosŏn sahoe kyŏngjesa,* Kaejosa, 1933. Alternately, that it is a record of the distribution of *chikchŏn.* See Kim Ch'ŏlchun, "Silla kwijok seryŏkŭi kiban," *Inmun kwahak* 7 (1962); Kang Chinch'ŏl, "Silla ŭi nogŭp taehayŏ," *Yi Hongjik paksa hoegap kinyŏm Hanguk sahak nonch'ong* 1969; Hatada Takashi, "Shiragi no sonraku," *Rekishigaku kenkyū* 227 (1959). The distribution of such land was not merely based upon office but, by extension, reflected one's bone rank and social standing.

39 The *nogŭp* system characterized the salary payments of the officialdom on and off from the Three Kingdoms period through early Koryŏ. Scholarly treatments of the *nogŭp* system are numerous. However the majority of scholars assert that *nogŭp* and *chikchŏn* are two different but coexisting land-allotment systems. The

Autumn, ninth [leap] month, twenty-sixth day. The King made a royal tour of Changsan Fortress. A wall was constructed around the minor capital of Sŏwŏn. Although the King wished to transfer the capital to Talgubŏl[40] this was never accomplished.

Year ten [690], spring, second month. Chief Minister Wŏnsa was removed for health reasons and so *Ach'an* Sŏnwŏn was named chief minister.

Winter, tenth month. Chŏnyasan-gun was established.

Year eleven [691], spring, third month, first day. Prince Yihong was conferred with the title of Crown Prince. Thirteenth day, there

---

distribution of the *nogŭp* was countrywide and its recipients and benefactors were Silla civil and military officials who were allotted land, generally according to rank. As to the form such distribution took, various scholarly theories hold sway. Notably, Pak Sihyŏng sees the *nogŭp* as only one aspect of the more general collective system of *chikchŏn*. Regarding the causal motivations of the system, there are three general theories. First, the theory which emphasizes the system as a means of mobilizing manpower to receive tribute, a theory that has become divided in turns over the nature of such mobilization, with competing theories emphasizing by turns: 1) a combination of *cho* (tax payments in kind), *cho* (different character; tax payments in cash), and *yong* (corvée duty), echoing the so-called *zu-diao-yong* taxation system of contemporary Tang; see Paek Namun (1933), *Chosŏn sahoe kyŏngjesa,* and Kang Chinch'ŏl, *Silla ŭi nogŭp taehayŏ;* 2) a combination of tax payments and manpower, see Kim Ch'ŏlchun "Silla kwijok seryŏkŭi kiban"; and 3) a combination of tribute and corvée duty, see Takeda Yukio and Kimura Makoto, both in "Shiragi no rokubusei to sonraku kōzō," *Rekishigaku kenkyū,* Bessatsu, 1979. Second, the theory that emphasizes control over the land with the aim of augmenting tax-gathering authority. See Pak Sihyŏng, *Chosŏn t'oji chedosa,* parts 1–2, 1960–1961; Yi Kyŏngsik, "Kodaechungseŭi sigŭpjeŭi kucho wa chŏn'gae," *Son Pogi paksa chŏngnyŏn kinyŏm Hanguk sahak nonch'ong,* Seoul: Chisik sanŏpsa, 1988; Nomura Tadao, "Shōsōin yori hakken seru Shiragi no minsei bunsho ni tsuite," *Shigaku zasshi* 62–4 (1953), Pak Sihyŏng above, Kim Yongsŏp, "Chŏngŭndaeŭi t'oji chedo," *Hangukhak ipmun,* Seoul, Haksulwŏn, 1983; and Yi Kyŏngsik, above, and further, it has been proposed that such taxes were gathered on the one-tenth of the land that was akin to public land, see Kim Yongsŏp above. Third, an intermediary theory between the two standpoints given above, proposing that *nogŭp* evolved from an earlier system for extricating manpower (*chŏnnogŭp*) to a later one for extricating the produce of the land (*hunogŭp*), see Kim Kihŭng, *Samguk mit t'ong'il sillagi sejeŭi yŏn'gu,* Yŏksa pip'yŏngsa, 1999.

40 Modern Taegu.

was a general amnesty. Sahwa-ju presented a white sparrow.[41] Namwŏn Fortress[42] was constructed.

Year twelve [692], spring. The bamboo withered.[43] Tang Zhongzong sent an envoy with a verbal message:

Because the awesome merits and lofty virtue of our Taizong, the Refined Emperor, were in excess throughout the ages, on the day when the Emperor passed away we bequeathed him the temple name of Taizong ["Great Progenitor"]. We now find it beyond the bounds of propriety that the late King of your country, Kim Ch'unch'u, was also conferred this title. By all means remedy this by changing his title at once.[44]

At this the King conferred with his ranking officials and said in reply:

It is by chance that the posthumous title of the former King [Kim] Ch'unch'u of our small country conflicts with the temple name of your sage ancestor [Taizong]. Now, given His Majesty's order to change it, how dare I disobey and not follow it? However, upon reflection, I realize that our former King Ch'unch'u was endowed with exceeding virtue and wisdom. Moreover while he

---

41 A white sparrow was one of a number of propitious omens believed in Chinese tradition to designate a virtuous reign. See Tiziana Lippiello, *Auspicious Omens and Miracles in Ancient China: Han, Three Kingdoms and Six Dynasties*, Mounumenta Serica Institute, Nettetal: Steyler Verlag, 2001.

42 Modern Namwŏn in North Cholla province, established as a minor capital in 685.

43 An inauspicious portent of the approaching death of King Sinmun.

44 Zhongzong was the seventh son of Tang Gaozong and the Empress Wu. He was named Emperor in 683 upon Gaozong's death but his mother quickly removed him from the throne. At the time of this supposed edict Zhongzong had already been deposed by his mother and confined to Fangling, so that it is highly doubtful he could have been the actual sender. *SY* contains a similar anecdote; only in that version it is Gaozong who sends a missive demanding King Muyŏl's temple name be changed. If we take *SY*'s version of the story to be the correct one, since Tang Gaozong died in the twelfth month of 683 (the third year of King Sinmun), it would be feasible that this request from Gaozong arrived with the Tang envoys that came to Silla in the first year of Sinmun's reign.

was still alive he obtained that excellent subject Kim Yusin and single-mindedly they governed and unified the Three Hans [kingdoms]. Nothing can surpass his meritorious achievements. Therefore at the time of his death, all the people of the country, unable to overcome their sorrow and longings, conferred on him this posthumous title, not realizing it would conflict with your sage ruler. Now learning of His Majesty's directive, we cannot overcome fear and trembling. Prostrating before you, I beseech that you make all this known in your report before the imperial court.

Following this there were no other imperial directives on this issue.[45]

Autumn, seventh month. The King died.[46] He was conferred the posthumous title of Sinmun and was buried to the east of Mount Nangsan.[47]

King Hyoso

King Hyoso ascended the throne. His personal name was Ihong {another source says Kong}, and he was the Crown Prince of King Sinmun. His mother was Queen Sinmok of the Kim lineage, the daughter of *Ilgilch'an* Kim Hŭmun {another source has it written

---

45 See *SY* 1:36–7a for its version of these events.
46 More precisely, according to an engraving upon a gilded-copper *sarira* box discovered within the stone pagoda at Hwangbok Monastery, Sinmun died on the second day of the seventh month of the third year (692) of the Tianshou era of Tang.
47 Sinmun's tomb can be found near the Sach'ŏnwang Monastery site in Paebandong, Kyŏngju city.

as Un}.[48] Tang [Empress Wu] Zetian sent an envoy with condolences and to perform mourning rites and invest the King as King of Silla, *Fuguo dajiangjun* [Great Bulwark General of the State], *Xing zuobaotaowei dajiangjun* [Acting General-in-Chief of the Left Guard of the Leopard Strategy], and Commander-in-Chief of Kyerim Prefecture. The name of the Left and Right Ministry of Law was changed to the Left and Right *Ŭibangbu* [Ministry of Law].[49] This was because the character *yi* conflicted with the character *yi* in the King's personal name.

Year one [692], eighth month. *Taeach'an* Wŏnsŏn was appointed chief minister. High Priest Tojŭng[50] returned from Tang and presented an astronomy chart.

Year three [694], spring, first month. The King personally held sacrifices at the Singung Shrine and proclaimed a general amnesty. Munyŏng was appointed extraordinary rank one. Kim Inmun died, while in Tang, at the age of sixty-six.[51]

Winter. Songak and Ujam fortresses were constructed.[52]

---

48 Sinmok became Sinmun's second Queen Consort in 683, replacing Chaŭi following the disgrace of that Queen's father Kim Hŭmdol. *SY* relates that Sinmok was the daughter of Kim Ungong, also known as Kim Hŭmun. On the engraved gilded-copper *sarira* box found in the stone pagoda of Hwangbok Monastery she is referred to as Queen Dowager Sinmok.

49 The *Ŭibangbu* was established in the fifth year (651) of Queen Chindŏk and in the seventh year (667) of King Munmu divided into sections of Left and Right.

50 At an early age Tojŭng voyaged to Tang where he studied in the *Vijñapti-mātratā* (Consciousness-only) School under his fellow Korean Buddhist Wŏnjŭk. In 692 Tojŭng returned to Silla and there introduced Wŏnjŭk's teachings, which were taken up and systematized by the monk T'aehyŏn.

51 Kim Inmun (629–694) was a noted aristocrat, scholar, and official. He was the son of King Muyŏl and the younger brother of King Munmu. *SY* relates that Kim Inmun died on board ship enroute back to Silla but this account seems doubtful. See Kim Inmun's biography in *SS* 44.

52 Songak Fortress was located in the modern region of Kaesŏng, Kyŏngi. It would later be established as the capital of Later Koguryŏ by the rebel leader Kungye. Ujam Fortress was located in modern Hyŏnbyŏng-ri, Kŭmch'ŏn-gun, North Hwanghae province, Democratic People's Republic of Korea (North Korea).

Year four [695]. The *cha* month[53] was designated the first month. Kaewŏn was appointed extraordinary rank one.

Winter, tenth month. There was an earthquake in the capital. Chief Minister Wŏnsŏn retired from office due to age. Two markets, the West and South markets, were established.[54]

Year five [696], spring, first month. *Ich'an* Tangwŏn was appointed chief minister.

Summer, fourth month. The western regions of the kingdom suffered from severe drought.

Year six [697], autumn, seventh month. A propitious ear of rice was offered from Wansan-ju as two stalks of rice from different furrows had grown into a single plant.

Ninth month. A banquet was given for various officials at Imhaejŏn.[55]

Year seven [698], spring, first month. *Ich'an* Ch'ewŏn[56] was named Adjutant Grand Commander of Udu-ju.

Second month. In the capital the earth shook and strong winds blew, snapping trees. Chief Minister Tangwŏn retired due to old age and so *Taeach'an* Sunwŏn[57] became chief minister in his

---

53 The eleventh month. It denotes the month wherein the moon appears in the handle of the constellation Ursa Major (the Big Dipper) that is in the *chabang* (northern) sky in the early evening. We know from *Jiu Tangshu* 6 that, with the calculation of a new calendar, Tang officially redesignated the eleventh month of the year 689 as the first month. The same change in Silla in 695 reflects its receipt of the Tang calendar.

54 Along with the East Market established during the reign of King Chijŭng (r. 500–514), these made up the three royally established markets of Silla.

55 The name of a royal hall located to the west of Anapchi Pond in the Silla capital of Kyŏngju. See Yi Kibaek, "Maenghaejŏnggwa Imhaejŏn," *Kogo misul* 129–30 (1976), reprinted in *Silla sasangsa yŏngu*, Seoul: Ilchokak, 1986, 287–92.

56 See Yi Kibaek, "Silla chipsabuŭi sŏngnip," *Silla chŏngch'i sahoesa yŏn'gu* (1974), 162.

57 Kim Sunwŏn was one of the most powerful political figures of Silla's middle period. See Hamada Kōsaku, "Shiragi no Seitoku daiō shinshō to chūdai no ōshitsu," *Kumatsushū* 3 (1980).

place.

Third month. Envoys from Japan arrived and so the King gave them an audience in Sungnyejŏn.[58]

Autumn, seventh month. There was flooding in the capital.

Year eight [699] spring, second month. White extended across the sky and a comet appeared out of the east. [The court] sent an envoy to Tang to present local products as tribute.

Autumn, seventh month. The water of the Eastern Sea turned the color of blood and it was five days before it returned to normal.

Ninth month. Noise from a naval battle in the Eastern Sea was heard as far as the capital. Drums and flutes in the armory sounded on their own.[59] Mihil, a man from Sinch'on, discovered a gold nugget of 100 *p'un*[60] weight and offered it [to the King]. He was thereupon awarded the title of *nambyŏn* first rank[61] together with one hundred sacks of grain rent.

Year nine [700]. The *in* month was named the first month.[62]

Summer, fifth month. *Ich'an* Kyŏngyŏng { *"yŏng"* also appears as *"hyŏn"*} plotted rebellion and was executed. The chief minister was implicated and removed from office.

Six month. *Sesŏng* [Jupiter] crossed the path of the moon.

---

58 *Shoku Nihongi* (book 1, Emperor Mommu, years 1–2) records that in the tenth month of 697 *Ilgilch'an* Kim P'ildŏk, along with *Nama* Kim Imsang and others, arrived in Japan, returning to Silla in the second month of 698. It would seem that *SS*'s record of envoys from Japan refers to the Japanese envoys who returned with the embassy of Kim P'ildŏk.

59 Bad portents presage the death of the King.

60 Approximately 37.5 grams or 1.3 ounces. A *p'un*, or pennyweight.

61 *Nambyŏn cheil.* Though the title is mentioned in *SS*, monographs, no details are provided. The title was also conferred upon Taeyŏngnang for his presentation of a fox in the fifteenth year (757) of King Kyŏngdŏk.

62 This appears to be related to the earlier attempts initiated by Empress Wu to realign the calendar.

The **Silla** Annals of the **Samguk Sagi**

Year ten [701], spring, second month. A comet crossed the path of the moon.

Summer, fifth month. *Ilgilch'an* Cheil, governor of Yŏngam-gun,[63] because he pursued personal gain at the expense of public good, was sentenced to a hundred lashes and banished to an island.

Year eleven [702], autumn, seventh month. The King died.[64] He was conferred the posthumous title of Hyoso and was buried to the east of Mangdŏk Monastery.[65] {*The Old History of Tang* records, "Ihong died in the second year [702] of the Changan era." In various *kogi* [ancient records] it is recorded, "He died in the *imin* year [702], seventh month, twenty-seventh day." *Zizhi tongjian* records, "He died in the third year [703] of the Dazu era." The *Zizhi tongjian* is in error.}

King Sŏngdŏk

King Sŏngdŏk assumed the throne. His personal name was Hŭnggwang. Originally his name was Yunggi but, as this shared a character with the name of [Tang] Xuanzong, this name was

---

63 Modern Yŏng'am-gun, South Cholla.

64 The engraving on the gilded-copper *sarira* box of Hwangbok Monastery stone pagoda accords with this, giving the King's death date as the twenty-seventh day, seventh month, of 702. However *Shoku Nihongi* 3 gives a slightly different date, recording that the Silla envoys arrived in 703 announcing the King's death.

65 The sixteenth-century *Sinjŭng tongguk yŏji sŭngnam* 21, remnants of Kyŏngju-bu, records that King Hyoso's tomb lies to the east of Kyŏngju in the village of Punam-ri. See also Kang Inyŏng, "Hanguk chŏngsin munhwa yŏn'guso," *Silla onŭng* 113–4 (1990), on Mangdŏk Monastery.

changed during the Xiantian era[66] {*History of Tang* records his name as Kim Chisŏng}.[67] He was the second son of King Sinmun and the younger brother, by the same mother, of King Hyoso. Because Hyoso had no sons the people of the country enthroned him. Upon hearing of the passing of Hyoso, [Empress Wu] Zetian of Tang observed mourning, closed court audiences for two days, and sent a delegation to express condolences as well as to invest the new King as King of Silla and had him inherit his older brother's title of *Changgun todok* [General and Commander-in-Chief].

Year one [702], ninth month. There was a general amnesty, officials were granted a one-grade promotion in office and title, and all the *chu* and *kun* were given a one-year exemption from taxes. *Ich'an* Wŏnhun[68] was appointed chief minister.

Winter, tenth month. In Samnyang-ju the acorns became chestnuts.

Year two [703], spring, first month. The King personally went to offer service at the Singung Shrine. [The court] sent an envoy to Tang to present local products as tribute.

---

66 According to *SS*, in the third month, eleventh year (712) of his reign, King Sŏngdŏk received an imperial order from the Tang Emperor demanding he change his name. The record of this also appears in *Tang Huiyao* (hereafter *TH*) 95. However *Jiu Tangshu* 199, "Record of Silla," records that, because King Sŏngdŏk's name conflicted with that of Tang Taizong, it was that late Emperor's consort, Empress Wu, who demanded it be changed. Regarding the origin of the demand, *Jiu Tangshu* is in error as Empress Wu died in 705.

67 In fact, neither *Jiu Tangshu* nor *Xin Tangshu* record King Sŏngdŏk's name as Kim Chisŏng. However *Cefuefu yuangui* 970, first month, year three (705) of the Shenlong era, does record "The Silla King Kim Chisŏng sent an envoy to offer tribute." This latter record, however, is nothing more than the mistaken notation of the name of the Silla King for the name of the envoy he sent. See Suematsu Yasukazu, "Kansanji mirokusonzō oyobi amidabutsu no kakōkōki," *Shiragishi no shomondai* (1954), 459.

68 *SY* relates that Wŏnhun was the grandfather of Kim Yangsang, later King Sŏndŏk (r. 780–785), and that his son, Kim Hyobang, married Lady Saso, daughter of King Sŏngdŏk (r. 702–737), making him a relation to King Sŏngdŏk by marriage.

Autumn, seventh month. There was a fire at Yŏngmyo Monastery.[69] There was a flood in the capital causing many to drown. Chief Minister Wŏnhun retired and *Ach'an* Wŏnmun became chief minister. An embassy from Japan, totaling 240 people, arrived.[70] [The court] sent *Ach'an* Kim Sayang to the Tang court.

Year three [704], spring, first month. Ungch'ŏn-ju presented a golden mushroom.[71]

Third month. The envoy to Tang, Kim Sayang, returned and presented a copy of the *Zuishengwang jing*.[72]

Summer, fifth month. The daughter of *Sop'an* Kim Wŏnt'ae,[73] the Minister of the Ministry of Transportation,[74] became Queen.

Year four [705], spring, first month. Chief Minister Wŏnmun died and *Ach'an* Sinjŏng became chief minister.

Third month. [The court] sent an envoy to Tang to present local products as tribute.

Summer, fifth month. There was a drought.

Autumn, eighth month. Wine and food were distributed to the

---

69 Yŏngmyo Monastery was located in the western area of the Silla capital of Kyŏngju. Nothing but a foundation stone remains today.

70 *Shoku nihongi* 3 records that in the first month of the Taiho era (703), Silla envoys Kim Pokho, Kim Hyowŏn, and others arrived in Japan with news of the Silla King's death. See note 64.

71 In Chinese tradition this is a propitious sign. *Hanshu* notes for the year 61 BCE that an imperial edict was issued following the appearance of several propitious phenomena, including a golden divine mushroom with nine stalks.

72 More fully, *Jin'guangming zuisheng wangjing*, a *sutra*, first translated into Chinese by the monk Yijing (635–713). See Kim Sanghyŏn, "Chip'il kŭmgwangmyŏng ch'oesŭng wanggyŏngso- kŭmgwangmyŏng ch'oesŭng wanggyŏng hyŏnch'u soin wŏnhyosoŭi chipp'yŏn," *Tongyanghak* 24 (1994): 260.

73 Kim Wŏnt'ae would seem to be the same person as Kim Wŏntae, mentioned in *SY*, though not much is known about him. Kim Sut'ae, "Silla chungdae chŏnchewanggwŏn kwa chingol kwijok," unpublished PhD dissertation, Sogang University, 1990, 99–105.

74 *Sŭngbu* (Ministry of Transportation) was responsible for transportation within the court and was headed by two officials. See *SS* 38.

elderly.

Ninth month. A royal decree was issued prohibiting the taking of life of living things.[75] [The court] sent an envoy to Tang to present local products as tribute.

Winter, tenth month. There was famine in the *chu* and *kun* of the eastern parts of the kingdom causing many to become vagabonds so that [the court] dispatched commissioners to distribute relief.

Year five [706], spring, first month. *Ich'an* Inp'um became extraordinary rank one. As the country suffered from famine, the granaries were opened to offer relief.

Third month. Numerous stars were seen falling in the western sky.

Summer, fourth month. [The court] sent an envoy to Tang to present local products as tribute.

Autumn, eighth month. Chief Minister Sinjŏng was removed due to illness and *Taeach'an* Mullyang[76] became chief minister. [The court] sent an envoy to Tang to present local products as tribute. [This year] the grains did not ripen well.

Winter, tenth month. [The court] sent an envoy to Tang to present local products as tribute.

Twelfth month. There was a general amnesty.

Year six [707], spring, first month. Many people were dying of starvation so that daily allotments of 3 *sŭng*[77] of millet were

---

75 To mean a prohibition against the killing of animals, in accordance with strict Buddhist scripture.

76 Kim Mullyang was named chief minister in 706 and died in the tenth month of 710. It would seem this is the same Kim Mullyang referred to as the father of Kim Taesŏng, the founder of Pulguk Monastery and Sŏkkuram. See *SY* 5, "Taesŏng, Twice a Dutiful Son, Reign of King Sinmun."

77 This is a second meaning for *sŭng; sŭng:* approximately 0.52 liters or 1 US pint (dry); 10 *sŭng* is equal to 1 *tu.* For earlier mention see also Book 7, n. 74.

The **Silla Annals** of the **Samguk Sagi**

distributed to each person through the seventh month.

Second month. There was a general amnesty. [The court] distributed seeds of five grains to the farmers according to need.

Winter, twelfth month. [The court] sent an envoy to Tang to present local products as tribute.

Year seven [708], spring, first month. Saböl-chu presented an auspicious mushroom.

Second month. There was an earthquake.

Summer, fourth month. *Chinsŏng* [Saturn] intruded on the moon. There was a general amnesty.

Year eight [709], spring, third month. Ch'ŏng-ju presented a white falcon.

Summer, fifth month. There was a drought.

Six month. [The court] sent an envoy to Tang to present local products as tribute.

Autumn, eighth month. There was an amnesty for criminals.

Year nine [710], spring, first month. A *Ch'ŏngu* [Celestial Dog] star fell to the north of Samnang Monastery.[78] [The court] sent an envoy to Tang to present local products as tribute. There was an earthquake. An amnesty was granted to criminals.

Year ten [711], spring, third month. There was heavy snowfall.

Summer, fifth month. The butchering of animals was prohibited.

Winter, tenth month. The King made a royal tour of inspection of the *chu* and *kun* in the south of the kingdom. Chief Minister Mullyang died.

Eleventh month. The King drew up guidelines for the officialdom and issued them to the officials.

Twelfth month. [The court] sent an envoy to Tang to present

---

78 Samnang Monastery was built in 597 and located in the Silla capital of Kyŏngju.

local products as tribute.

Year eleven [712], spring, second month. [The court] sent an envoy to Tang to present tribute.[79]

Third month. *Ach'an* Wimun[80] became chief minister. Great Tang sent an envoy Lu Yuanmin with an imperial directive to change King [Sŏngdŏk's] name.[81]

Summer, fourth month. The King made a visit to Onsu.[82]

Autumn, eighth month. Kim Yusin's wife was enfeofed *puin* [lady] and granted an annual allotment of 1,000 *sŏk* of grain.

Year twelve [713], spring, second month. *Chŏnsasŏ* [Office of Sacrifices] was established.[83] [The court] sent an envoy to Tang to present local products as tribute and Emperor Xuanzong came out to receive it at the royal tower gate.[84]

Winter, tenth month. Kim Chŏngjong, an envoy dispatched to Tang, returned home. He brought with him imperial edicts naming the King *Piaoqi jiangjun* [General of Calvary], *Xingzuo weiwei dajiangjun* [Lord Specially Advanced acting Grand General of the Left Awesome Guard], *Shichijie* [Commissioner with Special Powers], *Dadudu kyerimzhou juzhunshi* [Commander-in-Chief of Kyerim Prefecture and its Various Military Commissioners], Prefect of Kyerim Prefecture, Supreme Pillar of State, Duke of

---

79 The record of this is taken from *Cefu yuangui* 970, second month, year one (712) of the Taiji era.

80 Wimun was the grandfather of the future King Wŏnsŏng (r. 785–798).

81 King Sŏngdŏk's original given name was Yunggi, using the same two characters as the given name of Tang Xuanzong, Longji. In the eleventh month of that year the Silla King changed his personal name to Hŭnggwang.

82 This is in Asan in South Ch'ungch'ŏng.

83 An office under the Ministry of Rites and responsible for the direction of national ceremonial rites.

84 This reception of the Silla envoys is also recorded in *Cefu yuangui* 971. The tower gate referred to is the Chengtian Gate within the Tang royal palace complex in Changan.

Nangnang Commandery, and King of Silla.

Winter, tenth month. Chief Minister Wimun requested retirement due to age and this was granted.

Twelfth month. There was a general amnesty. Kaesŏng Fortress was constructed.[85]

Year thirteen [714], spring, first month. *Ich'an* Hyojŏng became chief minister.

Second month. [The court] changed *Sangmunsa* [Master in Charge of Diplomatic Correspondence] to *T'ongmun paksa* and charged him with composing royal letters and memorials.[86] Prince Kim Such'ung was sent to Tang to become an imperial resident guard. [Tang] Xuanzong presented him with a residence and silks, provided him with favors, and held a banquet [in his honor] in the imperial hall.

Second [leap] month. *Kŭpch'an* Pak Yu was sent to Tang with New Year's greetings, where he was granted the title of *Chaosan dafu* [Grand Master for Closing Court] and the office of *yuanwai fengyu* [supernumerary chief steward][87] and then returned.

Summer. There was a drought and an epidemic spread widely among the populace.

Autumn. In Samnyang-ju the mountain acorns turned to chestnuts.

Winter, tenth month. Tang Xuanzong held a banquet for our emissaries in the inner hall of the palace where he directed the

---

85 Located in modern Kaesŏng in North Korea. According to *SS* 35, under Koguryŏ rule the location was known as Tongbihol but its name was changed to Kaesŏng during the reign of Silla's King Kyŏngdŏk (r. 742–765). As is apparent, however, the name Kaesŏng is used in *SS* before its putative change under King Kyŏngdŏk.

86 *Sangmunsa* was a Silla government office responsible for the preparation of official diplomatic correspondence.

87 *Fengyu* (office of chief steward) refers to the two chief officers who headed each of the six services of the Tang Palace administration.

councilors of state and all officials of rank four and above, [including] the censorial offices,[88] to attend.

Year fourteen [715], spring, third month. [The court] sent to Tang a tribute mission headed by Kim P'unghu.

Summer, fourth month. Ch'ŏng-ju presented a white sparrow.

Fifth month. There was an amnesty.

Sixth month. There was a great drought and the King summoned the Buddhist devotee Yi Hyo of Yongmyŏng Peak in Hasŏ-ju to conduct a prayer for rain on the pond at Imch'ŏn Monastery.[89] Right after [the prayer] it rained for ten days.

Autumn, ninth month. Venus covered the star *Sŏja.*[90]

Winter, tenth month. Shooting stars intruded into the constellation *Ch'ami.*[91]

Twelfth month. A shooting star from *Ch'ŏnch'ang* entered *T'aemi.*[92] There was an amnesty for criminals. Prince Chunggyŏng was enfeofed Crown Prince.

Year fifteen [716], spring, first month. A shooting star intruded on the moon causing the moon to lose its luster.

Third month. [The court] sent an envoy to Tang to present local products as tribute. Queen Consort Sŏngjŏng {another source states Ŏmjŏng} was sent out [from the royal palace].[93] She was

---

88 See *AKS* 3:265, n. 123. One source renders this as various officials but in *AKS* and elsewhere it appears as censorial offices.

89 Located in the modern city of Kyŏngju.

90 Third of five stars in the *Pukkŭk* ("Pole Star"; Polaris) constellation.

91 Chinese: *Ziwei,* a constellation of ten stars located to the north of the clusters of *Chin* and *Ik* (Chinese: *Zhen* and *Yi;* in the vicinity of the Corvus constellation) within the "Vermillion Bird of the South" grouping.

92 *Ch'ŏnch'ang* designates one of the twenty-eight constellations of traditional East Asian astrology and was associated with grains. It is also designated as the constellation *Wi* (Chinese: *Wei*), one of the seven constellations within the "White Tiger of the West" grouping. It corresponds roughly to the Western constellation of Aries.

93 Sŏngjŏng was the daughter of Kim Wŏnt'ae and was married to King Sŏngdŏk in

granted five hundred bolts of colored silk, 200 *kyŏl*[94] of rice land, 5,780 *sŏm* of grain rent, and a residential house. The house, the former residence of Lord Kangsin, was bought and given to her. There were heavy winds that snapped trees and blew off roof tiles and destroyed Sungnye Hall. Kim P'unghu, who went to Tang as *hajŏngsa* [congratulatory envoy] for the new year, wished to return home. Before being sent off Tang conferred on him the title of *yuanwailang* [bureau vice director][95] and had him return.

Summer, sixth month. There was a drought so the Buddhist devotee Yi Hyo was again summoned to perform a prayer [for rain] and then it rained. There was an amnesty for criminals.

Year sixteen [717], spring, second month. [The court] established one person each as a *ŭibaksa* [professor of medicine] and as a *sanbaksa* [professor of mathematics].[96]

Third month. A new palace was constructed.

Summer, fourth month. There was an earthquake.

Sixth month. Crown Prince Chunggyŏng died and he was given the posthumous title of Hyosang.

Autumn, ninth month. *Taegam* Such'ung returned from Tang and presented to the King portraits of Confucius, as well as [of]

the third year of his reign to become Queen Paeso. Imjŏng was her posthumous name. The circumstances behind her expulsion from the royal palace are unclear, however it would appear to be a result of a power struggle. This is further hinted at by the fact that the daughter of Kim Sunwŏn became the consort of King Sŏngdŏk in the nineteenth year (720) of his reign, as well as the fact that Sŏngjŏng's son by King Sŏngdŏk, and designated Crown Prince, died in the following year, though the circumstances of his death are unknown.

94 *Kyŏl:* land measurement of approximately 8,025 square meters (9,600 square yards)

95 During the Sui dynasty this was a supernumerary position but by the Tang period it had become a regular position designating the second-in-command to the Bureau Director in one of the six ministries.

96 Academicians of medicine and mathematic calculations respectively and appointed to the National Academy.

the ten philosophers and seventy-two disciples.[97] They were immediately placed in the National Academy.

Year seventeen [718], spring, first month. Chief Minister Hyojŏng retired and *P'ajinch'an* Sagong became chief minister.

Second month. The King made a tour and looked into the *chu* and *kun* of the western region and personally inquired into the elderly, widows, widowers, orphans, and the childless elderly, and distributed goods according to need.

Third month. There was an earthquake.

Summer, sixth month. The pagoda at Hwangnyong Monastery was rattled.[98] For the first time a *nugak* [waterclock] was made.[99] [The court] sent an envoy to Tang to present tribute. [The Silla envoy] was conferred title of *shou zhonglangjiang* [acting commandant] and sent back.

Winter, tenth month. Shooting stars from the constellation *Myo* entered the constellation of *Kyu*, causing many stars to follow.[100] A Celestial Dog fell in the northeastern area. Various fortresses within the jurisdiction of the governor general of

---

97 *Munsŏnwang* (Chinese: *Wenxuanwang*) was one in a string of progressively illustrious posthumous titles granted to Confucius, this one by the Tang Emperor Xuanzong in 739. The ten philosophers were the ten most-noted disciples of Confucius, namely Yan Hui, Min Ziqian, Ran Boniu, Zhonggong, Zaiwo, Zigong, Ranyou, Zilu, Ziyou, and Zixia (see *Analects* 11.3). The seventy-two disciples designate the number of traditional disciples of Confucius.

98 See *SY* 3 for a more detailed explanation which indicates a thunderstorm may have been the cause.

99 *SS* 38 notes that in the seventeenth year (718) of King Sŏngdŏk the *Nugakchŏn* (Water Clock Office) was established and charged with timekeeping. The record here should note that the *Nugakchŏn*, rather than a *nugak*, was first created at this time. The Water Clock Office had a staff of six *paksa* (academicians) and one *sa* (low-ranking official).

100 *Myo* (Chinese: *Mao*; Pleiades) designates the eighteenth of the twenty-eight *xiu* (Chinese zodiacal constellations). *Kyu* (Chinese: *Kui*; Andromeda) is the fifteenth of the Chinese zodiacal constellations. *Kyu* is comprised of sixteen stars and its name derives from the character meaning "to stride" since its shape was supposed to resemble a person walking.

Hansan-ju were constructed.

Year eighteen [719], spring, first month. [The court] sent an envoy to Tang to offer New Year's greetings.

Autumn, ninth month. Mirŭk Monastery in Kŭmma-gun was rattled [by thunder].[101]

Year nineteen [720], spring, first month. There was an earthquake. Extraordinary Head Rank One Inp'um died and so *Taeach'an* Paebu was named extraordinary rank one.

Third month. The daughter of *Ich'an* [Kim] Sunwŏn was received as Queen.

Summer, fourth month. Heavy rains fell causing landslides in thirteen mountain locations and hail fell damaging rice seedlings.

Fifth month. Orders were given to the offices concerned to bury skeletal remains. Wansan-ju presented a white magpie.[102]

Sixth month. The royal consort was formally invested as *Wanghu* [Queen].

Autumn, seventh month. Ungch'ŏn-ju presented a white magpie. Hail damaged the crops. Chief Minister Sagong retired and *P'ajinch'an* Munnim became chief minister.

Year twenty [721], autumn, seventh month. Two thousand *chŏngbu* [adult males] from the Hasŭlla circuit region were conscripted to construct a great long wall at the northern border.[103]

---

101 This is in modern Iksan, North Chŏlla.

102 Like the white crow or white sparrow of Chinese tradition, this is seen to be a propitious omen linking the affairs of earth and heaven's will.

103 It has been postulated that the remnants of this wall can be seen along the border between Yŏnghŭng-gun and Chŏngp'yŏng-gun, South Hamgyŏng province, North Korea. See Ikeuchi Hiroshi, "Sinkō-ō no boshi junkyōhi to tōhokukyō," *Chōsen koseki chōsa tokubetsu hōkoku* 6 (1929). The motives for constructing such a wall at this time are tied to Silla efforts to ward off the emergence of the Parhae state in the northern regions of the former Koguryŏ territory, a situation that deeply concerned Tang as well.

Winter. There was no snow.

Year twenty-one [722], spring, first month. Chief Minister Munnim died and *Ich'an* Sŏnjong became chief minister.

Second month. There was an earthquake in the capital.

Autumn, eighth month. [The court] started to distribute *chŏngjŏn* [male adult land].[104]

Winter, tenth month. [The court] sent *Taenama* Kim Inil to Tang to offer New Year's greetings as well as to present local products. Walls were constructed at Mobŏl-gun to block the routes of Japanese pirates.[105]

Year twenty-two [723], spring, third month. The King dispatched an envoy to Tang and presented two beautiful women. One of them was named P'ochŏng, whose father was *Nama* Ch'ŏngsŭng, and the other was named Chŏngwan, whose father was *Taesa* Ch'unghun. They were provided with garments, utensils, *nobi* [slaves], horses, and carriages, and sent off with proper ceremony. [Tang] Xuanzong addressed them, "You are both royal maternal cousins, yet you have left your family and parted from your homeland [to journey here]. I could not bare to have you remain." With generous gifts he sent them back [to Silla].[106] On Chŏngwan's stele it is recorded, "They returned to

---

104 Land granted to able-bodied peasants and first distributed in 721. The precise nature of able-bodied land and the motivations behind its distribution are the focus of continued debate. See Paek Namun, *Chosŏn sahoe kyŏngjesa,* 1933; Pak Sihyŏng, *Chosŏn t'oji chedosa,* part 1, 1960; Kim Yongsŏp, "Chŏngŭndaeŭi t'oji chedo," *Hangukhak ipmun,* 1960; and Kim Kihŭng, *Samguk mit t'ong'il sillagiŭi seje yŏngu,* Seoul: Yŏksabip'yŏngsa, 1991.

105 Mobŏl-gun was centered in modern Kyŏngju, extending southward to modern Ulchu-gu, Ulsan city. See also *SS* 34. The wall at Mobŏl was a checkpoint and later became known as Kwanmun Fortress. Regarding Kwanmun Fortress or wall, see Chŏng Yŏngho, "Silla Kwanmunsŏng e taehan soso," *Komunhwa* 5 (1977) and Pak Pangyong, "Silla Kwanmunsŏng ŭi kŭmsŏngmun koch'al," *Misul charyo* 31 (1982).

106 According to Chinese sources these events occurred one year later. See *AKS* 3:269, n. 151.

Tang in the sixth year of King Hyosŏng, the first year [742] of the *ch'ŏnbo* [*tianbao*] era", so we cannot be certain which is correct.

Summer, fourth month. [The court] sent an envoy to Tang to present a *kwahama* [miniature native horse] and ox bezoar, ginseng, beautiful hair pieces, thin silks, *chohaju* [rosy-dawn silk], and *ŏaju* [fish-tooth silk], bells carved with images of hawks, seal pelts, gold, silver, and other [products][107] together with a memorial that said,

"My [your subject's] home is at the corner of the far sea and the land is at an out-of-the way place. From early on we have not had the treasures of the Quanzhou[108] merchants nor the tribute brought by the southern barbarians. I would not dare to soil Your Imperial Majesty with these local products nor with this feeble horse sully Your Imperial Stables. Should I venture to compare these offerings to the pig of Yan[109] or dare liken them to the cock of Chu,[110] it would be enough to make me tremble and perspire in shame."

There was an earthquake.

Year twenty-three [724], spring. Prince Sŭnggyŏng was elevated to Crown Prince. There was a general amnesty. Ungch'ŏn-

---

107 A miniature horse native to Korea. Fully grown its height would reach only about 90 centimeters. The name *kwahamal* ("under the fruit-tree horse") purportedly comes from the fact that, even astride the small horse, one could still pass with ease under the boughs of a fruit tree. Ox bezoar was highly valued for its supposed medicinal properties.

108 Quanzhou refers to Quanzhou in China's Fujian province. The city, which thrived with trade from Persia, became a byword for wealth and exotic abundance.

109 The story of the "pig of Yan" can be found in *Hou Hanshu* 63, "Biography of Zhu Fu." A "pig of Yan" might be likened to something one at first takes as precious but which in fact turns out to be quite ordinary.

110 Taken from *Yinwenzi,* a lengthy legalist tract by Yin Wen (350–284 BCE) found in *Hanshu.* A "Chu cock" refers to a local bird, likely a large wild pheasant of some sort, and reflects the idea that deep loyalty may be reflected even in the offer of seemingly unattractive objects.

ju presented an auspicious mushroom.

Second month. [The court] dispatched Kim Muhun to Tang to offer New Year's greetings. Upon Muhun's return [to Silla] Xuanzong gave him a letter stating:

"Every year you receive the calendar and arrive to offer tribute to the court. These thoughts that you cherish are truly praiseworthy. Further, looking upon your varied products here offered, and reflecting that they all have been brought across the high waves and wide plains, they are all precious and beautiful and express fully the thoughts of you [my subject's] heart. Accordingly, in response to your sincere offerings, I grant you silken robes with golden sashes and 2,000 bolts of colored and white silks, so please accept them when they reach you."

Winter, twelfth month. [The court] sent an envoy to Tang to present local products. Royal consort Sodŏk died.

Year twenty-four [725], spring, first month. A white rainbow appeared.

Third month. There was snow.

Summer, fourth month. Hail fell. Chief Minister Sŏnjong retired and *Ich'an* Yunch'ung became chief minister.[111]

Winter, tenth month. The earth trembled.

Year twenty-five [726], summer, fourth month. [The court] sent Kim Ch'ungsin to Tang to offer New Year's greetings.[112]

Fifth month. The King's younger brother, Kim Kŭnjil was sent

---

111 Yunch'ung served as chief minister from 725 to 737. One theory posits that Yunch'ung is the same person as Yunjung, the grandson of Kim Yusin. See Yi Kibaek, "Silla chipsabuŭi sŏngnip," *Silla chŏngch'i sahoesa yŏn'gu* (1974), 163–4.

112 Kim Ch'ungsin would appear to be the same person as Imperial Resident Guard Kim Ch'ungsin who, in 734, presented a petition to the Tang Emperor formally requesting he be sent home to Silla. See Kim Sut'ae, "Silla chungdae chŏnjewanggwŏn kwa chingol kwijok," unpublished PhD dissertation, Sŏgang University, 1990, 113.

to Tang to present tribute. Having been conferred with the title of vice commandant, he returned [home].

Year twenty-six [727], spring, first month. There was an amnesty for criminals. [The court] sent an envoy to Tang to offer New Year's greetings.

Summer, fourth month. *Ilgilch'an* Wiwŏn became *taeach'an* and *Kŭpch'an* Taeyang became *sach'an*.

Winter, twelfth month. Yŏngch'ang Palace was repaired. Extraordinary Rank One Paebu requested to retire due to age but it was not granted and he was given an arm rest and cane.

Year twenty-seven [728], autumn, seventh month. [The court] sent the King's younger brother, Kim Sajong, to Tang to present local products and a memorial requesting [Silla] youth be allowed to enter the [Tang] National Academy. An imperial edict granted this, also conferring upon Kim Sajong the title of *Guoyi* [Vice Commandant of the Assault-resisting Garrison][113] and retained him as an imperial resident guard. Extraordinary Rank One Paebu requested retirement due to age and this was granted. *Ach'an* Sagong was appointed extraordinary rank one.

Year twenty-eight [729], spring, first month. [The court] sent an envoy to Tang with New Year's greetings.

Autumn, ninth month. [The court] sent an envoy to Tang to present tribute.

Year twenty-nine [730], spring, second month. [The court] sent royal clansman Chiman to Tang for an imperial audience where he presented [the Tang Emperor with] five small horses, one dog, 2,000 *ryang* of gold,[114] 80 *ryang* of hair, and 10 *chang* of seal

---

113 More fully, the *guoyi duwei* (Korean: *kwaŭi towi*). Originally established during the Sui in 613 as special military units created separate from the regular militia units.

114 *Ryang* (Chinese: *liang*) equals approximately 28.4 grams or 1 ounce.

pelts. [Tang] Xuanzong then conferred on Chiman the title of *Taipuqing* [Chief Minister of the Court of the Imperial Stud],[115] and granted him a hundred bolts of silk, a purple cloak with a brocaded silk belt, and then retained him as an imperial resident guard.

Winter, tenth month. [The court] sent an envoy to Tang to present local products as tribute. Xuanzong presented gifts [to the envoys] in accordance with their ranks.

Year thirty [731], spring, second month. [The court] sent Kim Chiryang to Tang to offer New Year's greetings. [Tang] Xuanzong conferred on him the title of *Taipu shaoching yuanwaizhi* [Supernumerary Vice Minister of the Court of the Imperial Stud] and sixty bolts of silk before he sent him home. Xuanzong also handed down to him an imperial letter:

"Looking at your offerings of ox bezoar, gold and silver, and other products that you presented, as well as your memorial, all is in good order. Blessed are you and your wife and so are the good relations among the Three Hans [Korea]. Your country today is considered to be benevolent and righteous witnessing distinguished accomplishments for generations. In letters, as in rites and music, you manifest the style of a gentleman. Fulfilling your utmost loyalty brings forth the duty of assisting the ruler. You are truly a barricade defending the nation and a model of loyalty and righteousness. How could I speak of yours as the same as a parochial culture of a distant land. Moreover, you diligently cherish morality and report to the court with surpassing diligence. Crossing mountains and traversing the seas, though the road is long, you show no indolence but offer tribute of silk and

---

115 *Taipusi* (The Court of the Imperial Stud) was one of the nine courts of the imperial Chinese government apparatus.

treasures, and remain constant through the passage of time. In keeping our imperial laws, your state's merits have been set down in the records. Such a demonstration of sincerity is worthy of praise. Whether rising every dawn to contemplate, or at night without shedding my daytime attire, I still wait for a man of virtue. Were I to meet such a person face to face, I would long to open my heart. For this reason have I longed to meet you so that I might share with you my most cherished hopes. Now on the arrival of your envoy I know that, due to illness, you are unable to fulfill my orders. Knowing that we are so far apart in distance, my worries deepen. It is my hope the warming weather will nourish your health. I present to you 500 bolts of colored ornamental silk and 2,500 bolts of unpatterned silk. Please accept at once as I give you all this."

Summer, fourth month. There was an amnesty. [The King] distributed wine and food to the elderly. Three hundred battleships from Japan crossed the ocean and attacked our eastern coast. The King ordered generals to dispatch troops and greatly routed them.

Autumn, ninth month. [The King] ordered the officials to assemble at the gateway to the target to observe shooting arrows from moving chariots.

Year thirty-one [732], winter, twelfth month. *Kakkan* Sagong and *Ich'an* Chŏngjong, Yunch'ung, and Sain were each appointed generals.

Year thirty-two [733], autumn, seventh month. Tang Xuanzong, as Parhae-Malgal[116] crossed the sea to invade Dengzhou,[117]

---

116 Following the fall of Koguryŏ in 668, refugees from that state, under the leadership of a former Koguryŏ general named Tae Choyŏng, united with tribes of the Sokmal Malgal (Sumo Mohe) and, in the vicinity of Mount Tongmo (Mount Dongmou, near modern Dunhua in Jilin province), in 699 established the Parhae kingdom.

dispatched the Supernumerary Minister of the Court of the Imperial Stud Kim Saran to return [to Silla] to confer upon the Silla King the title Commander Unequalled in Honor, Governor General of Ninghai. When [Silla] dispatched troops to attack the Malgal's southern flanks,[118] they met a heavy blizzard [with snow] over one *ch'ŏk* deep blocking the mountain paths. Over half the [Silla] troops perished and the army retreated without any gains. Kim Saran belonged to royal lineage. Earlier, when he went to the Tang court, he showed respect and propriety and accordingly was retained as an imperial resident guard. At this time he was entrusted as an imperial envoy and dispatched [by Tang] to foreign lands.

Winter, twelfth month. [The court] sent the King's nephew [Kim] Chiryŏm to the Tang court with thanks for the imperial favor. Earlier the Emperor had granted the King gifts of a male and female white parrot, a cloak of fine purple silk, dishes crafted with gold, patterned silk with auspicious designs, fine thin silk in five colors, and other items totaling over 300 *tan*. The [Silla] King sent a memorial of gratitude:

The "Record of the Bohai-Mohe (Parhae-Malgal)" in *Jiu Tangshu* 199 describes Parhae as distinct from Koguryŏ, whereas the "Record of Bohai" in *Xin Tangshu* 219 describes Parhae as composed of the Sokmal Malgal peoples who had been subjugated by the remnant Koguryŏ population. Further, according to the account of *Xin Tangshu* 219, in 713 Tang enfeoffed Tae Choyŏng as *Bohai junwang* (Parhae Commandery Prince) and that, subsequently, the term Malgal to refer to Parhae was dropped. Nevertheless Chinese records after 713 continue to refer to that state as Bohai-Mohe (Parhae-Malgal). Regarding the history of Parhae, see the volume on Parhae (v. 10) of the series *Hanguksa,* Seoul: Kuksa p'yŏnch'an wiwŏnhoe, 1996.

117 Modern Dengzhou. A key port city on the northern shore of China's Shandong peninsula. It had been a launching point for several naval expeditions against Koguryŏ during the Sui and early Tang.

118 Here the term Malgal is being used interchangeably with Parhae. The Tang Emperor's instructions to the Silla King to attack Parhae to its north can also be found in *SS* 43, "Biography of Kim Yusin", part 1.

"Prostrating myself in deference to Your Majesty, with what revered culture and inspired arms do you administer justice and govern the state! The result shall be a millennium of prosperity and good fortune for all things. Wherever clouds and wind flow, there Your Majesty's surpassing virtue shall be received. Wherever the sun and moon illumine, there Your Majesty's deep benevolence shall be felt. Though your subject's land is separated [from Tang] by Pongnae and Pangho,[119] your imperial benevolence makes its way even to this far-off [corner]. Though our land does not face your own, your imperial favors are received even in this secluded place. Reading your rescript in prostration, I arise to open the jade-adorned box that holds within the rain and dew of heaven and is encircled by a band of phoenixes and *luan*[120] in the five colors. How exquisite too are the white and blue hues of these heavenly birds that bear testament to your favor. Perhaps they sing the songs of Changan, perhaps their talk is of your imperial grace. Gazing upon the varied and colorful silken patterns and the engravings upon the gold and silver treasures, one's eyes are dazzled and, listening, one's heart is filled with joy. The origins of merit of what was presented to you was really due to what my ancestors had achieved. The favor that I have received is beyond my worth and its effects shall extend to our furthest generations. My loyalty to you is insignificant like dust but your favor is as momentous as a mountain peak. Given my [lowly] status, how could I pay back this grace I have

---

119 Pongnae (Chinese: Penglai), or Mount Pongnae, refers to a mountain whose location is shrouded in legend. It was, from early in Chinese history, mythologized as a dwelling place of Eight Daoist Immortals. Pangho (Chinese: Banghu), or Mount Pangho, and also known as Mount Pangjang (Chinese: Bangzhang), was likewise described as a dwelling place of the Immortals in the Yellow Sea.

120 The phoenix and the *luan* or *simurgh* were fabulous and mythical birds of Chinese tradition.

received?"

Thereupon an imperial directive had [Kim] Chiryŏm entertained in the inner palace, granting [him] bolts of silk.

Year thirty-three [734], spring, first month. [The King] issued a directive to the officialdom personally to come through the north gate [of the royal palace] for audiences. The Imperial Resident Guard and *Zuolingjunwei yuanwei jiangjun* [Supernumerary Commander General of the Left Metropolitan Guard],[121] Kim Ch'ungsin, who had been sent to Tang, presented a petition [to the Tang Emperor]:

"The order that I, your subject, received from you was to carry your imperial credentials to my homeland [to the Silla King] to mobilize troops to drive out the Malgal and to continue to report to Your Majesty so long as operations continue. From the time I, your servant, received such orders, I took an oath to dedicate myself to them wholly. However, at that time, because Kim Hyobang,[122] who was to replace [me], had passed away, I continued my residency here and became an Imperial Resident Guard. My own sovereign, seeing that I have long resided at your imperial court, has sent his first cousin once removed, [Kim] Chongjil, to replace me. As this person has already arrived I feel the time appropriate for me to return immediately [to Silla]. Every time I consider your earlier imperial orders, I can not forget it day or night. Previously Your Majesty issued commands to my King Hŭnggwang [Sŏngdŏk], granting him the added title of Governor General of Ninghai and ordered him to attack the wicked bandits [Malgal]. Wherever the dignity of Your Majesty reaches, though it

---

121 The two *Lingjunwei* (Metropolitan Guards), prefixed Left and Right, were among the sixteen guards charged with protecting the Tang capital.

122 Kim Hyobang was the son of the *Kakkan* Wŏnhun. *SY,* royal tables, states that Hyobang was the father of Kim Yangsang, later King Sŏndŏk (r. 780–785).

be distant, it will seem near. If this is your imperial order, how could I dare not heed it? The scheming barbarians already regret their misdeeds. Eliminating evil requires one suppress its foundation and spreading the law demands foisting reform. In deploying troops righteousness is more precious than a trio of victories and to let go of one's enemies will lead to the risk of troubles in future generations.

Prostrating myself before you, I wish Your Majesty would have me return to my homeland, and I entreat Your Highness to appoint me a deputy to my King so that I might extend the imperial will to far lands and promulgate the imperial intentions once again there. How can this not but make even further known the imperial indignation? Undoubtedly the troops will become spirited and overturn the lair of these bandits. Then making peaceful this far corner, my small effort will become the nation's great gain. I and others shall once more embark over the blue seas to bring to your imperial court reports of victory. I wish that my merit, though light like a strand of hair, will pay back your grace which is as essential as rain and dew. In prostration, I hope that Your Majesty will consider this."

The Emperor consented to this request.

Summer, fourth month. [The court] sent *Taesin* Kim Tangaltan[123] to Tang to offer New Year's greetings. The Emperor held a banquet to see him in the inner palace, conferring on him the title of *Weiwei shaoching* [Vice Minister of the Court of the Imperial Regalia],[124] a scarlet cloak, a silver belt, and sixty bolts of fine silk. Earlier [the court] sent the royal nephew [Kim]

---

123 In one source his name is rendered as Kim Kaltan. See *AKS* 3:276, n. 185.

124 *Weiweiyuan* (The Court of the Imperial Regalia) was one of the Nine Courts of the Tang central government and charged with the manufacture, storage, and upkeep of weapons, tents, insignia, and other such military regalia.

Chiryŏm to Tang to express gratitude for the imperial favors and presented [to the Emperor] two small horses, three dogs, 5000 *ryang* of gold, 20 *ryang* of silver, sixty bolts of hemp cloth, 20 *ryang* of cow bezoar, 200 *kŭn* of ginseng, 100 *ryang* of hair locks, and 16 *chang* [of seal pelts]. At this time Chiryŏm received the title of *Honglushaoching yuanwaizhi* [Supernumerary Vice Minister of the Court of State Ceremonial].[125]

Year thirty-four [735], spring, first month. The planet *Hyŏnghok* [Mars] intruded on the moon. [The court] sent Kim Ŭich'ung to Tang to offer New Year's greetings.

Second month. *Pusa* [Deputy envoy] Kim Yŏng died in Tang and he was conferred the posthumous title of *Guanglu shaoching* [Vice Minister of the Court of Imperial Entertainments].[126] When Ŭich'ung returned [to Silla] there was an imperial edict granting the territory south of the P'ae [Taedong] River as part of Silla.[127]

Year thirty-five [736], summer, sixth month. [The court] sent an envoy to Tang with New Year's greetings and accordingly attached a memorial expressing gratitude:

"I have reverently received your gracious decree granting the territory south of the P'ae River. Though I, your subject, was born and reared in a distant corner across the sea, I have benefited from the culture of your most sagely court. Despite my sincere intentions, I have no accomplishments worthy of display, and

---

125 *Honglusi* (The Court of State Ceremonial) was one of the Nine Courts of the Tang central government and in charge of important formal functions such as court receptions of foreign dignitaries and state funerals.

126 *Guanglusi* (The Court of Imperial Entertainments) was one of the Nine Courts of the Tang central government and under the general supervision of the Ministry of Rites.

127 Here the P'ae River is believed to be the modern Taedong River in North Korea. This may be seen as an attempt by Tang to use Silla to counter the rising power of Parhae. In the third year (782) of King Sŏndŏk, Silla established the P'ae River Garrison (P'aegang-jin) in the region as its northern line of defense.

though I faithfully and loyally apply myself to my tasks, my efforts fall short of success. However, Your Majesty has granted to me the grace that is as essential as rain and dew and issued your imperial rescript that shines as bright as the sun and moon. You have granted me, your subject, territory, whereby to expand my province, thereby bringing such lands under cultivation according to the seasons and providing new farmlands and mulberry fields [for silk production]. I, upholding your imperial will, though deeply indebted with your imperial grace and, although I grow weary and turn to dust, I shall find no way to repay such goodwill."

Winter, eleventh month. [The court] sent the King's younger cousin, *Taeach'an* Kim Sang to the Tang court. As he died en route, the Emperor was deeply grieved, and conferred upon him the posthumous title of *Weiwiqing* [Chief Minister of the Court of Imperial Regalia]. [The court] sent *Ich'an* Yunch'ung, Sain, and Yŏngsul to P'yŏngyang and Udu-ju to inspect the topography.

A dog ascended the drum tower of a wall and cried for three days.

Year thirty-six [737], spring, second month. [The court] sent *Sach'an* Kim P'ojil to Tang to offer New Year's greetings and to present local products. The King died.[128] His posthumous title was Sŏngdŏk and he was buried south of Ich'a Monastery.[129]

---

128 Tang sources all record that in the second month of 737 the official Xing Chou was appointed as an envoy to confer investiture as King of Silla upon Sŏngdŏk's successor (later King Hyosŏng). Therefore it has been argued that the year of Sŏngdŏk's death was, in all likelihood, 736. See Suematsu Yasukazu, *Shiragishi no shomondai* (Tokyo: The Tōyō Bunko Publications, Ser. A, No. 36, 1954), 413–28. Also, Michael C. Rogers, "The Thanatochronology of Some Kings of Silla," *Monumenta Serica* 29 (1960): 336–7.

129 *SY* 1 records, "His tomb was to the south of Tongch'on, perhaps in the Yangjang Valley." See Kang Inyŏng, *Silla onŭng* 127. In any case, no relation can be found between his tomb and an Ich'a Monastery.

The Silla
Annals of the
Samguk Sagi

Kings Hyosŏng, Kyŏngdŏk,
Hyegong, and Sŏndŏk

Book

9

King Hyosŏng

King Hyosŏng ascended the throne. His personal name was Sŭnggyŏng and he was the second son of King Sŏngdŏk. His mother was Queen Sodŏk. There was a general amnesty.

Third month. The *sŭng* [deputy] of the *Sajŏngbu* [Office of Surveillance][1] and the deputy of the Left Ministry of Law were all changed to *chwa* [deputy]. *Ich'an* Chŏngjong became extraordinary rank one and *Ich'an* Ŭich'ung became chief minister

Summer, fifth month. There was a great earthquake.

Autumn, ninth month. A shooting star entered the *T'aemi* constellation.

Winter, tenth month. *Sach'an* P'ojil, who had been to Tang, returned.

Twelfth month. [The court] sent an envoy to Tang to present tribute.

Year two [738], spring, second month. When the Tang Emperor Xuanzong learned that King Sŏngdŏk had died, he grieved for a long time and sent *Zuozanshan dafu* [Left Grand Master Admonisher] Xing Shou as Vice Minister of the Court for Dependencies to offer condolences and mourning rites and posthumously conferred on the deceased King [the title] *Taizi taibao* [Grand Guardian of the Heir Apparent] and enfeofed the

---

1   This office surveyed officials and was set up in 659. See *SS* 38.

succeeding King as Commander Unequalled in Honor, King of Silla. [Xing] Shou was about to depart when the Crown Prince [through lesser-ranked] officialdom together wrote poetry, and the Emperor himself wrote a preface [for the] poems, to send [with Xing Shou for the Tang Emperor].

The Emperor told Shou, "Silla is called a country of gentlemen and, like China, they truly know writing well. Because you are a true scholar, we entrust you with these credentials to carry so fittingly lecture on the meaning of the classics so they will know the high level of Confucianism in our country [Tang]." As our countrymen [Silla people] play go [*paduk*] well, [the Emperor] directed *Shuaifu bingcao canzhun* [Administer of the Guard Commandant Military Service Section] Yang Jiying to go as a deputy. All those highly skilled in go in our country are his followers. Thereupon the King lavishly rewarded [Xing] Shou and others with treasures made of gold and [herbal] medicines. Tang sent an envoy to enfeof by imperial decree Lady Pak as royal consort.[2]

Third month. [The court] sent Kim Wŏnhyŏn to Tang with New Year's greetings.

Summer, fourth month. The Tang envoy Xing Shou presented to the King *Lao Tzu, Daodejing*, and other books. A white rainbow pierced the sun.[3] The river at Soburi-gun[4] changed to blood [red].

Year three [739], spring, first month. The King paid respects at the shrine of his father and grandfather. Chief Minister Ŭich'ung

---

2   See *AKS* 3:280, n. 9. *SS 1977* 149 notes that in the year 740 Lady Kim was enfeofed and believes the entry here is in error. Kim Sut'ae in his dissertation believes King Hyosŏng had two consorts, one was Lady Pak and the other a Lady Kim.

3   As a white rainbow symbolizes war and the sun symbolizes the King, this is an omen noting danger to the king. See *AKS* 3:281, n. 12.

4   This is in Puyŏ, Ch'ungnam.

died and *Ich'an* Sinch'ung became chief minister. Sŏnch'ŏn Palace was completed. The King granted to Xing Shou 30 *ryang* of yellow gold, fifty bolts of cloth, and 100 *kŭn* of ginseng.

Second month. The King's younger brother Hŏnyŏng was appointed *p'ajinch'an*.

Third month. The King received *Ich'an* [Kim] Sunwŏn's daughter Hyemyŏng to be his consort.[5]

Summer, fifth month. *P'ajinch'an* Hŏnyŏng was named Crown Prince.

Autumn, ninth month. Wansan-ju presented a white magpie. A fox cried in Wŏlsŏng Palace but a dog bit and killed it.

Year four [740], spring, third month. Tang sent an envoy to enfeof Lady Kim, making her a royal consort.

Summer, fifth month. Saturn intruded on great star *Hŏnwŏn*.[6]

Autumn, seventh month. A woman wearing violet clothes came out from under Yegyo Bridge, slandered court politics, passed by the gate to Lord Hyosin's [house], and then suddenly disappeared.

Eighth month. *P'ajinch'an* Yŏngjong plotted a rebellion and was executed. Earlier Yŏngjong's daughter became a royal concubine and the King indulgently loved her and daily showered her with favors. The royal consort became jealous and, with her relatives, planned to kill her. Yŏngjong resented the royal consort and her family clique and so this plot occurred.

Year five [741], summer, fourth month. [The King ordered] leading ministers Chŏngjong and Sain to inspect the archery troops.

---

5   *SY* states the royal consort Hyemyŏng was the daughter of *Kakkan* Chinjong. In 720 *SS* notes another daughter of Sunwŏn became royal consort. If this is true then the King is marrying his mother's sister.

6   This is a group of stars north of Ursa Major.

Year six [742], spring, second month. There was an earthquake in the northeastern region and a noise like thunder.

Summer, fifth month. A shooting star intruded into the Orion constellation. The King died. His posthumous name was Hyosŏng. According to his last will, his coffin was burned south of Pŏmnyu Monastery and his bones were scattered in the East Sea.

King Kyŏngdŏk

King Kyŏngdŏk was enthroned. His personal name was Hŏnyŏng and he was the younger brother by the same mother of King Hyosŏng. As Hyosŏng had no children, Hŏnyŏng became the Crown Prince and therefore he inherited the throne. His consort was the daughter of *Ich'an* Sunjŏng.

Year one [742] winter, tenth month. An envoy from Japan arrived but he was not received.

Year two [743], spring, third month. In the residence of Lord Churyŏk a cow gave birth at one time to three calves. The Tang Emperor Xuanzong sent *Zanshan dafu* [Grand Master Admonisher] Wei Yao to offer condolences and mourning rites and invest the King as King of Silla and to inherit the former King's official titles decreeing:

"To Hŏnyŏng, the younger brother of the late Silla King, Kim Sŭnggyŏng, *Kaifu yidongsansi* [Commander Unequalled in Honor] Commissioned with Extraordinary Power, *Dadudu Jilinzhou juzhunshi* [Grand Commander-in-Chief of Kyerim Various Military Affairs], and *Chijie Yonghae zhunshi* [Military Commander of the Yŏnghae Army Commissioned with Extraordinary Power].

For many generations you cherished benevolence and always let your heart maintain propriety so that the wise Jizi [Kija]'s teachings and rulings became even brighter. You earlier inherited the regulations and rites and attire of China. Carrying gifts across the sea, we communicated frequently like clouds as companions. For generations you have been subjects [of mine] and on many occasions have demonstrated loyalty. Recently your older brother inherited the throne but as he died without sons to succeed, you, his younger brother, inherited [the throne]. I believe this is in accord with the standards of conduct. Treating you like a cherished guest, I honorably invest you. Properly maintain the early achievements of your kingdom and uphold the royal name of [your] country. Moreover, in adding special favor, I bestow upon you Chinese official titles. You may inherit your brother's titles of King of Silla, Commander Unequalled in Honor, *Shichijieh* [Commissioned with Extraordinary Power], Grand Commander-in-Chief of Kyerim Various Military Affairs, and concurrent Military Commander of the Yŏnghae Army Commissioned with Special Power."

[The Emperor] also granted one set of the *Classic of Filial Piety* annotated by His Majesty the Emperor.

Summer, fourth month. [The King] received *Sŏburhan* Kim Ŭich'ung's daughter as his royal consort.[7]

Autumn, eighth month. There was an earthquake.

Winter, twelfth month. The King sent his brother to Tang with New Year's greetings. The Emperor conferred on him the title of *Zuoqingdao shuaifu yuanwai changshi* [Senior Historian of Left Qing Province, Military Service Section] and granted him a green

---

7   See *AKS* 3:283, n. 28. She is also known as Lady Manwŏl, the second consort of King Hyosŏng, and also called Queen Kyŏngmok. As the previous consort of King Kyŏngdŏk bore no children, she left the court and this woman appears.

official cloak and a silver belt and sent him back.

Year three [744], spring, first month. *Ich'an* Yu Chŏng became chief minister.

Lunar second month. [The court] sent an envoy to Tang with New Year's greetings and also presented local products.

Summer, fourth month. The King personally held sacrifices at the Singung Shrine. [The court] sent an envoy to Tang to present horses.

Winter. A phantom star appeared in the middle of the sky whose size was a 5 *tu* vessel[8] and, after ten days, it disappeared.

Year four [745], spring, first month. *Ich'an* Kim Sain became extraordinary rank one.

Summer, fourth month. In the capital hail fell as big as eggs.

Fifth month. There was a drought. As Chief Minister Yu Chŏng retired, *Ich'an* Taechŏng became chief minister.

Autumn, seventh month. [The court] repaired the Eastern Palace and established [renamed] the *Sajŏngbu* [Office of Surveillance], *Sonyŏngajŏn* [Office of Youth Management], and *Yegungjŏn* [Office of Palace Management].[9]

Year five, [746], spring, second month. [The court] sent an envoy to Tang with New Year's greetings and to present local products.

Summer, fourth month. There was a general amnesty and a great feast offered [to peasants]. It was permitted that one hundred fifty people be [ordained] monks.

Year six [747], spring, first month. The name of the office of *Chungsi* [Chief Minister] was changed to *Sijung* [Chief Minister].

---

8   *Tu* (Chinese: *tou*), approximately 5,178 cubic centimeters or 316 cubic inches, often translated a "peck."

9   The *Sajŏngbu* originally started in King Muryŏl's reign. See also Yi Kidong, "Silla chungdae ŭi kwallyoche wa kolp'umche," *Kolp'um*. See *AKS* 3:284, n. 35.

[The court] placed *paksa* [professors] of various fields and *chogyo* [instructors] in various schools in the National Academy. [The court] sent an envoy to Tang with New Year's greetings and to present local products.

Third month. King Chinp'yŏng's tomb was rattled [by thunder].

Autumn. There was a drought.

Winter. There was no snow. As peasants starved and there was an epidemic [the court] sent out officials to the ten circuits to comfort [and to assist].

Year seven [748], spring, first month. A Celestial Dog [meteor][10] fell to the ground.

Autumn, eighth month. The Queen Dowager changed her residence to the new palace of Yŏngmyŏng. For the first time [the court] set up one position as a *chŏngch'al* [inspector] to examine the misdeeds of officials. [The court] sent *Ach'an* Chŏngjŏl and others to inspect the northern frontier borders. [The court] created Taegok Fortress and fourteen *kun* and *hyŏn*.[11]

Year eight [749], spring, second month. A strong wind uprooted trees.

Third month. [The court] established one *ch'ŏnmun paksa* [astronomy professor][12] and six *nugak paksa* [water-clock professors].[13]

Year nine [750], spring, first month. Chief Minister Taejŏng gave up his post and *Ich'an* Choryang became chief minister.

Second month. [The court] established the *Ŏyongsŏng* [Office of Royal Attendants][14] with two positions of *pongŏ* [chief

---

10 See above, Book 7, n. 109.
11 See also "Silla hadae ŭi P'aegangjin," in *Kolp'umje.*
12 This official handled meteorological matters.
13 This office was in charge of time.
14 This was an office of royal administration that supervised all royal attendants.

stewards] there.

Year eleven [752], spring, third month. *Kŭpch'an* Wŏnsin and Yongbang became *taeach'an*.

Autumn, eighth month. The position of *Agwan* [Adjutant] of the Eastern Palace was established.

Winter, tenth month. Three functionary positions were added to the Ch'angbu [Ministry of Granaries].[15]

Year twelve [753], autumn, eighth month. An envoy arrived from Japan. As he was arrogant with no propriety, the King did not receive him so he returned [home].[16] Mujin-ju presented a white pheasant.

Year thirteen, [754], summer, fourth month. There was hail as big as eggs.

Fifth month. [The court] erected a memorial stele to King Sŏngdŏk. Udu-ju presented an auspicious fungus.

Autumn, seventh month. The King commanded officials to repair Yŏnghŭng Monastery and Inyŏn Monastery.

Eighth month. There was a drought and locusts. Chief Minister Choryang retired.

Year fourteen [755], spring. Since grain was scarce, people starved. [A man named] Hyangdŏk from Ŭngch'ŏn-ju was poor and as he was unable to support [his father], he cut flesh from his thigh to feed him. When the King learned of this, he presented him with a generous reward and had an official erect a filial gate [at his village] to proclaim [his filial piety.] The stupas at Mangdŏk Monastery swayed. {The Tang text *Xinle guoji* [*Silla Kukki*], by Linghu Cheng, stated: "Because this country [Silla] constructed

---

15 This office oversaw the country's finances.

16 A similar entry can be found in the *Shoku Nihongi*. See *AKS* 3:287, n. 49.

this temple for Tang, therefore it took this name.[17] The two stupas faced each other with a height of thirteen stories. Then suddenly they shook, moving to and from each other as if they wished to fall down, for several days. As this year was the [An] Lushan rebellion, I suppose this may be the cause.}

Summer, fourth month. [The court] sent an envoy to Tang with New Year's greetings.

Autumn, seventh month. There was an amnesty for criminals and an inquiry was made into the old and sick, widows and widowers, and the orphaned and alone, with grain bestowed accordingly. *Ich'an* Kim Ki became chief minister.

Year fifteen [756], spring, second month. Extraordinary Rank One Kim Sain, because recently calamities and strange events frequently occurred, sent a memorial unsparingly discussing the state of current government affairs. The King happily accepted it. The King learned that Xuanzong was in Shu[18] and so he sent an envoy to Tang to cross the Yangzi River to go to Chengdu to present tribute products. Xuanzong personally composed and wrote [in his own calligraphy] a five-character ten-verse poem to give to the King and said, "In commending you, the Silla King, for your annual presentation of tribute to my court and practicing well the etiquette of rites and music, and fulfilling the obligations of a true subject, I am granting this poem":

The universe is composed of the sun and stars
All phenomena in the universe rotate around the central axis
Jade and silk pervade throughout the world
Crossing mountains and seas, all come to [Changan] the capital

---

17 Mangdŏk means "longing for virtue," or, in this case, "China."
18 This is the Sichuan area of China.

Though deemed to be separated by land and seas
They have diligently served China for a long time
Far away where the land comes to an end
It [Silla] sits in the far corner of the vast ocean
Yet known as a country of principle and righteousness
How can one say its mountains and rivers are different
The envoys depart carrying customs and teachings
People arrive to learn laws and practices
Literati know how to uphold decorum
Those with fidelity and faith know how to promote Confucian learning
Their sincerity will reflect in Heaven
Wise indeed, its virtue will not stand in isolation
Holding banners erect as if raising livestock[19]
Their generous gifts are comparable to their great devotion
Giving increasing weight to lofty goals
So as not to be deterred by unexpected hardships

At this time, when the Emperor was in Shu, Silla, not thinking that 1,000 *li* was too far, presented tribute to where [the Emperor] was. Therefore, pleased with this utmost sincerity, [the Emperor] granted him this poem which has the passage "Giving increasing weight to lofty goals, so as not to be deterred by unexpected hardships." Does it not have the same meaning as that from the ancient poem, "Unyielding grass in a strong wind, a time of turmoil brings forth loyal and upright subjects"?[20]

---

19 Taken from *Shijing,* this refers to the pastoral life of the "Eastern Barbarians." The next line also is borrowed from *Shijing.*

20 This passage comes from a poem Tang Taizong gave to one of his subjects; see *Jiu Tangshu* 63. This, in turn, draws on a phrase that a Later Han Emperor gave to a subject, as noted in *Hou Hanshu* 50.

In Xuanhe,[21] when the envoy Kim Puŭi went to the [Song] imperial court, he carried a woodblock of this poem to Bianjing[22] and showed it to *Quanban baoshi*[23] Li Bing. Li Bing presented it to the Emperor and the Emperor had it shown to the Two Administrations and various scholars. He [Bing] conveyed the Emperor's words, "The poem offered by the *Chinbong sirang*[24] is without a doubt the work of Emperor Ming [Xuanzong]," and he was pleasantly surprised.

Summer, fourth month. Large hail fell. A certain Taeyŏngrang presented a white fox and received the title of *nambyŏn* first rank.

Year sixteen [757], spring, first month. Extraordinary Rank One Sain, because of illness, resigned and *Ich'an* Sinch'ung became extraordinary rank one.

Third month. The monthly stipend given to officials in the central and local offices was abolished and the granting of village stipends [*nogŭp*] was restored.

Autumn, seventh month. [The court] again repaired Yŏngch'ang Palace.

Eighth month. Two functionary positions were added to the *Chobu* [Ministry of Taxation].

Winter, twelfth month. Sabŏl-chu was changed to Sang-ju, which consisted of[25] one *chu*, ten *kun*, and thirty *hyŏn*. Samnyang-ju was changed to Yang-ju which consisted of one *chu*, one minor capital, twelve *kun,* and thirty-four *hyŏn*. Ch'ŏng-ju was changed

---

21 This is the Song emperor Huizong (r. 1119–1125).

22 This is Kaifeng, the Song capital.

23 This is an office in charge of foreign guests which retained scholars in attendance to welcome foreign envoys.

24 This refers to Kim Puŭi, who was second in command on this mission. See *AKS* 3:289, n. 68.

25 Yŏng is the original but its exact meaning is still open to debate. Here it is rendered as "consisted of," but some suggest "jurisdiction over."

to Kang-ju which consisted of one *chu*, eleven *kun*, and twenty-seven *hyŏn*. Hansan-ju was changed to Han-ju which consisted of one *chu*, one minor capital, twenty-seven *kun*, and forty-six *hyŏn*. Suyang-ju was changed to Sakchu which consisted of one *chu*, one minor capital, eleven *kun*, and twenty-seven *hyŏn*. Ungch'ŏn-ju was changed to Ung-ju which consisted of one *chu*, one minor capital, thirteen *kun*, and twenty-nine *hyŏn*. Hasŏ-ju was changed to Myŏng-ju which consisted of one *chu*, nine *kun*, and twenty-five *hyŏn*. Wŏnsan-ju was changed to Chŏn-ju which consisted of one *chu*, one minor capital, ten *kun*, and thirty-one *hyŏn*. Mujin-ju was changed to Mu-ju which consisted of one *chu*, fourteen *kun*, and forty-four *hyŏn*. {"Yang-ju" in another source is written as "Yang-ju" using a different character}.

Year seventeen [758], spring, first month. As Chief Minister Kim Ki died, *Ich'an* Yŏmsang became chief minister.

Second month. A royal decree stated, "Officials in the central or local offices who have requested and completed sixty days of leave shall be [subject] to review to remove them from those offices."

Summer, fourth month. [It was decided], "Among the medical officials, select one person who researches medicine thoroughly and place him in the *Naegongbong*."[26] Two positions were established as *yullyŏng paksa* [law professors].[27]

Autumn, seventh month, twenty-third day. A prince was born. Thunder and lightening struck a Buddhist monastery in sixteen places.

Eighth month. [The court] sent an envoy to Tang with tribute products.

---

26 This was an office that directly attended the King for medical purposes.
27 This office oversaw criminal and administrative legal matters.

The **Silla Annals** of the **Samguk Sagi**

Year eighteen [759], spring, first month. The *kam* [director] of the *Pyŏngbu* [Ministry of Military Affairs] and the *kyŏng* [director] of the *Ch'angbu* [Ministry of Granaries] became *sirang* [attendant gentlemen], and the *taesa* [grand secretary] became *nangjung* [gentleman of the interior]; the *saji* [secretary] of the Chancellery Office was changed to *wŏnoerang* [vice director], the *sa* [scribe] of the Chancellery Office was changed to *rang* [gentleman of the interior]. The *taesa* [grand secretary] of the *Chobu* [Ministry of Taxation], *Yebu* [Ministry of Rites], *Sŭngbu* [Ministry of Transportation], and *Sŏnbu* [Ministry of Shipping]; *yŏnggaekpu* and *chwauŭibangbu* [senior and junior sections] of the Ministry of Law, *Sajŏngbu* [Office of Surveillance], *Wihwabu* [Ministry of Personnel Affairs], *Yejakchŏn* [Department of Buildings and Maintenance], and *taehakkam, taedosŏ, yŏngch'anggung,* etc. became *chubu* [recorders]. The *taesa* [grand secretary] of the *Sangsasŏ* [Office of Gifts], *Chŏnsasŏ* [Office of Sacrifices], *Ŭmsŏngsŏ* [Office of Music], *Kongjangbu* [Ministry of Works], the *ch'aejŏn,* and others became *chusŏ* [scribes].

Second month. The *saji* [secretary] of the *Yebu* [Ministry of Rites] became *sarye* [director of rites] and the *saji* [secretary] of the *Chobu* [Ministry of Taxation] became *sago* [warehousemen], the *saji* [secretary] of the *yŏnggaekpu* became *saŭi* [ceremonial official], the *saji* [secretary] of the *Sŭngbu* [Ministry of Transportation] became *samok* [director of pasturage], the *saji* [secretary] of the *Sŏnbu* [Ministry of Shipping] became *saju,* the *saji* [secretary] of the *Yejakpu* [Department of Buildings and Maintenance] became *sarye* [manager of regulations], the *nosaji* [secretary of the crossbow section] of the *Pyŏngbu* [Ministry of Military Affairs] became *sabyŏng* [manager of arms], and the *chosaji* [secretary of taxation] of the *Ch'angbu* [Ministry of Granaries] became *sach'ang* [director of granaries].

Third month. A comet appeared lasting until autumn when it disappeared.

Year nineteen [760], spring, first month. East of the capital as there was a noise like the beating of a drum, the populace called it "the spirit's drum."

Second month. Inside the palace they dug a large pond and south of the palace, over Munch'ŏn Stream, they built two bridges—Wŏnjŏng Bridge and Ch'unyang Bridge.

Summer, fourth month. As Chief Minister Yŏmsang retired from his office, *Ich'an* Kim Ong became chief minister.

Autumn, seventh month. Prince Kŏnun was enfeoffed Crown Prince.

Year twenty [761], spring, first month, first day. A rainbow went through the sun, making an earring.

Summer, fourth month. A comet appeared.

Year twenty-one [762], summer, fifth month. [The court] constructed six fortresses, Ogok, Hyugam, Hansŏng, Changsae, Chisŏng, and Tŏkkok and placed at each a *t'aesu* [governor].[28]

Autumn, ninth month. [The court] sent an envoy to Tang with tribute goods.

Year twenty-two [763], summer, fourth month. [The court] sent an envoy to Tang to present tribute products.

Autumn, seventh month. In the capital there was a strong wind that blew tiles and uprooted trees.

Eighth month. Peach and plum blossoms bloomed again. Extraordinary Rank One Sinch'ung and Chief Minister Kim Ong resigned from their offices. *Taenama* Yi Sun was one of the King's favorite officials but suddenly one day he gave up living in the

---

28 The forts were north of the Yesŏng River and south of the Taedong River in today's Hwanghae province: Ogok is in Sŏhŭng, Hyugam in Pongsan, Hansŏng in Chaeryŏng, Changsae in Suan, Chisŏng in Haeju, and Tŏkkok in Koksan.

secular world and retreated [entered] to the mountains [to become a recluse.] Although several times he was called back, he would not return but shaved his head becoming a monk. In the name of the King he established Tansok Monastery[29] and lived there. Later when he heard that the King liked music, he immediately went to the palace gate and admonishingly said, "I heard that in ancient times Jie and Zhou[30] became dissipated in wine and women and would not desist from enjoying lewd music and so their rule deteriorated and their kingdoms perished. If the front cart overturns, the following cart must be cautious. Prostrating, I wish that Your Majesty would correct your excesses and start anew to prolong the kingdom's existence." Upon hearing this, the King was moved and stopped [his] amusements. Leading him to a room, [the King] listened for several days on the profound principles of Buddhism and ways of governing a country and then stopped.

Year twenty-three [764], spring, first month. *Ich'an* Manjong became extraordinary rank one and *Ach'an* Yangsang became chief minister.

Third month. A comet appeared in the southeast and a dragon was seen under Mount Yangsan and suddenly it flew away.

Winter, twelfth month, eleventh day. [So many] comets in various sizes appeared that those who watched could not count [the number].

Year twenty-four [765], summer, fourth month. There was an earthquake. [The court] sent an envoy to Tang with tribute products. The Emperor conferred on the envoy the title *jianjiao*

---

29   This is in Kyŏngnam, Sanch'ŏn-gun, east of Mount Chiri.
30   Jie was the last monarch of the Xia Kingdom and Zhou was the last of the Shang kings.

libu shangshi [acting minister of rites].

Sixth month. A shooting star intruded into the *Sim* constellation.[31] In this month the King died. His posthumous title was Kyŏngdŏk and he was buried on the peak west of Miji Monastery.[32] {According to the ancient record, "He died in 765, the first year of Yŏngt'ae." According to *Jiu Tangshu* and *Zizhi tongjian*, "The Silla King Hŏnyŏng died in *Dali* second year [767]." Why this error?}

King Hyegong

King Hyegong was enthroned. His personal name was Kŏnun and he was King Kyŏngdŏk's oldest son. His mother was Lady Kim Manwŏl, the daughter of *Sŏburhan* Ŭich'ung. As the King was eight years old when he was enthroned, the Queen Dowager ruled as regent.

Year one [765]. There was a general amnesty. The King went to the Confucian College [Taehak] and ordered the *paksa* [professor(s)] to lecture on the meaning of the *Shangshu* [*Ancient Writings*].

Year two [766], spring, first month. Two suns appeared side by side.[33] There was a general amnesty.

Second month. The King personally held sacrifices at the

---

31 See *AKS* 3:292, n. 88 for additional information.

32 According to *SY* he was buried south of Kyŏnji Monastery and later reinterred here. See *AKS* 3, n. 89.

33 According to *SY* 5:12a this occurred in the nineteenth year (760) of King Kyŏngdŏk's reign and was interpreted as an omen of disaster.

Singung Shrine. A cow in the house of Lord Yangni gave birth to a calf with five legs with one leg facing upward. In Kang-ju there was a landslide forming a pond that was over 50 *ch'ŏk* wide and the water was dark blue.[34]

Winter, tenth month. A sound like drumming came from the sky.

Year three [767], summer, sixth month. There was an earthquake.

Autumn, seventh month. [The court] sent *Ich'an* Kim Ŭngŏ to Tang with local products of tribute and then requested orders to invest [the new King]. The Emperor came to Zichen Hall and held a banquet to see [Kim Ŭngŏ]. Three stars fell on the royal palace garden hitting each other. They were bright like fire and then scattered.

Ninth month. In Kimp'o-hyŏn the rice on the stalks all became rice.[35]

Year four [768], spring. A comet appeared in the northeast. Tang Daizong sent *Cangbu langzhong* [Granaries Bureau Director] Gui[36] Chongjing as *yushi zhongcheng* [concurrent vice censor-in-chief] to carry a letter of investiture to confer on the King the title *Kaibu yidong sansi* [Commander Unequalled in Honor], King of Silla, and at the same time invested the King's mother Lady Kim as [Royal] Consort Dowager.

Summer, fifth month. Pardons were extended to those below the crime carrying the death penalty.

---

34 See *SY* 2:11b for a similar account.

35 See *SY* 2:11b for a similar account. This means the rice came off the stalk, losing its covering, and became rice.

36 It was customary for Chinese envoys to engage in private trading. Gui alone did not do this thereby winning the respect of the Silla people. On this particular visit one of his deputies wrote *Xinle guoji* (*Silla Kukki*). See *AKS* 3:294, n. 99.

Sixth month. In the capital there was lightning and hail damaging the grass and trees. As a large star fell south of Hwangnyong Monastery the noise of the land shaking was like thunder. The springs and wells all went dry and a tiger entered the royal palace.

Autumn, seventh month. *Ilgilch'an* Taegong and his brother *Ach'an* Taeryŏm together rebelled and gathered a crowd that encircled the royal palace for thirty-three days. The royal troops attacked and suppressed them and executed their three generations: paternal, maternal, and wife's relatives.[37]

Ninth month. [The court] sent an envoy to Tang to present tribute.

Winter, tenth month. *Ich'an* Sinyu became extraordinary rank one and *Ich'an* Kim Ŭngŏ became chief minister.

Year five [769], spring, third month. [The court] feasted the various officials in Imhae Hall.

Summer, fifth month. There was [an infestation of] locusts and a drought. [The King] commanded each official to recommend people from among those that they knew.

Winter, eleventh month. More than eighty rats from Ch'iak-hyŏn[38] headed toward P'yŏngyang. There was no snow.

Year six [770], spring, first month. The King traveled to Sŏwŏn minor capital and examined and freed those guilty in the *chu* and *hyŏn* through which he passed.

Third month. It rained dirt.

Summer, fourth month. The King returned from Sŏwŏn minor capital.

---

37 Normally this means four generations above and four generations below but in this instance we believe it to be as translated. See also *AKS* 3:296, n. 102.

38 This is in Hwanghae, Yŏnbaek-gun.

The *Silla Annals* of the *Samguk Sagi*

Fifth month, sixteenth day. A comet appeared north of *Ogŏ* [Five-Cart] constellation and then disappeared on the twelfth day of the sixth month. On the twenty-ninth day a tiger entered the *Chipsasŏng* [Chancellery Office] and it was captured and killed.

Autumn, eighth month. As *Taeach'an* Kim Yung rebelled, he was executed.

Winter, eleventh month. There was an earthquake in the capital.

Twelfth month. Chief Minister Ŭngŏ retired and *Ich'an* Chŏngmun became chief minister.

Year eight [772], spring, first month. [The court] sent Kim P'yosŏk to Tang with New Year's greetings. Daizong conferred on him the post of *weiwei yuanwei shaoqing* [supernumerary vice minister of the awesome guard] and sent him back.

Year nine [773], summer, fourth month. [The court] sent an envoy to Tang with New Year's greetings and he presented gold, silver, ox bezoar, fish-tooth silk, rosy-dawn silk, and other local goods.

Sixth month. [The court] sent an envoy to Tang to express gratitude. Daizong greeted him in Yanying Hall.

Year ten [774], summer, fourth month. [The court] sent an envoy to Tang with tribute goods.

Autumn, ninth month. *Ich'an* Yangsang became extraordinary rank one.

Winter, tenth month. [The court] sent an envoy to Tang with New Year's greetings. [The Emperor] greeted him in Yanying Hall and conferred on him the title *yuanweiweiweiqing* [supernumerary minister of the awesome guard] and sent him back.

Year eleven [775], spring, first month. [The court] sent an envoy to Tang with tribute products.

Third month. *Ich'an* Kim Sun became chief minister.

Summer, sixth month. [The court] sent an envoy to Tang. As *Ich'an* Kim Ŭngŏ revolted, he was executed.

Autumn, eighth month. *Ach'an* Yŏmsang, with Chief Minister Chŏngmun, plotted to rebel but were executed.

Year twelve [776], spring, first month. [The King] decreed that the former names of all the government offices shall be restored. The King traveled to Kamŭn Monastery[39] to view the ocean.

Second month. The King went to the *Kukhak* [National Academy] to listen to lectures.

Third month. [The court] increased the number of functionaries to eight in the *Ch'angbu* [Ministry of Granaries].

Autumn, seventh month. [The court] sent an envoy to Tang to present local products.

Winter, tenth month. [The court] sent an envoy to Tang with tribute goods.

Year thirteen [777], spring, third month. There was an earthquake in the capital.

Summer, fourth month. There was another earthquake. Extraordinary Rank One Yangsang presented a memorial unsparingly criticizing the state of government.

Winter, tenth month. *Ich'an* Chuwŏn became chief minister.

Year fifteen [779], spring, third month. There was an earthquake in the capital that wrecked people's houses, killing more than a hundred people. Venus intruded on the moon. [The court] held a Hundred-Seat Assembly.

Year sixteen [780], spring, first month. There was a yellow fog.

Second month. It rained dirt. The King was enthroned at a young age. Growing up he indulged in music and women and

---

39 Kamŭn Monastery with its two stupas is still standing near the East Sea. See *AKS* 3:297, n. 114.

played around without restraint [causing] the government to lose discipline and control. Calamities and strange events frequently arose as people became rebellious against dynastic decadence. *Ich'an* Kim Chijŏng rebelled and assembled many [followers] to surround forcefully and enter the palace.

Summer, fourth month. Extraordinary Rank One Kim Yangsang and *Ich'an* Kyŏngsin raised troops to execute Chijŏng and others but the King and his queens were killed by the rebellious troops. Yangsang and others conferred the King's posthumous name as King Hyegong. His first consort was Queen Sinbo, the daughter of *Ich'an* Yusŏng and the second consort was the daughter of *Ich'an* Kim Chang. The sources have lost the dates they became consorts.

King Sŏndŏk

King Sŏndŏk was enthroned [780]. He was of the Kim lineage with the personal name of Yangsang [but] was the tenth-generation descendant of King Naemul. His father was *Haech'an* [*Pajinch'an*] Hyobang[40] and his mother was Lady Saso of the Kim lineage and daughter of King Sŏngdŏk. His consort was Lady Kujok, the daughter of *Kakkan* Yangp'um. {Another source says the daughter of *Ach'an* Ŭigong.}

There was a general amnesty. [The King] posthumously invested his father to be Great King Kaesŏng and his mother to be

---

40 According to *SY*, he was an imperial resident guard in Tang in 735. He was also King Sŏngdŏk's son-in-law (702–737). See *AKS* 3:275, n. 183.

Queen Dowager Chŏngŭi and he made his wife to be Queen. *Ich'an* Kyŏngsin became extraordinary rank one, *Ach'an* Ŭigong became chief minister. The *Pongŏ* [Chief Steward] of the *Ŏryongsŏng* [Office of Royal Travel] was changed to *kyŏng* [director]—and then *kyŏng* [director] was changed to *kam* [director].

Year two [781], spring, second month. The King personally held sacrifices at the Singung Shrine. [The court] sent an official to inspect the *chu* and *kun* south of the P'aesu River.

Year three, spring, leap first month. [The court] sent an envoy to Tang with tribute goods.

Second month. The King went to Hansan-ju to inspect and resettled people and their households to P'aegang-chin.[41]

Autumn, seventh month. [The court] held a major military inspection on the plains of Sirim.

Year four [783], spring, first month. *Ich'an* Ch'esin became military governor of Taegok-chin.[42]

Second month. Three *ch'ŏk* of snow fell in the capital.

Year five [784], summer, fourth month. The King wished to abdicate. However ranking officials sent memorials three times opposing this and so he gave up [the idea].

Year six [785], spring, first month. Tang Dezong dispatched *Hubu langzhong* [Director of the Ministry of Finance] Gai Xun carrying a warrant to invest the King *Jianjiao taiwei jilinjucishi yŏnghae junshi* [Acting Guardian, Prefect of Kyerim, Commissioner of the Yŏnghae Army, King of Silla]. This month, as the King was sick and remained in bed for a long time not

---

41 See Fujita Ryūsaku, "Shiragi kyūshū gokyō kō," *Chōsengaku ronkō* (1963), and Yi Kidong, "Silla hadae ŭi P'aegang-chin," *Kolp'umje*. P'aegang-chin was becoming an administrative and military center.

42 This is in Hwanghae, P'yŏngsan (also called P'aegang-chin).

getting up, he issued the [following] statement:

From the start I have lacked talent and virtue. I had no wish to take the throne but, as it was difficult to decline the invitation, I became King. Since I have been on the throne, the years have not been prosperous and the lives of the peasants have become destitute. This is all because my virtue did not match the hopes of the peasants and my polices could not correspond to the will of Heaven. I always wanted to abdicate the throne and retire to live a private life. Because the ranking officials of the state and many subjects, always with sincerity, dissuaded me, I could not follow my own wishes until now. But now I have suddenly fallen ill with no expectation of getting well. Life and death are fated. In looking back why should I have regrets? After I die please follow Buddhist practicies, cremate my remains, and scatter my bones in the Eastern Sea.

On the thirteenth day he died and his posthumous title was Sŏndŏk.

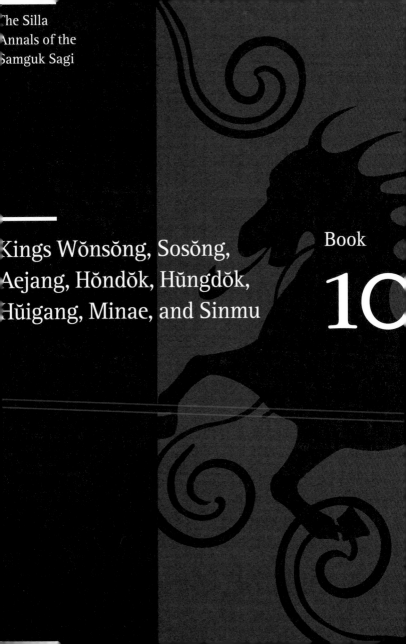

The Silla
Annals of the
Samguk Sagi

Kings Wŏnsŏng, Sosŏng,
Aejang, Hŏndŏk, Hŭngdŏk,
Hŭigang, Minae, and Sinmu

Book

10

King Wŏnsŏng

King Wŏnsŏng was enthroned [785]. His personal name was Kyŏngsin and he was a twelfth-generation descendant of King Naemul. His mother was Lady Kyeo of the Pak lineage and his Queen was the daughter of *Kakkan* Sinsul of the Kim lineage.[1] Earlier, late in King Hyegong's reign, when rebellious ministers were rampant, Sŏndŏk [then] was extraordinary rank one and became a leading advocate for the removal of the treasonous close to the King. Kyŏngsin, supporting this, earned merit in pacifying the rebellions. Upon Sŏndŏk becoming King, Kyŏngsin at once became extraordinary rank one.

When [King] Sŏndŏk died with no sons, the ranking officials, after deliberations, wanted to enthrone the King's cousin [Kim] Chuwŏn.[2] Chuwŏn lived 20 *li* north of the capital. [At that time]

---

1 According to *SY* 1:13a, chronology section, King Wŏnsŏng was called Kyŏngsin or Kyŏngch'uk in the Chinese history *Tangshu*. His father was Hyoyang Taeagan and posthumously honored as Myŏngdŏk Naewang. His mother was Lady In or Chio and posthumously named Queen Somun. She was the daughter of Ch'anggŭn Iki. His consort was Lady Sukchŏng, the daughter of *Kakkan* Sinsul.

2 Kim Chuwŏn's birth date is unclear. A late-Silla *chingol* aristocrat, he was a sixth-generation descendant of King Muyŏl. In King Hyegong's thirteenth year he became *ich'an* and later advanced into the Ministry of Military Affairs. When he failed to become King he went to the Kangnŭng area and became known as the King of Myŏngju-gun. He was the progenitor of the Kangnŭng Kim lineage. His descendants, antagonists of the central court, became powerful regional strongmen in the Kangnŭng area and received the royal surname Wang from the Koryŏ Dynastic Founder. See Ch'oe Pyŏnghŏn, "Silla hadae sahoe ŭi tongyo," *Hanguksa* 3, and Kim Chŏngsuk, "Kim Chuwŏn segye ŭi sŏngnip kwa p'yŏngchŏngchan'an," *Paeksan hakpo* 28.

encountering a great rain, Alch'ŏn Stream flooded, preventing Chuwŏn from crossing. Some said, "As kingship is a great position and clearly not something people can determine, is not today's heavy rain perhaps Heaven's way of saying it does not want Chuwŏn to be enthroned? Now Extraordinary Rank One Kyŏngsin is the brother of the former King[3] and he, from the start, enjoys a reputation of being virtuous and carries the bearing of a King." Thereupon the people discussed this together, agreeing to enthrone him as King, and immediately the rain stopped. The people of the kingdom all cried out long live the King [*mansei*— ten thousand years].[4]

Second month. [The King] posthumously invested his great-great-grandfather *Taeach'an* Pŏpsŏn as Great King Hyŏnsŏng and his great-grandfather *Ich'an* Ŭigwan as Great King Sinyŏng, his grandfather *Ich'an* Wimun as Great King Hŭngp'yŏng, his deceased father *Ilgilch'an* Hyoyang as Great King Myŏngdŏk, his mother of the Pak lineage as Queen Dowager Somun, and his son Ingyŏm as Crown Prince.

He tore down the two shrines to Great King Sŏngdŏk and Great King Kaesŏng.[5] Great Founding King [Sijo-wang], Great King Taejong, Great King Munmu, his grandfather Great King Hŭngp'yŏng, and his father Great King Myŏngdŏk were placed in the Five Ancestral Shrines.[6] He promoted all military and civil officials by one rank and appointed Minister of Military Affairs

---

3   As King Sŏndŏk was a tenth-generation descendant of King Naemul and King Wŏnsŏng was a twelfth-generation descendant, and they had different mothers, they were not immediate brothers.

4   *SY* 2:12a–13a provides a more detailed account of this enthronement.

5   Kaesŏng is King Sŏngdŏk's father. See the entry for King Sinmun's seventh year, fourth month.

6   Silla kings were enfeofed in the Five Ancestral Shrines. Chinese emperors were enfeofed in the Seven Ancestral Shrines. See *AKS* 3:302, n. 11.

Ich'an Ch'ungnyŏm to be extraordinary rank one and *Ich'an* Chegong to be chief minister. [Then] Chegong resigned and *Ich'an* Segang became chief minister.

Third month. The King sent the former Queen, Queen Dowager Kujok, to an attached palace and gave her 34,000 *sŏk* of grain. P'aegan-chin presented a red crow. [The court] changed the title of *ch'onggwan* [adjutant grand commander] to be called *todok* [commander-in-chief].[7]

Year two [786], summer, fourth month. In the eastern part of the kingdom hail fell damaging all the mulberry trees and barley. [The court] sent Kim Wŏnjŏn to Tang to present local products. [Tang] Tezong sent a decree stating:

"I, the Emperor, hereby decree to the King of Silla Kim Kyŏngsin: The letter and tribute that Kim Wŏnjŏn brought on his arrival, on examining them, were found to be all appropriate. The customs of your country esteem good faith and aspire to be incorruptible. [Moreover] from early on supporting my state [China], you have honored the imperial name and influence, thereby soothing the frontiers into submission and subjecting everyone under Confucian influence, thus giving rise to the practice of the ritual of propriety. As your enfeofed land is at peace, you have turned toward the imperial palace with all sincerity and attend court audiences without failure. You frequently send official envoys and continue to observe tribute presentations. Even through the ocean is vast and wide and the land road is long and far-reaching, the exchange of precious gifts has continued in accordance with old precedents. I truly commend and am deeply moved by your loyalty. Since I rule directly over all the world like a parent to the people, with fitting laws and

---

7 See treatise section on government offices in *SS* 40.

shared culture from the capital to the provinces, effecting the promised grand harmony and jointly advancing benevolence and longevity, may you fittingly maintain peace in your domain, endeavor to sustain human security, and forever be a loyal subject of the frontier, keeping your far-away country at peace. Accordingly, I now grant thirty bolts of various silks, one suit of clothes, and one silver bowl. Please fittingly receive this. To your Queen, twenty bolts of various silks, one suit made of gold thread on silk, and one shallow silver plate. To the extraordinary rank one,[8] one set of clothes and one silver plate. To the two next *chaesang* [councilors of state] each, one set of clothes and a shallow silver plate. Please fittingly accept and distribute these. As the summer is still very hot, I hope you will take good care of yourself. Please extend my regards to your high ministers and below, though I can not convey all my thoughts in this letter."

Autumn, seventh month. There was a drought.

Ninth month. As the people in the royal capital were confronting famine, [the court] sent out 33,240 *sŏk* of rice to aid them.

Winter, tenth month. [The court] again sent out 33,000 *sŏk* [of rice] to aid them. *Taesa* Muo presented fifteen volumes on military tactics and two volumes of *Hwaryŏngdo*.[9] He was given the post of magistrate of Kurap-hyŏn.[10]

Year three [787], spring, second month. There was an

---

8 In the text this appears as *taejaesang* (chief councilor of state) but this is most likely *sangdaedŭng* (extraordinary rank one). See *AKS* 3:303, n. 19.

9 From the title, literally, it may mean "Illustrations of Ornamental Bells."

10 This is in Hwanghae, Kurap-hyŏn. *SY* 2:13a–b reports that the Emperor of Japan planned to attack Silla but, hearing that King Wŏnsŏng possessed a magical flute, he offered 50 *yang* of gold for the instrument. The King denied that he had the flute but the Emperor sent a second envoy the following summer with the same request. The King still denied the story although he had the hidden the flute in a royal vault.

The Silla Annals of the Samguk Sagi

earthquake in the capital. The King personally held sacrifices at the Singung Shrine. There was a general amnesty.

Summer, fifth month. Venus appeared in the day.

Autumn, seventh month. Locusts damaged the grain.

Eighth month, first day [*sinsa*]. There was a solar eclipse.

Year four [788], spring. [The court] instituted, for the first time, the *tokső samp'umgwa* [examination of reading of texts in three gradations], thereby those who were versed in the ideas of the *Zuo Commentary of the Spring and Autumn Annals, The Book of Rites,* and *The Book of Documents,* and could explicate the *Analects* and the *Book of Filial Piety* received the top rank. Those who were versed in the Five Rites and could read the *Analects* and the *Book of Filial Piety* received the middle rank. And those well versed in the Five Rites and who could read the *Book of Filial Piety* received the bottom [rank]. Those who were widely versed in the five classics, three histories, and the books of the philosophers of *Zhou* [One Hundred Schools],[11] should be specially appointed to a higher rank. Earlier [the court] selected people based only on their ability in archery. Coming to this, it has changed.

Autumn. In the western part of the kingdom there was a drought and there was a locust [infestation]. As there were many robbers, the King dispatched officials to go and suppress them.

Year five [789], spring, first month, first day, *kapchin.* There was a solar eclipse. As the people of Hansan-ju were facing famine, the King sent millet to aid them.

Autumn, seventh month. Frost fell, damaging the grain.

Ninth month. When Chaok became *sosu* [deputy magistrate] of Yanggŭn-hyŏn, *chipsasa* [scribe of the chancellor's office] Moch'o

---

11 The classics are *Book of Documents, Book of Songs, Book of Changes, Book of Rites,* and *Spring and Autumn Annals.* The three histories are *Shiji, Hanshu,* and *Hou Hanshu.*

protested saying, "As Chaok is not under a civil registration, he is not suitable to hold a regional office." The chief minister disputed this saying, "Even though he is not under a civil registration, as he once entered Tang becoming a student, does not this not also make him employable?" The King agreed to this.

| Commentary | Only after study does one know the way, and only after knowing the way does the essence of things become clearly apprehended. Therefore, serving the government after studying lies in this. By first mastering the root, the end can be correct. Therefore if you serve after you have studied, when it comes to handling matters you will do first what is basic and the rest will fall in place. Figuratively speaking, it is like pulling up a large rope net and the rest will follow. On the contrary, those who do not study do not know that all affairs have an order with a beginning and an end, essentials and non-essentials, and only focus on trivial things—not knowing what to do. [Officials] will see gains only by extorting the people or harshly scrutinizing to elevate themselves. Although they try to benefit the country and help the people, on the other hand, they harm them. Therefore *Xueji* [*Liji*] ends with the words, "Attend to what is fundamental" and *Shangshu* states, "Without study you stand facing a wall and your management of affairs will be full of trouble."[12] Accordingly Chancellor Moch'o's single statement can be a model for generations to come.

Year six [790], spring, first month. Chonggi became chief minister. To build up Pyŏkkol Dike,[13] people from Chŏnju and seven *chu* were mobilized to work [on the project]. Ungch'ŏn-ju

---

12 For the *Shangshu* translation see Legge's translation of the *Shangshu,* part v, book 20, verse 16.
13 See *SS* 2:15a. When first constructed in Kimje (Chŏnbuk), it was 1,800 *p'o.*

presented a red crow.

Third month. *Ilgilch'an* Paek Ŏ was dispatched as an envoy to the northern country [Parhae]. There was a great drought.

Summer, fourth month. Venus and Mercury appeared together in the eastern constellation.[14]

Fifth month. [The court] sent out grain to aid the starving people in two *chu,* Hansan and Ungch'ŏn.

Year seven [791], spring, first month. The Crown Prince died. He was posthumously named Hyech'ung. As *Ich'an* Chegong rebelled, he was executed. The wife of Hyangsŏng, the *taesa* of Ungch'ŏn-ju, gave birth to boy triplets.

Winter, tenth month. As 3 *ch'ŏk* of snow fell in the capital, there were people who froze to death. Chief Minister Chonggi resigned and *Taeach'an* Chunong became chief minister.

Eleventh month. There was an earthquake in the capital. *Naesŏng sirang* [Executive of Palace Administration] Kim Ŏn became *ach'an,* third level.[15]

Year eight [792], autumn, seventh month. The court sent an envoy to Tang to present the beautiful woman Kim Chŏngnan.[16] She was the most beautiful woman in the country and her body gave off a fragrance.

Eighth month. The court enfeofed Prince Ŭiyŏng as Crown Prince. Extraordinary Rank One Ch'ungnyŏm died and *Ich'an* Segang became extraordinary rank one. Chief Minister Chunong resigned because of illness and *Ich'an* Sungbin became chief

---

14 This constellation was one of twenty-eight constellations located in the southern sky and comprised of eight stars. See *AKS* 3:306, n. 39.

15 This was a rank in the late-Silla rank system. In addition to *ach'an,* three levels were created above called second level, third level, and, the highest, fourth level. See Pyŏn T'aesŏp, "Silla kwandŭng ŭi sŏnggyŏk," *Yŏksa kyoyuk* 1 (1956).

16 See *AKS* 3:306, n. 42. See Kwŏn Tŭkyŏng, *Kodae Hanjung waegyosa,* Seoul: Ilchokak, 1997.

minister.

Winter, eleventh month, first day, *imjae.* There was a solar eclipse.

Year nine [793], autumn, eighth month. A strong wind broke trees and flattened rice. *Naema* Kim Noe presented a white pheasant.

Year ten [794], spring, second month. There was an earthquake. Crown Prince Ŭiyŏng died and posthumously was named Hŏnp'yŏng. Chief Minister Sungbin died and *Chapch'an* Ŏnsŭng[17] became chief minister.

Autumn, seventh month. Construction started on Pongŭn Monastery.[18] Hansan-ju presented a white crow. West of the palace Mangŭn-ru [tower] was erected.

Year eleven [795], spring, first month. [The King] enfeofed Chunong, the son of Crown Prince Hyech'ung, Crown Prince.

Summer, fourth month. As there was a drought, the King personally examined the records of those imprisoned. On coming to the sixth month, it rained.

Autumn, eighth month. Frost fell, damaging grain.[19]

Year twelve [796], spring. Since a famine and epidemic hit the capital, the King opened the granary to aid.

Summer, fourth month. Chancellor Ŏnsŭng became Minister of the Ministry of Military Affairs and *Ich'an* Chiwŏn became chief minister.

Year thirteen [797], autumn, ninth month. In the eastern part of the kingdom locusts damaged the grain and heavy rains caused landslides. Chief Minister Chiwŏn resigned and *Ach'an* Kim Samjo

---

17 Ŏnsŭng was the son of Ingyŏm and brother of Chunong, the future King Sosŏng.
18 See also *SY* 2:14b for a similar entry.
19 *SY* 2:13b notes that a Tang envoy visited Kyŏngju for one month.

became chief minister.

Year fourteen [798], spring, third month. A tower bridge south of the palace burned and two pagodas at Mangdŏk Monastery crashed against each other.[20]

Summer, sixth month. There was a drought and the wife of *Taesa* Sŏk Namo of Kulcha-kun[21] gave birth to quadruplets, three boys and one girl.

Winter, twelfth month, twenty-ninth day. The King died. He was posthumously named Wŏnsŏng and, according to his wishes, his coffin was elevated and cremated south of Pongdŏk Monastery.[22] {*Tangshu* states "In Zhenyuan fourteenth year [797] Kyŏngsin died." *Tongjian* states, "In Zhenyuan sixteenth year [800] Kyŏngsin died." By investigating this history [the *Samguk sagi*] the *Tongjian* is in error.}[23]

King Sosŏng

King Sosŏng {another source says Sosŏng [by another character]} was enthroned. His personal name was Chunong and he was the son of King Wŏnsŏng's Crown Prince Ingyŏm. His mother was of

---

20 According to Yi Kibaek, *Silla chŏngch'i,* construction on dikes in Yŏngch'ŏn was completed at this time.

21 This is in Kyŏngnam, Ch'angwŏn.

22 According to *SY* 2:14b he is buried west of Mount T'ot'oham with a stele inscription written by Ch'oe Ch'iwŏn standing nearby. Pongdŏk Monastery is in Kyŏngju where its foundation can still be seen.

23 See *Xin Tangshu* 220, Silla chuan, and *Zizhi tongjian* 235, zhenyuan 16, 800. See also *AKS* 3:310, n. 61, which provides yet a third date, 799, according to *Samguk yusa.*

the Kim lineage and his consort was Lady Kyehwa of the Kim lineage, the daughter of *Taeach'an* Sungmyŏng.[24]

In the first year of King Wŏnsŏng's reign, he had enfeofed his son Ingyŏm to be Crown Prince, but [Ingyŏm] died in the seventh year. Wŏnsŏng raised Ingyŏm's son in the palace. In the fifth year he went to Tang as an envoy and received the title of *taeach'an;* in the sixth year, as *p'ajinch'an,* he became a councilor of state [*chaesang*]. In the seventh year he became chief minister and in the eighth year he became Minister of the Ministry of Military Affairs. In the eleventh year he became Crown Prince and, when King Wŏnsŏng died, he succeeded to the throne.

Year one [799], spring, third month. Ch'ŏng-ju, Kŏro-hyŏn, became a stipend village.[25] Naengjŏng-hyŏn magistrate Yŏmch'ŏl presented a white deer.

Summer, fifth month. The King posthumously enfeofed his late father Crown Prince Hyech'ung as Great King Hyech'ung. An Udu-ju governor sent an official who reported, "There is a strange animal that looks like a cow. Its body is long and tall with a tail over 3 *ch'ŏk*. It has no fur but a long nose."[26] From Hyŏnsŏng Stream it headed to Osigyang.

Autumn, seventh month. People obtained a ginseng root 9 *ch'ŏk* in length. Considering it very strange, [the court] sent it to Tang to present to the Emperor, but Emperor Dezong said it was not ginseng and would not receive it.

Eighth month. The King enfeofed his mother Lady Kim as Queen Dowager Sŏngmok. Hansan-ju presented a white crow.

---

24 According to *SY* 1:13a, his mother was Queen Sŏngmok and his Queen was Queen Dowager Kyehwa, the daughter of Lord Sungmyŏng.

25 Kŏro-hyŏn is in Kyŏngnam, Kŏje. The state awarded stipends to students at the National Academy.

26 This seems to be an elephant.

Year two [800], spring, first month. The King enfeofed his consort Lady Kim to be Queen and made Ch'ungbun a chief minister.

Summer, fourth month. There was a violent wind that broke trees and blew away tiles. The blinds hanging at Sŏran Hall blew off to an unknown place. The two gates, Imhae and Inhwa, both collapsed.

Sixth month. The Prince was enfeofed as Crown Prince. The King died and was posthumously named Sosŏng.

King Aejang

King Aejang was enthroned. His personal name was Ch'ŏngmyŏng and he was King Sosŏng's Crown Prince. His mother was Lady Kyehwa of the Kim lineage. As he came to the throne at the age of thirteen, *Ach'an* Minister of the Ministry of Military Affairs Ŏnsŭng acted as regent. Earlier when King Wŏnsŏng died, Tang Dezong had sent Director of the Board of Honors, concurrent Vice Censor-in-Chief Wi Dan to carry imperial credentials of condolences and enfeof the new King Chunong as Commander Unequalled in Honor, acting Grand Guardian, King of Silla. Wi Dan, on reaching Yunzhou, hearing that the King [Sosŏng] had died, he returned home.[27]

Autumn, seventh month. The King's name was changed to Chunghŭi.[28]

---

27 Yunzhou is in Shandong, China. See *Jiu Tangshu* 13, zhenyuan 16, and 199.
28 According to *Jiu Tangshu* and *Xin Tangshu* his name was Chunghŭng.

Eighth month. The King gave the position of deputy magistrate of Tuhil-hyŏn[29] to Yang Yŏl who had been an imperial resident guard and student in Tang China. Earlier when Dezong had gone to Fengdian [Shanxi] to escape a rebellion, [Yang]Yŏl, accompanying the Emperor during his flight, displayed merit. The Emperor conferred on him the position of *youzanshandufu* [right grand master admonisher] and returned him [to Silla]. Therefore the King singled him out and appointed him.

Year two [801], spring, second month. The King paid respects at *Sijomyo* [The Founder's Tomb] and separately established two shrines for Great King Taejong and Great King Munmu. He took Great King Sijo [Founder King], his great-great-grandfather Great King Myŏngdŏk, great-grandfather Great King Wŏnsŏng, his grandfather Great King Hyech'ung, and his father Great King Sosŏng, forming the Five Shrines. [The King] appointed Ministry of the Ministry of Military Affairs Ŏnsŭng an official in the Office of Royal Attendants, and shortly after he became extraordinary rank one. [The King] proclaimed general pardons.

Summer, fifth month, first day, *imsul*. There was supposed to be a solar eclipse but it did not occur.

Autumn, ninth month. Mars intruded on the moon and meteors fell like rain. Mujin-ju presented a red crow and Udu-ju presented a white pheasant.

Winter, tenth month. As there was severe cold, the pine and bamboo trees all died. The kingdom of T'amna sent an envoy presenting tribute.[30]

Year three [802], spring, first month. The King personally held

---

29 According to *Sinjŭng Tongguk yŏji sŭngnam* 35 and 40, during the Paekche period there was a Tuhil-hyŏn both in Naju and Hŭngyang.

30 T'amna first surrendered to Silla in 662 and then, in 679, declared its independence but subordinate to Silla.

sacrifices at the Singung Shrine.

Summer, fourth month. The daughter of *Ach'an* Kim Chubyŏk[31] entered the rear palace [to become a royal concubine].

Autumn, seventh month. There was an earthquake.

Eighth month. [The court] constructed Haein Monastery on Mount Kaya.[32] Samnyang-ju presented a red crow.

Winter, twelfth month. The King elevated Kyunjŏng[33] to be *taeach'an*, making him a false prince, hoping to send him as a hostage to the kingdom of Wa but Kyunjŏng declined this.

Year four [803], summer, fourth month. The King visited the southern suburbs to inspect the barley crop.

Autumn, seventh month. With Japan, the court concluded an agreement for the exchange of envoys and friendly ties.

Winter, tenth month. There was an earthquake.

Year five [804], spring, first month. *Ach'an* Susŭng became chief minister.

Summer, fifth month. Japan sent an envoy who presented 300 *ryang* of yellow gold.[34]

Autumn, seventh month. The court held a major military inspection on the banks of Alch'ŏn Stream. Samnyang-ju presented a white magpie. [The court] renovated Imhae Hall and newly constructed Mansu Chamber in the Eastern Palace [of the Crown Prince]. In Udu-ju, Nansan-hyŏn, a boulder that laid flat

---

31 The name appears as Pubyŏk in *Samguksa chŏryo*.

32 Tradition holds that, initially, followers of the monk Ŭisang practiced Hwaŏm beliefs here, but around this time, with changes in Silla society, the temple became a Sŏn center. See Ch'oe Wŏnjik, "Silla hadae ŭi Haeinsa wa hwaŏmjong," *Hanguksa yŏngu* 49 (1985).

33 He is the younger brother of King Sosŏng and figures prominently in Silla politics in subsequent years. See *Sae kuksa sajŏn* 227.

34 Although *SS* lists four occasions in King Aejang's reign when Japan sent envoys to Silla, only this entry is noted in *Nihon koki*, book 12, twenty-third year.

up-righted itself. At Pup'o in Ungch'ŏn-ju, Sodae-hyŏn, the water changed into the color of blood.

Ninth month. Two pagodas at Mangdŏk Monastery [crashed into] each other as if in battle.

Year six [805], spring, first month. The King's mother Lady Kim was enfeofed Queen Dowager and his consort Lady Pak was enfeofed Queen. This year Tang Emperor Dezong died. [Emperor] Xunzong sent Director of the Ministry of War, concurrent *Bingfu langzhong yushi dafu* [Vice Censor-in-Chief] Yuan Chifeng to announce mourning and also invest the King as Commander Unequalled in Honor, acting Grand Guardian, Commissioned with Extraordinary Powers, Grand Commander-in-Chief of Kyerim and Military Affairs, Regional Chief of Kyerim, concurrent Commissioner with Special Powers, Military Commander of Chonglong Sea and Military Matters, King of Silla; and invest his mother Lady Suk as consort dowager[35] {Sungmyŏng, the King's maternal grandfather, was a thirteenth-generation descendant of King Naemul. As his mother's surname was Kim, to use the father's name Suk is in error},[36] and invested his wife Lady Pak as consort.

Autumn, eighth month. [The court] announced more than twenty official regulations.[37]

Winter, eleventh month. There was an earthquake.

Year seven [806], spring, third month. A Japanese envoy arrived and was given an audience in Chowŏn Hall. The King decreed, "The new construction of temples is prohibited but the

---

35 See *Jiu Tangshu* 14, zhenyuan 21:2 and 99; *Tang huiyao* 95; and *Xin Tangshu* 220.

36 This confusion might have been intended, on the part of Silla, to conceal the endogamy practiced by the Silla court.

37 See Yi Kidong, "Silla hadae wangwi kyesŭng kwa chŏngch'i kwajŏng" in *Silla kolp'um* 153–4.

The **Silla Annals** of the **Samguk Sagi**

repair of [existing] temples is permitted. Also the use of elegant silk in Buddhist functions and utensils made of gold and silver is forbidden. Accordingly, this decree should be made widely known and implemented by the offices concerned." Tang Xianzong let Imperial Resident Guard, Prince Kim Hŏnch'ung, return to [Silla] and gave him the title of *shibushujian* [probationary director of the Palace Library].

Autumn, eighth month. The King sent an envoy to Tang to present tribute.[38]

Year eight [807], spring, first month. *Ich'an* Kim Hŏnch'ang {*ch'ang* is also written as *chŏng*} became chief minister.[39]

Second month, the King went to Sungnye Hall to listen to music.

Autumn, eighth month. There was a heavy snow.

Year nine [808], spring, second month. A Japanese envoy arrived. The King, with great courtesy, received him. [The King] sent Kim Yŏkki to Tang to present tribute. Yŏkki said [to the Emperor], "In Zhenyuan sixteenth year, an imperial decree invested my late King Kim Chunong to be King of Silla. His mother Lady Sin became consort dowager and his wife Lady Suk became royal consort. When Wi Tan, the envoy carrying the investiture, was on his way, on hearing that the King had died, [he] returned home. As that investiture is in the *Zhongshusheng* [Central Secretariat], and I am returning to my country, may I request Your Majesty to please give it to me to take back?" The Emperor commanded:

---

38 *SY* 2:14b reports that there was an early snow in Kyŏngju in the middle of the eighth month.

39 See *SS* 10:13a–b, King Hŏndŏk, fourteenth year, third month. This may actually be two different individuals. See Yi Kibaek, "Silla hadae ŭi chisasŏng," *Silla chŏngch'i sahoe* 174, and Yi Kidong, "Silla hadae ŭi wangwi kyesŭng kwa chŏngch'i," *Silla kolp'um* 156.

Regarding the investiture of Kim Chunong and others, as I have commanded the *Honglusi* [Court of State Ceremonial] to obtain it from the Central Secretariat, accordingly when it reaches that office, give it to Kim Yŏkki ordering him to take it back home.

Thereupon he commanded that the King's uncle Ŏnsŭng[40] and his brother Chunggong and others be given ritual lances[41] and commanded that they be given according to the regulations of their country. {Lady Sin was the daughter of Kim Sinsul. Because *sin* [spirit] has the same sound as *sin* [notify], to call her Lady Sin [notify] is an error.} The King sent officials to the twelve circuits to demarcate the boundaries of all the *kun* and *ŭp*.

Autumn, seventh month. On the first day, *sinsa,* there was a solar eclipse.

Year ten [809], spring, first month. The moon infringed on the Hyades constellation.

Summer, sixth month. In the salt storage at Mount Sŏhyŏng Fortress there was crying that sounded like a cow. At Pyŏksa Monastery a toad ate a snake.

Autumn, seventh month. [The King] sent *Taeach'an* Kim Yukchin[42] to Tang to give thanks for favors and local products. There was a great drought. The King's uncle Ŏnsŭng and his younger brother *Ich'an* Cheong, leading troops into the palace, started a rebellion, killing the King. The King's brother Ch'emyŏng, defending the King, was killed at the same time. The King was posthumously titled Aejang.

40　This is his father's younger brother.
41　Ritual lances were given to noble houses and meritorious subjects.
42　Kim Yukchin received the appointment of *sudae namgyŏng* in 801.

King Hŏndŏk

King Hŏndŏk was enthroned. His personal name was Ŏnsŭng and he was the younger brother of King Sosŏng by the same mother. In King Wŏnsŏng's sixth year [790], he was commissioned as envoy to Great Tang and [upon returning] received the title of *taeach'an*. In the seventh year [791], because he executed a rebellious official,[43] he became *chapch'an*. In the tenth year [794] he became chief minister and in the eleventh year [795], as *ich'an,* he became a councilor of state. In the twelfth year [796] he became Minister of the Ministry of Military Affairs. In King Aejang's first year [800] he became *Kakkan* and in the second year [801] Official of the Office of Royal Attendants and shortly after extraordinary rank one. Coming to this time he was enthroned and his consort was Lady Kwisŭng, the daughter of *Kakkan* Yeyŏng.[44] *Ich'an* Kim Sungbin became extraordinary rank one.

Autumn, eighth month. There was a general amnesty. [The King] sent *Ich'an* Kim Ch'angnam and others to Tang to announce mourning. [Tang Emperor] Xunzong sent Vice Director of the Bureau of Operations, acting Vice Censor-In-Chief Cui Ting, and [the Emperor's Silla] hostage Kim Sasin[45] as a deputy to carry credentials for mourning and memorial services and invested the enthroned King as Commander Unequalled in Honor, acting Grand Guardian, Grand Commander-in-Chief of Kyerim, Commissioner with Special Power and Military Affairs, Grand Commander-in-Chief of Chonglong Sea and Military Matters,

---

43 The official was *Ach'an* Chaegong.
44 According to *SY* 1:13a, she was the daughter of *Kakkan* Ch'unggong and posthumously known as Queen Dowager Hwanga.
45 When he went to Tang is unclear. See Kwŏn Tŭkyŏng, above, who has written about both Kim and Cui.

Supreme Pillar of State, King of Silla; and his wife, Lady Chŏng, to be consort, and granted to *Taejaesang* [Chief Councilor of State] Kim Sungbin and three others ritual lances. {On examination, the royal consort was the daughter of *Kakkan* Yeyŏng but the present reference to the Chŏng lineage is unclear.}[46]

Year two [810], spring, first month. *P'ajinch'an* Yangjong became chief minister. Hasŏ-ju presented a red crow.

Second month. The King personally held services in the Singung Shrine. He dispatched officials to mend the dikes throughout the kingdom.

Autumn, seventh month. A shooting star entered *Chami* [Chinese: *Ziwei*]. [Minor capital] Sŏwŏn-gyŏng [Chŏng-ju] presented a white pheasant.

Winter, tenth month. [The King] sent Prince Kim Hŏnjang to Tang and he presented gold and silver Buddhist statues as well as Buddhist *sutras* and respectfully said, "We pray for [Emperor] Xunzong's happiness." A shooting star entered *Wangnang* [star].

Year three [811], spring, first month. Chief Minister Yangjong resigned because of illness and *Ich'an* Wŏnhŭng became chief minister.

Second month. *Ich'an* Ungwŏn became governor of Wansan-ju.

Summer, fourth month. The King, for the first time, went to P'yŏngŭi Hall to oversee government affairs.

Year four [812], spring. Kyunjŏng became chief minister. As *Ich'an* Ch'ungyong became seventy years old, the King give him a small table and cane.

Autumn, ninth month. [The King] sent *Kŭpch'an* Sungjŏng to

---

46 This is similar to the case cited for the mothers of King Sosŏng and King Aejang. Tang regarded marriage between people with the same surname as uncivilized.

the North Country [Parhae] as head envoy.

Year five [813], spring, first month. *Ich'an* Hŏnch'ang became governor of Mujin-ju.

Second month. [The King] paid respects at the Dynastic Founder's Shrine. There was a fire at Hyŏndŏk Gate.

Year six [814], spring, third month. The King hosted ranking officials at Sungnye Hall. As the merry-making reached a peak the King played the *kŏmungo* and *Ich'an* Ch'ungyŏng danced.

Summer, fifth month. In the western part of the kingdom, as there was a major flood, [the King] sent officials to inquire into the conditions of the people flooded in *chu* and *kun* and he exempted them from taxes for one year.

Autumn, eighth month. In the capital there was wind and fog making it like night. The governor of Mujin-ju, Hŏnch'ang, returned [to the capital] and became chief minister.

Winter, tenth month. The wife of the grand secretary of Kŏmmo gave birth to boy triplets.

Year seven [815], spring, first month. [The court] sent envoys to Tang. [Emperor] Xunzong saw them in audience, entertained them, and gave out gifts by rank.

Summer, fifth month. Snow fell.

Autumn, eighth month, first day, *kihae*. There was a solar eclipse. In the *chu* and *kun* of the western region there was a great famine. As bandits rose up in great numbers, [the court] sent troops to subdue them. A large star appeared between *Iksŏng* and *Chinsŏng* and moved west. Its light stretched for 6 *ch'ŏk* and was about 2 *ch'on* wide.[47]

Year eight [816], spring, first month. Chief Minister Hŏnch'ang

---

47 *Ch'on:* one tenth of a *ch'ŏk*, approximately 3 centimeters (somewhat more than 1 inch).

became governor of Ch'ŏng-ju and Changyŏ instead became chief minister. As this was a year of drought, there was a famine and many people starved with 170 people going to eastern Zhejiang [in China] seeking food.[48] In Tangŭn-hyŏn in Hansan-ju a boulder that was 10 *ch'ŏk* long, 8 *ch'ŏk* wide, and 3½ *ch'ŏk* tall moved by itself over 100 *po*.

Summer, sixth month. Two pagodas at Mangdŏk Monastery [tumbled into each other] as if in a fight.

Year nine [817], spring, first month. *Ich'an* Kim Ch'unggong became chief minister.

Summer, fifth month. As there was no rain, [the King] prayed at the mountains and streams everywhere and, reaching autumn, the seventh month, it rained.

Winter, tenth month. As many people died of starvation, [the King] instructed the *chu* and *kun* to open granaries to aid them. [The King] sent Prince Kim Changnyŏm to Tang to present tribute.[49]

Year ten [818], summer, sixth month, first day, *kyech'uk*. There was a solar eclipse.

Year eleven [819], spring, first month. As *Ich'an* Chinwŏn was seventy years old, [the King] gave him a small table and a cane. *Ich'an* Hŏnjŏng[50] was not able to move because of illness and, although he was not yet seventy, [the King] gave him a purple sandalwood cane decorated with gold.

Second month. Extraordinary Rank One Kim Sungbin died and

48 This is in China, see *Jiu Tangshu* 199 and *Tanghuiyao* 95.
49 In Ch'oe Ch'iwŏn's writings it is mentioned that when Kim traveled to Tang he was blown off course and landed in eastern Zhejiang. See *AKS* 3:320, n. 120.
50 He is Kim Hanjŏng, grandson of King Wŏnsŏng and son of Kim Yeyong. See *AKS* 3:320, n. 121.

Ich'an Kim Sujung[51] became extraordinary rank one.

Third month. As bandits arose all over, [the court] ordered the governors and *taesu* [chief magistrates] of the various *chu* and *kun* to capture them.

Autumn, seventh month. *Yunzhou jiedushi* [Military Commissioner of Yunzhou] Li Shidao of T'ang rebelled. [Emperor] Xianzong, wanting to suppress him, sent Military Commissioner of Yangzhou Zhou Kong to mobilize and dispatch our troops. The King, receiving this imperial command, ordered Sunchŏn-gun General Kim Ungwŏn to lead 30,000 armed soldiers to help.

Year twelve [820]. As there was a drought in the spring and summer, there was starvation in the winter.

Eleventh month. The court sent envoys to Tang to present tribute. [Tang] Muzong received them in Linde Hall and entertained them, giving gifts according to rank.

Year thirteen [821], spring. As people were starving, [some] sold their children and grandchildren to survive.[52]

Summer, fourth month. Chief Minister Kim Ch'unggong died[53] and *Ich'an* Yŏnggong became chief minister. Hŏnch'ang, governor of Ch'ŏng-ju, was changed to become governor of Ungch'ŏn-ju.

Autumn, seventh month. Two boulders in the P'aesu River and Namch'ŏn [stream crashed into] each other as if in battle.

Winter, twelfth month, twenty-ninth day. There was loud thunder.[54]

---

51 He is King Hŏndŏk's younger brother and will become King Hŭngdŏk.

52 According to *SY* 2:14b, heavy snow fell in the third month.

53 This is obviously in error as Ch'unggong is noted in the following year (822) as leading troops to suppress Kim Hŏnch'ang's rebellion. See also Yi Kibaek, "Silla hadae ŭi chipsasŏng," *Silla chŏngch'i sahoe* 183.

54 According to *Cefu yuangui* 17, Tang pirates were capturing Silla people and enslaving them. In the third month of this year Sŏl P'yŏng requested this be

Year fourteen [822], spring, first month. The King's younger brother by the same mother, Sujong, became *Pugun* [Crown Prince] and entered Wŏlchi Palace.[55] {Sujong also appears as Susŭng in another source}.

Second month. Five *ch'ŏk* of snow fell, causing trees to wither.

Third month. The governor of Ungch'ŏn-ju, Hŏnch'ang, rebelled because his father Chuwŏn could not become King. He called his kingdom Changan and proclaimed the reign title of Kyŏngun first year. He threatened to place under his control the governors of the four *chu* of Mujin [Kwangju], Wansan [Chŏnju], Ch'ŏng-ju [Chinju], and Sabŏl [Sangju] and the officials in charge of the minor capitals at Kugwŏn [Ch'ungju], Sŏwŏn [Ch'ŏng-ju], and Kŭmgwan [Kimhae] and the magistrates of the various *kun* and *hyŏn*. The governor of Ch'ŏng-ju, Hyangyŏng, managed to flee to Ch'uhwa-gun. Those in Hansan-[ju], Udu-[ju], Samnyang-[ju], P'aegang Garrison, and Pugwŏn minor capital, and others,[56] first detecting Hŏnch'ang's planned rebellion, raised troops to protect themselves. On the eighteenth, Ch'oe Ung, a *changsa* [high official] of Wansan-[ju], helping Yŏngch'ung, the son of *Ach'an* Chŏngnyŏn, and others fled to the royal capital to report [this]. The King at once conferred on Ch'oe Ung the rank of *kŭpch'an* and *t'aesu* [chief magistrate] of Sokham-gun and conferred on Yŏngch'ung the rank of *kŭpch'an*. Later, after he selected eight

---

stopped. Also in this year Toŭi, a Sŏn cleric, returned from China. Koreans of that time were not especially interested in his style of Buddhism but, persevering, his disciples established his teachings at Porim Monastery in Changhung. See Ch'oe Pyŏnghŏn, "Silla hadae sŏnjong kusanp'a ŭi sŏngnip," *Hanguksa yŏngu* 7 (1972).

55 Pugun is another name for Crown Prince and Wŏlchi Palace is an attached palace for the use of the Crown Prince. See Yi Kidong, "Silla Hŭngdŏkwangdae ŭi chŏngch'i wa sahoe," *Kuksagwan nonch'ong* 21 (1991): 112–3.

56 Ch'uhwa-gun is in Kyŏngnam, Miryang; Udu-ju is in Kangwŏn, Ch'unch'ŏn; Samnyang-ju is in Kyŏngnam, Yangsan; P'aegang Garrison is in Hwanghae, Kimch'ŏn; and Pugwŏn minor capital is in Kangwŏn, Wŏnju.

officers to guard all directions of the royal capital, he dispatched troops with *Ilgilch'an* Chang Ung being the first sent out and *Chapch'an* Wi Kong and *P'ajinch'an* Cherŭng following him. *Ich'an* Kyunjŏng, *Chapch'an* Ungwŏn, and *Taech'an* Ujing, and others led three armies to suppress [the rebellion]. *Kakkan* Ch'unggong and *Chapch'an* Yunŭng guarded Munhwagwanmun [Fortress].[57]

Two Hwarang, Myŏnggi and Anrak, each requested to join an army. Myŏnggi, with a group of followers, went to Hwangsan[58] and Anrak went to Simiji Garrison. Thereupon Hŏnch'ang sent his generals to occupy strategic roads and wait [for the government armies]. Chang Ung, meeting rebel forces in Todong-hyŏn, attacked and defeated them. Wi Kong and Cherŭng joined Chang Ung's army and attacked and defeated Samnyŏn Mountain Fortress[59] and then advanced their troops to Mount Songni where they attacked rebel forces and destroyed them. Kyunjŏng and others fought the rebels at Mount Sŏngsan[60] and wiped them out. The various armies, together on arriving at Ungjin, engaged the enemy in a great battle, killing and capturing countless numbers. Hŏnch'ang barely escaped with his life, entering into the fortress and firmly defending it.

The various armies encircled and attacked for ten days. When the fortress was about to fall, Hŏnch'ang, knowing he could not escape, committed suicide. His followers severed his head and stored it separate from his body. When the fortress fell, they took his body from an old mound to [posthumously] punish him. They

---

57 This is Modaegun Fortress, also known as Kwanmun Fortress. Its remains can be seen in Kyŏngju's Wadong-myŏn. See *AKS* 3:322, n. 139.
58 This is in Ch'ungnam.
59 This is in Ch'ungbuk, Poun.
60 This is in Kyŏngbuk, Sŏngju.

put to death his clan members and his faction, as well as others, numbering over 239 people and freed the people [under his control].

Later [the court] evaluated merit [in the battles], giving government titles and awards by rank. *Ach'an* Nokchin[61] was conferred with the rank of *taeach'an* but he declined and would not receive [the rank]. Because Kulcha-hyŏn in Samnang-ju was located near the rebels but refused to join them, it was exempted from tax payments for seven years.

Prior to this, in the pond south of the office of the chief magistrate of Ch'ŏng-ju, there was a strange bird that was 5 *ch'ŏk* tall, black in color, had a head like a five-year-old child, a beak 1½ *ch'ŏk* long, eyes like a person, and its pouch was as big as a 5 *sŭng* vessel; after three days it died. It was an omen of Hŏnch'ang's defeat.

Chŏnggyo, the daughter of *Kakkan* Ch'unggong, was invited to be the consort of the Crown Prince. Deep in the P'aesu River Valley a fallen tree produced a stump that [grew] 13 *ch'ŏk* in one night with a girth of 4½ *ch'ŏk*.

Summer, fourth month, thirteenth day. The color of the moon was like blood.

Autumn, seventh month, twelfth day. The sun had a dark halo pointing from south to north.

Winter, twelfth month. [The court] sent Chup'il to Tang to present tribute.

Year fifteen [823], spring, first month, fifth day. There were insects in Sŏwŏn-gyŏng [minor capital] that fell from the sky. On the ninth day there were three types of insects: white, black, and

---

61 Although his family name is unclear, he is the son of Ilgil and will become extraordinary rank one in King Hŏndŏk's reign. See SS 45:3b–5b.

red. Braving snow, they crawled around but when they saw the sun, they stopped.

Two *Kakkan,* Wŏnsun and P'yŏngwŏn, reached seventy and reported their retirement. The King presented them with small tables and canes.

Second month. The court combined Susŏng-gun and Tangŭn-hyŏn.

Summer, fourth month, twelfth day. A shooting star rose from the *Ch'ŏnsi* constellation and infringed on *Chejwa* and passed the space northeast of *Ch'ŏnsi* and by *Chingnyŏ* and *Wangnyang* and, reaching *Kakto* constellation,[62] split into three. It gave off a noise like the beating of a drum and disappeared.

Autumn, seventh month. There was snow.

Year seventeen [825], spring, first month. Hŏnch'ang's son Pŏmmun, with Mount Kodal bandit Susin and one hundred other people, plotted a rebellion and, wishing to establish a capital at P'yŏngyang,[63] he attacked Mount Pukhan-ju. Governor Ch'ongmyŏng led troops capturing and killing them. {P'yŏngyang is modern day [Koryŏ] Yangju. A penance writing at Changŭi Monastery[64] written by [Koryŏ] T'aejo has the phrase, "It is former Koguryŏ territory, the sacred mountain of P'yŏngyang."}

Third month. A woman in Mujin-ju, Mamiji-hyŏn,[65] gave birth to a child with two heads, two bodies, and four arms. When she

---

62 *Ch'ŏnsi,* in the northeast sky, is believed to be in charge of marketing, trading, and killing. *Chingnyŏ* and *Wangnyang* represent the weaver maid and the princely youth who, figuratively, are united once a year. *Kakto* is a constellation of six stars. See *AKS* 3:324, n. 147–9.

63 Mount Kodal is in Kyŏnggi, Ich'ŏn. P'yŏngyang seems to indicate a place called South P'yŏngyang, which is where Mount Pukhan is located. See *chiriji* section (1) in *Koryŏsa chiriji.*

64 Changŭi Monastery was built at Pukhansan-ju by King Muyŏl to honor the spirit of two Silla Hwarang, Changch'unnang and P'arang. See *SY* 1:37a.

65 Mujin-ju, Mamiji-hyŏn, is in Chŏnnam, Changhŭng.

gave birth the sky was [filled] with loud thunder.

Summer, fifth month. [The court] sent Prince Kim Hŭn[66] to Tang to present tribute and, appealing to the Emperor, said, "Please allow earlier National University students Ch'oe Ijŏng, Kim Sukchŏng, Pak Kyeŏp, and others to return home and allow newly arrived people to the court Kim Yunbu, Kim Ipchi, Pak Yangji, and twelve others to stay as imperial resident guards, and request admitting them to the National Academy to study, and pay for their expenses and board from the *Honglusi*."[67]

The Emperor agreed to this.

Autumn. Samnang-ju presented a white crow. The wife of *Naema* Hwangchi from Udu-ju, Taeyanggwan-gun, gave birth at one time to two boys and two girls. [The court] gave them 100 *sŏk* of grain.

Year eighteen [826], autumn, seventh month. The court ordered Paegyŏng, chief magistrate of Ujam,[68] to mobilize 10,000 people of the *chu* and *kun* north of Hansan to construct a wall 300 *li* long along the P'aesu River.

Winter, tenth month. The King died. His posthumous name was Hŏndŏk and he was buried north of Ch'ŏllim Monastery.[69] {According to *Kogi*, "He was on the throne for eighteen years and died in *Baoli* second year [826] *Bingwu* [*pyŏngu*] fourth month. *Xin Tangshu* states, "[Sometime] between *Zhangging* and *Baoli*, the

---

66 Kim Hŭn (803–849), a ninth-generation descendant of King Muyŏl returned from Tang with titles and became magistrate of Namwŏn and subsequently an *ich'an*. Later he supported Chang Pogo and then retired to live with monks at Mount Sobaek.

67 The *Honglusi* was a Chinese agency in charge of foreign ties.

68 Ujam is in Hwanghae, Kimch'ŏn.

69 Ch'ŏllim Monastery is in Tongch'ŏn-dong, Kyŏngju.

Silla King Ŏnsŭng died. *Zizhi tongjian*[70] and *Jiu Tangshu*[71] say he died in *Dahe* fifth year [831]. How could [they] make this mistake?}

King Hŭngdŏk

King Hŭngdŏk was enthroned. His personal name was Sujong which was later changed to Kyŏnghwi. He was King Hŏndŏk's younger brother by the same mother.

Winter, twelfth month. As the royal consort Lady Changhwa died, she was posthumously enfeofed Queen Chŏngmok.[72] As the King, unable to forget [the Queen], was unhappy and despondent, ranking officials wrote memorials appealing to the King to take another consort, but the King responded, "Even birds are sad when they lose their mates, how can I so unfeelingly again marry so soon after I have lost such a superb companion?"

And so to the end he did not follow their request and did not go near women in attendance once. Those attending the King were eunuchs and that was all. {Lady Changhwa, surnamed Kim, was the daughter of King Sosŏng.}

Year two [827], spring, first month. The King personally held services at the Singung Shrine. Tang Emperor Wenzong, hearing that King Hŏndŏk died, stopped the court, sent condolences, and ordered Office of the Heir Apparent, Vice Censor-in-Chief, Yuan Ji

---

70 *Zizhi tongjian,* vol. 244 (831).
71 *Jiu Tangshu,* vol. 199.
72 She appears to be a royal relative, as she was the daughter of King Sosŏng, making her a first cousin.

to carry credentials for mourning and a memorial service and invest the succeeding King as Commander Unequalled in Honor, acting Grand Guardian, Commissioner with Extraordinary Power, Grand Commander-in-Chief of Kyerim, Grand Commander-in-Chief of Chonglong Sea and Military Matters, King of Silla, his mother Lady Pak as consort dowager, and his wife Lady Pak as consort.

Third month. Kudŏk [a descendant of former] Koguryŏ, who went to Tang, returned [to Silla] carrying Buddhist sutras. The King assembled monks from various temples and went to welcome him.

Summer, fifth month. Frost fell.

Autumn, eighth month. Venus appeared. In the capital there was a great drought. Chief Minister Yŏnggong retired.

Year three [828], spring, first month. *Taeach'an* Kim Ujing became chief minister.

Second month. [The court] sent an envoy to Tang offering tribute.

Third month. It snowed 3 *ch'ŏk* deep.

Summer, fourth month. Ch'ŏnghae Commissioner Kungbok, whose surname was Chang[73] {another name was Pogo}, went to Xuzhou in Tang where he became a general. He later returned [to Silla], had an audience with the King, and garrisoned 10,000 soldiers at Ch'ŏnghae. {Ch'ŏnghae is the present Wando.}

A wizard from Hansan-ju, P'yoch'ŏn-hyŏn, muttered to himself that there is an art to becoming rich quick and many

---

73 Chang Pogo has captured the imagination of many historians. See Yi Kidong, "Chang Pogo wa kŭūi haesang hwaldong" (hereafter "Chang Pogo"), *Chang Pogo ŭi sinyŏngu*, 1985. Kungbok was Chang Pogo. He also was known as Kungp'a. See *SY* 2:15a–16a; *SS* 44:12a–13a. Also see Edwin O. Reischauer's translation, *Ennin's Travels in T'ang China*, New York: Ronald Press, 1955.

people were deluded by him. When the King heard this he said, "To punish one who confuses the masses with trickery is the law of the former Kings" and sent discarding the man to a distant island.

Winter, twelfth month. [The court] sent envoys to Tang to present tribute goods. Wenzong summoned them for an audience in Linde Hall, gave them a banquet, and presented gifts according to rank. As the envoy to Tang, Taeryŏm, returned with seeds of tea trees, the King had them planted on Mount Chiri. Although there was tea from Queen Sŏndŏk's time, by this time it became very popular.

Year four [829], spring, second month. Tangŭn-gun became Tangsŏng Garrison and [the court] sent *Sach'an* Kŭkchŏng to oversee it.

Year five [830], summer, fourth month. As the King became ill, there were prayers and he allowed the ordination of 150 people to become monks.

Winter, twelfth month. [The court] sent an envoy to Tang to present tribute.

Year six [831], spring, first month. There was an earthquake. Chief Minister Ujing resigned his post and *Ich'an* Yunbun became chief minister. [The court] sent Prince Kim Nŭngyu, along with eight monks, to the Tang court.

Autumn, seventh month. *Chinbongsa* [Royal Envoy] Nŭngyu and his party who went to Tang, on returning, drowned in the ocean.

Winter, eleventh month. [The court] sent an envoy to Tang to present tribute.

Year seven [832]. In the spring and summer there was a drought turning the fields into dust. The King did not go to court but [daily] reduced his ordinary meals and gave pardons to those imprisoned throughout the country.

Autumn, seventh month. It finally rained.

Eighth month. As famine became severe, robbers rose up all over.

Winter, tenth month. The King ordered officials to relieve and aid the peasants.

Year eight [833], spring. Within the kingdom a great famine occurred.

Summer, fourth month. The King paid his respects at the Founder's Shrine.

Winter, tenth month. Peach blossoms and plum trees blossomed again. Many people died of infectious disease.

Eleventh month. Chief Minister Yunbun retired from his office.

Year nine [834], spring, first month. Ujing again became chief minister.

Autumn, ninth month. The King went to the foot of Mount Sŏhyŏng and [held] a large military review and watched archery at Mup'yŏng Gate.

Winter, tenth month. The King inspected the *chu* and *kun* in the southern part of the kingdom and made inquiries into the conditions of the elderly, widows, widowers, orphans, and elderly without children and presented grain and clothing accordingly.

Year ten [835], spring, second month. *Ach'an* Kim Kyunjŏng became extraordinary rank one. Chief Minister Ujing, because his father Kyunjŏng became councilor of state, sent a memorial requesting to be relieved from his office and *Taeach'an* Kim Myŏng became chief minister.

Year eleven [836], spring, first month, first day, *sinch'uk*. There was a solar eclipse. [The court] sent Prince Kim Ŭijong to Tang to express gratitude and be an imperial resident guard.

Summer, sixth month. A comet appeared in the east.

Autumn, seventh month. Venus intruded on the moon.

Winter, twelfth month. The King died. His posthumous title was Hŭngdŏk. [The court], according to his will, buried him together in a tomb with Queen Changhwa.

King Hŭigang

King Hŭigang was enthroned. His personal name was Cheryung {another source says Cheong}. He was the son of *Ich'an* Hŏnjŏng {another source says Ch'ono}, who was the grandson of Great King Wŏnsŏng, and his mother was Lady P'odo.[74] His consort, Lady Munmok, was the daughter of *Kalmunwang* Ch'unggong. Prior to this, at the death of King Hŭngdŏk, his cousin Kyunjŏng and Cheryung, the son of [another] cousin, each wanted to become ruler. Coming to this Chief Minister Kim Myŏng, and *Ach'an* Ihong, Pae Hwŏnbaek, and others supported Cheryung. *Ach'an* Ujing, along with a nephew Yejing and Kim Yang, supported [Ujing's] father Kyunjŏng and they all entered the palace and fought. Kim Yang was shot by an arrow but, together with Ujing and others, fled while Kyunjŏng was killed. Thereafter Cheryung was able to be enthroned.

Year two [837], spring, first month. A general amnesty was extended to those imprisoned with crimes lesser than the death penalty. The King's deceased father was posthumously enfeofed Great King Iksŏng and his mother, Lady Pak, as Queen Dowager

---

74 According to *SY,* royal tables, his mother was Lady Mido, also called Lady Simnae or Lady Pari. See *AKS* 3:331, n. 189.

Sunsŏng. Chief Minister Kim Myŏng was appointed extraordinary rank one and *Ach'an* Ihong became chief minister.

Summer, fourth month. The Tang [Emperor] Wenzong let return home Prince Kim Ŭijong who had been an imperial resident guard. As *Ach'an* Ujing spoke out about his resentment over the death of his father Kyunjŏng, Kim Myŏng, Ihong, and others considered this inappropriate.

Fifth month. Ujing, fearful that harm would reach him, together with his wife and children, fled to the entrance of Hwangsan Garrison and took a boat where he sought help from Kungbok, the Chief Magistrate of Ch'ŏnghae Garrison.

Sixth month. Kyunjŏng's brother-in-law *Ach'an* Yejing, along with *Ach'an* Yangsun, escaped and joined Ujing. Tang Wenzong presented brocade, by rank, to Kim Ch'ungsin and others who had been imperial resident guards.

Year three [838], spring, first month. Extraordinary Rank One Kim Myŏng and Chief Minister Ihong and others raised troops to stage a rebellion and killed the King's confidants. The King, realizing he could not protect himself, hanged himself in the palace. His posthumous title was Hŭigang and he was buried at Sosan Mountain.

King Minae

King Minae was enthroned. His surname name was Kim and his personal name was Myŏng. He was the great-grandson of Great King Wŏnsŏng and the son of *Taeach'an* Ch'unggong. He held various posts up to extraordinary rank one and, together with

Chief Minister Ihong, they persecuted the King, killing him. He then enthroned himself to be the king. His deceased father posthumously became Great King Sŏngang, his mother, Lady Kwibo of the Pak lineage, became Queen Dowager Sŏnŭi, and his wife, Lady Kim, became Queen Yunyong. *Ich'an* Kim Kwi became extraordinary rank one and *Ach'an* Hŏnsung became chief minister.

Second month. Kim Yang recruited soldiers and went to Ch'ŏnghae Garrison to see Ujing. While *Ach'an* Ujing was in Ch'ŏnghae Garrison, he learned that Kim Myŏng had usurped the throne and said to the Ch'ŏnghae Garrison Commissioner Kungbok, "Kim Myŏng, after killing the King, enthroned himself. As Ihong murdered the King and my father, I cannot live under the same heaven with him. I appeal to let me borrow your troops to avenge the King and my father." Kungbok said, "Ancients of the past said, 'A person who sees an injustice and does nothing is [a person] without courage.' Although I may be unworthy, I will follow on your order." Then, entrusting 5,000 soldiers to his friend Chŏng Nyŏn, he said, "If it were not for you, we could not suppress this rebellion."[75]

Winter, twelfth month. Kim Yang became *P'yŏngdong* [Pacifying East] General and, together with Yŏmjang, Chang Pyŏn, Chŏng Nyŏn, Nakkŭm, Chang Kŏnyŏng, and Yi Sunhaeng, led troops. On arriving at Muju, Ch'ŏrya-hyŏn, the King had Director Kim Minju send troops to engage in battle and sent Nakkŭm and Yi Sunhaeng to attack with three thousand cavalry on a charge, wounding and killing nearly all [the enemy].

Year two [839], spring leap month, first month. The troops marched day and night and arrived on the nineteenth at Talbŏl

---

75 See *SS* 44 for the biography of Chang Pogo.

Hill. The King, hearing that soldiers had arrived, ordered *Ich'an* Taehǔn, *Taeach'an* Yullin, Ŏkhun, and others to lead the troops to resist them. Once again there was a great victory, in a single battle killing more than half the King's [forces]. At this time the King was in the western suburbs [of the capital] under a large tree. All of his entourage was scattered and, alone, not knowing what to do, he ran into Wŏryu residence where the soldiers sought him out and killed him. His ranking officials, with proper rituals, buried him. His posthumous title was Minae.

King Sinmu

King Sinmu was enthroned. His personal name was Ujing and he was the son of Extraordinary Rank One Kyunjŏng who was the grandson of Great King Wŏnsŏng. Ujing was a younger cousin of King Hŭigang. Yejing[76] and others had already cleaned the palace and, welcoming him with propriety, then enthroned him. He posthumously enfeofed his grandfather *Ich'an* Yeyŏng {or Hyojin} to be Great King Hyegang, his deceased father to be Great King Sŏngdŏk, his mother, Lady Chingyo of the Pak lineage, to be Queen Dowager Hŏnmok, and his son, Kyŏngŭng, to be Crown Prince. He enfeofed Kungbok, the commander of Ch'ŏnghae Garrison, to be *Kamŭi* [Feeling Righteous] *kunsa* [army commander] and gave him an actual *sigŭp* of 2,000 households. Ihong, frightened, abandoned his wife and children and fled, hiding in

---

76 Some suggest he may be Ujing's nephew, others surmise a cousin. See *AKS* 3:332, n. 194.

the mountain forests, but the King sent his horsemen to seek him out, capture, and kill him.

Autumn, seventh month. [The court] sent an envoy to Tang and gave slaves to the *jiedushi* [military commissioner] of Ziqing. When the Emperor heard this, feeling pity for poor people who came from such a distant place, [he] ordered they be sent back home. The King was bedridden with an illness and dreamed that Ihong shot an arrow in his back. Waking up, the King had a tumor on his back. On the twenty-third of this month, the King died. His posthumous title was Sinmu and he was buried northwest of Chehyŏng Mountain.

| Commentary | The Commentaries of Ouyang Xiu[77] state, "Lord Huan of Lu killed Lord Yin and enthroned himself. Lord Xuan killed Zichi and enthroned himself. And then Lord Li of Zheng sent out the Crown Prince Hu and enthroned himself. Kongsun Piao of Wei threw out his ruler Kan and enthroned himself. The sage [Confucius], in the *Spring and Autumn Annals,* states that the fact that he did not delete all of them becoming rulers and instead related the reality of the events is because he wanted the later generations to know this." Onsung of Silla killed [King] Aejang and ascended the throne. Kim Myŏng killed [King] Hŭigang and ascended the throne. Ujing killed [King] Minae and ascended the throne. Now these facts have all been recorded, which was also the intent of the *Spring and Autumn Annals.*

---

77 A Song scholar (1007–1073) who compiled *Xin Tanghsu.*

The Silla
Annals of the
Samguk Sagi

Kings Munsŏng, Hŏnan,
Kyŏngmun, Hŏngang, and
Chŏnggang and Queen
Chinsŏng

Book
11

King Munsŏng

King Munsŏng was enthroned. His personal name was Kyŏngŭng. He was King Sinmu's Crown Prince. His mother was Lady Chŏnggye {another source says Queen Dowager Chŏngjong}.[1]

Eighth month.[2] There was a general amnesty and an edict stated, "The commander of Ch'ŏnghae Garrison, Kungbok,[3] once raised troops to help my late father and destroy a major rebel in an earlier reign. How could I forget his outstanding merit?" Thereupon he conferred on him the title of general of Chinhae [Calming the Seas] and presented him with ceremonial dress.

Year two [840], spring, first month. Yejing[4] became extraordinary rank one, Ŭijong became chief minister, and Yangsun[5] became *ich'an*.

Summer. From the fourth month to the sixth month there was no rain. Tang Wenzong ordered the *Honglusi* to deport all the hostages as well as those whose [terms] of stay had expired.

---

1 *SY,* royal tables, indicates his mother's name was Chinjong. And in another section she is called Chingye. "Chin" may have been miswritten for "Chŏng".
2 *SY* 2:14b indicates that the sky was dark at this time.
3 Ch'ŏnghae Garrison (modern Wando in Chŏnnam) was the center of Chang Pogo's power.
4 He is a brother of Kim Chŏnggyun. He relied on Chang Pogo and in 839, with Kim Yang, overthrew King Minae and enthroned King Sinmu.
5 Ŭijong earlier had traveled to Tang China and Yangsun was close to Chang Pogo. See *SS* 44:8b.

[Those returned to Silla] numbered, all together, 105 people.[6]

Winter. There was famine.

Year three [841], spring. There was an epidemic in the capital. *Ilgilch'an* Hongp'il plotted a rebellion. When the plan was discovered he escaped to a sea island where [officers] tried to capture him but failed.

Autumn, seventh month. Tang [Emperor] Wuzong decreed that the returned Silla official who had formerly entered Tang as *Xuanwei fushi* [Vice Commissioner of the Pacification Commission], *Chongyanzhou dudufu* [Adjutant of the Chongyanzhou Area Command], and given a "Red Fish Badge," Kim Ungyŏng,[7] was now made *Zizhou changshi* [administrator of Zizhou] and an imperial envoy and sent to invest the King as Commander Unequalled in Honor, acting Grand Guardian, Grand Commander-in-Chief of Kyerim, Commissioner with Special Power and Military Affairs, Grand Commander-in-Chief of Chonglong Sea and Military Matters, King of Silla; and his wife Lady Pak was named consort.[8]

Year four [842], spring, third month. The King received the daughter of *Ich'an* Wihŭn as his consort.[9]

Year five [843], spring, first month. Chief Minister Ŭijong resigned his position because of illness and *Ich'an* Yangsun

---

6   The accuracy of the placement of this entry is in doubt as, according to the *Jiu Tangshu,* Wenzong died in the fifth year (840) of Kaisheng. *Honglusi* was one of nine Tang bureaus and was responsible for overseeing foreign matters.

7   Kim had passed the state examination in Tang in 821. See Sin Hyŏngsik, "Sukwi haksaeng ko," *Yŏksa kyoyuk* 11–2 (1969). Using a Silla official as envoy to represent Tang in the investiture of a Silla king is a departure from custom.

8   *SY* 1:13b says his wife was Queen Dowager Somyŏng, but it is uncertain if this is Lady Pak. In the fourth year the King married the daughter of Kim Yang who also may be Queen Dowager Somyŏng.

9   Wihŭn was Kim Yang. See *SS* 44:8b. His daughter is King Munsŏng's second Queen. Kim Yang opposed and then helped assassinate Chang Pogo. See "Chang Pogo."

became chief minister.

Autumn, seventh month. Five tigers entered the garden of the Singung Shrine.

Year six [844], spring, second month, first day. There was a solar eclipse and Venus infringed on *Chinsŏng* [Saturn].

Third month. In the capital there was hail. Chief Minister Yangsun retired and *Taeach'an* Kim Yŏ[10] became chief minister.

Autumn, eighth month. [The court] established Hyŏlgu Garrison with *Ach'an* Kyehong as *chindu* [garrison chief].[11]

Year seven [845], spring, third month. The King wanted to marry the daughter of Ch'ŏnghae Garrison Commander Kungbok, making her his second consort. The court officials remonstrated saying, "The tie between a husband and wife is a cardinal relationship of man. Because of the Tushan family the Xia rose; [12] because of Xin, Yin flourished;[13] because of Miss Pa, Zhou collapsed;[14] and because of Liji, Jin experienced disorder.[15] Because a country's rise and fall may depend on this, how can we not be careful? Now as Kungbok is an islander, how can his daughter be a royal consort?" The King agreed.

---

10   His lineage is unclear but he will hold this post until he dies three years later.

11   Hyŏlgu Garrison is on Kanghwa Island in modern Kyŏnggi. This garrison was probably established for defense purposes. The position of *chindu* (garrison chief) is unclear, although it probably means in charge of the garrison.

12   When King Wu of Xia traveled in the eastern part of his domain, he married a Tushan lineage member. She gave birth to Chi. All subsequent kings of Xia were descendants of King Wu.

13   Xin is the name of a country. King Yang of Yin married a woman from there and all later kings of Yin were descendants of this union.

14   King Yu of Zhou loved a woman from the country of Pa with the surname of Shi. He abandoned his family for her and ultimately lost his kingdom. See *Shiji* 4, Zhou, King Yu, third year.

15   In China's Spring and Autumn period (770–476 BCE), Lord Xian took as his wife a woman from Li. She gave birth to two sons but they both died. See *Zuozhuan*, Zhanggong, twenty-eighth year.

Winter, eleventh month. There was thunder but no snow.

Twelfth month, first day. Three suns appeared in a row.

Year eight [846], spring. Kungbok of Ch'ŏnghae, resentful toward the King for not marrying his daughter, staged a rebellion from his garrison. The court officials were about to suppress him but feared an unforeseeable disaster. They considered leaving him alone but his crime was unforgiveable. They fretted and worried not knowing what to do. Yŏmjang from Muju, who was known for his bravery,[16] came to the court saying, "If the court officials favor to allow me, I will not trouble even one soldier but with my bare hands sever and offer up Kungbok's head." The King agreed to this. Yŏmjang pretended to betray his country and surrendered to Ch'ŏnghae Garrison. Kungbok, liking stalwart soldiers and without harboring any doubts, treated Yŏmjang as an honored guest and together with him drank, becoming quite happy. When Kungbok became drunk, Yŏmjang took Kungbok's sword and beheaded him. He then summoned [Kungbok's] followers and admonished them. Prostrate, none dared to move.[17]

Year nine [847], spring, second month. The court repaired again two halls, P'yŏngŭi Hall and Imhae Hall.

Summer, fifth month. *Ich'an* Yangsun and *P'ajinch'an* Hŭngjong and others staged a rebellion and were executed.

Autumn, eighth month. An [unknown] Prince was enfeofed Crown Prince. Chief Minister Kim Yŏ died. *Ich'an* Wihŭn became chief minister.

---

16 He had worked earlier with Kim Yang to remove King Minae and enthrone King Sinmu. See *SY* 2:15a–16a.

17 There is some doubt over when this event took place. *Shoku Nihongi* 11, *showa* 9, records that this happened in the third year (841) of King Munsŏng's reign. *Ennin's Diary, chuan* 4, *Huichang* fifth year, seventh month, ninth day, records it happening also at this time. If so, that would explain why Kim Yang had his daughter marry in 842. See "Chang Pogo."

Year ten [848], spring and summer. There was a drought. Chief Minister Wihŭn retired. *P'ajinch'an* Kim Kyemyŏng[18] became chief minister.

Winter, eleventh month. In the sky there was a sound like thunder.

Year eleven [849], spring, first month. Extraordinary Rank One Yejing died. *Ich'an* Ŭijŏng[19] became extraordinary rank one.

Autumn, ninth month. *Ich'an* Kim Sik and Taehŭn[20] and others staged a rebellion but were captured and executed. *Taeach'an* Hŭllin was sentenced for his involvement.

Year twelve [850], spring, first month. Saturn [appeared to] enter the moon. In the capital it rained dirt with strong winds uprooting trees. [The King] pardoned those in prison charged with crimes lesser than the death penalty.

Year thirteen [851], spring, second month. [The court] abolished Ch'ŏnghae Garrison and moved the people to Pyŏkkol-gun.[21]

Summer, fourth month. Frost fell. *Ach'an* Wŏnhong,[22] the [Silla] envoy to Tang, returned carrying Buddhist sutras and the tooth of the Buddha. The King went to the suburbs [of the capital]

---

18 He is the son of King Hŭigang and the father of King Kyŏngmun. His wife was Lady Kwanghwa, the daughter of King Sinmu. Although little is known about his personal life, he remained chief minister until 862 and died in 864. See Yi Kidong, "Silla hadae wangwi kyesŏng kwa chŏngch'i kwajŏng," *Yŏksa hakpo* 85 (1980) and *Kolp'um.*

19 A man named Ŭijŏng went to Tang in 839. There is also another person with that name in King Hŏnan's reign. It is unclear if these are both the same man. See Yi Kibaek, "Silla hadae ŭi chipsasŏng," *Silla chŏngch'i,* and *Kolp'um* 170–1.

20 There is a possibility that Taehŭn fought with Kim Yang at Taegu in King Minae's second year (839). He might have been an ally to King Sinmu in toppling King Minae and has rebelled here with King Munsŏng's elevation.

21 This is in Chŏnbuk, Kimje. Some see this as the final destruction of the remnants of Chang Pogo's power. Others see it as the end of Yŏmjang's strength. See Ch'oe Kŭnyŏng, *T'ongil Silla sidae ŭi chibang seryŏk yŏngu,* Seoul: Sinsowon, 1990, 145.

22 See also *SY* 3:28a.

to meet him.

Year fourteen [852], spring, second month. *P'ajinch'an* Chillyang became governor general of Ungch'ŏn-ju. The *Chobu* [Ministry of Taxation] had a fire.[23]

Autumn, seventh month. [The court] repaired again Myŏnghak Tower.

Winter, eleventh month. The Crown Prince died.

Year fifteen [853], summer, sixth month. There was a great flood.

Autumn, eighth month. Locusts caused destruction in the *chu* and *kun* of the southwest.

Year seventeen [855], spring, first month. [The court] dispatched officials to inquire into the conditions of the peasants in the southwestern [region].

Winter, twelfth month. *Chingaksŏng*[24] had a fire. Saturn [appeared to] enter the moon.

Year nineteen, autumn, ninth month. The King was ill and sent down his last injunction stating:

"In spite of my insignificant ability, I have occupied the highest office. Above I have feared committing crimes against Heaven and below I am anxious about disappointing the people. Day and night I live in fear like crossing a deep stream on thin ice. Only by relying on the close assistance of scholars and the officialdom and through their efforts, I did not lose the royal position. Now it has been ten days since I have suddenly become ill. Moreover, I am on the verge of losing my faculties and fear I

---

23 This office oversaw the collection of taxes and the administration of corvee labor conscription. It was also known as *Chobu* and *Taebu.* It employed about fifteen people.

24 This was an agency that oversaw the royal treasury, employing about seventeen people.

will disappear before the morning dew. I believe the great undertaking of my earlier ancestors cannot be done without a ruler and the many tasks of defending the country cannot be abandoned for even a short time. Reflecting upon this, I believe *Sŏburhan* Ŭijŏng,[25] a grandson of the former King and my paternal uncle, is filial and fraternal, bright and witty, and generous and humane. For a long time he has held high offices and assisted in royal governance. Above he may be able to serve the ancestral shrines and below he may be able to look after the people's livelihood. Now I may be relieved of a heavy task, and entrust it to a wise and virtuous person. As I have found the [right] person to entrust [the throne], what worry should I have? Moreover, life and death, beginning and ending, is the great law of nature. Whether life is long or short is Heaven's will. To die is to follow this principle, but those living do not need to be excessively sorry. You, my many officials, exert your utmost to fulfill your loyalty. Send off those who have died, respect those who live, and without fail do not deviate from what is right. Please proclaim my cherished ideas, making them known throughout the kingdom."

After seven days the King died and was posthumously called Munsŏng. He was buried at Kongjakchi.[26]

---

25 This is the future King Hŏnan.
26 This location is unclear. According to the current Ministry of Culture, King Munsŏng's tomb is beside the tomb of King Chinji in Sŏaktong, Kyŏngju.

King Hŏnan

King Hŏnan was enthroned. His personal name was Ŭijŏng {another source says Ujŏng} and he was a younger brother of King Sinmu by a different mother. His mother was Lady Chomyŏng, the daughter of King Sŏngang.[27] The King was enthroned according to King Munsŏng's will. There was a general amnesty and *Ich'an* Kim An became extraordinary rank one.

Year two [858], spring, first month. The King personally held services in the Singung Shrine.

Summer, fourth month. Frost fell.

From the fifth month to the seventh month there was no rain. On the shore of a river south of Tangsŏng-gun[28] a large fish appeared that was 40 *po* long and 6 *ch'ŏk* high.

Year three [859], spring. As grain was expensive, people were starving. The King sent officials to relieve and aid them.

Summer, fourth month. [The King] instructed that dikes be completely repaired and agriculture be encouraged.

Year four [860], autumn, ninth month. The King met his ranking officials in Imhae Hall and he allowed the royal relative Ŭngnyŏm,[29] who was fifteen, to attend.[30] The King, wanting to see his thoughts, suddenly asked, "You have been going around studying for some time, haven't you seen a truly good-hearted

---

27 *SY* 1:13b claims Hŏnan ruled for three years and his mother was Lady Hŭmyŏng. King Sŏngang was also known as King Minae.

28 This is in Kyŏnggi, Hwasŏng-gun.

29 He was the son of Kim Kyemyŏng and succeeded King Hŏnan as King Kyŏngmun. His mother was Kwanghwa or Lady Kwangŭi. According to Ch'oe Ch'iwŏn, in "Ch'owŏlsan taesong puksap'i," he was both a Hwarang and an instructor in the National Academy. See *Kolp'um* 172.

30 According to *SY* 2:16a, he became *kuksŏn* (native practitioner) at the age of eighteen when this banquet was held.

person?"

He [Ŭngnyŏm] replied, "I early on saw three men who I believe had good conduct."

The King inquired, "What did they do?"

And he [Ŭngnyŏm] replied, "One was a member of a noble family but with other people he never went first and deferred to those below him. One was from a rich family and could wear extravagant clothes but was always happy wearing hemp cloth. One person possessed power and glory but he never used this over other people. This is what I have seen."

The King, on hearing this, without a word, whispered into the Queen's ear saying, "I have seen many men but none have been like Ŭngnyŏm." Thinking he would like to marry one of his daughters to him, he turned around and said to Ŭngnyŏm, "It is my hope that you have enough self-esteem, as I have daughters and would like to escort you to their sleeping quarters." Then he set up wine and as they drank together, he casually said, "I have two daughters, the oldest is now twenty and the younger is nineteen, which would you like to marry?"

Ŭngnyŏm declined but hesitatingly thanked him and returned home to consult with his parents, who said, "We have heard that the King has two daughters and in appearance the oldest cannot be compared with the youngest. It would be better for you to marry the youngest." However, still in doubt, he could not make up his mind and so asked a monk at Hŭngnyun Monastery.[31] The monk said, "If you marry the oldest you will obtain three blessings. On the other hand, if you marry the youngest, you will encounter three disadvantages." Ŭngnyŏm then appealed, "I do not dare to make this decision by myself. Only Your Majesty can

---

31 *SY* 2:16a identifies the monk to be in charge of the Hwarang.

make the command and I will obey."

Thereupon the King sent out the oldest daughter to marry him.

Year five [861], spring, first month. As the King was ill in bed with no sign of recovery, he summoned his confidants and said:

"I, unfortunately, have no sons but only daughters. Although our country does have the earlier history of two female queens, Sŏndŏk and Chindŏk, because of the dangers of a hen who cries in the morning, this cannot be the rule.[32] My son-in-law Ŭngnyŏm, even though he is young, is endowed with the virtue of maturity. If you enthrone and serve him, certainly he will not harm the continuation of the excellent royal undertaking. When I die, do not let this go to waste."

He died on the twenty-ninth of this [first] month. His posthumous title was Hŏnan and he was buried at Kongjakchi.

King Kyŏngmun

King Kyŏngmun was enthroned.[33] His personal name was Ŭngnyŏm {another source writes another Ŭng character or the character Ŭi}. He was the son of *Ach'an* Kim Kyemyŏng who was the son of King Hŭigang. His mother was Lady Kwanghwa {another source says Kwangŭi}. His consort was Lady Yŏnghwa of the Kim lineage.

Year one [861], third month. The King went to Mup'yŏng Gate

---

32 See Queen Chindŏk, book 5, n. 33. This is based on the idea that dangers occur when the hen crows in the morning.

33 According to *SY* 2:16a–b, he slept with snakes at night and grew two donkey ears on his head.

and there was a general amnesty.

Year two [862], spring, first month. *Ich'an* Kim Chŏng became extraordinary rank one and *Ach'an* Wijin became chief minister. The King personally held services at the Singung Shrine.

Autumn, seventh month. [The court] sent an envoy to Tang to present tribute.

Eighth month. The envoy to Tang, *Ach'an* Puryang, and his party drowned in the sea.

Year three [863], spring, second month. The King went to the National Academy and ordered those of *paksa* and below to lecture on the meaning of the classics[34] and he presented gifts according to rank.

Winter, tenth month. Peach and plum trees blossomed.

Eleventh month. There was no snow. The King received the younger sister of Lady Yŏnghwa as his second consort. Later the King asked the monk from Hŭngnyun Monastery, "What did you mean when you formerly spoke of three blessings?" The monk replied, "Because the King and Queen at that time were happy that you had the same intention [to marry], their love grew even deeper, that was the first. Accordingly, you were able to succeed to the throne, that was the second. In the end you were able to marry the youngest daughter who you originally wanted, that is the third." The King had a big laugh.[35]

Year four [864], spring, second month. The King went to Kamŭn Monastery to view the sea.[36]

---

34 The National Academy started in 682 as the highest educational unit. In King Kyŏngdŏk's reign it became known as the *Taehak* (Confucian College) and then its name was changed back to *Kukhak* (National Academy) in King Hyegong's reign. It was subordinate to the Board of Rites. See *SS* 38 under *Kukhak*.

35 *SY* 2:16b again provides a slightly different account and notes that the King rewarded the monk with the position of *taedŏk* and gave him 130 *ryang* of gold.

36 This can be seen as a service to the spirits of nature.

Summer, fourth month. An envoy from Japan arrived.

Year five [865], summer, fourth month. The Tang [Emperor] Yizong sent the envoy Office of the Heir Apparent, *Taizi youyude* [Vice Censor-in-Chief], Hu Guihou and Assistant Grand Recorder for Splendid Happiness, *Pushi guanglu zhubu jiancha yushi* [Investigating Censor], Pei Guang[37] to offer condolences and hold mourning services for the former King. They also presented 1,000 bolts of cloth as a condolence. They invested the enthroned King as Commander Unequalled in Honor, acting Grand Guardian, Grand Commander-in-Chief of Kyerim, Commissioner with Special Power and Military Affairs, Pillar of State, King of Silla. They also presented to the King the office of *kwango,*[38] a waymark, 500 bolts of brocade, two sets of clothes, and seven gold and silver vessels; they gave the Queen fifty bolts of brocade, one set of clothes, and two silver vessels; they gave the Crown Prince forty bolts of brocade, one set of clothes, and one silver vessel; they gave to the chief councilor of state thirty bolts of brocade, one set of clothes, and one silver vessel; and they gave to the deputy councilor of state twenty bolts of brocade, one set of clothes, and one silver vessel.

Year six [866], spring, first month. [The King] posthumously enfeofed his father as Great King Ŭigong, and his mother, Lady Kwanghwa of the Pak lineage, as Queen Dowager Kwangŭi, and his wife, Lady Kim, as Royal Consort Munŭi, and his son, Chŏng, as Crown Prince. On the fifteenth he went to Hwangnyong Monastery to view the lanterns and offered a banquet to the government officials.

---

37 He was a Silla man who had passed the state examination.

38 This is a credential of office.

The **Silla Annals** of the **Samguk Sagi**

Winter, tenth month. *Ich'an* Yunhŭng,[39] with his younger brothers Sukhŭng and Kyehŭng, plotted a rebellion. When it was uncovered they fled to Taesan-gun. The King ordered they be captured and beheaded the entire family.

Year seven [867], spring, first month. The court repaired again Imhae Hall.

Summer, fifth month. There was an epidemic in the capital.

Autumn, eighth month. There was a great flood and the grain did not grow.

Winter, tenth month. [The court] dispatched officials to go out to different circuits to inquire into the conditions of the people.

Twelfth month. A guest star invaded Venus.

Year eight [868], spring, first month. *Ich'an* Kim Ye and Kim Hyŏn[40] and others plotted a rebellion but were [captured and] executed.

Summer, sixth month. The pagoda at Hwangnyong Monastery shook.[41]

Autumn, eighth month. [The court] repaired again Chowŏn Hall

Year nine [869], autumn, seventh month. The King sent Prince *Sop'an* Kim Yun and others to Tang to express gratitude and presented two horses, 100 *ryang* of gold dust, 200 *ryang* of silver, 15 *ryang* of ox bezoar, 100 *kŭn* of ginseng, ten bolts of large-flowered brocade, ten bolts of small-flowered brocade, twenty bolts of morning-fog brocade, forty bolts of forty-*sung* white

---

39 He was at one time an official in the minor capital of Namwŏn.

40 Kim Ye was the younger brother of King Munsŏng and participated in a dedication ceremony at Ch'angnim Monastery. Kim Hyŏn might be his brother. See Ch'oe Pyŏnghŏn, "Silla hadae sahoe ŭi tongyo," *Hanguksa* 3 (1978): 492.

41 Until the pagoda was destroyed by the Mongols in 1229, *SY* claims it was hit by lightning five times.

cloth, forty bolts of thirty-*sung* sack-cloth shirts, 150 *ryang* of 4½ *ch'ŏk* head hair, 300 *ryang* of 3½ *ch'ŏk* head hair, ten each of gold head pins and multicolored, variegated broaches, twenty each of eagle-design golden heaters and multicolored reddish sword bags, thirty new-eagle gold-design multicolored sword bags, twenty eagle silver-design reddish sword bags, thirty new-eagle silver-design multi-colored sword bags, twenty hawk gold-design reddish sword bags, thirty new-hawk silver-design multicolored sword bags, twenty hawk silver-design reddish sword bags, thirty new-eagle silver-design multicolored sword bags,[42] 200 gold-flowered-eagle peddler gongs, 200 gold-hawk peddler gongs, fifty pairs of gold eagle-tail tubes, fifty pairs of gold hawk-tail tubes, fifty pairs of silver eagle-tail tubes, 100 pairs of bound-eagle dark-purple knotted skins, 100 pairs of bound-hawk dark-purple knotted skins, thirty turquoise hairpins with gold needle tubes, thirty gold-flower silver needle tubes, and 1,500 pins. He also sent exchange student Yi Tong[43] and two other [students] to accompany royal envoy Kim Yun and go to Tang to study. He gave 300 *ryang* of silver for buying books.

Year ten [870], spring, second month. [The court] sent *Sach'an* Kim In to Tang as an imperial resident guard.

Summer, fourth month. There was an earthquake in the capital.

Fifth month. The royal consort died.

Autumn, seventh month. There was a great flood.

Winter. There was no snow. Many people in the kingdom [suffered] from epidemics.

Year eleven [871], spring, first month. The King ordered the

---

42 This is redundant.

43 He first went to Tang in 875 and passed the state examination for foreigners. See Ch'oe Ch'iwŏn's essay, "Silla wang yŏ tang kangsŏ kodaebu sangjang," *Tongmunsŏn* 47.

offices concerned to rebuild the pagoda at Hwangnyong Monastery.

Second month. The court repaired again Wŏlsang Tower.

Year twelve [872], spring, second month. The King personally held services at the Singung Shrine.

Summer, fourth month. There was an earthquake in the capital.

Autumn, eighth month. Locusts ravaged the grain in the *chu* and *kun* in the kingdom.

Year thirteen [873], spring. As people were starving, an epidemic [spread]. The King dispatched officials to relieve and aid them.

Autumn, ninth month. The nine-story pagoda at Hwangnyong Monastery was completed. It was 22 *chang* high.[44]

Year fourteen [874], spring, first month. Extraordinary Rank One Kim Chŏng died and Chief Minister Wijin became extraordinary rank one. Inhŭng became chief minister.

Spring, fourth month. Tang [Emperor] Xizong sent an envoy with an imperial edict.

Fifth month. *Ich'an* Kŭnjong plotted a rebellion and invaded the palace. [The King] sent out his palace guards to attack and destroy them. Kŭnjong, with his group, escaped from the fortress at night but were pursued, captured, and executed by being pulled apart by several carts.[45]

Autumn, ninth month. [The court] again repaired

---

44 *SY* 3:17b–19b provides a detailed entry on this pagoda and notes it was 42 *ch'ok* above an iron base and 183 *ch'ok* below. See also *Sourcebook* 1:87–9 for an English translation.

45 This punishment, used originally in China, disappeared after Tang, but is noted as occurring in Koryŏ in King Kongmin's reign, twenty-third year (1374), *Koryŏsa chŏryo* (hereafter *KSC*), Tokyo: Hōsa bunkō edition, Gakushuin, 1960, 29; and in King U's reign, eighth year (1382), *Koryŏsa* (hereafter *KS*), Seoul: Yonsei edition, Kyŏngin, 1972, biography 26, Ch'oe Yŏngjŏn.

Wŏlchŏngdang. Ch'oe Ch'iwŏn[46] passed the state examination in Tang.

Year fifteen [875], spring, second month. Both the capital and the eastern part of the country had an earthquake. A comet appeared in the east for twenty days and then vanished.

Summer, fifth month. A dragon was seen in a well in the palace and then, shortly after, cloud and fog enveloped all over and the dragon flew away.

Autumn, seventh month, eighth day. The King died, and was posthumously known as Kyŏngmun.

King Hŏngang

King Hŏngang was enthroned. His personal name was Chŏng and he was King Kyŏngmun's Crown Prince. His mother was Queen Munŭi and his consort was Lady Ŭimyŏng.[47] The King, by nature, was intelligent and witty and loved to read books. Once he saw something, he could repeat it all. On being enthroned he appointed *Ich'an* Wihong to be extraordinary rank one and *Taeach'an* Yegyŏm to be chief minister.[48] There was a general amnesty for those throughout the kingdom who committed crimes below those requiring punishment by the death penalty.

---

46 See *SS* 46:3a–6b. He was eighteen when he passed the examination.
47 According to *SY* 1:14a, his mother was Queen Dowager Munja, also called Ŭimyŏng, but this second name probably was the name for the King's wife.
48 Wihong was the younger brother of King Kyŏngmun and King Hŏngang's uncle. *SY* 2:19a says he was the husband of Queen Chinsŏng. As for Yegyŏm, *SS* 12:3a indicates that King Sindŏk's father was one Yegyŏm and *SS* 12:14b indicates that his stepfather was Yegyŏm.

Year two [876], spring, second month. A banquet for monks was held at Hwangnyong Monastery[49] where they set up Hundred-Seat Assembly services to lecture on the sutras. The King personally went to listen to them.

Autumn, seventh month. The King sent envoys to Tang to present tribute.

Year three [877], spring, first month. Our great King T'aejo [the founder of Koryŏ] was born in Songak-gun.[50]

Year four [878], summer, fourth month. Tang [Emperor] Xizong sent an envoy with an investiture to enfeof the King Commissioner with Extraordinary Power, Commander Unequalled in Honor, acting Grand Guardian, Grand Commander-in-Chief of Kyerim, Commissioner with Special Power and Military Affairs, King of Silla.

Autumn, seventh month. [The court] sent an envoy to the Tang court but [on the way] heard of the Huang Zhao [rebel] uprising and so stopped.[51]

Eighth month. An envoy from the kingdom of Japan arrived. The King received him in Chowŏn Hall.

Year five [879], spring, second month. The King went to the National Academy and ordered those of *paksa* and below to lecture on the classics.

Third month. The King inspected the *chu* and *kun* in the eastern part of the kingdom where four men, who came from nowhere, went in front of the royal carriage singing and dancing. Their appearance was appalling and their clothes and head scarves were strange. Contemporaries called them the spirits of the mountains

---

49 See *AKS* 3:353, n. 78.
50 T'aejo (Wang Kŏn) was born in 877 and died in 943.
51 From 874 to 884 Huang Zhao led a peasant rebellion that started in Szechuan and spread across the country, contributing to the collapse of Tang.

and seas.[52] {*Kogi*[53] says this event occurred in the year the King was enthroned.}

Summer, sixth month. *Ilgilch'an* Sinhong rebelled but was [captured and] executed.

Winter, tenth month. The King went to Chullye Gate to observe archery.

Eleventh month. The King went hunting on Hyŏlsŏng Plain.

Year six [880], spring, second month. Venus intruded on the moon. Chief Minister Yegyŏm retired and *Ich'an* Mingong[54] became chief minister.

Autumn, eighth month. Ung-ju presented an auspicious stalk of rice.

Ninth month, ninth day. The King and his attendants climbed Wŏlsan Tower and looked out in four directions. The people's houses in the capital were lined up row after row and music and song was played continuously.[55] The King turned and said to Chief Minister Mingong, "I have heard that among the people, their houses have tiled roofs and none have thatch, and that they cook their food with charcoal, not firewood. Is this true?" Mingong replied, "I too once heard that it was like this." And then went on to say, "Since Your Majesty has ascended the throne, the

---

52 *AKS* 3:354, n. 82. See also *SY* 2:17b–18b which relates how, when the King went to Kaeunp'o, several people who were the sons of the Dragon of the Eastern Sea sang and danced in front of the King. See also Yi Usŏng, "Samguk yusa sojae ch'ŏyong sŏrhwa ŭi ilgoch'al," *Kim Chaewŏn paksa hwangap kinyŏm nonch'ong* 89–127. Yi Yongbŏm, "Ch'ŏyong sŏrhwa ŭi ilgoch'al," *Chindan hakpo* 32 (1969): 31–4, suggests these may have been merchants who drifted from Tang China.

53 *Kogi* is mentioned more than twenty times in the *Annals*. It may be a composite of earlier works or just signify earlier sources. See Yi Kangnae, "Samguk sagi wa Kogi," *Yongbong nonch'ong* 17–8 (1989): 83–107.

54 Mingong is mentioned in a stele composed in 1814, "Silla Kyŏngsun wang chŏnbi mun," as the great grandfather of King Kyŏngsun and the grandson of King Munsŏng.

55 See also *SY* 1:11a and 2:17b for similar descriptions.

The **Silla Annals** of the **Samguk Sagi**

forces of yin and yang are balanced, and the wind and rain have been timely. The years have been prosperous and the people have enough to eat. The borders have been peaceful and still and the people on the streets have been happy. This is because of Your Majesty's virtue [merit]." The King, delighted, replied, "This is the result of your help. What merit have I?"

Year seven [881], spring, third month. The King held a banquet for his ranking officials at Imhae Hall. As they became light-hearted from drinking, the King played the *kŏmungo* and his attendants each presented their own verses. Everyone truly enjoyed [themselves] to the end.

Year eight [882], summer, fourth month. The King of Japan sent an envoy who presented 300 *ryang* of yellow gold and ten bright pearls.

Winter, twelfth month. A woman from Komi-hyŏn[56] gave birth to boy triplets.

Year nine [883], spring, second month. The King visited Samnang Monastery[57] and ordered the civil officials to each compose a poem.

Year eleven [885], spring, second month. A tiger entered the palace grounds.

Third month. Ch'oe Ch'iwŏn returned [from China].

Winter, tenth month, *imja* day. Venus was seen in the sky during the day. [The King] sent an envoy to Tang to congratulate [the Emperor] on the defeat of the bandit Huang Zhao.

Year twelve [886], spring. Pukchin [Northern Garrison]

---

56 Komi-hyŏn's exact location is unclear but Yi Pyŏngdo, *SS* 194, suggests it might be in Chŏnnam, Yŏngam.

57 *SY* 5:10a mentions the monk Kyŏnghong living at this temple. Recently a stele from the temple was discovered in Kyŏngju and is presently housed at Tanguk University's museum.

announced, "People from Chŏkkuk[58] entered the garrison, took a piece of wood, suspended it from a tree, and left." Then the (Northern Garrison people) took the wood and presented it. On the wood were fifteen characters that said, "People from Poro and Hŭksu want to have peaceful relations with Silla."[59]

Summer, sixth month. The King was ill and pardoned those imprisoned throughout the kingdom. He also held at Hwangnyong Monastery a Hundred-Seat Assembly and lectures on the sutras.

Autumn, seventh month, fifth day. The King died. His posthumous title was Hŏngang. He was buried southeast of Pori Monastery.

King Chŏnggang

King Chŏnggang was enthroned. His personal name was Hwang and he was the second son of King Kyŏngmun.[60]

Eighth month. *Ich'an* Chunhŭng became chief minister. In the western part of the kingdom there was a severe drought and crops withered.

Year two [887], spring, first month. [The court] set up a Hundred-Seat Assembly at Hwangnyong Monastery and the King personally went to listen to the lectures. When *Ich'an* Kim Yo of Han-ju staged a rebellion, [the court] dispatched troops to

---

58 Yi Kibaek suggests Pukchin is in the Samch'ŏk area in "Koryŏ T'aejosi ŭi chin," *Koryŏ pyŏngjesa yŏngu,* Seoul, 1975, 230. Chŏkkuk is probably Parhae.

59 Yi Pyŏngdo, *SS* 195, suggests that Poro was a Jurchen tribe in Anbyŏn and Hŭksu was another Jurchen tribe in the same area.

60 According to *SY* 1:14a, King Chŏnggang was the brother of King Minae.

suppress it.

Spring, fifth month. The King fell ill and addressed Chief Minister Chunhŭng saying:

My illness is critical and I certainly will not get better. Unfortunately I have no heir to succeed me. However, my younger sister, Man, by nature is bright and sharp and in blood and in build is similar to a man. As this is also like the earlier precedent of [Queens] Sŏndŏk and Chindŏk, it would be possible for you to enthrone her.

Autumn, seventh month, fifth day. The King died.[61] His posthumous title was Chŏnggang and he was buried southeast of Pori Monastery.[62]

Queen Chinsŏng

Queen Chinsŏng was enthroned. Her personal name was Man and she was the younger sister of King Hŏngang.[63] {In Ch'oe Ch'iwŏn's *Munjip* [*Collected Writings*], book 2, the entry "Sach'ujŭngp'yo [letter to thank for posthumous awards]" states, "I, T'an [Queen Chinsŏng], offer the following, 'By imperial decree my deceased father Ŭng [Kyŏngmun] posthumously becomes *T'aesa* [Grand Preceptor] and my deceased brother Chŏng [Hŏngang] becomes *T'aebu* [Grand Mentor].'"[64] The *Nap chŏng*

---

61 *SY* 1:14a claims he died the same year (886) he was enthroned.
62 His tomb is alleged to be east of South Mountain in Namsandong in Kyŏngju, although some claim this to be King Sŏndŏk's tomb.
63 *SY* 1:14a says her name was Manhŏn and her husband was Wihong.
64 Ŭng is King Kyŏngmun and the positions of *t'aesa* and *t'aebu* are the highest

jŏlp'yo [Letter accepting the way][65] states, "My older brother King Chŏng suddenly died on Guangqi third year [887], seventh month, fifth day, putting behind his blessed reign.[66] As my young nephew Yo was not even a year old, my older brother Hwang [Chŏnggang] temporarily took control of this frontier country [Silla]. But not even one year passed before he left the world for a distant place, giving up this bright age."

According to this entry, King Kyŏngmun's name was Ŭng, although the *Annals* call him Ŭngnyŏm. And Queen Chinsŏng's personal name is T'an but the *Annals* say Man. Again King Chŏnggang died in Guangqi third year but the *Annals* say he died in the second year.[67] It is unknown which is correct.} There was a general amnesty and the various *chu* and *kun* were exempted from paying taxes for one year. [The court] set up a Hundred-Seat Assembly at Hwangnyong Monastery and the Queen personally went to listen to Buddhist sermons.

Winter. There was no snow.

Year two [888], spring, second month. A boulder at Soryang-ri moved on its own. The Queen, in her youth, had been intimate with *Kakkan* Wihong. Coming to this he still constantly came to the palace to carry out business at will.[68] [The Queen] commanded him with the priest Taegu to collect *hyangga* verse into a volume entitled *Samdaemok*.[69] When Wihong died, the Queen

---

honorary ranks.

65 This was written by Ch'oe Ch'iwŏn. These essays were ordinarily written when conveying memorial tablets.

66 Guangqi third year is 887. There is some confusion because King Chŏnggang died in this year, not Chŏng, King Hŏngang.

67 This is additional confusion, above, because *SS* 11:12b and 31:47b state he died in the third year.

68 *SY* 2:19a states that Wihong was her lover and she made him her spouse after she became Queen.

69 *SY* 2:17a–b notes in King Kyŏngmun's reign that four Hwarang visited a scenic

posthumously named him Great King Hyesŏng. After this she secretly brought into her palace two or three young, handsome men for licentious activities and conferred on these men important offices, commissioning them with state affairs. From this time sycophants had their way, bribes were publicly passed, and rewards and punishments were not fair. The discipline of the country collapsed and became loose. At this time there was an unknown person who, in disguise, criticized the politics of the age by composing some writings on placards and putting them by the roads to the court.[70] The Queen ordered people to investigate this but they were unable to find [anyone]. Someone told the Queen, "This certainly must be the work of a man of letters who could not fulfill his ambition and I suspect it is probably done by the recluse Kŏin of Taeya.[71] The Queen ordered that Kŏin be imprisoned in the capital. When he was about to be punished, Kŏin out of indignation wrote on the prison wall, "Lord Yu wept and for three years there was a drought. Zuoyan was overcome by sorrow and in the fifth month dew fell. Now deep in my heart my anguish is like those of the past. But heaven makes no reply and only stays blue."[72] Suddenly, that evening, clouds and fog formed, there was thunder and lightning, rain and hail fell. The Queen, frightened, had Kŏin set free.

Third month, *musul* day, the first day of the month. There was

---

spot and composed patriotic songs. They also asked Taegu, a famous monk, to compose some songs. This is probably the same individual here. The *Samdaemok* is not extant but probably was a collection of Silla verse from its three periods.

70 See *SY* 2:17a for a more elaborate description of these events.

71 *SY* 2:17a identifies him as Wang Kŏin. His name also appears at the end of Sŏl Ch'ong's biography in *SS* 44. Taeya is in Kyŏngnam, Hapch'ŏn.

72 *SY* 2:19a provides a slightly different verse. Lord Yu lived in Han China in Tunghai. He protested the imprisonment and death of a woman, and for three years there was drought until she was rehabilitated. See *Hanshu* 71. Zuoyan was from Chi and was slandered and imprisoned.

a solar eclipse. As the Queen fell ill, she ordered [her officials] to [review] the records of those imprisoned, pardoning those charged with crimes below the death penalty. She permitted the ordination of sixty people to become monks. The Queen's illness then abated.

Summer, fifth month. There was a drought.

Year three [889]. As the various *chu* and *kun* all over the kingdom ceased to send in taxes in kind, the government warehouses became empty and government revenue dried up. The Queen dispatched officials to press [payment]. Thereupon bandits rose all over. With this Wŏnjong and Aeno, based in Sabŏl-ju, rebelled. The Queen ordered *Nama* Yŏnggi to capture them. Yŏnggi looked off and saw the bandit's ramparts and fearful, he could not advance. *Ch'onju* [village head] Uryŏn fought hard and died. The Queen ordered that Yŏnggi be killed and that Uryŏn's son, who was more than ten years old, succeed him as village head.

Year four [890], spring, first month. The sun had a halo of five rings. On the fifteenth the Queen went to Hwangnyong Monastery to see the Yŏndŭng Festival.

Year five [891], winter, tenth month. The Pugwŏn bandit leader Yanggil sent his lieutenant Kungye, leading over 100 horsemen, to attack the villages east of Pugwŏn and over ten *kun* and *hyŏn* under Myŏng-ju's jursdiction.[73]

Year six [892]. The bandit Kyŏnhwŏn, from his base in Wansan-ju, declared on his own the founding of Later Paekche. The *kun* and *hyŏn* southeast of Mu-ju surrendered to him.[74]

Year seven [893]. The court sent *Pyŏngbu Sirang* [Attendant

---

73 Yanggil developed his center of power in the border area of modern Kangwŏn, Kyŏngsang, and Ch'ungch'ŏng provinces. Kungye emerged under him. See *SS* 50:1a–2b. Myŏngju is in Kangwŏn, Kangnŭng.

74 Kyŏnhwŏn was a key figure at this time. See *SS* 50:7b. He prockained himself king or Later Paekche.

Gentleman] of the Ministry of Military Affairs Kim Ch'ŏhŭi to Tang to present a waymark but he drowned in the ocean.

Year eight [894], spring, second month. Ch'oe Ch'iwŏn presented a ten-point memorial on current affairs which the Queen happily received.[75] Ch'iwŏn became *ach'an*.

Winter, tenth month. Kungye, going from Pugwŏn, entered Hasŭlla leading over 600 people and calling himself *changgun* [general].[76]

Year nine [895], autumn. Kungye attacked and captured two *kun,* Chŏjok and Sŏngchŏn, and destroyed Puyak, Ch'ŏlwŏn, and more than ten *kun* and *hyŏn* under the Han-ju jurisdiction.[77]

Winter, tenth month. The Queen appointed Yo, King Hŏngang's son by a concubine, to be Crown Prince. Earlier, King Hŏngang had gone off hunting. On the way, he spotted a girl who in appearance was beautiful and the King in his heart loved her. He commanded her to be placed in the rear carriage and on reaching an improvised palace, he had illicit relations with her. At once she became pregnant and gave birth to a son. When he grew up his appearance was distinguished and his name was Yo. Chinsŏng,

---

75 The contents of this proposal are unknown but they most likely attacked the *kolp'um* rank order and the growing power of the monarch. See Yi Kibaek, "Kolp'um ch'eje ha ŭi yugyojŏk chŏngch'i inyŏm," *Silla sidae ŭi kukka pulgyo wa yugyo,* Seoul: Hangok yŏnguwŏn, 1978, 164–6; Pak Chonggŭn, "Ch'oe Ch'iwŏn ŭi chŏngch'i inyŏm kwa chonggyo kwan," *Yŏksa kyoyuk nonjip* 3, 41–3; and Ch'oe Kyŏngsuk, "Ch'oe Ch'iwŏn yŏngu," *Pusan hakpo* 5:24–31.

76 In the biography section of *SS* it states that Kungye had over thirty-five hundred followers. This discrepancy may be explained by arguing that Kungye left with six hundred followers but arrived at Myŏngju with thirty-five hundred. For information on Kungye see Hugh H.W. Kang, "The Development of the Korean Ruling Class from Late Silla to Early Koryŏ," unpublished PhD dissertation, University of Washington, 1964; Kim Ch'ŏlchun, "Husamguk sidae chibae seryŏk ŭi sŏnggyŏk," *Hangguk kodae sahoe yŏngu,* 1975, 256; and Cho Insŏng, "T'aebong ŭi Kungye chŏnggwŏn yŏngu," unpublished PhD dissertation, Sogang University, 1990, 31–2.

77 Chŏjok is in Kangwŏn, Injae; Sŏngchŏn is in Kangwŏn, Hwach'ŏn; and Puyak is in Kangwŏn, P'yŏnggang

learning this, called him into the palace and patting him on his back said, "My brothers' and sisters' bone structure is different from others. On this child's back there are two protruding bones. This is truly King Hŏngang's son." She then ordered the offices concerned to prepare a ceremony to invest him with all honors.

Year ten [896]. Bandits arose in the southwestern [region] of the kingdom. As they wore red trousers to distinguish themselves from others, people called them the "Red Trouser Bandits." Ravaging the *chu* and *hyŏn,* they reached even Moryang-ni in the western ward of the capital where they plundered the houses of the people and left.

Year eleven [897], summer, sixth month. The Queen addressed her attendants saying, "In recent years the peasants have been impoverished and bandits have risen up. This is because of my lack of virtue. I have made up my mind to abdicate the throne to a wise person." The throne was passed to the Crown Prince Yo. Thereupon the court sent an envoy to Tang with a memorial stating, "I humbly offer these words, 'To occupy Xizhong's office was not my fate. To guard the integrity of Yanling has been my good plan.[78] My nephew Yo is my deceased brother Chŏng's son and is nearly fifteen years old, endowed with the capacity to advance the dynasty. We have no leisure to search outside and have decided to recommend from within [the court]. Recently he has already temporarily governed and has pacified the calamities of the kingdom.'"[79]

---

78 Xizhong was an official who governed the east when Yao was King in China and is used here as a metaphor for ruling Korea. See *Shujing.* Yanling was a palace where the kings of Wu were enfeofed. See *Tzochuan,* Xiangong, fourteenth and thirty-first year.

79 The original, drafted by Ch'oe Ch'iwŏn, is in *Tongmunsŏn.* This is an excerpt. See *AKS* 3:362, n. 133.

Winter, twelfth month, *ŭlsa* day. The Queen died in the northern palace. Her posthumous title was Chinsŏng and she was buried at Mount Hwangsan.[80]

<hr />

80 The northern palace is mentioned in *SY* 2:11b in King Hyegong's reign. A Haein Monastery document contends that the Queen died at that temple. See *Haeinsa*, Seoul, 1975, 104. As for Mount Hwangsan, *SY* 1:14a states the Queen was cremated and placed west of Moryang-ri. Some suggest the mountain may be in Yangsan.

The Silla
Annals of the
Samguk Sagi

Kings Hyogong, Sindŏk, Kyŏngmyŏng, Kyŏngae, and Kyŏngsun

Book

12

King Hyogong

King Hyogong was enthroned. His personal name was Yo and he was the son of King Hŏngang by a concubine. His mother was of the Kim lineage.[1] There was a general amnesty and the [King] promoted the military and civil officials in the government each by one rank.

Year two [898], spring, first month. [The King] made his mother Lady Kim to be Queen Dowager Ŭimyŏng. *Sŏburhan* Chunhŭng became extraordinary rank one and *Ach'an* Kyegang[2] became chief minister.

Autumn, seventh month. Kungye seized P'aesŏ-do [circuit] and more than thirty fortresses under Hansan-ju's administration and then, finally, made as his capital Songak-gun.[3]

Year three [899], spring, third month. The King married the daughter of *Ich'an* Yegyŏm making her his consort.

Autumn, seventh month. The bandit leader Yanggil of Pugwŏn, fearing that Kungye would double-cross him, planned to attack Kungye with the castle lord of Kugwŏn and more than ten others. When they advanced their troops to below Pinoe Fortress,

---

1   According to *SY* 1:14a, her name was Queen Dowager Munja, but *SY* gives the identical name to King Hŏngang's mother.
2   The official rank of *ach'an,* according to the *SS* 38, was below that prescribed for the post of chief minister. See *AKS* 3:3, n. 64.
3   *SY* 1:14a and *SS* 50 claim this occurred in King Hyogong's first year.

Yanggil's troops fled.[4]

Year four [900], winter, tenth month. Bandit leaders Ch'ŏnggil, Sinhwŏn,[5] and others from Kugwŏn, Ch'ŏng-ju, and Koeyang[6] and others surrendered with their fortresses to Kungye.

Year five [901]. Kungye proclaimed [himself] King.[7]

Autumn, eighth month. The Later Paekche King Kyŏnhwŏn attacked Taeya Fortress but it did not fall. He moved his troops south of Kŭmsŏng[8] and plundered some border villages and then withdrew.

Year six [902], spring, third month. Frost fell. *Taeach'an* Hyojong became chief minister.[9]

Year seven [903]. Kungye wanted to move his capital. Arriving at Ch'ŏrwŏn and Puyang, he viewed their topography [geomancy].

Year eight [904]. Kungye established government offices based on the Silla system. {Although names of the offices followed Silla, there were others that were different.} He named the country Majin with the reign year Mut'ae first year. More than ten *chu* and *hyŏn* in the P'aegang circuit surrendered to Kungye.

Year nine [905], spring, second month. Shooting stars fell like rain.

Summer, fourth month. Frost fell.

Autumn, seventh month. Kungye moved his capital to

---

4 Again the biography section *SS* 50 provides a slightly different account noting over thirty fortress chiefs attacking Kungye and this event occurring in 897, not 899 as stated here. P'aesŏ-do is in western Hwanghae.

5 He also appears as Sinhwŏn, by other characters, in the biography section.

6 For Ch'ŏngju see Kim Kaptong, "Koryŏ kŏngukki ŭi Ch'ŏngju seryŏk kwa Wang Kŏn," *Hanguksa yŏngu* 48 (1985), and *Namal yŏch'o ŭi hojok kwa sahoe pyŏndong yŏngu,* 1990, 28. Koeyang is in Ch'ungbuk, Koesan.

7 According to *SY,* Kungye called his kingdom "Koryŏ." See *AKS* 3:365, n. 11.

8 Kŭmsŏng is in Chŏnnam, Naju.

9 He was the son of *Sŏburhan* Ingyŏng and father of King Kyŏngsun. He won fame as a Hwarang who expressed a lot of compassion. See *SY* 5:20a.

Ch'ŏlwŏn.

Eighth month. Kungye sent his troops to attack and seize our border towns reaching northeast of Chungnyŏng [Pass]. The King, learning that his territory was daily dwindling and extremely concerned but lacking the strength to stop it, ordered the various castle lords not to go out and fight, but firmly guard and defend [themselves].

Year ten [906], spring, first month. *P'ajinch'an* Kim Sŏng became extraordinary rank one.

Third month. Kim Munul, who formerly went to Tang, passed the state examination and achieved positions up to Bureau Vice Director of the *Gongbu* [Ministry of Works], *Yiwangfu* [Princely Establishment], and *ziyicanjun* [adjutant], returned as *cemingshi* [imperial diplomat] with orders of [royal] investiture.

From the fourth month to the fifth month of summer there was no rain.

Year eleven [907]. Spring and summer were without rain. More than ten fortresses south of Ilsŏn-gun[10] were all taken over by Kyŏnhwŏn.

Year twelve [908], spring, second month. A comet appeared in the east.

Third month. Frost fell.

Summer, fourth month. It rained hail.

Year thirteen [909], summer, sixth month. Kungye ordered his generals to lead battleships and capture Chindo-gun.[11] They also destroyed the fortress on Koi Island.[12]

---

10 Ilsŏn-gun is in Kyŏngbuk, Sŏnsan.
11 Chindo-gun is in Chŏnnam, Chindo
12 Koi Island is in Chŏnnam, Sinan. The Japanese monk Ennin stopped at this site earlier. See Reischauer, *Ennin's Travels in T'ang China,* diary 4, Huichang seventh year.

Year fourteen [910]. Kyŏnhwŏn personally led 3,000 infantry and cavalry and encircled Naju Fortress for ten days without seizing it. When Kungye sent his naval force to attack, Kyŏnhwŏn pulled his troops and retreated.[13]

Year fifteen [911], spring, first month, first day, *pyŏngsul.* There was a solar eclipse. As the King fell for a concubine of base status and neglected state affairs, the leading minister Ŭnyŏng remonstrated but the King would not listen. [Ŭn]yŏng seized the concubine and killed her. Kungye changed the name of his state to T'aebong and established the reign year of Sudŏk manse [long live maritime virtue].[14]

Year sixteen [912], summer, fourth month. The King died, his posthumous title was Hyogong and he was buried north of Saja Monastery.[15]

King Sindŏk

King Sindŏk was enthroned. His surname was Pak, his personal name was Kyŏnghŭi, and he was a distant descendant of King Adalla. His father was Yegyŏm {another source writes different characters}. Serving Great King Chŏnggang, he became

---

13 Wang Kŏn was active in this engagement. *SS* 50 claims this occurred in the fifteenth year, 911, not 910. See Hugh. H.W. Kang, "The First Succession Struggle of Koryŏ in 945: A Reinterpretation," *The Journal of Asian Studies* 36:3 (May 1977).

14 This is a phrase adapted from Chinese cosmology of the five elements. See *AKS* 3:368, n. 27.

15 *SY* 1:14b states his bones were placed east of Kujije. According to the Bureau of Cultural Treasures, *Munhwa yujŏk ch'ongnam* 2 (1977), 76, King Hyogong's tomb was in Paeban-dong, Kyŏngju.

taeach'an.[16] His mother was Lady Chŏnghwa and his consort was Lady Kim, the daughter of Great King Hŏngang.[17] When King Hyogong died he had no sons and so the people of the kingdom supported [Sindŏk] to be enthroned.

Year one [912], fifth month. [The King] posthumously invested his father as Great King Sŏnsŏng, his mother as Queen Dowager Chŏnghwa, his consort as Queen Ŭisŏng, and his son, Sŭngyŏng, as Crown Prince, and appointed *Ich'an* Kyegang to be extraordinary rank one

Year two [913], summer, fifth month. Frost fell and there was an earthquake.

Year three [914], spring, third month. Frost fell. Kungye changed the name of his reign from Sudŏk manse to Chŏnggae first year.

Year four [915], summer, sixth month. The waters in Ch'amp'o and the Eastern Sea collided with each other, causing waves over 20 *ch'ŏk* high for three days and then stopped.[18]

Year five [916], autumn, eighth month. Kyŏnhwŏn attacked Taeya Fortress to no avail.

Winter, tenth month. There was an earthquake that sounded

---

16 According to *SS* 11 he already was *taeach'an* in King Hŏngang's reign.

17 Some contend that, as the younger brother of King Hyogong's queen, he used this opportunity to change his name from Kim to Pak. See Hideo Inoue, "Shiragi bokushioki no seiritsu," *Shiragi kiso kenkyū,* 1974, 321–74. According to *SY* 1:14b, his original name was Sujong. King Adalla was the last of the Pak lineage to be king. Since King Adalla is reputed to have had no heirs, King Sŏndŏk may have descended through Adalla's sister's family or through his maternal family. *SY* states that Sŏndŏk's adopted father was Yegyŏm and his father was Munwŏn igan, posthumously honored as Great King Hŭngyŏm. According to *SS* 11:10a–b, Yegyŏm, a *taeach'an*, became a chief minister in King Hŏngang's reign, which makes the statement here appear inaccurate. Lady Chŏnghwa was the daughter of *Kakkan* Sunhong and, in *SY* 1:14b, she is listed as Lady Chinhwa. *SY* also gives three possible names for Sŏndŏk's Queen: Chasŏng, Ŭisŏng, or Hyoja.

18 This phenomenon is also listed in *SY* 2:20a and most likely indicates rather severe tidal changes or the aftermath of a tsunami.

like thunder.

Year six [917], spring, first month. Venus infringed on the moon.

Autumn, seventh month. The King died, his posthumous title was Sindŏk and he was buried at Chuksŏng.[19]

King Kyŏngmyŏng

King Kyŏngmyŏng was enthroned. His personal name was Sŭngyŏng and he was King Sindŏk's Crown Prince. His mother was Queen Ŭisŏng.[20]

Year one [917], eighth month. The King appointed his brother *Ich'an* Winŭng to be extraordinary rank one and *Taeach'an* Yuryŏm to be chief minister.

Year two [918], spring, second month. *Ilgilch'an* Hyŏnsŭng rebelled but was [captured and] executed.

Summer, sixth month. As the people under Kungye's command suddenly changed their minds to support T'aejo, Kungye fled but was killed by his subordinates. T'aejo was enthroned calling this the first year of his reign.[21]

Autumn, seventh month. The bandit leader of Sang-ju Ajagae sent an emissary to surrender to T'aejo.[22]

---

19 *SY* 1:14b states his bones were interred south of Ch'amhyŏn.
20 *SY* 1:14b states his mother's name was Chasŏng.
21 See *SS* 50 and *KS* for a detailed account.
22 The identity of Ajagae has sparked considerable interest. *SY* 2:29a claims Kyŏnhwŏn's father was named Ajagae and was a descendant of King Chinhŭng's queen. He farmed in Sangju and became a military leader there. Given the fierce opposition between T'aejo Wang Kŏn and Kyŏnhwŏn at this time, some contend it

Year three [919]. The bow strings on a statue in Sach'ŏnwang Monastery were severed and dogs painted on a wall mural made sounds like barking.[23] Extraordinary Rank One Kim Sŏng became *kakkan* and Chief Minister Ŏnong became *sach'an*.[24] Our T'aejo moved his capital to Songak-gun.

Year four [920], spring, first month. The King and T'aejo exchanged envoys to conclude amicable ties.

Second month. Kang-ju General Yun Ung surrendered to T'aejo.[25]

Winter, tenth month. Later Paekche ruler Kyŏnhwŏn led 10,000 infantry and cavalry attacking and capturing Taeya Fortress and then had his troops proceed to Chillye.[26] The King sent *Ach'an* Kim Yul to seek help from T'aejo. T'aejo ordered his generals to go out and assist. [Kyŏn]hwŏn, on hearing this, withdrew.

Year five [921], spring, first month. Kim Yul reported to the King, "Last year I was commanded to go to Koryŏ as an envoy where the Koryŏ King asked me, 'I have heard that in Silla there are three treasures, the so-called 16 foot tall Buddha statue, the nine-story pagoda, and the hallowed belt. The Buddha and pagoda are still there but I do not know if the hallowed belt still

---

would be difficult to see Kyŏnhwŏn's father siding with Wang Kŏn. See An Chŏngbok, *Tongsa kangmok*. See also Sin Hoch'ŏl "Hu Paekche ŭi chibae seryŏk e taehan punsŏk," *Yi Pyŏngdo paksa kinyŏm* 138. Kim Sanggi, "Kyŏnhwŏn ŭi kahyang e taehayŏ," *Tongbangsa nonch'ong*, 1974, argues that Kyŏnhwŏn did not come from Sangju but from Kwangju.

23 *SY* 2:20b reports similar activity. Sach'ŏnwang Monastery was built in 679 with the idea of expelling Tang. The remains of the monastery can be seen in Kyŏngju. See *AKS* 3:372, n. 49.

24 Here, too, people holding the post of *sach'an* were not eligible to be chief minister.

25 Yun Ung was a regional strongman in the Chinju region. His son Ilgang went as a hostage to Wang Kŏn and became an *ach'an*. *KS* 1:15b.

26 Chillye is probably near the modern Ch'angwŏn or the Kimhae area. See Ch'oe Pyŏnghŏn, "Sillamal Kimhae chibang ŭi hojok seryŏk kwa sŏnjong," *Hanguksaron* 4 (1978): 403-4.

exists.' I was not able to answer."

The King, hearing this, questioned his ranking officials, "What sort of treasure is this hallowed belt?" None knew about it. At that time there was a monk at Hwangnyong Monastery who was over ninety years old and he said, "I once heard of the treasured belt. It was worn by Great King Chinp'yŏng. It was handed down from many generations and stored in the Southern Warehouse." The King, accordingly, ordered the warehouse to be opened but they were unable to find it. Then on another day they held a [Buddhist] service and later they could find it. The belt, adorned with gold and jade, was very long and not what an ordinary person could wear.[27]

| Commentary | In ancient times sitting in the Mingtang,[28] holding the inherited imperial seal and lining up the nine *ting* [vessels] was thought to be the grand affair of the Emperor. Lord Han [Han Yu] discussing it said, "[Bringing on] the [good] heart of heaven and man and raising the foundation of eternal peace certainly cannot be achieved by these three treasures.[29] Upholding the three treasures and making them important, is it not the verbal [adornments] of a braggart?" Moreover, what Silla calls the three treasures, is this nothing more than an artificial extravagance? How must this be a necessity for the state? Mencius said, "The

---

27 *SY* 1:25b and 3:19a also present this discussion on the three treasures. Each of the three treasures is also discussed in separate entries: the Buddha in 3:16a–17b, the pagoda in 3:17b–19b, and the belt in 1:25b. Kim Kyŏngsun gives the belt to Wang Kŏn in 937. See also *KS* 2:12b. According to *SY* the belt measured ten arm-spans in length and had sixty-two jade pendants.

28 The Hall of Rites was the hall from which China's ancient kings conducted ancestral rites and also the place where the officials and lords of the early kingdoms met. See *AKS* 3:374–5, n. 60.

29 Lord Han refers to Tang scholar Han Yu. See *AKS* 3:375, n. 63. The three vessels means the *Myŏngdang* (Hall of Rites), *okchae* (seal of state), and nine *chong* (administrations).

The **Silla Annals** of the **Samguk Sagi**

princes' treasures are three: land, people, and government." The *Chushu* said,[30] "The state of Chu has nothing it considers a treasure except only what is good it considers a treasure." If this comes from within, it is sufficient to bring good to one state. To extend it to the outside, it is sufficient to benefit the world, and, besides this, what can be said about treasures? [Our] T'aejo heard of this conversation among the people of Silla and only asked about it, but did not consider it to be of value.[31]

Second month. The Talgo people, *pyŏlbu,* [a part] of the Malgal, came pillaging the northern frontier. At that time T'aejo's General Kyŏngwŏn, garrisoned in Sak-chu, led his cavalry attacking and greatly defeating them so that not a single horse escaped. The King was pleased and sent envoys conveying a letter of thanks to T'aejo.[32]

Summer, fourth month. In the capital there was a strong wind uprooting trees.

Autumn, eighth month. There were locusts and a drought.

Year six [922], spring, first month. Wŏnbong, General of Haji Fortress,[33] and Sunsik, General of Myŏng-ju Fortress, surrendered to T'aejo. As T'aejo valued their surrender, he raised Wŏnbong's base to be called Sun-ju and gave Sunsik the surname of Wang. This month Hong Sul, General of Chinbo Fortress, surrendered to

---

30 See *AKS* 3:375, n. 65. It notes that this quote appears to come from the *Daxue.*

31 *SY* 3:19a–b provides a slightly different interpretation, asserting that Wang Kŏn believed these treasures were somewhat like the nine sacred vessels of Zhou, which provided that kingdom with protection from outside invaders, and so withdrew his idea of taking over Silla because of the existence of these three treasures. These treasures clearly were connected with state legitimacy and seen as forces protecting the state from outside intruders.

32 See also *KS* 1:16a. This event occurred in the Anbyŏn region. Kyŏngwŏn became one of Wang Kŏn's merit subjects. Sak-chu is in modern Kangwŏn, Ch'unch'ŏn.

33 This is in Kyŏngbuk, Andong.

T'aejo.[34]

Year seven [923], autumn, seventh month. General of Myŏngji Fortress, Sŏngdal, and General of Kyŏngsan-bu, Yangmun, and others surrendered to T'aejo.[35] The King sent Attendant Gentleman of the Ministry of Granaries Kim Ak and *Noksa ch'amgun* [Registrar for the Military] Kim Yugyŏng to the Later Tang court to present local products.[36] [Later Tang Emperor] Changzong presented gifts according to rank.

Year eight [924], spring, first month. [The court] sent an envoy to the Later Tang court to present tribute. Ch'ŏn-ju *chŏltosa* [Military Commissioner] Wang Ponggyu also sent an envoy to present tribute.[37]

Summer, sixth month. [The court] sent *Chaosan dafu*[38] [Attendant Gentleman of the Ministry of Granaries] Kim Ak to Later Tang to present tribute. Changzong conferred on him the position of *Chaoyi Dafu*[39] *Si* [Honorary] *Weiweijing* [Chief Minister

---

34 *Bong* in Wŏngbong's name is written by another character in *KS* 1:16b. In 929 Wŏnbong, unable to withstand attacks from Kyŏnhwŏn, surrendered to him. Sunsik performed meritorious resistance to Kyŏnhwŏn in 935. *"Sun"* means to submit, indicating the idea of his submission. Wang is the royal surname indicating a fictive kinship with the royal family. See Cho Insŏng, "T'aebong ŭi Kungye chŏnggwŏn yŏngu," unpublished PhD dissertation, Sogang Univerity, 1990. Hong Sul, who later will occupy Ŭisŏng, is clearly a force in the area. See also Hatada Takashi, "Kōrai ōchō seiritsuki no fu to gozoku," *Hōseishi kenkyū* 10 (March 1959). Hatada places Chinbo Fortress in Kyŏngbuk, Ch'ŏngsong.

35 Myŏngji Fortress is in Kyŏnggi, P'och'ŏn, and Kyŏngsan-bu is in Kyŏngbuk, Sŏngju.

36 See also *KS* 1:17a. The name Kim Ak appears several times below and in the employ of Later Paekche and Koryŏ, although the characters differ. See Yi Kidong, "Namal Yŏch'o kŭnsi kigu wa munhwa kigu ŭi hakjang," *Kolp'um.* See also *AKS* 3:378, n. 80.

37 Ch'ŏnju appears to be another name for Kang-ju or modern Chinju. Wang Ponggyu's title appears to be a Tang title and he seems to be a regional strongman in the Chinju area, exerting considerable independence, see also Kim Sanggi, "Namal chibang kunung ŭi taejung t'onggyo," *Hwang Ŭidon,* 60–1.

38 This is a Tang honorary title at the grade rank of five lower.

39 This is a Tang honorary title at the grade rank of five upper.

The Silla Annals of the Samguk Sagi

of the Court of Imperial Regalia].

Autumn, eighth month. The King died. His posthumous title was Kyŏngmyŏng. He was buried north of Hwangbok Monastery.[40] T'aejo sent an envoy to express condolences and observe mourning services.

King Kyŏngae

King Kyŏngae was enthroned. His personal name was Wiŭng and he was the younger brother by the same mother of King Kyŏngmyŏng.

Year one [924], ninth month. [The King] sent an envoy bearing greetings to T'aejo.

Winter, tenth month. [The King] personally held services at the Singung Shrine. There was a general amnesty.

Year two [925], winter, tenth month. General of Koul-bu, Nŭngmun, surrendered to T'aejo.[41] He was commended and assured before being allowed to return. This is because his fortress was very close to the capital of Silla.[42]

Eleventh month. The Later Paekche ruler Kyŏnhwŏn sent his nephew Chinho to Koryŏ as a hostage. When the King heard this he sent an envoy to T'aejo saying, "As Kyŏnhwŏn is fickle, he has lied many times and cannot be trusted as a friend." T'aejo

---

40 According to SY 1:14b, his bones were placed west of Mount Sŏngdŭnging.
41 Koul-bu is in Kyŏngbuk, Yŏngch'ŏn. Pu is a higher unit of administration than chu or kun.
42 See See also KS 1:18b and Hatada, "Kōrai ōchō seiritsuki no fu to gozoku."

concurred.[43]

Year three [926], summer, fourth month. Chinho suddenly died.[44] Kyŏnhwŏn, believing he was [intentionally] killed by Koryŏ, in anger mobilized troops, advancing them to Ungjin. T'aejo ordered his various fortresses to guard firmly and not to go out [to fight]. The King sent an envoy saying, "Since Kyŏnhwŏn, in violation of the agreement, has mobilized his forces, Heaven will certainly not assist him. If you, great King, boldly display your power, Kyŏnhwŏn will certainly destroy himself." T'aejo addressed his envoy, "It is not that I am afraid of Kyŏnhwŏn but only that I am waiting for his evil to be complete for him to topple himself."

Year four [927], spring, first month. As T'aejo personally led the invasion of [Later] Paekche,[45] the King dispatched troops to assist.

Second month. [The court] sent Attendant Gentleman of the Ministry of Military Affairs Chang Pun and others to the Later Tang court with local products. The [Emperor] conferred on Chang Pun the title of Imperial Secretary of the Ministry of Public Works and to his deputy, Gentleman of the Interior of the Ministry of Military Affairs Pak Surhong, he conferred the title of concurrent *yushi zhongcheng* [vice censor-in-chief], and to *P'angwan* [Administrative Assistant] of the Ministry of Granaries Bureau Vice Director Yi Ch'ungsik, the post of current attendant censor.[46]

Third month. The pagoda at Hwangnyong Monastery shook,

---

43 See also *SS* 50 and *SY* 2:30b. Chinho appears to have been from Kyŏnhwŏn's wife's family and, accordingly, from the Kwangju area. Wang Kŏn also sent his nephew Wang Sin to Kyŏnhwŏn as a hostage. See *KS* 1:18b.

44 See also *KS* 1:19a. Kyŏnhwŏn killed, in retaliation, Wang Sin.

45 Wang Kŏn was in the Yongju area at this time. See *KS* 1:19b.

46 Later Chang Pun would go to China representing Koryŏ. See *AKS* 3:381–2, n. 98.

tilting toward the north. T'aejo personally led in the destruction of Kŭnam Fortress.[47] [Later] Tang Mingzong gave *Kwŏnji* [Provisional] Administrator of Kang-ju Wang Ponggyu the honorary rank of *huaihua taijiangjun* [civilizing grand general].[48]

Summer, fourth month. Administrator of Kang-ju Wang Ponggyu sent envoy Im Ŏn to Later Tang to present tribute. Mingzong summoned him to Zhongxing Hall and gave gifts.[49] Tolsan and others, four *hyang* [villages] under Kang-ju's control, all submitted to T'aejo.[50]

Autumn, ninth month. As Kyŏnhwŏn attacked our army at Koul-bu, the King asked T'aejo for help and he ordered his officers to lead 10,000 strong troops to assist. Because the relief troops had not yet arrived, Kyŏnhwŏn in the eleventh month suddenly invaded the capital. The King, Queen, and relatives of the court were on an excursion to P'osŏk-chong enjoying a banquet and, unaware that the enemy troops had intruded, they were startled and did not know where to go [to hide]. The King and Queen fled to the rear palace and the royal relatives, the court officials, and the prominent officials as well as men and women fled in all directions, hiding. Among those who were captured by the enemy, regardless of whether they were noble or humble, all were frightened and with sweat flowing down, they groveled and even though they begged to be enslaved, they could not escape. Kyŏnhwŏn set his troops free to plunder public and private property, seizing everything. He entered the palace and ordered

---

47 See *KS* 1:19b. Kŭnam Fortress is identified as Kŭnp'um Fortress and is in modern Kyŏngbuk, Mungyŏng.

48 This is a Tang honorary title at the grade rank three.

49 *KS* 1:22a says that Im Ŏn went from Koryŏ and Chinese sources claim he went from Silla. See *AKS* 3:383, n. 108.

50 See also *KS* 1:20a–b. These were in the Kyŏngnam, Namhae, region.

the close officials to look for the King. The King, his consort, and several concubines were in the rear palace and were dragged out and sent to military camps. He forced the King to commit suicide and raped the consort. He let his subordinates molest the concubines. They then enthroned the King's brother as temporary *kuksa* [preceptor of state]. He was King Kyŏngsun.[51]

King Kyŏngsun

King Kyŏngsun was enthroned. His personal name was Pu and he was a descendant of Great King Munsŏng and the son of *Ich'an* Hyojong. His mother was Queen Dowager Kyea.[52] He was chosen by Kyŏnhwŏn and enthroned. The corpse of the former King was carried and placed in state in the Sŏdang where the King, together with the various officials, wailed loudly [in mourning] and they offered the posthumous title of Kyŏngae. He was buried on South Mountain at Haemong-nyŏng [Pass]. T'aejo sent an envoy offering condolences and observing mourning services.

Year one [927], eleventh month. [The King] posthumously conferred on his father the title of Great King Sinhŭng and on his mother Great Queen Dowager.

---

51 Sin Hoch'ŏl, "Silla ŭi myŏlmang kwa Kyŏnhwŏn," *Ch'ungbuk sahak* 2 (1989) suggests that Kyŏnhwŏn's purpose was to dissolve the alliance that developed between Silla and Koryŏ, and also to restore the Silla throne to the more legitimate Kim clan. *KS* asserts that the new King Kyŏngsun was related to the former King Kyŏngae through his mother. See also Chang Tongik, "Kim Pu ŭi ch'aeksang pugo e taehan ilgoch'al," *Yŏksa kyoyuk nonjip* 3 (1982).

52 She was the daughter of King Hŏngang and became Queen Dowager after Kyŏngsun was enthroned.

Twelfth month. Kyŏnhwŏn invaded Taemok-gun, burning completely the fields and the grain stored on the open fields.[53]

Year two [928], spring, first month. The Koryŏ General Kim Sang fought with the bandit Hŭngjong of Chop'al Fortress[54] but, unable to defeat him, he died in battle.

Summer, fifth month. The Kang-ju General Yu Mun surrendered to Kyŏnhwŏn.

Sixth month. There was an earthquake.[55]

Autumn, eighth month. Kyŏnhwŏn ordered General Kwanhŭn to build a fortress at Yangsan.[56] T'aejo ordered Wang Ch'ung, the General of Myŏngji Fortress, to lead troops to attack pursuing them. Kyŏnhwŏn advanced and camped beneath Taeya Fortress and sent his troops to cut down and seize the crops in Taemok-gun.[57]

Winter, tenth month. Kyŏnhwŏn attacked and seized Mugok Fortress.[58]

Year three [929], summer, sixth month. The monk Mahura from Ch'ŏnjuk-kuk [India] reached Koryŏ.[59]

Autumn, seventh month. Kyŏnhwŏn attacked Ŭisŏng-pu Fortress.[60] The Koryŏ General Hong Sul went out to fight but could not win and died in battle. Wŏnbong, a Sun-ju general, surrendered to Kyŏnhwŏn.[61] When T'aejo heard this he was angry,

---

53 Taemok-gun is in Kyŏngbuk, Ch'ilgok. *KS* 1:21a records this as occurring in the ninth month.
54 Chop'al Fortress is in Kyŏngnam, Hapch'ŏn.
55 *KS* 1:25b situates the earthquake in Pyŏkchin-gun.
56 Yangsan is in Ch'ungbuk, Yŏngdong.
57 See also *KS* 1:25a.
58 Mugok Fortress is in Kyŏngbuk, Kunwi.
59 See also *KS* 1:26a.
60 Ŭisŏng Fortress is in Kyŏngbuk, Ŭisŏng.
61 *SS* 50 notes this occurring in the first month.

however because of Wŏnbong's former merit he forgave him and only demoted Sun-ju to a *hyŏn*.

Winter, tenth month. Kyŏnhwŏn encircled Kaŭn-hyŏn[62] but, unable to win, he withdrew.

Year four [930], spring, first month. General Sŏnp'il of Chaeam Fortress[63] surrendered to Koryŏ. T'aejo, with generous courtesy, attended him, calling him honored father. Earlier, when T'aejo was about to have friendly ties with Silla, Sŏnp'il had guided him. Now, coming to this, he surrendered. Mindful of his earlier meritorious act, and moreover because of his age, [T'aejo] gave him special favors and rewards.[64] T'aejo fought with Kyŏnhwŏn below Mount Pyŏngsan in Koch'ang-gun. In a great victory he killed and captured many. Yŏngan, Hagok, Chingmyŏng, Songsaeng, and more than thirty *kun* and *hyŏn* in succession surrendered to T'aejo.[65]

Second month. T'aejo sent an envoy to announce the victory [to Silla]. The King, in acknowledgment, sent an envoy to request a meeting [with T'aejo].

Autumn, ninth month. The villages of the *chu* and *kun* on the east coast of the kingdom all surrendered to T'aejo.

Year five [931], spring, second month. T'aejo led more than fifty horsemen. Reaching the capital he requested to meet with the King. The King, with the officialdom, went to welcome him in the suburbs and then, entering the palace, they met with each other. Sharing deep affection and courtesy, they held a banquet in Imhae

---

62 Kaŭn-hyŏn is in Kyŏngbuk, Mungyŏng.

63 Chaeam Fortress is in Kyŏngbuk, Ch'ŏngsong.

64 For Sŏnp'il's biography see *KS* 92:19b.

65 In this battle over 8,000 were killed or captured. See *KS* 1:20b. Hagok's location may be Kyŏngnam, Ulchu, although Yi Pyŏngdo, *SS* 1977 208, believes both Hagok and Chingmyŏng to be Andong. Koch'ang-gun and Yŏngan are in Andong and Songsaeng is in Ch'ŏngsong.

Hall. Mellowed by wine, the King spoke, "I have not been helped by Heaven as chaos has spread over my country. Kyŏnhwŏn's reckless conduct at will has destroyed my country. What is more pitiful than this?" With tears falling he wept ceaselessly and among his attendants there were none who did not sob. T'aejo also shed tears, consoling them. He stayed there several weeks before returning home. The King sent him off to Hyŏlsŏng Fortress and presented his cousin Yu Ryŏm as a hostage to accompany T'aejo. As the troops under T'aejo were orderly and fair without committing any misconduct, all the men and women of the capital congratulated each other saying, "Earlier, when that guy Kyŏn came, it was like meeting a cruel tiger, but now with Lord Wang, it is like seeing your parents."

Autumn, eighth month. T'aejo sent an envoy to present to the King multi-colored silk, a horse saddle, and gave to the various officials and officers silk and cloth according to rank.[66]

Year six [932], spring, first month. There was an earthquake.

Summer, fourth month. [The court] sent Attendant Gentleman of the Chancellery Office Kim Pul and deputy envoy *Sabingyŏng* [Director of the Court of State Ceremonial] Yi Yu to [Later] Tang to present tribute.

Year seven [933]. [Later] Tang [Emperor] Mingzong sent an envoy to Koryŏ with a memorial.[67]

Year eight [934], autumn, ninth month. *Argo* appeared.[68] More than thirty *kun* and *hyŏn* in the Un-ju region surrendered to

---

66 See also *KS* 2:1a–2a. T'aejo Wang Kŏn seems to have stayed in Kyŏngju two-to-three months and seems to have given, in addition to cloth, tea and incense.

67 For details of the memorial see *KS* 2:3b–6a. Later Tang enfeoffed Wang Kŏn as King of Koryŏ.

68 See *AKS* 3:388, n. 160. *Argo* is *noinsŏng* star. If the star is not seen, it supposedly is a harbinger of possible chaos.

T'aejo.[69]

Year nine [935], winter, tenth month. The King saw that the land all over the country had been taken over by others, the kingdom was weak, isolated, and unable to ensure peace. So, with his officials, he planned to take the land and surrender to T'aejo. In deliberations among the ranking officials, some approved and some disapproved [of this action]. The royal Prince declared, "A kingdom's existence certainly depends upon Heaven's will. Now, together with loyal officials and upright scholars, and rallying the people's support to stand firm, only after exhausting all means can we give up. How can we, in one day, lightly abandon to a person a thousand-year mandate?" The King said, "Isolated and in peril like this, our strength is unable to preserve [the country]. Already we can no longer be stronger or weaker and, if this leads to letting innocent people die, this is something I am unable to bear." Thereupon he had Attendant Gentleman Kim Ponghyu take a letter requesting submission to T'aejo. The Prince, weeping, bid farewell to the King and went directly to Mount Kaegol where, using a grotto for shelter, he wore hemp and ate coarse food to the end of his life.[70]

Eleventh month. T'aejo received the King's letter and sent high state councilor Wang Ch'ŏl and others to welcome him. The King led his officialdom and set off from the royal capital to submit to T'aejo. The procession of carriages filled with fragrances and adorned horses stretched for over 30 *li*.[71] The roads were crowded

---

69 The Un-ju area is in Ch'ungnam, Hongsŏng.
70 See *SY* 2:22a for a similar account. *SY* states that the Crown Prince Maŭi made these statements and the King's youngest son, Pŏmgong, who shaved his head, becoming a monk at Pŏpsu Monastery and Haein Monastery. Mount Kaegol is another name for Diamond Mountain.
71 These adjectives indicate carriages filled with beautiful women and horses loaded with treasures.

as spectators formed like a thick wall. T'aejo went out to the suburbs to provide an honor welcome and presented the King with the best mansion east of the palace. [T'aejo] also gave in marriage his oldest daughter Princess Nangnang to the [former King].[72]

Twelfth month. [Kim Pu] was enfeofed Lord Chŏngsŭng, ranking him above the Crown Prince, and given a stipend of 1,000 *sŏk* [of rice]. [T'aejo] also gave to [Kim Pu's] attending officials and generals, and employed them. Silla was renamed Kyŏngju, making it the Lord [Chŏngsŭng's] *sigup*.[73]

Earlier, when Silla submitted, T'aejo was extremely pleased and at once treated [the King] with generous courtesy. He had a man tell him, "Now Your Majesty has given your kingdom to me, this is a great gift indeed. It is my hope that [Your Majesty] will marry into mine and we can establish the ties of father-in-law and son-in-law." Kim Pu responded, "My uncle *Chapkan* Ŏngnyŏm was Administrator of Taeya-gun and has a daughter who in both her virtue and appearance is [exceedingly] beautiful. There is no one better to be your Queen." T'aejo accordingly married her and had a son. This is [Koryŏ] Hyŏnjong's father who was posthumously enfeofed Anjong.

Coming to [Koryŏ] Kyŏngjong, Great King Hŏnhwa, he accepted Lord Chŏngsŭng's daughter as his consort, and he enfeofed Lord Chŏngsŭng as *sangboryŏng* [honored father]. In Great Song, the fourth year of Xingguo, *wuyin,* Kim Pu died.[74] His

---

72 See also *SY* 2:22a–b and *KS* 2:8b–9b. Wang Ch'ŏl was one of Wang Kŏn's meritorious officers. Kim Pu, besides marrying this daughter, also married another one of Wang Kŏn's daughters, Lady Sŏngmu, whose mother was of the Pak lineage.

73 For a discussion of *sigŭp* see Ha Hyŏngang, "Koryŏ sigŭp ko," *Yŏksa hakpo* 26 (1965).

74 See *AKS* 3:390–1, n. 163. This was 978.

posthumous title was Kyŏngsun {another source says Hyoae}. People in the country say from Sijo [the founder] to now is divided into three ages. From the start to the twenty-eighth King Chindŏk is called the Early Age. From Muyŏl to Hyegong, a period of eight kings, is called the Middle Age, and from Sŏndŏk to Kyŏngsun, a period of twenty kings, is called the Later Age.

| Commentary | Silla's Pak and Sŏk lineages each were born from eggs. The Kim lineage descended from heaven in a golden case, and some say they rode on a golden cart. These tales are too fantastic to be believed. However, among the people they have been passed on and taken to be fact.

During the period of Zhenghua,[75] our dynasty sent Minister Yi Charyang to the Song court with tribute. I, [Kim] Pusik, went to assist the envoy as a literary attache. Entering into Youshen Hall I saw a room with a statue of a female immortal. The academician of the hall, Wang Po, said, "This is your country's deity, didn't you know that?" He then spoke, "In ancient times there was a lady of the imperial household who, although [she] was without a husband, became pregnant. As people became suspicious [of this], she set herself adrift on the sea. Reaching Chinhan she gave birth to a son who became the first ruler of Haedong [Korea]. The lady became an immortal of the land and resided for a long time in Sŏndo Mountain.[76] This is her statue."[77] I also saw, in a funeral ode to the Eastern Deity Hallowed Mother written by the Great Song envoy Wang Xiang, state the phrase, "Gave birth to the wise who founded the kingdom," and I knew the Eastern Deity goddess was the Hallowed Mother of Sŏndo Mountain. However, I did not

---

75   This is the Song period, 1111–1117.
76   This is located in Kyŏngju.
77   For a similar account see *SY* 5:6a–7a.

know at what time her son became king.[78]

Now, looking at those beginnings, those who were at the top were frugal for their own sakes and liberal for others. They established offices sparingly and conducted affairs simply and with utmost sincerity served China. They sent envoys to the court passing through mountains and oceans in a ceaseless succession and always sent youth to the [Chinese] court as imperial resident guards and to enter the National University to study. Thereupon, taking on the customs of the sages and reforming the conventions of [our] backward area, it became a kingdom with propriety and principle. Moreover, relying on the august authority of the [T'ang] imperial forces, they pacified Paekche and Koguryŏ, turning those lands into our local governance [*kun* and *hyŏn*]. This can be called the zenith of [our] flourishing. Upholding the laws of the Buddha without knowing its adverse effects led the countryside to be [filled] with pagodas and shrines, causing the people to seek refuge as monks. As soldiers and peasants gradually dwindled, and the kingdom daily deteriorated, how could the nation escape from disorder and collapse?

Coming to this time [King] Kyŏngae added to this with his wild pursuits and, together with palace women and attendants, went out to enjoy P'osŏk-chong, holding a wine banquet and joyfully partying, unaware that Kyŏnhwŏn had intruded. This is no different from Han Qinhu being outside the palace gates or Zhang Lihua being in the tower.[79]

Although the final submission of [King] Kyŏngsun to T'aejo was inescapable, it is still commendable. If he had fought to death

---

78 According to *SY* 5:6a–b, her son was Hyŏkkŏse.

79 These are two incidents that brought the end of the Chen and the rise of the Sui. Han Qinhu led 500 troops to take the Chen ruler. Zhang Lihua was a favorite of the Chen ruler who diverted his attention away from government affairs.

resisting [T'aejo's] royal forces, exhausting the people's strength and reducing them to nothing, then certainly this would have destroyed the dynasty and harm would have spread to innocent people. But, not waiting for a command, he took the palace treasures and the local government [*kun* and *hyŏn*] to [T'aejo]. His merit to the court and virtue in saving people is truly great. Formerly when Qian turned over Wuyue to Song,[80] Su Zizhan [Shi] called him a loyal subject. Now Silla's merit and virtue far surpasses that of Wuyue.

Our T'aejo had many queens and consorts and his children and grandchildren were numerous. Hyŏnjong being a maternal descendant of the Silla [royal lineage] ascended the [Koryŏ] throne and all who succeeded to the throne since then have been his descendants. How can this not be repayment for this unostentatious virtue?[81]

---

80 Qian offered Wuyue land to Song. Su is Su Shi, a renowned Song scholar.

81 *SY* 2:22b–23a notes that the twelfth-century Koryŏ historian Kim Kwanŭi claims T'aejo married the daughter of one Yi Chŏngsin and from this union came the future kings of Koryŏ. Ha Hyŏngang casts doubt on the veracity of Kim Kwanŭi's records in "Koryŏ sidae ŭi yŏksa kyesŭng ŭisik," *Ihwa sahak yŏngu,* 1975.

Glossary of Titles and Offices

Note | Below are first Korean titles and offices found in *The Silla Annals* followed by a list of Chinese titles and offices found in both *The Koguryŏ Annals* and *The Silla Annals*.

• Korean Titles:

Ach'an: Sixth-degree bureaucratic rank

Agan: Sixth-degree bureaucratic rank

Ch'ach'aung: Shaman; term for early Silla rulers

Ch'aechŏnggam: Director of Adornments and Lacquer

Chaesang: Councilor of State

Ch'amgun: Military

Ch'angbu: Ministry of Granaries

Changgwan: Chief

Changsa: High Official

Chapch'an: Third-degree bureaucratic rank

Chegam: Deputy Director

Chi...sa: Administrator of ...

Chinbongsa: Royal Envoy

chingol: true bone

Chinju: Garrison Chief

Chipsabu: Chancellery Office

Chipsasa: Scribe in the Chancellor's Office

cho: grain rents

Chobu: Ministry of Taxation

Chŏltosa: Military Commissioner

chŏngbu: male adults

Ch'onggwan: Adjutant Grand Commander

Chŏnggwan: Scribal Inspector

chŏngjŏn: male adult land

Ch'onju: Village Head

Chŏnsasŏ: Office of Sacrifices

Chowi: Seventeenth-degree bureaucratic rank

chu: province

Chubu: Recorder

Chuju: Chief (first century)

Chungsi: Chief Minister

Chwa: Deputy, *also* Senior

Chwa i Pangburyŏng: Senior Minister of the Ministry of Law

Haengchwa P'yodowi Taejanggun: Acting General-in-Chief of the Left Guard of the Leopard Strategy

haenggun: field army

Hajŏngsa: Congratulatory Envoy

Hyŏllyŏng: Hyŏn Magistrate

hyŏn: county

Ibangbu: Ministry of Law

Ibŏlch'an: First-degree bureaucratic rank

Ich'ŏkch'an: Second-degree bureaucratic rank

Ilgich'an: Seventh-degree bureaucratic rank

Isagŭm: Lit. "teeth;" successor Prince

Kalmunwang: Honorary title for royal relative

Kam: Director

Kilsa: Fourteenth-degree bureaucratic rank

kolp'um: bone-rank system

Kongjangbugam: Director of the Ministry of Works

Kŏsŏgan [Chin(han)]: King; also a general term of respect for people of rank

Kukhak: National Academy

Kuksa: Preceptor of State

kun: prefecture; also military district

Kunju: Chief (first century); Military Governor

Kunsa: Army Commander

Kŭppŏlch'an: Ninth-degree bureaucratic rank

Kwidang: Noble Banner

Kwŏnji: Provisional

Kyŏng: Director

Kyŏngjŏng: Capital Banner

Maripkan: Title for early rulers of Silla

Naema (also *Nama*): Eleventh-degree bureaucratic rank
Naesŏng Sirang: Executive of Palace Administration
Nangdang: Junior Banner
Nangjung: Gentleman of the Interior
Nangnang Kungong: Duke of Lelang Commandery
nogŭp: stipend villages
Noksa: Registrar
Nugakchŏn: Water Clock Office

Ŏryongsŏng: Office of Royal Attendants

P'ajinch'an: Fourth-degree bureaucratic rank
pangni: ward
P'angwan: Administrative Assistant
Pi: Consort
Pongŏ: Chief Steward
Pŏpsa: Dharma Master
pu: district
Puguk Taejanggun: Great Bulwark General of the State
Pugun: Crown Prince
Puin: Royal Consort
Pusa: Deputy Envoy
P'yogi Changgun: General of Cavalry
Pyŏngbu: Ministry of Military Affairs
Pyŏngburyŏng: Minister of the Ministry of Military Affairs
Pyŏngsŏn: Naval

Rang: Gentleman of the Interior

Sa: Scribe
Sabingyŏng: Director of the Court of State Ceremonial
Saji: Secretary
Sajijŏl: Commissioner with Special Powers
Sajŏngbu: Office of Surveillance
Sanbaksa: Professor of Mathematics
Sangboryŏng: Honored Father
Sangdaedŭng: Extraordinary Rank One
Sangdŭng: Member of the Hwabaek council
Sangjuguk: Supreme Pillar of State

Sangmunsa: Master in Charge of Diplomatic Correspondence
Sanokkwan (chwa): Right Office (oversaw stipends and salaries)
Sasin: Mayor
sigŭp: tax village
Sijo: Founder Ancestor
Sijomyo: Dynastic Founder's Shrine
Sima: Adjutant
Sirang: Attendant Gentleman
Siwigam: Director of Royal Bodyguard
Sŏburhan: First-degree bureaucratic rank
Sŏdang: Oath Banner
Sogam: Junior Director
sogyŏng: minor capital
Sŏnbusŏ: Office of Shipping
Sŏngju: Fortress Commander; Castle Lord (after 900)
Sonyŏngamjŏn: Office of Youth Management
Soo: Sixteenth-degree bureaucratic rank
Sosa: Thirteenth-degree bureaucratic rank
Sukwi: Imperial Resident Guard
Sŭng: Deputy
Sŭngbu: Ministry of Transportation

Tae chaesang: High State Councilor
Taebi: Royal Consort Dowager
Taebo: Silla title
Taeach'an: Fifth-degree bureaucratic rank
Taedang: Grand Banner
Taedŏk: Prestige title given to monks
Taedodok Kyerimju Chegunsa: Commander-in-Chief of Kyerim Prefecture and its Various Military Commissioners
Taegam: Director
Taehak: Confucian College
Taejanggun: Grand Generals
Taenaema (also *Taenama*): Tenth-degree bureaucratic rank
Taeo: Fifteenth-degree bureaucratic rank
Taesa: Grand Secretary; Commissioner; Fortress Commander
Taesin: Leading Minister
Taesŏsŏng: Central Secretariat
T'aesu: Chief Magistrate

Taewanghu: Queen Dowager

Tangju: Chief

Todok: Governor (prior to 672, commander-in chief; after that date, governor-general)

Togwan: Area Commander-in-Chief

T'ongmun paksa: Master in Charge of Diplomatic Correspondence

Ŭibaksa: Professor of Medicine

Ŭibangbu: Ministry of Law

Umsŏngsŏ: Office of Music

Umuwi: Right Militant Guard

ŭp: town

Usang: Junior Minister

Wangbi: Royal Consort

Wangdaehu: Queen Dowager

Wanghu: Queen

Wihwabu: Ministry of Personnel Affairs

Wiwidaejanggun: General-in-Chief of the Awesome Guard

Wŏnoerang: Vice Director

Yebu: Ministry of Rites

Yegungjŏn: Office of Palace Management

Yejakpu (chŏn): Department of Buildings and Maintenance

Yuktup'um: Head-rank six

Yullyŏng Paksa: Professor of Laws

• Chinese Titles:

Andong jiangjun: General Pacifying the East [Andong]

Anfu dashi: Pacification Commander-in-Chief

Beijiang: Adjunct Commander

Bingbu shilang: Vice Minister of the Ministry of War

Bingfu: Minister of War

Bishujian: Director of Royal Palace Library

Cangbu: Granaries Bureau

Chaosan dafu: Grand Master for Closing Court
Chaoxian junwang: Chaoxian Commandery Prince
Chegi dajiangjun: Great General of Horse and Chariot
Cheji jiangjun: General of Chariot and Horse
Chifang: Bureau of Operations
Chijieh : Commissioned with Special Powers
Chishi: Appointed Emissary
Cishi: Regional Chief or Prefect

Daifujing: Chamberlain for the Palace Reserves
Daijiangjun: Grand General
Dajiangjun: Generalissimo for the Eastern Expedition
Daliqing: Minister of the Court of Judicial Review
Dashijia: Chamberlain of the Ministry of Husbandry
Dazongguan: Grand Commandant
Dianzhong jiangjun: General of the Palace
Dongyi duhu: Protector-General of the Eastern Tributaries
Dudu: Commander-in-Chief
Dudu liaohaiju junshi: Commander-in-Chief of the Liao Region
Dudufu: Area Command
Duhufu: Protectorate General
Duwei: Garrison Commander

Fudazongguan: Assistant Commander-in-Chief
Fujun dajiangjun: Great General of the Pacification Army
Fuzongguan: Assistant Area Commander-in-Chief

Gongpu shangsu: Minister of Works
Guanglu daifu: Grand Master for Splendid Happiness
Guoyi duwei (or *Guoyi*): Vice-Commandant of one of the Assault-resisting
               Garrisons

Hongluqing: Chief Minister of the Court of State Ceremonial
Honglusi: Court of State Ceremonial
Hou-wei: Reserve Guards
Huben langjiang: Gentleman Brave as a Tiger
Hudongyi: Protector of the Eastern Tributaries

Jia sanji changshi: Honorary Cavalry Attendant-in-Ordinary

Jiangjun: General

jianjiao: acting

Jiangzuo jiang: Chamberlain for the Palace Buildings

Jia sangji changshi: Honorary Cavalier Attendant-in-Ordinary

Jiedushi: Military Commission

Juanliangshi: Provision Transport Commissioners

Jungong: Commandery Duke

Junshi: Commander-in-Chief

Junxian: Administrative structure

Junwang: Commander Prince

Kaifuyitongsansi: Commander Unequalled in Honor

Kaiguogong: Dynasty-founding Duke

Kong: Duke

Kuishushi: Commissioner of Provisions and Transport

Langjiang: Vice Commandant

Langzhong: Director

Liaodongjun kaiguo gong: Dynasty-founding Duke of the Liaodong Commandery

Liaohaiju junshi: Commander-in-Chief of the Liao Region

ling: concurrent

Lingdong: General Pacifying the East [Lingdong]

Linghu dongyi: Protector of the Eastern Tributaries

Linghu dongyi zhongliangjiang: Concurrent Protector of the Eastern Tributaries and Leader of the Court Gentlemen

Lingping erzhou: Arbiter of the Two Provinces

Lingzuo youfu: Palace Military Headquarters

Nangnangkong: Duke of Lelang

Ningdong jiangjun: General Pacifying the East [Ningdong]

Piaoqi dajiangjun: Grand General of the Cavalry

Pijiang: Assistant General

Pushe: Vice Director

Sanji changshi: Cavalier Attendant-in-Ordinary

Shangjuguo: Supreme Pillar of State

Shang kaifu yitong sansi: Commander Unequaled in Honor (superior)

Shangshu: Imperial Secretary

Shangshu qibulang: Director of the Ministry of Works of the Department of State Affairs

Shangshu youcheng: Assistant Director of the Right of the Department of State Affairs

Shaochangbo: Junior Executive Attendant

Shaofujian: Director of Imperial Manufactures

Shaoqing: Vice Minister

she: acting

shi: probationary

Shichijie: Commissioner with Special Powers

Shiyushi: Attendant Censor

Shizhong: Palace Attendant

Sifeng: Board of Honors

Sikong: Minister of Works

Silie: Minister of Personnel

Sima: Adjutant

Sinongcheng: Assistant Minister of the Court of National Granaries

Sinongqing: Chief Minister of the Court of National Granaries

Siping tai changpo: Grand Executive Attendant of the Ministry of Works

Sizai shaoqing: Vice Minister of the Court of Imperial Entertainments

Taichangcheng: Aide for Ceremonials

Taifu: Grand Mentor

Taishuo: Governor

Taiwei: Grand Guardian

Taizi: Heir Apparent

Taizitaibao: Grand Guardian of the Heir Apparent

Tejin liaodong dudu: Lord Specially Advanced Commander-in-Chief

Tun-wei: Encampment Guards

Weifushi: Commissioner of Pacification

Wei-wei: Awesome Guards

Weiwei qing: Chief Minister of the Court of Imperial Regalia

Wu-wei: Militant Guards

Xianling: District Chief

Xiang: Councilor

Xiao-ji wei (also *Xiao-wei*)*:* Courageous Cavalry Guards

Xiaowei: Concurrent Commandant

The **Silla Annals** of the **Samguk Sagi**

Xingjun dazongguan jian anfudashi: Expeditionary Commander-in-Chief and Pacification Commissioner-in-Chief

Xingjun guanji tongshishiren: Acting Secretarial Receptionist of the Expeditionary Army

Xingjun zongguan: Expeditionary Commander

Xingpu shangshu: Minister of the Ministry of Justice

Xingzhun: Adjutant

Xuantu jungong: Xuantu (Hyŏndo) Commandery Duke

Yezhe pushe: Receptionist Vice Director

Yingping erzhou: Arbiter of the Two Provinces

Yingzhou cizhi: Regional Chief of Yingzhou

Yinqing guanglu dafu: Grand Master of Imperial Entertainments with Silver Seal and Blue Ribbon

Yi-wei: Standby Guards

Youji jiangjun: Mobile Corps Commander

Youlingjun zhonglangjiang: Commandant of the Right Metropolitan Guard

Youtunwei: Right Encampment Guards

Youwei jiangjun: General of the Right Guard

Youxiang: Director of the Secretariat

You-wei: Protective Guards

Youyiwei: Right Standby Guards

Youyouwei: Right Protective Guards

Youwuhouwei: Right Militant Reserve Guards

Yuanshuai: Marshal

Yuanwai: Supernumery

Yuanwai Sanjishilang: Supernumerary Gentleman Cavalier Attendant

Yuanwailang: Vice Director

Yuanwai sanji shilang: Supernumerary Gentleman Cavalier Attendant

Yuanwai tongzheng: Grand Executive Attendant of the Ministry of Works as a Supernumerary and Supplemental Official

Yunhui: Cloud-like Flags

Yushi zhongcheng : Vice Censor-in-Chief

Yuying: Imperial Command

Zanshandafu: Grand Master Admonisher

Zhangshi: Administrator, Aide

Zhangshi zuo lingzuoyoufu: Aide of the Left Palace Military Headquarters

Zhanshi zuoweishuai: Left Defense Guard Commandant of the Household of the

Heir Apparent

Zhechongfu: Assault-resisting Garrison

Zhengdong dajiangjun: Generalissimo for the Eastern Expedition

Zhengdong jiangjun: East-attacking General

Zhengqing: Chief Minister

Zhenshoshi: Grand Defender

Zhifang langzhong: Director of the Bureau of Operations

Zhongliangjiang: Leader of the Court Gentlemen

Zhonghu: Mentor

Zhongshushengling: Director of the Secretariat

Zhongshusheng shihong: Director of the Chancellery

Zhongwei: Commander-in-Ordinary

Zhuguo: Pillar of State

Zhunshi: Military Commander

Zongcheng: Prince of State

Zongcheng guowang: Loyal Sincerity; True Loyalty

Zongguan: Commander

Zuoguanglu dafu: Left Grand Master of Splendid Happiness

Zuojiang: Left Leader

Zuoshuzi: Grandee

Zuowei zhonglangjiang: Commandant of the Left Soaring Hawk Guard

Zuowuwei: Left Militant Guards

Zuowuwei jiangjun: General of the Left Militant Guard

Zuoxiang: Left Administrator

Zuoxiaowei: Left Courageous Guards

Zuoxiaowei dajiangjun: General-in-Chief of the Left Courageous Guard

Zuoyiwei: Left Standby Guards

Zuozhangshi: Senior Administrator

Weights and Measures

Chang [Chinese: *Zhang*] approximately 10 *ch'ŏk*.

Chi [Chinese] approximately 36 centimeters (14 inches)

Chih see *Ch'ŏk*

Ch'ing approximately 9 kilograms (19.8 pounds)

Ch'ŏk prior to Tang (seventh century), approximately 24 centimeters (approximately 9.5 inches), and from Tang forward, approximately 30.5 centimeters (12 inches).

Ch'on one tenth of a *ch'ŏk*, from Tang (seventh century) forward, approximately 3 centimeters (somewhat more than 1 inch)

Chun approximately 15 kilograms (33 pounds)

Hu approximately 44 liters (40 quarts-US dry; 10 gallons-US dry; 5 pecks-US; 1.25 bushels-US)

Kŭn approximately 600 grams (1.3 pounds)

Kyŏl land measurement of apprimately 8,025 square meters (9,600 square yards)

Kyŏng approximately 6.1 hectares (15.1 acres)

Li approximately .75 kilometer (.5 mile)

P'il bolt (of cloth); as of 665 1 bolt is 2 *ch'ŏk* (61 centimeters/24 inches) wide and 7 *po* (paces; prior to Tang [seventh century], approximately 10 meters/32.8 feet) long

Po one pace; prior to Tang (seventh century), 1 *po* was about 6 *ch'ŏk*—with 1 *ch'ŏk* approximately 24 centimeters (approximately 9.5 inches), so 1 *po* was approximately 1.44 meters (approximately 4.7 feet). From Tang forward, 1 *po* equalled 5 *ch'ŏk*—with 1 *ch'ŏk* approximately 30.5 centimeters (12 inches), so 1 *po* was approximately 1.53 meters (5 feet).

P'un approximately 37.5 grams (1.3 ounces); "pennyweight"

Ryang [Chinese: *Liang* or *Tael*] approximately 28.4 grams (1 ounce)

Shi see *Sŏk*

Sim approximately 2.03 meters (80 inches)

Sŏk [Chinese: *Shi* or *Tan*] ("stone"): approximately 60.5 kilograms (133 pounds)

Sŏm approximately 61 liters (55.4 quarts-US dry; 13.8 gallons-US dry; 6.9 pecks-US; 1.73 bushels-US)

Sŭng cloth measurement, 80-warp thread equals one *sung;* for a second meaning, *Sŭng:* approximately 0.52 liters or 1 US pint (dry); 10 *sŭng* is equal to 1 *tu.*

Tan see *Sŏk*

Tu [Chinese: *Tou*] approximately 5.2 liters (316 cubic inches); while often translated as "peck," *tu* is approximately .6 US peck.

Tuan bolts (of cloth)

Bibliography

English language sources:

Best, Jonathan W., *A History of the Early Korean Kingdom of Paekche,* Cambridge, MA: Harvard University Asia Center, 2006.

Best, Jonathan W., "The *Samguk sagi*'s Anomalous Reference to the Japanese Queen Himiko," *Proceedings of the 10ᵗʰ ISKS International Conference on Korean Studies* 73–7.

Feng Yu-lan, *A Short History of Chinese Philosophy,* New York: Free Press, 1960.

Hucker, Charles O., *A Dictionary of Official Titles in Imperial China,* Palo Alto, CA: Stanford University Press, 1985.

Jamieson, John C., "The Samguk Sagi and the Unification Wars," unpublished PhD dissertation, University of California, Berkeley, 1969.

Kang, Hugh H.W., "The Development of the Korean Ruling Class from Late Silla to Early Koryŏ," unpublished PhD dissertation, University of Washington, 1964.

Kang, Hugh H.W., "The First Succession Struggle of Koryŏ in 945: A Reinterpretation," *The Journal of Asian Studies* 36:3 (May 1977).

Lee Ki-baik (Yi Kibaek), translated by Edward W. Wagner with Edward J. Shultz. *A New History of Korea,* Cambridge, MA: Harvard University Press, 1984 .

Lee Kidong (Yi Kidong), "The Indigenous Religions of Silla: Their Diversity and Durability," *Korean Studies* 28 (2004).

Lee, Peter H., trans., *Lives of Eminent Korean Monks: The Haedong Kosŭng Chon,* Cambridge, MA: Harvard University Press, 1969.

Lee, Peter H., ed., *Sourcebook of Korean Civilization,* vol. 1, New York: Columbia University Press, 1993.

Lee, Peter H., and Wm. Theodore de Bary, eds., *Sources of Korean Tradition,* New

York: Columbia University Press, 1997.

Legge, James, trans., *Li Chi: Book of Rites,* New Hyde Park, NY: University Books, 1967.

Lippiello, Tiziana, *Auspicious Omens and Miracles in Ancient China: Han, Three Kingdoms, and Six Dynasties,* Mounumenta Serica Institute, Nettetal, Germany: Steyler Verlag, 2001.

McBride, Richard D. II, "Silla Buddhism and the Hwarang Segi Manuscripts," *Korean Studies* 31 (2007).

Park Sungnae, "Portentography in Korea," *Journal of Social Sciences and Humanities* 46 (1977).

Reischauer, Edwin O., *Ennin's Travels in T'ang China,* New York: Ronald Press, 1955.

Rogers, Michael C., "The Thanatochronology of Some Kings of Silla," *Monumenta Serica* 29 (1960).

Schafer, Edward H., *The Golden Peaches of Samarkand: A Study of T'ang Exotics,* Berkeley: University of California Press, 1963.

Sima Qian, and James Legge, trans., *Shiji* (*Records of the Historian*).

Vermeersch, Sem, *The Power of the Buddhas,* Cambridge, MA: Harvard University Asia Center, 2008.

Waley, Arthur, *The Analects,* New York: Vintage Books, 1989.

Waley, Arthur, *Book of Songs,* New York: Grove Press, 1987.

Watson, Burton, *Records of the Grand Historian,* New York: Columbia University Press, 1990.

Primary Sources:

Academy of Korean Studies, trans., *Samguk Sagi,* Seoul: Choun munhasa, 1996.

An Chŏngbok, *Tongsa kangmok,* 1778.

Cefu yuangui.

Ch'oe Ch'iwŏn, *Kyewŏn P'ilgyŏng chip*, ca. 885.

Ch'oe Ch'iwŏn, *Sasan pimyŏng.*

Ch'oe Ch'iwŏn, "Silla Wang Yŏ Tang Kangsŏ Kodaebu Sangjang," *Tongmunsŏn* 47.

Chŏng Yagyong, *Pyŏnjin Pyŏlgo.*

Daodejing.

Hou Hanshu.

Inoue Hideo, trans., *Sankuo shiki* (*Samguk sagi*), Tokyo: Heibonsha, 1980.

Iryon, *Samguk Yusa* (*The Memorabilia of the Three Kingdoms*), Seoul: Minjok munhwa ch'ujinhoe, 1973.

Jiu Tangshu.

Koryŏsa, Yonsei edition, Seoul: Kyŏngin, 1972.

Koryŏsa chŏryo, Hōsa bunko edition, Tokyo: Gakushuin, 1960.

Nihon Shoki.

Pak, M.N., and L.R. Kontsevich, trans., *Samkuk Sagi.* Moscow: Izd-vo vostochnoi litry, 1959.

Samguksa chŏryo.

Samguk sagi, Hanguk Kojŏn Ch'ongsŏ edition, Seoul: Minjok munhwa ch'ujinhoe, 1973.

Samguk sagi, P'yŏngyang: Kojŏn yŏnguso, 1958–9.

Sanguoji.

Shiji (*Records of the Historians*).

Shoku Nihongi.

Shujing (*Classic of Documents*).

Sinjŭng Tongguk yŏji sŭngnam (1530), Kojŏn kugyok edition, Seoul, 1964.

Tongmunsŏn (1478), Seoul: Taehan kongnonsa, 1970.

Xin Tangshu.

Yi Chaeho, trans., *Samguk sagi,* Seoul: Kwangsin, 1989.

Yi Pyŏngdo, trans., *Samguk sagi,* Seoul: Ulyu munhwasa, 1977.

Yi Sŭnghyu, *Chewang ungi (Rhymed Prose of the Imperial Ruler).* 1287.

Yijing.

Zizhi Tongjian, Beijing: Gaige, 1991.

Secondary Sources:

Chang Tongik, "Kim Pu ŭi ch'aeksang pugo e taehan ilgoch'al," *Yŏksa kyoyuk nonjip* 3 (1982).

Cho Insŏng, "Kwanggaet'o wangnangbi t'onghae pon Koguryŏ ŭi sumyoje." *Hanguksa simin kangchwa* 3 (1988).

Cho Insŏng, "T'aebong ŭi Kungye chŏnggwŏn yŏngu," unpublished PhD dissertation, Sogang University, 1990.

Ch'oe Chaesŏk, *Hanguk kodae sa yŏngu,* Seoul: Ilchisa, 1987.

Ch'oe Kŭnyŏng, *T'ongil Silla sidae ŭi chibang seryŏk yŏngu,* Seoul: Sinsowon, 1990.

Ch'oe Kwangsik, *Kodae Hanguk ŭi kukka wa chesa,* Seoul: Hangilsa, 1994.

Ch'oe Kwangsik, "Samguk Sagi sojae nogu ŭi sŏnggyŏk," *Sach'ong* 25 (1981).

Ch'oe Kyŏngsuk, "Ch'oe Ch'iwŏn yŏngu," *Pusan sahak* 5 (1981).

Ch'oe Pyŏnghŏn, "Silla hadae sahoe ŭi tongyo," *Hanguksa* 3, Seoul: P'yŏnch'an wiwŏnhoe, 1993.

Ch'oe Pyŏnghŏn, "Silla hadae sŏnjong kusanp'a ŭi sŏngnip," *Hanguksa yŏngu* 7 (1972).

Ch'oe Pyŏnghŏn, "Sillamal Kimhae chibang ŭi hojok seryŏk kwa sŏnjong,"

Hanguksaron 4 (1978).

Ch'oe Wŏnjik, "Silla hadae ŭi Haeinsa wa hwaŏmjong," *Hanguksa yŏngu* 49 (1985).

Chŏng Kubok, "Koryŏ sidae sahaksa yŏngu," unpublished PhD dissertation, Sŏgang University, 1985.

Chŏng Kubok, "Samguk sagi ŭi wŏnjŏn ch'aryŏ," in *Samguk sagi ŭi wŏnjŏn kŏmt'o,* Sŏngnam: Hanguk chŏngsin munhwa yŏnguwŏn, 1995.

Chŏng Yŏngho, "Silla Kwanmunsŏng e taehan soso," *Komunhwa* 5 (1977).

Ch'ŏn Kwanu, *Ko Chosŏnsa: Samhansa yŏngu,* Seoul: Ilchokak, 1989.

Chŏn Tŏkjae, "Sa-yuk segi nongŏp saengsallyŏk ŭi paltal kwa sahoe pyŏndong," *Yŏksa wa hyŏnsil* 4 (1990).

Chu Podon, "Silla chunggo ŭi chibang t'ongch'i chojik e taehayŏ," *Hanguksa yŏngu* 23 (1979).

Fujita Ryūsaku, "Shiragi kyūshū gokyō kō," *Chōsengaku ronkō* (1963).

Ha Hyŏngang. "Koryŏ sidae ŭi yŏksa kyesŭng ŭisik," *Ihwa sahak yŏngu* (1975).

Ha Hyŏngang, "Koryŏ sigŭp ko," *Yŏksa hakpo* 26 (1965).

Hamada Kōsaku, "Shiragi no gokugaku to kentō ryugakusei," *Kumatsushū* 2 (1980).

Hamada Kōsaku, "Shiragi no seitoku daiō shinshō to chūdai no ōshitsu," *Kumatsushū* 3 (1980).

Hatada Takashi, "Kōrai ōchō seiritsuki no fu to gozoku," *Hōseishi kenkyū* 10 (March 1959).

Hatada Takashi, "Sangoku shiki Shiragi hongi ni mieru Wa," *Nihon bunka to Chōsen* (1975).

Hatada Takashi, "Shiragi no sonraku," *Rekishigaku kenkyū* 227 (1959).

Ikeuchi Hiroshi, "Sinkō-ō no boshi junkyōhi to tōhokukyō," *Chōsen koseki chōsa tokubetsu hōkoku* 6 (1929).

Imanishi Ryū, *Shiragishi kenkyū,* Tokyo, 1933.

Im Pyŏngt'ae, "Silla sogyŏnggo," *Yŏksa hakpo* 35–6 (1967).

Inoue Hideo, "Shiragi bokushioki no seiritsu," *Shiragi kiso kenkyū* (1974).

Inoue Hideo, "Shiragi seiji taisei no hensen katei," *Kodaishi kōza* 4 (1962).

Kang Chinch'ŏl, "Silla ŭi nogŭp e taehayŏ," in *Yi Hongjik paksa hoegap kinyŏm Hanguk sahak nonch'ong,* Seoul: Singu munhwasa, 1969.

Kang Inyŏng, *Silla onŭng,* Sŏngnam: Hanguk chŏngsin munhwa yŏnguso, 1990.

Kim Sanghyŏn, "Chip'il kŭmgwangmyŏng ch'oesŭng wanggyŏngso-kŭmgwangmyŏng ch'oesŭng wanggyŏng hyŏnch'u soin wŏnhyoso ŭi chipp'yŏn," *Tongyanghak* 24 (1994).

Kang Sŏngwŏn, "Silla sidae panyŏk ŭi yŏksajŏk sŏnggyŏk," *Hanguksa yŏn'gu* 43 (1983).

Kim Ch'ŏlchun, "Husamguk sidae chibae seryŏk ŭi sŏnggyŏk," in *Hangguk kodae sahoe yŏngu,* Seoul: Seoul National University Press, 1975.

Kim Ch'ŏlchun, "Koryŏ chunggi ŭi munhwa ŭisik kwa sahak sŏnggyŏk," *Hanguksa yŏngu* 9 (1973).

Kim Ch'ŏlchun, "Silla kwijok seryŏk ŭi kiban," *Inmun kwahak* 7 (1962).

Kim Ch'ŏlchun, "Silla sangdae sahoe ŭi Dual Organization," *Yŏksa hakpo* 1–2 (1952).

Kim Chŏnghak, "Anapchi chapki," *Pangmulgwan sinmun* 130 (1982).

Kim Chŏngsuk, "Kim Chuwŏn segye ŭi sŏngnip kwa p'yŏngchŏngchan'an," *Paeksan hakpo* 28.

Kim Chŏngsuk, "Silla munhwa e nat'anan tongmul ŭi sangjing," *Silla munhwa* 7 (1990).

Kim Kaptong, "Koryŏ kŏngukki ŭi ch'ŏngju seryŏk kwa Wang Kŏn," *Hanguksa yŏngu* 48 (1985).

Kim Kaptong, *Namal yŏch'o ŭi hojok kwa sahoe pyŏndong yŏngu.* Seoul: Kodae minjok munhwa, 1990.

Kim Kihŭng, "Samguk mit t'ong'il Silla-gi seje ŭi yŏngu," *Yŏksa pip'yŏngsa* (1999).

Kim Sanggi, "Kyŏnhwŏn ŭi kahyang e taehayŏ," *Tongbangsa nonch'ong* (1974).

Kim Sanggi, "Namal chibang kunung ŭi taejung t'onggyo," *Hwang Ŭidon sŏnsaeng kohŭi kinyŏm sahak nonch'ong,* Seoul: Tongguk University Press, 1960.

Kim Sut'ae, "Silla chungdae chŏnche wanggwŏn kwa chingol kwijok," unpublished PhD dissertation, Sogang University, 1990.

Kim Sut'ae, "Silla sinmunwangdae chŏnjaewanggwŏn ŭi hangnipgwa Kim Hŭmdol ran," *Hanguk munhwa* 9 (1992).

Kim T'aekkyun, "Ch'unch'ŏn Maekkuk sŏl e kwanhan yŏngu," *Paeksan hakpo* 30–1 (1985).

Kim T'aesik, "Haman Anŭm-guk ŭi sŏngjang kwa pyŏnjŏn," *Hanguk sahak yŏngu* 86 (1994).

Kim T'aesik, *Kaya yŏnmaengsa,* Seoul: Ilchokak, 1993.

Kim T'aesik, "Paekche ŭi Kaya chiyŏk kwangyesa," in *Paekche ŭi chungang kwa chibang.* Taejŏn: Ch'ungnam University, 1997.

Kim T'aeshik, "Tae Kaya ŭi segye wa tosŏlji." *Chindan hakpo* 81 (1996).

Kim Tujin, "Silla Sŏk T'arhae sinhwa ŭi sŏngnip kiban," *Hangukhak nonch'ong* 8 (1980).

Kim Wŏryong, "Samguk sidae ŭi kaesi e kwanhan ilgoch'al," *Tonga yŏngu* 7 (1967).

Kim Wŏryong, "Saro yukch'on kwa Kyŏngju kobun," *Yŏksa hakpo* 70 (1976).

Kim Yongsŏp, "Chŏngŭndae ŭi t'oji chedo," *Hangukhak immun,* Seoul: Haksulwŏn, 1983.

Kimura Makoto, "Shiragi gun kansei no kakuritsu katei to sonshisei," *Chōsenshi kenkyūkai ronbunshū* 13 (1976).

Kimura Makoto, "Shiragi no rokuyusei to sonraku kōzō," *Rekishigaku kenkyū,* Bessatsu: 1979.

Kuksa taesajŏn, Seoul: Ch'ŏnga Publishing, 1983.

Kwŏn Chuhyŏn, "Ana Kaya sŏngip kwa palchŏn," *Kyemyŏng sahak* 4 (1993).

Maema Kōsaku, "Shiragi ō no seji to kimei ni tsuite," *Tōyō gakuhō* 15:2 (1925).

Mishina Shoei, *Sangoku yūshi kōchō*, Tokyo, 1975.

No T'aedon, "P'ilsabon Hwarang segi ŭi saryojŏk kach'e," *Yŏksa hakpo* 147 (1995).

No T'aedon, "Samguk sidae pu e kwanhan yŏngu," *Hanguksaron* 2 (1975).

Nomura Tadao, "Shōsōin yori hakken seru Shiragi no minsei bunsho ni tsuite," *Shigaku zasshi* 62:4 (1953).

Paek Namun, *Chosŏn sahoe kyŏngjesa*, Tokyo: Kaejosa, 1933.

Pak Chonggŭn, "Ch'oe Ch'iwŏn ŭi chŏngch'i inyŏm kwa chonggyo kwan," *Yŏksa kyoyuk nonjip* 3 (1982).

Pak Pangyong, "Silla kwanmunsŏng ŭi kŭmsŏngmun koch'al," *Misul charyo* 31 (1982).

Pak Sihyŏng, *Chosŏn t'oji chedosa*, part 1, P'yŏngyang: Kwahagwŏn, 1960.

Pak Sihyŏng, *Chosŏn t'oji chedosa*, part 2, P'yŏngyang: Kwahagwŏn, 1961.

Pyŏn T'aesŏp, "Silla kwandŭng ŭi sŏnggyŏk," *Yŏksa kyoyuk* 1 (1956).

Sin Hoch'ŏl, "Hu Paekche ŭi chibae seryŏk e taehan punsŏk," *Yi Pyŏngdo paksa kinyŏm.* Seoul: Ilchokak, 1991.

Sin Hoch'ŏl, "Silla ŭi myŏlmang kwa Kyŏn Hwŏn," *Ch'ungbuk sahak* 2 (1989).

Sin Hyŏngsik, *Hanguk kodaesa ŭi Silla yŏngu*, Seoul: Ilchokak, 1984.

Sin Hyŏngsik, "Silla pyŏngburyŏng ko," *Yŏksa hakpo* 61 (1974).

Sin Hyŏngsik, "Silla ŭi tae Tang kyosŏpsang e nat'anan sukwi e taehan ilgoch'al," *Yŏksa kyoyuk* 9 (October 1966).

Sin Hyŏngsik, "Sukwi haksaeng ko," *Yŏksa kyoyuk* 11–2 (1969).

Suematsu Yasukazu, "Kansanji miroku sonzō oyobi Amida butsu no kakōkōki," *Shiragishi no shomondai* (1954).

Suematsu Yasukazu, "Kyū sangoku shiki to Sangoku shiki," *Seikyu shiso* 2 (1966).

Suematsu Yasukazu, *Shiragishi no shomondai,* 36, Tokyo: The Tōyō Bunko Publications, 1954.

Takeda Yukio, "Shiragi koppinsei no saikentō," *Tōyō bunka kenkyū* 67 (1975).

Takeda Yukio, "Shiragi no rokubusei to sonraku kōzō," *Rekishigaku kenkyū,* Bessatsu, 1979.

Yi Chonguk, "Namsan sinsŏngp'irul taehae pon Silla ŭi chibang t'ongch'i cheje," *Yŏksa hakpo* 64 (1974).

Yi Chonguk, "Saroguk ŭi sŏngjang kwa Chinhan," *Hanguksa yŏngu* 25 (1979).

Yi Chonguk, *Silla kukka hyŏngsŏngsa yŏngu,* Seoul: Ilchogak, 1982.

Yi Chonguk, *Silla sangdae wangwi kyesŭng yŏngu,* Taegu: Yeungnam University Press, 1980.

Yi Chonguk, "Silla sanggogi ŭi yuk ch'on kwa yuk pu," *Chintan hakpo* 49 (1980).

Yi Hyŏnhye, *Samhan sahoe hyŏngsŏng kwajŏng yŏngu.* Seoul: Ilchogak, 1984.

Yi Kangnae. "Samguk sagi wa kogi," *Yongbong nonch'ong* 17–8 (1989).

Yi Kibaek, "Kim Taemun kwa kŭ ŭi sahak," *Yŏksa hakpo* 77 (1978).

Yi Kibaek, "Kodae kukka ŭi yŏksa insik," *Hanguksaron* 6 (1979).

Yi Kibaek, "Koryŏ t'aejo-si ŭi chin," *Koryŏ pyŏngjesa yŏngu,* Seoul, 1975.

Yi Kibaek, *Silla chŏngch'i sahoesa yŏngu,* Seoul: Ilchokak, 1974.

Yi Kibaek, *Silla sasangsa yŏngu.* Seoul: Ilchokak, 1986.

Yi Kibaek, *Silla sidae ŭi kukka pulgyo wa yugyo,* Seoul: Hanguk yŏnguwŏn, 1978.

Yi Kibaek, "Uri yŏksarŭl ŏdyekye polkŏs inga?" *Samsŏng munhwa mungo* (1976).

Yi Kidong, "Chang Pogo wa kŭ ŭi haesang hwaldong," *Chang Pogo ŭi sinyŏngu* (1985).

Yi Kidong, *Hanguk kodae ŭi kukka wa sahoe,* Seoul: Ilchokak, 1985.

Yi Kidong, "Silla Hŭngdŏkwangdae ŭi chŏngch'i wa sahoe," *Kuksagwan nonch'ong* 21 (1991).

Yi Kidong, *Silla kolp 'umje sahoe wa hwarangdo*. Seoul: Ilchogak, 1984.

Yi Kyŏngsik, "Kodae-Chungse ŭi sigŭpje ŭi kuchowa chŏn'gae," *Son Pogi paksa chŏngnyŏn kinyŏm Hanguk sahak nonch 'ong*, Seoul: Chisik sanŏpsa, 1988.

Yi Mungi, "Silla siwibu ŭi sŏngnip kwa sŏnggyŏk," *Yŏksa kyoyuk nonjip* 9 (1986).

Yi Sungŏn, "Silla sidae sŏngsi choedŭk kwa kŭ ŭimi," *Hanguksaron* 6 (1980).

Yi Pyŏngdo, "Silla ŭi kiwŏn munje," *Hanguk kodaesa yŏngu*, Seoul: Pagyongsa, 1976.

Yi Pyŏngdo, *Hanguksa: Kodaep'yŏn*, Seoul: Ŭlyu munhwasa, 1959.

Yi Sŏngsi, "Shiragi 6 tang no saikentō," *Chōsen gakuhō* 92 (1979).

Yi Usŏng, "Samguk yusa sojae Ch'ŏyong sŏrhwa ŭi ilgoch'al," *Kim Chaewŏn paksa hwangap kinyŏm nonch 'ong*, Seoul, 1969.

Yi Ut'ae, "Hanguk kodae ŭi ch'ŏkto," *T'aedong kojŏn yŏngu* 1 (1984).

Yi Ut'ae, "Silla ch'on kwa ch'onju," *Hanguksaron* 7 (1981).

Yi Yongbŏm, "Ch'ŏyong sŏrhwa ŭi ilgoch'al," *Chindan hakpo* 32 (1969).

Yun Mubyŏng and Sŏng Chuyŏk, "Paekche sansŏng ŭi sindohyŏng," *Paekche yŏngu* 8 (1977).

Shultz, Edward J., "Kim Pusik kwa Samguk sagi," *Hanguksa yŏngu* 73 (June 1991).

Index

P Circle P stand for person

L Circle L for location

A

Chingnyŏ (constellation) 341

chingol (True Bone) 16, 17, 162, 165, 267, 278, 317, 407, 425

Chingong ⓟ 198, 211, 249, 250

Chingyo ⓟ 350

Chinhan 25

Chinho ⓟ 395, 396

Chinhŭm ⓟ 177, 183, 187

Chinhŭng ⓟ (King) 115, 122, 124, 128, 131, 132, 133, 139, 390

Chinji ⓟ (King) 24, 132, 133, 134, 140, 166, 257, 361

Chinjong 293, 355

Chinjŏng ⓟ 134

Chinju (garrison chief) 68, 141, 150, 168, 170, 183, 187, 207, 239, 254, 338, 391, 394, 407

Chijŭng 62, 81, 105

Chinp'yŏng ⓟ (King) 132, 133, 144, 147, 157, 166, 297, 392

Chinsŏng ⓟ (Queen) 335, 370, 375, 376, 379, 381

Chin sŏng (Saturn) 269, 357

Chinsun ⓟ 183, 197, 240

Chinwang ⓟ 176, 232

Chinwŏn ⓟ 336

Chipsabu (Chancellery Office) 164, 407

Chipsasŏng ⓟ (see Chipsabu) 309, 337, 359

Chiri (Mount) 305, 345

Chiryang ⓟ 79, 280

Chiryŏm ⓟ (see Kim Chiryŏm) 282, 284, 286

Chisang ⓟ 253

Chisŏng (Fortress) 266, 304

Chisorye ⓟ 52, 59

Chiwŏn ⓟ 13, 324

Ch'iyang (Fortress) 107

Chiyu 63

Chobu (Ministry of Taxation) 134, 301, 303, 360, 407

Chobun ⓟ (Isagŭm) 65, 69, 71, 74, 77, 80, 81

Ch'oe Ch'iwŏn ⓟ 114, 131, 325, 336, 362, 368, 370, 373, 375, 376, 379, 380, 421, 422, 426

Ch'oe Ijŏng ⓟ 342

Ch'oe Ung ⓟ 338

Chŏjok ⓟ 379

Choju ⓟ 199

Chŏkkuk ⓛ 374

Chŏksu 240

Ch'ŏlbu ⓟ 121, 122

Ch'ŏlch'ŏn ⓟ 184, 236

Ch'ŏlgwan (Fortress) 239

Ch'ŏllim (Monastery) 342

Ch'ŏlwŏn ⓛ 196, 379, 387

Ch'ŏmhae ⓟ (Isagŭm) 71, 72, 74

Chŏmnyangbu ⓟ 37

Chŏmsŏngdae ⓛ 92

constellation) 41, 197

Ch'ŏnsŏng (Fortress) 239

Chŏnyasan-gun ❶ 259

Chŏn (Yŏn) Namsan ❷ 198

Ch'op'al ❶ 48

Chop'al (Fortress) 399

Ch'ŏrya-hyŏn ❶ 349

Choryang ❷ 297, 298

Chosaeng ❷ 113

Chosŏn ❶ 14, 24, 66, 258, 259, 276, 426

Chowi 37, 408

Chowŏn (Hall) 164, 330, 367, 371

chu 7, 42, 44, 45, 53, 62, 63, 65, 106, 115, 116, 126, 132, 148, 149, 168, 190, 194, 195, 228, 237, 239, 254, 255, 256, 258, 266, 268, 269, 274, 301, 302, 308, 312, 322, 323, 335, 337, 338, 342, 346, 360, 369, 371, 376, 378, 380, 386, 395, 400, 408

Chu (Fortress) 118

Chu (State) 218, 277, 393

Chu (Term) 114

chuda 49

Ch'uhwa-gun ❶ 338

Chujae (Fortress) 141

Chujam (Fortress) 236

chuju (magistrate) 114

Chuju (chief) 42, 408

Chukchang (Tomb) 79

Chukchi ❷ 161, 164, 177, 183, 197, 205, 211

Chukchuk ❷ 151

Chuksŏng ❶ 390

Chullye (Gate) 372

Chumong ❷ 27

Ch'unbu ❷ 128

Ch'unch'ŏn ❶ 24, 38, 68, 97, 105, 158, 167, 338, 393

Chunch'ŏn ❶ 38

Ch'ungbun ❷ 327

Ch'unggong ❷ 333, 336, 337, 339, 340, 347, 348

Chunggong ❷ 332

Chunggyŏng ❷ 272, 273

Chunghŭi ❷ 327

Ch'unghun ❷ 276

Ch'unghwŏn ❷ 68

Ch'ungji ❷ 189

Chungji ❷ 174

Chungmo ❷ 206

Ch'ungnyŏm ❷ 319, 323

Chungnyŏng ❷ 60, 152, 387

Ch'ungsang ❷ 172, 176, 183

Chungsi (Chief Minister) 164, 185, 296, 408

Chungsin ❷ 183, 205, 206

Ch'ungsŭng ❷ 189

Ch'ungyŏng ❷ 334, 335

dog 143, 244, 269, 274, 279, 286, 287, 293, 297, 391

Dong Baoliang ℗ 172

dragon 25, 26, 30, 38, 60, 73, 75, 100, 106, 108, 109, 118, 125, 142, 244, 305, 370, 372

drought 33, 34, 42, 44, 46, 52, 54, 61, 62, 64, 65, 67, 73, 76, 78, 81, 82, 89, 90, 91, 96, 99, 103, 106, 108, 116, 129, 135, 139, 142, 148, 263, 267, 269, 271, 272, 273, 296, 297, 298, 308, 320, 321, 323, 324, 325, 332, 336, 337, 344, 345, 359, 374, 377, 378, 393

Duke of Lu ℗ 87

Duke of Ying 196, 198, 199, 226, 227, 230

Du Shuang ℗ 225

Dynastic Founder's Shrine 36, 41, 44, 49, 52, 59, 61, 62, 65, 66, 69, 71, 73, 76, 77, 80, 82, 88, 93, 96, 97, 100, 103, 105, 335, 410

E

earthquake 41, 46, 51, 61, 64, 69, 71, 81, 90, 93, 99, 103, 116, 123, 140, 148, 190, 194, 207, 244, 263, 269, 273, 274, 275, 276, 277, 291, 294, 295, 305, 307, 309, 310, 321, 323, 324, 329, 330, 345, 368, 369, 370, 389, 399, 401

Eastern Okchŏ ℒ 29

Eastern Palace 241, 298, 329

Eastern Sea 150, 264, 313, 372, 389

Eastern Ye ℒ 34, 51

egg 25, 39, 47, 296, 298, 404

elderly 46, 75, 80, 96, 268, 274, 281, 346

epidemic 50, 54, 61, 64, 66, 90, 102, 271, 297, 324, 356, 367, 368, 369

extraordinary rank one 121, 122, 134, 136, 149, 156, 158, 167, 169, 242, 249, 262, 263, 268, 275, 279, 296, 299, 301, 304, 305, 308, 309, 310, 312, 317, 318, 319, 320, 323, 328, 333, 336, 337, 340, 346, 348, 349, 350, 355, 359, 362, 365, 369, 370, 385, 387, 390, 391, 409

F

falcon 241, 269

famine 50, 73, 103, 116, 268, 320, 321, 324, 335, 336, 346, 356

Fengdian (Shanxi) 328

fire 51, 55, 70, 75, 104, 137, 187, 194, 201, 267, 335, 360

fish 60, 73, 90, 94, 109, 135, 150, 168, 211, 213, 218, 235, 309, 356, 362

Fitful Glitter (Mars) 241

Five Tombs 30

flood 37, 44, 48, 49, 62, 89, 101, 104, 107, 136, 168, 264, 267,

318, 335, 360, 367, 368

fog 79, 98, 108, 310, 335, 367, 370, 377

fox 66, 246, 264, 293

frogs 149

frost 51, 53, 59, 61, 65, 66, 76, 83, 96, 97, 99, 116, 139, 142, 216, 321, 324, 344, 359, 362, 386, 387, 389

Fujian ❶ 277

G

Gai Xun ❷ 312

Gaochang (Koch'ang) 151

Gao (Kan) ❷ 218

Gaozong ❷ 157, 163, 165, 169, 178, 182, 191, 195, 196, 204, 206, 214, 220, 237, 249, 256, 260

Gaozu ❷ 140, 141, 156, 160, 193, 198

granaries 34, 42, 44, 48, 68, 89, 103, 116, 154, 203, 224, 245, 268, 298, 303, 307, 310, 336, 394, 396, 407, 411, 414

Gui ❶ 243, 307

Gui Jongjing ❷ 307

Guoxie (the National University) 160

H

Haedong (Korea) 13, 90, 119, 404

Haegok ❶ 195

Haein (Monastery) 329, 381, 402

Haemong-nyŏng (pass) 398

Haeron ❷ 139, 140

Hago 29

Hagok ❷ 400

hail 46, 49, 55, 61, 66, 68, 76, 83, 97, 99, 104, 148, 275, 278, 296, 301, 308, 319, 357, 377, 387

Haji (Fortress) 393

Haju ❶ 176, 177, 183

Hallim ❷ 194

Hamhŭng ❶ 29

Han 23, 24, 27, 29, 32, 34, 51, 71, 72, 114, 121, 124, 127, 153, 156, 159, 164, 185, 198, 218, 224, 231, 237, 260, 300, 392, 405

Han Chirhŏ 159

Han China ❶ 24, 34, 377

Han China ❶ 24, 34, 377

Han Commanderies 29

Hangi ❶ 47, 49, 64, 72, 205

Hangibu ❷ (coment) 37

Hanji ❶ 144

Hansan-ju ❷ 169, 190, 199, 200, 233, 275, 302, 312, 321, 324, 326, 336, 344, 385

Han-shu 232

Kim Wŏnt'ae 🅟 267, 272

Kim Yang 🅟 347, 349, 355, 356, 358, 359

Kim Ye 🅟 367

Kim Yo 🅟 374

Kim Yŏ 🅟 357, 358

Kim Yŏkki 🅟 331, 332

Kim Yŏng 🅟 286

Kim Yonghaeng 🅟 121

Kim Yudon 🅟 229

Kim Yugyŏng 🅟 394

Kim Yukchin 🅟 332

Kim Yul 🅟 391

Kim Yunbu 🅟 342

Kim Yung 🅟 309

Kim Yusin 🅟 14, 121, 125, 142, 152, 153, 155, 158, 159, 161, 166, 167, 169, 181, 183, 185, 189, 190, 196, 197, 223, 236, 261, 270, 278, 282

King Mu 🅟 188, 191

King Sŏngdŏk 🅟 286

Kinju 🅟 200

Kirim 🅟 (Isagŭm) 80, 81

kiwŏn 128, 428

Koch'ang-gun 🅛 400

Kŏch'ilbu 🅟 123, 125, 132

Kodal (Mount) 341

Koegok (Fortress) 73, 76

Koeyang 🅟 386

kogan 126, 176, 200

Kogi 77, 144, 342, 372, 427

Koguryŏ 🅛 12, 13, 14, 15, 25, 27, 29, 34, 37, 38, 70, 72, 80, 89, 90, 92, 94, 95, 96, 97, 98, 99, 101, 102, 104, 105, 106, 107, 108, 119, 120, 123, 124, 125, 138, 141, 142, 150, 151, 152, 153, 154, 155, 156, 161, 165, 167, 175, 177, 182, 183, 186, 189, 190, 191, 192, 194, 195, 196, 197, 198, 199, 201, 204, 206, 207, 214, 226, 227, 232, 233, 237, 238, 239, 242, 250, 262, 271, 275, 281, 282, 341, 344, 405, 282

Koguryŏ Annals 12, 15, 99, 102, 104, 139, 199, 250, 407

Koho (Fortress) 141, 142

Koi (Island) 387

Kŏin 🅟 377

Kojang 🅟 (P'ojang) 152

Kŏjin 🅟 158

Kokha (winding river) 38

Kolbŏl 🅛 70

Kolchŏng 🅟 65, 69, 71

kolp'um 15, 16, 24, 87, 95, 115, 130, 156, 162, 165, 296, 330, 331, 359, 362, 379, 394, 408

Komi-hyŏn 🅛 373

Kŏmil 🅟 174

Kŏmmo 🅟 335

Kŏmul (Fortress) 188

kŏmungo 335, 373

346, 360, 369, 371, 376, 378, 379, 395, 400, 401, 405, 406, 408

Kŭnam (Fortress) 397

Kungbok ⓟ (see Chang Pogo) 344, 348, 349, 350, 355, 357, 358

Kungmo (Fortress) 204

Kungnyang ⓟ 64

Kungwan ⓟ 183, 189, 190, 198, 205, 242, 251, 252

Kungye ⓟ 262, 378, 379, 385, 386, 387, 388, 389, 390, 394

Kŭnjong ⓟ 52, 369

kunju (chief) 42, 44,

kunju (military commanders) 62

kunju (military governor) 115, 116

Kunju 116, 175, 408

kŭppŏlch'an 37, 408

Kurap-hyŏn ⓛ 320

Kurye ⓛ 102

Kusuhye ⓟ 61, 62

Kuyang (Fortress) 41, 63

Kuyul ⓟ 200

Kwach'on (Stream) 186

Kwahyŏn ⓛ 106

kwallyojŏn (emolument land) 258

Kwan (Fortress) 379

Kwanggaet'o ⓟ 89, 190

Kwanggyŏm ⓟ 76

Kwanghwa ⓟ 359, 362, 364, 366

Kwangmyŏng ⓟ 74

Kwangsŏk ⓛ 102

Kwanhŭn ⓟ 399

Kwanjang ⓟ 171, 242, 256

Kwi Banner (see also Kwidang) 197

Kwibo ⓟ 349

Kwisan ⓟ 137

Kwisŭng ⓟ 333

Kyea ⓟ 398

Kyebaek ⓟ 170, 171, 172

Kyegang ⓟ 385, 389

Kyegi ⓟ 45

Kyego ⓟ 125

Kyegŭm Banner ⓟ 175, 176, 183, 198

Kyehong ⓟ 357

Kyehŭng ⓟ 367

Kyehwa ⓟ 326, 327

Kyeo ⓟ 317

Kyerim 42, 74, 81, 121, 188, 232, 237, 262, 270, 294, 295, 312, 330, 333, 344, 356, 366, 371, 410

Kyerim chapjŏn 121

Kyerimzhou 270

Kyerip (Pass) 59

Kyet'an ⓛ 175

Kyewŏn ⓟ 13, 59, 61

Kyŏna (Fortress) 107

kyŏng (Capital) 255

Ministry of Military Affairs 118, 123, 134, 140, 182, 251, 303, 317, 324, 326, 327, 328, 333, 379, 396, 409

Ministry of Personnel Affairs (Ibu) 134, 252, 303, 411

Mirŭk (Monastery) 275

Misahŭn ⓟ 92, 96, 97, 100, 103

Misap'um ⓟ 92, 93

Misil ⓛ 115

Mo (Mount) 104, 117

Mobŏl-gun ⓛ 276

Moch'o ⓟ 321

Moch'ŏk ⓟ 173, 174, 322

Modae ⓟ 106, 107

Mojam ⓟ 204

Mokch'ul (Island) 42

Moro (Fortress) 101

Moryang ⓟ 37

Moryang-ri ⓛ 381

Morye ⓟ 119, 120

Mosan (Fortress) 63, 140

mountain slides 73, 84, 101

Mudŏk ⓟ 121, 187

Mugok (Fortress) 399

Muhol ⓟ 176

Muhyul ⓟ 37

Mujin-gun ⓛ 256

Mukhoja ⓟ 119, 120

Mullyang ⓟ 268, 269

Munch'ŏn (Stream) 239, 304

Munch'ung ⓟ 167, 168, 176, 197, 205

Munhun ⓟ 183, 185, 190, 196, 197, 239

Munhŭng ⓟ 166, 257

Munhwagwanmun ⓟ (Fortress) 339

Munjŏng ⓟ 159, 166

Munju ⓟ 102, 187

Munmok ⓟ 347

Munmu ⓟ (King) 134, 162, 249, 254, 257

Munmyŏng ⓟ 166, 181

Mullim ⓟ 275, 276

Munp'um ⓟ 176

Munsŏng ⓟ (King) 355, 356, 358, 359, 361, 362, 367, 372, 398

Munŭi ⓟ 366, 370

Munwang ⓟ 159, 160, 161, 167, 168, 176, 191

Munyŏng ⓟ 172, 183, 190, 198, 205, 253, 262

Muo ⓟ 320

Mup'yŏng (Gate) 346, 364

Muryŏk ⓟ 121, 122, 125, 126

Musan (Mount) 24, 158

mushroom 267, 269, 278

music 36, 37, 124, 125, 130, 190, 200, 256, 280, 299, 303, 305, 310, 331, 372, 411

musin 30, 37

musin ● (Kogurŏ King)   37

Musŏn ●   244

Musu ●   176

Muyŏl ● (King)   117, 140, 165, 166,
    178, 181, 191, 195, 201, 212,
    213, 214, 216, 219, 220, 257,
    260, 262, 317, 341, 342, 404

Muzong ●   337

Myŏnggi ●   339

Myŏnghak (Tower)   360

Myŏnghwal (Fortress)   24, 93, 96,
    102, 126, 137

Myŏng-ju ●   302, 378, 393

Myŏngnong ●   126

Myŏngsŏn ●   44

Myŏngwŏn ●   81

V

321, 323, 344, 347, 357, 367, 372, 373, 390

Vimala ❷ 131

W

Wa (Wae) 26, 28, 29, 33, 34, 39, 41, 42, 50, 60, 61, 64, 66, 70, 72, 78, 79, 80, 82, 83, 88, 89, 91, 92, 93, 94, 96, 98, 100, 102, 104, 105, 107, 108, 194, 207, 225, 228

Waibing ❷ 31, 32

Wangbong (River) 237

Wang Ch'ŏl ❷ 402, 403

Wang Ch'ung ❷ 399

Wanghŭng (Monastery) 175

Wangnyang (constellation) 26, 341

Wang Po ❷ 404

Wang Ponggyu ❷ 394, 397

Wang Shiyi ❷ 139

Wang Wendu ❷ 175

Wang Yi 234

Wang Xiang ❷ 404

Wansan-ju ❶ 126, 128, 254, 263, 275, 293, 378

Wasajŏng 237

Wei Zheng 143

Wen (Duke) 206, 207, 277

Wenguan cilin (see also Sogyŏng) 256

Wenzong ❷ 343, 345, 348, 355, 356

Western Capital 198

Western Country (see also India) 246

West Sea 236

Wi Dan ❷ 327

Wihong ❷ 370, 375, 376

Wihŭn ❷ 356, 358, 359

Wihwabu (see Ministry of Personnel Affairs) 134, 303, 411

Wijin ❷ 365, 369

Wi Kong ❷ 339

Wiman Chosŏn ❶ 29

Wimun ❷ 270, 271, 318

wind 17, 38, 43, 50, 62, 67, 70, 76, 83, 97, 99, 104, 108, 136, 142, 186, 217, 219, 230, 238, 263, 273, 283, 297, 300, 304, 324, 327, 335, 359, 373, 393

Winŭng ❷ 390

Wiŭng ❷ 395

Wŏlchi Palace 338

Wŏlchŏngdang ❶ 370

Wŏlmyŏng ❷ 158

Wŏlsŏng (Fortress) 40, 45, 46, 50, 78, 83, 100, 105, 125, 167, 293

wolves ❷ 99, 218

Wŏnbong ❷ 393, 394, 399, 400

Wŏnch'ŏn ❷ 234, 235

Wŏngi ❷ 196